The
History
of
Freemasonry

The History of Freemasonry

of

Freemasonry

Its Legendary Origins

Albert Gallatin Mackey

PORTLAND HOUSE

This 2002 edition is published by Portland House an imprint of
Random House Value Publishing, Inc., a division of Random House Publishing, Inc.,
280 Park Avenue, New York, New York 10017.

Random House
New York • Toronto • London • Sydney • Auckland
http://www.randomhouse.com/

Printed and bound in the United States

ISBN 0-517-21474-1

9 8 7 6 5 4 3 2 1

CONTENTS

INTRODUCTION

Of all the institutions which have been established for the purpose of improving the condition of mankind, Freemasonry stands preeminent in usefulness as it is in age. Its origin is lost in the abyss of unexplored antiquity. No historical records, no traditionary accounts, can with certainty point out the precise time, the place, or the particular manner of its commencement. While some have endeavored to discover its footsteps amongst the master-builders and artists engaged in the construction of the first Jewish temple, others have attempted to trace it to the Eleusinian mysteries, which are said to have taught the immortality of the soul and the other sublime truths of natural religion. Some again have ascribed its rise to the sainted heroes of the Crusades; while others have endeavored to penetrate the mysteries of the Druids, and to discover its origin amongst the wise men of that institution.

—— De Witt Clinton

HE fraternal order of Free and Accepted Masons, or the Freemasons, is a secret society, yet its influence and effect on Western society have been great. Many of the Founding Fathers of the United States—George Washington, Thomas Jefferson, John Hancock, Benjamin Franklin, and Paul Revere—were Masons. Simón Bolívar, the great freedom fighter of South America, and Giuseppe Garibaldi, Italy's distinguished patriot, were also members, as were the great writers Voltaire and Goethe, and the composers Franz Joseph Haydn and Amadeus Mozart. However, the order's ultimate purpose has always been shrouded in the self-imposed mystery that surrounds the organization as well as the wild conjecture about it that arose from the fear of the ignorant. Accusations that the Freemasons have cultivated the occult sciences—particularly alchemy, astrology, and ceremonial magic—have pursued the order throughout its history. While, without a doubt, some branches of the organization have endeavored to

explore the realms of esotericism, it was merely a means to an end, not an end in itself.

Order out of chaos is the famous motto of the Freemasons. It means the occasion of rising beyond one's aimless animal nature and attaining a higher plane of existence. To learn the way to that plane, to follow the proper paths, and to continue the journey and complete the wondrous voyage to a higher self and the unity of the whole, are the ultimate goals of a Freemason.

The mythology and symbolism of Freemasonry is very rich and complex. As the age of the society is unknown, its history blends facts with traditions and legends. Until the end of the seventeenth century, these apocryphal stories of Freemasonry—called the *Legend of the Craft,* or the *Legend of the Guild*—were believed with implicit faith by its members. The object of this book, Albert Gallatin Mackey's *The History of Freemasonry: Its Legendary Origins,* is to present a complete survey of the mythical and allegorical narratives of Freemasonry and to show that these Masonic legends contain the germs of historical truth often mingled with a symbolic idea, and almost always reflect in their unadorned form the true philosophic spirit of the Order.

Most scholars today believe the origins of modern Freemasonry can be traced to ancient Rome, where an organization of workmen formed under the name of the *Collegium Artificum,* or *Collegium Fabrorum*—the College of Artificers, or the College of Workmen. This brotherhood consisted of builders and architects and was the prototype of the guilds and incorporations of the Middle Ages. The college flourished under the Roman empire, which sent its members, endowed with skill in architecture and the spirit of confraternity, to the various provinces that the Romans had conquered. In all these provinces, but principally in Northern Italy, Gaul, and Britain, they established similar colleges or associations, in which they transmitted to the native inhabitants their knowledge of the art of building and impressed them with their spirit of fraternal cooperation in labor.

After the fall of the empire and the transition of the provinces into independent and sovereign states, these colleges of workmen evolved into organizations of builders—masons and architects—who in Italy assumed the name of Traveling Freemasons, in Gaul that of the *Mestrice des Maçons,* in Germany that of the *Steinmetzen,* in England that of the Guilds and Companies, and in Scotland that of the Lodges and Incorporations. These associations of builders and architects were bound together by regulations very similar to and evidently derived from those that governed the Roman Colleges, with other rules suggested by change of conditions and circumstances.

The associations, though mainly made up of professional workmen, sometimes admitted nonprofessionals—men of wealth, distinction, or learning—into their ranks as honorary members. At the end of the seventeenth century the number of these nonprofessional members greatly increased, and by the early eighteenth century they had completely changed the character of the Masonic organizations, known at that time as Lodges. The operative element—the practical application of the rules of architecture to the construction of public and private edifices—was entirely eliminated, and the Lodges were no longer companies of builders, but fraternities of speculative philosophers. The new institution of Speculative Freemasonry retained no relation to the practical purposes of operative Freemasonry other than the memory of its descent and the retention of its technical language and the tools of the art. These, however, were subjected to new and symbolic interpretations, adapted to the worship of God as the Grand Architect of the universe.

This transition from the operative to the speculative form of Masonry was complete by the year 1717, when the Grand Lodge of Free and Accepted Masons was established in London. From England the change passed over to other Lodges as Freemasonry spread to the United States, South America, and throughout the rest of the world.

In *The History of Freemasonry: Its Legendary Origins* you will find the lore and mythology that is the philosophical and ritual foundation upon which Freemasonry is built and from which its three great principles—brotherly love, charity, and truth—have evolved. Albert Gallatin Mackey is an excellent guide through this compelling exploration of the Masonic tradition. Included are excerpts from many rare and hard-to-find original manuscripts sacred to the Masons—including the Halliwell Poem, the oldest Masonic document in existence, dating from the late fourteenth to the middle fifteenth century—and a learned discussion of the origin, significance, and meaning of these works. Mackey recounts the various stories that explore Freemasonry's origins, ranging from its beginnings with Abraham, the Old Testament patriarch, to the builders of the Tower of Babel, to King Solomon and the builders of the Temple of Jerusalem. He also explores the possible associations of the Freemasons with the Knights Templars of the Crusades, the Druids, the Rosicrucians, and the Assassins—a secret Muslim sect. Throughout, this erudite and illuminating book investigates the subject with detail and completeness.

Albert Gallatin Mackey was born on March 12, 1807, in Charleston, South Carolina. He was the youngest son of Dr. John Mackey, a physician, editor, and teacher, who also published the periodical *The Investigator* from 1812 to 1817. After teaching for a time, Albert Mackey followed in his father's footsteps and attended the South Carolina Medical College, Charleston, from which he graduated in 1832. He practiced medicine in Charleston and became a teacher at the Medical College, but in 1854 his growing interest in Freemasonry impelled him to give up his practice and devote his energies to his Masonic activities.

Mackey eventually became the grand secretary of the Grand Lodge, grand high priest of the Grand Chapter, grand master of the Grand Council, and general grand high priest of the General Grand Chapter of the United States. The last decade of his life was spent in Washington, D.C., where he devoted himself to the continuance of his work as secretary general of the Supreme Council of the 33rd Degree. He died on June 20, 1881, at Old Point Comfort, Virginia.

While Mackey attained high official positions in the Masonic order, he is remembered today for his writings on Freemasonry. In 1849 he established *The Southern and Western Masonic Miscellany,* a weekly magazine, and in 1858–60 he published "Quarterly," which he dedicated to the same interests. He was also the author of many books on Freemasonry. His first book was *A Lexicon of Freemasonry* (1845), followed by *The Mystic Tie* (1849), *The Ahiman Rezon, or Book of Constitutions of the Grand Lodge of South Carolina* (1852), *Principles of Masonic Law* (1856), *The Book of the Chapter* (1858), *A Text Book of Masonic Jurisprudence* (1859), *History of Freemasonry in South Carolina* (1861), *Manual of the Lodge* (1862), *Cryptic Masonry* (1867), *Mackey's Masonic Ritualist* (1869), *The Symbolism of Freemasonry* (1869), *Encyclopedia of Freemasonry* (1874), and *Masonic Parliamentary Law* (1875). He was working on the present volume, *The History of Freemasonry,* when he died. Many of Mackey's books, particularly the *Encyclopedia of Freemasonry,* are considered among the most authoritative and definitive works on the subject.

HISTORY
OF
FREE MASONRY

CHAPTER I

N the study of Freemasonry there are two kinds of statements which are presented to the mind of the inquiring scholar, which are sometimes concurrent, but much oftener conflicting, in their character.

These are the historical and the traditional, each of which appertains to Freemasonry as we may consider it in a different aspect.

The historical statement relates to the Institution as we look at it from an exoteric or public point of view; the traditional refers only to its esoteric or secret character.

So long as its traditional legends are confined to the ritual of the Order, they are not appropriate subjects of historical inquiry. They have been invented by the makers of the rituals for symbolic purposes connected with the forms of initiation. Out of these myths of Speculative Masonry its philosophy has been developed; and, as they are really to be considered as merely the expansion of a philosophic or speculative idea, they can not properly be posited in the category of historical narratives.

But in the published works of those who have written on the origin and progress of Masonry, from its beginning to the present time, the legendary or traditional has too much been mingled with the historical element. The effect of this course has been, on adversely prejudiced minds, to weaken all claims of the Institution to an historical existence. The doctrine of "false in one thing, false in all," has been rigidly applied, and those statements of the Masonic historian which are really authentic have been doubted or rejected, because in other portions of his narrative he has been too credulous.

Borrowing the technical language of archæology, I should say that the history of Masonry[1] may be divided into two periods—the prehistoric and the historic. The former is traditional, the latter documentary. Each of these divisions must, in any historical inquiry, be clearly defined. There is also another division, into esoteric and exoteric history. The first is exclusively within the arcana of the Order, and can not, as I have said, be the subject of historical investigation. The second properly comes within the sphere of historical study, and is subjected to all the laws of historical criticism.

When we are treating of Freemasonry as one of the social organizations of the world—as one of those institutions which are the results of civilization, and which have sprung up in the progress of society; and, finally, when we are considering what are the influences that the varying conditions of that society have produced upon it, and what influences it has reciprocally produced upon these varying conditions—we are then engaged in the solution of a historical problem, and we must pursue the inquiry in a historical method and not otherwise. We must discard all speculation, because history deals only with facts.

If we were treating the history of a nation, we should assert nothing of it as historical that could not be traced to and be verified by its written records. All that is conjectured of the events that may have occurred in the earlier period of such a nation, of which there is no record in contemporaneous or immediately subsequent times, is properly thrown into the dim era of the prehistoric age. It forms no part of the authentic history of the nation, and can be dignified, at its highest value, with the title of historical speculation only, which claims no other credence than that which its plausibility or its probability commands.

Now, the possibility or the probability that a certain event may have occurred in the early days of a nation's existence, but of which event there is no record, will be great or little, as dependent on certain other events which bear upon it, and which come within the era of its records. The event may have been possible, but not probable, and then but very little or no importance would be im-

---

[1] In the progress of this work I shall use the terms *Masonry* and *Freemasonry* without discrimination, except on special, and at the time specified, occasions.

puted to it, and it would at once be relegated to the category of myths. Or it may have been both possible and highly probable, and we may be then permitted to speculate upon it as something that had exerted an influence upon the primitive character or the subsequent progress of the nation. But, even then, it would not altogether lose its mythical character. Whatever we might predicate of it would only be a plausible speculation. It would not be history, for that deals not in what may have been, but only in that which actually has been.

The progress in these latter days of what are called the exact sciences has led, by the force of example and analogy, to a more critical examination of the facts, or, rather, the so-called facts, of history.

Voltaire said, in his *Life of Charles XII. of Sweden*, that "incredulity is the foundation of history." Years passed before the axiom in all its force was accepted by the learned. But at length it has been adopted as the rule of all historical criticism. To be credulous is now to be unphilosophical, and scholars accept nothing as history that can not be demonstrated with almost mathematical certainty.

Niebuhr began by shattering all faith in the story of Rhea Sylvia, of Romulus and Remus, and of the maternal wolf, which, with many other incidents of the early Roman annals, were consigned by him to the region of the mythical.

In later times, the patriotic heart of Switzerland has been made to mourn by the discovery that the story of William Tell, and of the apple which he shot from the head of his son, is nothing but a mediæval fable which was to be found in a great many other countries, and the circumstances of which, everywhere varying in details, still point to a common origin in some early symbolic myth.

It is thus that many narratives, once accepted as veracious, have been, by careful criticism, eliminated from the domain of history ; and such works as Goldsmith's Histories of Greece and Rome are no longer deemed fitting text-books for schools, where nothing but truth should be taught.

The same rules of critical analysis which are pursued in the separation of what is true from what is false in the history of a nation should be applied to the determination of the character of all statements in Masonic history. This course, however, has, unhappily, not been generally pursued. Many of its legends are unquestionably founded, as I shall endeavor hereafter to show, on a historical basis ; but quite as many, if not more, are made up out of a mixture of truth and fiction, the distinctive boundaries of which it is difficult to define ; while a still greater number are altogether mythical, with no appreciable element of truth in their composition. And yet, for nearly two centuries, all of these three classes of Masonic legendary lore have been accepted by the great body of the Fraternity, without any discrimination, as faithful narratives of undoubted truthfulness.

It is this liberal acceptation of the false for the true, and this ready recognition of fables as authentic narratives whereby imaginative writers have been encouraged to plunge into the realms of absurdity instead of confining themselves to the domain of legitimate history, that have cast an air of romance over all that has hitherto been written about Freemasonry. Unjustly, but very naturally, scholars have been inclined to reject all our legends in every part as fabulous, because they found in some the elements of fiction.

But, on the other hand, the absurdities of legend-makers, and the credulity of legend-readers, have, by a healthy reaction, given rise to a school of iconoclasts (to whom there will soon be occasion to refer), which sprang up from a laudable desire to conform the principles of criticism which are to govern all investigations into Masonic history to the rules which control profane writers in the examination of the history of nations.

As examples of the legends of Masonry which have tempted the credulity of many and excited the skepticism of others, those almost universally accepted legends may be cited which attribute the organization of Freemasonry in its present form to the era of King Solomon's temple—the story of Prince Edwin and the Grand Lodge congregated by him at the city of York in the 10th century—and the theory that the three symbolic degrees were instituted as Masonic grades at a period very long anterior to the beginning of the 18th century.

These statements, still believed in by all Masons who have not made the history of the Order an especial study, were, until recently, received by prominent scholars as veracious narratives. Even Dr. Oliver, one of the most learned as well as the most prolific of Masonic authors, has, in his numerous works, recognized them as his toric truths without a word of protest or a sign of doubt, except, perhaps, with reference to the third legend above mentioned, of which he says, with a cautious qualification, that he has "some doubts whether the Master's degree, as now given, can be traced three centuries backwards."[1]

But now comes a new school of Masonic students, to whom, borrowing a word formerly used in the history of religious strifes, has been given the name of "iconoclasts." The word is a good one. The old iconoclasts, or image-breakers of the 8th century, demolished the images and defaced the pictures which they found in the churches, induced by erroneous but conscientious views, because they thought that the people were mistaking the shadow for the substance, and were worshipping the image or the picture instead of the Divine Being whom it represented.

And so these Masonic iconoclasts, with better views, are proceeding to destroy, by hard, incisive criticism, the intellectual images which the old, unlettered Masons had constructed for their veneration. They are pulling to pieces the myths and legends, whose fallacies and absurdities had so long cast a cloud upon what ought to be the clear sky of Masonic history. But they have tempered their zeal with a knowledge and a moderation that were unknown to the iconoclasts of religion. These shattered the images and scattered the fragments to the four winds of heaven, or they burnt the picture so that not even a remnant of the canvas was left. Whatever there was of beauty in the work of the sculptor or painter was forever destroyed. Every sentiment of æsthetic art was overcome by the virulence of religious fanaticism. Had the destructive labors of these iconoclasts been universal and long continued, no foundation would have been left for building that science of Christian symbolism, which in this day has been so interesting and so instructive to the archæologist.[2]

Not so have the Masonic iconoclasts performed their task of critical reformation. They have shattered nothing; they have destroyed nothing. When in the course of their investigations into true Masonic history, they encounter a myth or a legend, replete, ap-

---

[1] " Dissertation on the State of Masonry in the Eighteenth Century."

[2] Thus the Emperor Leo, the Isaurian, caused all images and pictures to be removed from the churches and publicly burnt—an act of vandalism not surpassed by that Saracen despot who (if the story be true) ruthlessly committed the books of the Alexandrian library to the flames as fuel for the public baths.

parently, with absurdities or contradictions, they do not consign it to oblivion·as something unworthy of consideration, but they dissect it into its various parts; they analyze it with critical acumen; they separate the chaff from the wheat; they accept the portion that is confirmed by other and collateral testimony as a legitimate contribution to history; what is undoubtedly fictitious they receive as a myth, and either reject it altogether as an unmeaning addition to a legend, or give it an interpretation as the expression of some symbolic idea which is itself of value in a historical point of view.

That lamented archæologist, Mr. George Smith, late of the British Museum, in speaking of the cuneiform inscriptions excavated in Mesopotamia, and the legends which they have preserved of the old Babylonian empire, said:[1] "With regard to the supernatural element introduced into the story, it is similar in nature to many such additions to historical narratives, especially in the East; but I would not reject those events which may have happened, because, in order to illustrate a current belief, or add to the romance of the story, the writer has introduced the supernatural."

It is on this very principle that the iconoclastic Masonic writers, such as Hughan and Woodford, are pursuing their researches into the early history of Freemasonry. They do not reject those events related in the old legends, which have certainly happened, because in them they find also mythical narratives. They do not yield to the tendency which George Smith says is now too general, "to repudiate the earlier part of history, because of its evident inaccuracies and the marvelous element generally combined with it."[2] It is in this way, and in this way only, that early Masonic history can be rightly written. Made up, as it has been for centuries past, of a commingled tissue of historical narrative and legendary invention, it has been heretofore read without judicious discrimination. Either the traditional account has been wholly accepted as historical, or it has been wholly rejected as fabulous, and thus, in either case, numerous errors have been the consequence.

As an example of the error which inevitably results from pursuing either of these methods of interpretation, one of which may be distinguished as the school of gross credulity, and the other as that of great skepticism, let us take the legend of the Temple origin of

---

[1] " Chaldean Account of Genesis," p. 302.   [2] Ibidem.

Masonry—that is to say, the legend which places the organization of the Institution at the time of the building of the temple at Jerusalem.

Now, the former of these schools implicitly receives the whole legend as true in all its details, and recognizes King Solomon as the first Grand Master, with Hiram of Tyre and Hiram as his Wardens, who, with him, presided over the Craft, divided into three degrees, the initiation into which was the same as that practiced in the lodges of the present day, or at least not very unlike it.

Thus Dr. Anderson, who was the first to publicly promulgate this legend and the theory founded on it, says, in the second edition of his "Constitutions," that Hiram Abif, "in Solomon's absence, filled the chair as Deputy Grand Master, and, in his presence, was the Senior Grand Warden";[1] and, again, that "Solomon partitioned the Fellow Crafts into certain lodges, with a Master and Wardens in each";[2] and, lastly, that "Solomon was Grand Master of all Masons at Jerusalem. King Hiram was Grand Master at Tyre, and Hiram Abif had been Master of Work."[3] The modern rituals have made some change in these details, but we evidently see here the original source of the legend as it is now generally believed by the Fraternity.

Indeed, so firmly convinced of its truth are the believers in this legend, that the brand of heterodoxy is placed by them on all who deny or doubt it.

On the contrary, the disciples of the latter school, whose skepticism is as excessive as is the credulity of the former, reject as fabulous everything that tends to connect Freemasonry with the Solomonic temple. To the King of Israel they refuse all honor, and they contemptuously repudiate the theory that he was a Masonic dignitary, or even a Freemason at all. One of these Pyrrhonists has gone so far as to defile the memory of the Jewish monarch with unnecessary and unmerited abuse.

Between these two parties, each of which is misdirected by an intemperate zeal, come the iconoclasts—impartial inquirers, who calmly and dispassionately seek for truth only. These disavow, it is true, the authenticity of the Temple legend in its present form. They deny that there is any proof which a historian could, by applying the just canons of criticism, admit as competent evidence, that Freemasonry was organized at the building of the temple of Solomon,

---

[1] Anderson, "Constitutions," 2d ed., chap. iii., p. 12.   [2] Ibid., p. 13.   [3] Ibid., p. 15.

and hence they look for its origin at some other period and under different circumstances.

But they do not reject the myth connected with the temple as being wholly unworthy of consideration. On the contrary, they respect this legend as having a symbolic significance, whose value can not be overestimated. They trace its rise in the Old Constitutions; they find it plainly alluded to in the *Legend of the Craft;* and they follow it in its full development in the modern rituals. They thus recognize the influence that the story of the temple and its builders has exerted on the internal construction of the Order, and hence they feel no disposition to treat it, notwithstanding its historical inaccuracy, with contumely.

Knowing what an important part the legends and symbols of Freemasonry have performed in the progress of the Institution, and how much its philosophic system is indebted to them for all that is peculiar to itself, they devote their literary energies, not to the expurgation of this or any other myth or legend, but to the investigation of the questions how and when it arose, and what is its real significance as a symbol, or what foundation as a narrative it may have in history. And thus they are enabled to add important items to the mass of true Masonic history which they have been accumulating.

In short, the theory of the iconoclastic school is that truth and authenticity must always, and in the first place, be sought; that nothing must be accepted as historical which has not the internal and external evidences of historical verity, and that in treating the legends of Masonry—of almost every one of which it may be said, " Se non vero, è ben trovato"—*if it is not true, it is well invented* —we are not to reject them as altogether fabulous, but as having some hidden and occult meaning, which, as in the case of all other symbols, we must diligently seek to discover. But if it be found that the legend has no symbolic significance, but is simply the distortion of a historical fact, we must carefully eliminate the fabulous increment, and leave the body of truth to which it had been added, to have its just value.

Such was the method pursued by the philosophers of antiquity; and Plato, Anaxagoras, and Cicero explained the absurdities of the ancient mythologists by an allegorical mode of interpretation.

To this school I have for years been strongly attached, and in the composition of this work I shall adopt its principles. I do not fear that the claims of Freemasonry to a time-honored existence will be injured by any historical criticism, although the era in which it had its birth may not be admitted to be as remote as that assigned to it by Anderson or Oliver.

Iconoclastic criticism can not depreciate, but will rather elevate, the character of the Institution. It will relieve it of absurdities, will often explain the cause of anachronisms, will purify the fabulous element, and confine it within the strict domain of history.

It was a common reproach against the great Niebuhr that he had overthrown the whole fabric of early Roman history, and yet Dr. Arnold, the most competent of critics, has said of him that he had built up much more than he had destroyed, and fixed much that modern skepticism had rejected as fabulous on firmer historic grounds.

Following such a method as that pursued by the most learned of modern historians, it will be necessary, for a faithful and comprehensible investigation of the history of Masonry, to discriminate between the two periods into which it is naturally divided,

The PREHISTORIC and

The HISTORIC.

The HISTORIC embraces the period within which we have authentic documents in reference to the existence of the Order, and will be considered in the second part of this book.

The PREHISTORIC embraces the period within which we have no authentic memorials, and when we have to depend wholly on legends and traditions.

The legendary history of Masonry will, therefore, be commenced in the next chapter.

CHAPTER II

THE LEGENDARY HISTORY OF FREEMASONRY

N the history of every ancient nation there is a prehistoric and a historic period.

The prehistoric period is that which has no records to prove the truth of the events that have been attributed to it. It is made up of myths and legends, founded—some of them, in all probability — on a distortion of historical facts, and some of them indebted entirely to imagination for their invention.

The historic period is that which begins with the narration of events which are supported by documents, either contemporary with the events or so recently posterior to them as to have nearly all the validity of contemporary evidence.

Just such a division of periods as this we find in the history of Freemasonry.

The prehistoric period, more commonly styled the legendary history, embraces the supposed history of the rise and progress of the Institution in remote times, and details events said to have occurred, but which have no proof of their occurrence other than that of oral tradition, unsupported by that sort of documentary evidence which is essentially necessary to give a reliable character to an historical statement.

The historic period of Freemasonry commences with the time when written or printed records furnish the necessary testimony that the events narrated did actually occur.

In treating of the history of nations, scholars have found great difficulty in precisely defining the point of separation between the prehistoric and the historic periods. As in natural history, it is almost impossible to define the exact line of demarkation between any two consecutive classes of the kingdoms of nature so as to distinguish the highest species of a vegetable from the lowest of an animal organization, so in political history it is difficult to tell when the prehistoric period ends and the historic begins.

In Freemasonry we meet with the same embarrassment, and this embarrassment is increased according to the different standpoints from which we view the institution.

If we adopt the theory (as has been done by a few writers too iconoclastic in their views) that Speculative Masonry never was anything but that which its present organization presents, with Grand Lodges, Grand Masters, and a ritual of distinct degrees, then we are compelled to place the commencement of the historic era at that period which has been called the *Revival* in the second decade of the 18th century.

If, with more liberal views, we entertain the opinion that Speculative Masonry was founded on, and is the offspring of, the Operative system of the Stonemasons, then we must extend our researches to at least the Middle Ages, where we shall find abundant documentary evidence of the existence and character of the Operative parent to which the Freemasonry of the present day, by a well-marked transition, has succeeded.

Connecting the written history of the Operative Masons with that of its speculative offshoot, we have an authentic and continuous history that will carry us back to a period many centuries anterior to the time of the so-called Revival in the year 1717.

If I were writing a history of Speculative Masonry merely, I should find myself restricted to an era, somewhere in the 17th century, when there is documentary evidence to show that the transition period began, and when the speculative obtruded into the Operative system.

But as I am really writing a history of Freemasonry, of which the Operative and the Speculative systems are divisions, intimately connected, I am constrained to go farther, and to investigate the rise and the progress of the Operative art as the precursor and the founder of the Speculative science.

The authentic details of the condition of Operative Masonry in the Middle Ages, of its connection, if it had any, with other organizations, and its transmutation at a later period into Speculative Masonry, will constitute the historic narrative of Freemasonry.

Its prehistoric narrative will be found in the myths and legends which were, unfortunately, for a long time accepted by the **great** body of the Craft as a true history, but which, though still credited by many, are yet placed by most modern Masonic scholars in their proper category.

These legends, some of which are preserved in the rituals, and some are becoming almost obsolete, have a common foundation in that traditional narrative which is known as the *Legend of the Craft*,[1] and which must first be understood before we can with satisfaction attempt to study the legendary history of the Institution.

But this legend is of such length and of so much importance that it demands for its consideration a separate and distinct chapter.

I, by no means, intend to advance the proposition that all the myths and legends now taught in the Lodges, or preserved in the works of Masonic writers, are to be found in the *Legend of the Craft*, but only the most important—those that are still recognized by the more credulous portion of the Fraternity as genuine and authentic narratives—receive their first notice in the *Legend of the Craft*, although they are indebted for their present, fuller form, to a development or enlargement, subsequently made in the course of the construction of the modern ritual.

---

[1] The Rev. Bro. Woodford calls it the " Legend of the Guild." But I prefer the title here used, because it does not lead to embarrassing questions as to the relation of the mediæval Guilds to Freemasonry.

CHAPTER III

THE OLD MANUSCRIPTS

NDERSON tells us, in the second edition of the *Book of Constitutions*, that in the year 1719, "at some private Lodges several very valuable manuscripts concerning the Fraternity, their Lodges, Regulations, Charges, Secrets, and Usages, were too hastily burnt by some scrupulous Brothers, that these papers might not fall into strange hands." [1]

Fortunately, this destruction was not universal. The manuscripts to which Anderson alludes were undoubtedly those Old Constitutions of the Operative Masons, several copies of which, that had escaped the holocaust described by him, have since been discovered in the British Museum, in old libraries, or in the archives of Lodges, and have been published by those who have discovered them.[2]

These are the documents which have received the title of "Old Records," "Old Charges," or "Old Constitutions." Their general character is the same. Indeed, there is so much similarity, and almost identity, in their contents as to warrant the presumption that they are copies of some earlier document not yet recovered.

The earliest of these documents is a manuscript poem, entitled the *Constitutiones artis geometriæ secundum Eucleydem*, which is preserved in the British Museum, and which was published in 1840 by Mr. Halliwell, in his *Early History of Freemasonry in England*. The date of this manuscript is supposed to be about the year 1390. A second and enlarged edition was published in 1844.

The next of the English manuscripts is that which was published

---

[1] Anderson's "Constitutions," 1738, p. 111.

[2] Among these writers we must not omit to mention Bro. William James Hughan, *facile princeps* of all Masonic antiquarians, who made, in 1872, a valuable contribution to this literature, under the title of "The Old Charges of the British Freemasons," the value of which is enhanced by the learned Preface of Bro. A. F. A. Woodford.

in 1861 by Bro. Matthew Cooke from the original in the British Museum, and which was once the property of Mrs. Caroline Baker, from whom it was purchased in 1859 by the Curators of the Museum. The date of this manuscript is supposed to be about 1490.

All the English Masonic antiquarians concur in the opinion that this manuscript is next in antiquity to the Halliwell poem, though there is a difference of about one hundred years in their respective dates. It is, however, mere guesswork to say that there were not other manuscripts in the intervening period. But as none have been discovered, they must be considered as non-existent, and it is impossible even to conjecture, from any groundwork on which we can stand, whether, if such manuscripts did ever exist, they partook more of the features of the Halliwell or of the Cooke document, or whether they presented the form of a gradual transmission from the one to the other.

The Cooke MS. is far more elaborate in its arrangement and its details than the Halliwell, and contains the *Legend of the Craft* in a more extended form.

In the absence of any other earlier document of the same kind, it must be considered as the matrix, as it were, in which that Legend, in the form in which it appears in all the later manuscripts, was moulded.

In the year 1815, Mr. James Dowland published, in the *Gentleman's Magazine*,[1] the copy of an old manuscript which had lately come into his possession, and which he described as being "written on a long roll of parchment, in a very clear hand, apparently early in the 17th century, and very probably is copied from a manuscript of an earlier date." Although not as old as the Halliwell and Cooke MSS., it is deemed of very great value, because it comes next to them in date, and is apparently the first of that series of later manuscripts, so many of which have, within the past few years, been recovered. It is evidently based on the Cooke MS., though not an exact copy of it. But the later manuscripts comprising that series, at the head of which it stands, so much resemble it in details, and even in phraseology, that they must either have been copies made from it, or, what is far more probable, copies of some older and common original, of which it also is a copy.

---

[1] *Gentleman's Magazine*, vol. 85, p. 489, May, 1815.

The original manuscript which was used by Dowland for the publication in the *Gentleman's Magazine* is lost, or can not now be found. But Mr. Woodford and other competent authorities ascribe the year 1550 as being about its date.

Several other manuscript Constitutions, whose dates vary from the middle of the 16th to the beginning of the 18th century, have since been discovered and published, principally by the industrious labors of Brothers Hughan and Woodford in England, and Brother Lyon in Scotland.

The following list gives the titles and conjectural dates of the most important of these manuscripts :[1]

Halliwell MS.	supposed, 1390.
Cooke MS.	" 1490.
Dowland MS.	" 1500.
Landsdowne MS.	" 1560.
York MS., No. 1	" 1600.
Harleian MS., No. 2054	" 1625.
Grand Lodge MS.	" 1632.
Sloane MS., No. 3848	certain, 1646.
Sloane MS., No. 3323	" 1659.
Harleian MS., No. 1942	supposed, 1660.
Aitcheson-Haven MS.	certain, 1666.
Edinburgh-Kilwinning MS.	supposed, 1670.
York MS., No. 5	" 1670.
York MS., No. 6	" 1680.
Lodge of Antiquity MS.	certain, 1686.
York MS., No. 2	" 1693.
Alnwick MS.	" 1701.
York MS., No. 4	" 1704.
Papworth MS.	supposed, 1714.

All of these manuscripts begin, except the Halliwell poem, with an invocation to the Trinity. Then follows a descant on the seven liberal arts and sciences, of which the fifth, or Geometry, is said to be Masonry. This is succeeded by a traditional history of Masonry, from the days of Lamech to the reign of King Athelstan of England. The manuscripts conclude with a series of "charges," or regulations, for the government of the Craft while they were of a purely operative character.

---

[1] I have relied on the excellent authority of Rev. A. F. A. Woodford for the dates. See Hughan's "Old Charges of the British Freemasons," p. xii.

The traditional history which constitutes the first part of these "Old Records" is replete with historical inaccuracies, with anachronisms, and even with absurdities. And yet it is valuable, because it forms the germ of that system of Masonic history which was afterward developed by such writers as Anderson, Preston, and Oliver, and from whose errors the iconoclasts of the present day are successfully striving to free the Institution, so as to give its history a more rational and methodic form.

This traditional history is presented to us in all the manuscripts, in an identity of form, or, at least, with very slight verbal differences. These differences are, indeed, so slight that they suggest the strong probability of a common source for all these documents, either in the oral teaching of the older Masons, or in some earlier record that has not yet been recovered. The tradition seems always to have secured the unhesitating belief of the Fraternity as a true relation of the origin and the progress of Masonry, and hence it has received the title of the *Legend of the Craft.*

From the zealous care with which many manuscripts containing this legend were destroyed in 1719 by "scrupulous brothers" who were opposed to its publication, we might believe that it formed a part of the esoteric instructions of the Guild of Operative Masons. If so, it lost this secret character by the publication of Roberts's edition of the "Constitutions" in 1722.

In the earlier German and French Masonic records, such as the *Ordenung der Steinmetzen* at Strasburg in 1462, and the *Reglements sur les Arts et Metiers* at Paris in the 12th century, there is no appearance of this legend. But it does not follow from this that no such legend existed among the French and German Masons. Indeed, as it is well known that early English Operative Masonry was derived from the continent, it is natural to suppose that the continental Masons brought the legend into England.

There is, besides, internal evidence in the English manuscripts of both French and German interpolations. The reference in the Legend to Charles Martel connects it with the French Masonry of the 12th century, and the invocation to the "Four Crowned Martyrs"[1] in the Halliwell MS. is undoubtedly of German origin.[2]

---

[1] Die heiligen Vier gekrönten, "Ordenung der Steinmetz, zu Strasburg, 1459," and in all the other German Constitutions.

[2] Findel thinks that this invocation to the Four Crowned Martyrs "must be regarded

The importance of this Legend in the influence that it exerted for a long period on the Craft as the accredited history of the Institution makes it indispensably necessary that it should form a part of any work that professes to treat of the history of Masonry.

For this purpose I have selected the Dowland MS., because it is admitted to be the oldest of those that assumed that general form which was followed in all the subsequent manuscripts, between which and it there is no substantial difference.

---

as a most decided proof of the identity of the German and English Stonemasons, and of their having one common parentage." (" Geschichte der Frei Maurerei." Lyon's translation, p. 31.) Woodford does not concur with this view, but I think without good reason.

CHAPTER IV

THE LEGEND OF THE CRAFT

HE might of the Father of Kings,[1] with the wisdome of his glorious Son, through the grace of the goodness of the Holy Ghost, there bene three persons in one Godheade, be with us at our beginninge, and give us grace so to governe us here in this mortall life liveinge, that we may come to his kingdome that never shall have endinje. Amen.

"Good Breetheren and Followes: Our purpose is to tell you how and in what manner this worthy science of Masonrye was begunne, and afterwards how it was favoured by worthy Kings and Princes, and by many other worshippfull men. And also to those that be willinge, wee will declare the charge that belongeth to any true Mason to keepe for in good faith. And yee have good heede thereto; it is well worthy to be well kept for a worthy craft and a curious science.

" For there be Seaven liberall Sciences, of the which seaven it is one of them. And the names of the Seaven Seyences bene these: First is Grammere, and it teacheth man to speake truly and write truly. And the second is Rhethoricke; and teacheth a man to speake faire in subtill termes. And the third is Dialectyke; and teacheth a man for to discern or know truth from false. And the fourth is Arithmeticke; and that teacheth a man for to recken and to accompte all manner of numbers. And the fifth is called Geometrie; and that teacheth mett and measure of earth and of all other things; of the which science is called Masonrye. And the sixth science is called Musicke; and that teacheth a man of songe and voice, of tongue and orgaine, harpe and trompe. And the seaventh science is called Astronomye; and that teacheth a man the course of

---

[1] In the Landsdowne, and most of the other MSS., the formula is "the Father of the Heavens," or " of Heaven."

the sunn, moone and starrs. These be the Seaven liberall Sciences, the which bene all founded by one Science, that is to say Geometrie. And this may a man prove, that the science of the work is founded by Geometrie, for Geometrie teacheth a man mett and measure, ponderation and weight, of all manner of things on earth, for there is no man that worketh any science, but he worketh by some mett or measure, nor no man that buyeth or selleth, but he buyeth or selleth by some measure or by some weight, and all these is Geometrie. And these use merchants and all craftsmen, and all other of the Seaven Sciences, and in especiall the plowman and tillers of all manner of grounds, graynes, vynes, flowers and setters of other fruits; for Grammere or Retricke, neither Astronomie nor none of all the other Seaven Sciences can no manner find mett nor measure without Geometrie. Wherefore methinketh that the science of Geometrie is most worthy, and that findeth [1] all other.

"How that these worthy Sciences were first begunne, I shall you tell. Before Noye's flood, there was a man called Lameche, as it is written in the Byble in the iiijth chapter of Genesis; and this Lameche had two wives, and the one height Ada, and that other height Sella; by his first wife Ada he gott two sons, and that one Jabell and thother Tuball, and by that other wife Sella he got a son and a daughter. And these four children founden the beginning of all sciences in the world. And this elder son Jabell found the science of Geometrie, and he departed flocks of sheep and lambs in the field, and first wrought house of stone and tree,[2] as is noted in the chapter above said. And his brother Tuball found the science of musicke, songe of tonge, harp and orgaine. And the third brother, Tuball Cain, found smithcraft of gold, silver, copper, iron and steele; and the daughter found the craft of Weavinge. And these children knew well that God would take vengeance for synn, either by fire or by water; wherefore they writt their science that they had found in two pillars of stone, that they might be found after Noye's flood. And that one stone was marble, for that would not burn with fire; and

---

[1] Used in its primitive Anglo-Saxon meaning of "to invent, to devise." Geometry invented or devised all the other sciences.

[2] This is an instance of the inaccuracy of these old records in historical lore. So far from Jabal being the first who "wrought house of stone and tree," he was the originator of the nomadic life, in which such buildings are never used. He invented tents, made most probably of skins, to be the temporary residence of a pastoral people, led by the exigency of a want of food to remove their flocks from time to time to new pastures.

that other stone was clepped laterns,[1] and would not drown in noe water.

"Our intent is to tell you trulie how and in what manner these stones were found that these sciences were written in. The great Hermarynes, that was Cuby's son, the which Cub was Sem's son, that was Noy's son. This Hermarynes afterwards was called Harmes, the father of wise men; he found one of the two pillars of stone, and found the science written there, and he taught it to other men. And at the making of the Tower of Babylon there was Masonrye first made much of. And the Kinge of Babylon that height Nemrothe,[2] was a mason himself; and loved well the science, and it is said with masters of histories. And when the City of Nyneve and other cities of the East should be made, Nemrothe, the King of Babylon, sent thither three score Masons at the rogation of the King of Nyneve, his cosen. And when he sent them forth, he gave them a charge on this manner. That they should be true each of them to other, and that they should love truly together, and that they should serve their lord truly for their pay; soe that the master may have worshipp and all that long to him. And other moe charges he gave them. And this was the first time that ever Masons had any charge of his science.

"Moreover when Abraham and Sara his wife went into Egipt, there he taught the Seaven Sciences to the Egiptians; and he had a worthy scoller that height Ewclyde,[3] and he learned right well and was a master of all the vij Sciences liberall. And in his days it befell that the lord and the estates of the realme had soe many sonns that they had gotten, some by their wives and some by other ladyes of the realme; for that land is a hott land and a plentious of generacion. And they had not competent livelode to find with their children, wherefor they made much care, and then the king of the land made a great Counsell and a Parliament, to witt, how they might find their children honestly as gentlemen; and they could find no manner of good way. And then they did crye through all the realme, if there were any man that informe them, that he should come to them, and he should be soe rewarded for his travail, that he should hold him pleased.

---

[1] This word is a corruption of the Latin "later," *brick*. [2] Nimrod.

[3] Bro. Matthew Cooke, in his Notes to the MS. which he was the first to publish, and which thence bears his name, protests against being held responsible for the chronology which makes Abraham and Euclid contemporaries. It will hereafter be seen that this legend of Euclid is merely a symbol.

"After that this crye was made, then came this worthy clarke Ewclyde and said to the king and all his great lords, ' If yee will take me your children to governe, and to teach them one of the Seaven Scyences, wherewith they may live honestly as gentlemen should, under a condition, that yee will grant me and them a commission that I may have power to rule them after the manner that the science ought to be ruled.' And that the kinge and all his Counsell granted to him anone and sealed their commission. And then this worthy Doctor tooke to him these lord's sonns, and taught them the scyence of Geometrie in practice, for to work in stones all manner of worthy worke that belongeth to buildinge churches, temples, castells, towres, and mannors, and all other manner of buildings ; and he gave them a charge in this manner.

"The first was that they should be true to the Kynge, and to the Lord that they owe. And that they should love well together and be true each one to other. And that they should call each other his fellowe or else brother and not by servant nor his knave, nor none other foul name. And that they should deserve their paie of the lord or of the master that they serve. And that they should ordaine the wisest of them to be master of the worke and nether for love nor great lynneage, ne riches ne for no favour to lett another that hath little conning for to be master of the lord's worke, wherethrough the lord should be evill served and they ashamed. And also that they should call their governors of the worke, Master, in the time that they worke with him. And other many moe charges that longe to tell. And to all these charges he made them to sweare a great oath that men used in that time ; and ordayned them for reasonable wages, that they might live honestly by. And also that they should come and semble together every yeare once, how they might worke best to serve the lord for his profitt and to their own worshipp ; and to correct within themselves him that had trespassed against the science. And thus was the seyence grounded there ; and that worthy Mr. Ewclyde gave it the name of Geometrie. And now it is called through all this land, Masonrye.

"Sythen longe after,[1] when the children of Israell were coming into the land of Beheast,[2] that is now called amongst us, the country of

---

[1] Since then long after—long after that time.
[2] The Land of Promise, or the Promised Land. " Beheste Promissio," says the Promptorium Parvulorum.

Jhrlm.   Kinge David began the Temple that they called *Templum D'ni*, and it is named with us the Temple of Jerusalem.   And the same Kinge David loved Masons well and cherished them much, and gave them good paie.   And he gave the charges and the manners as he had learned of Egipt given by Ewclyde, and other charges moe that ye shall heare afterward.   And after the decease of Kinge David, Solomon, that was David's sonn, performed out the Temple that his father begonne ; and sent after Masons into divers countries and of divers lands ; and gathered them together, so that he had fourscore thousand workers of stone, and were all named Masons.   And he chose out of them three thousand that were ordayned to be masters and governors of his worke.   And furthermore there was a Kinge of another region that men called Iram,[1] and he loved well Kinge Solomon and he gave him tymber to his worke.   And he had a sonn that height Aynon,[2] and he was a Master of Geometrie, and was chief Master of all his Masons, and was Master of all his gravings and carvinge, and of all manner of Masonrye that longed to the Temple ; and this is witnessed by the Bible, *in libro Regum*, the third chapter. And this Solomon confirmed both charges and the manners that his father had given to Masons.   And thus was that worthy Science of Masonrye confirmed in the country of Jerusalem, and in many other kingdoms.

" Curious craftsmen walked about full wide into divers countryes, some because of learning more craft and cunning, and some to teach them that had but little cunnynge.   And soe it befell that there was one curious Mason that height Maymus Grecus,[3] that had been at the making of Solomon's Temple, and he came into France, and there he taught the science of Masonrye to men of France.   And there was one of the Regal line of France that height Charles Martell ;[4] and he was a man that loved well such a science, and drew to this Maymus Grecus that is above-said, and learned of him the science, and tooke upon him the charges and manners ; and afterwards by the

---

[1] It is scarcely necessary to explain that this is meant for Hiram.

[2] The true origin and meaning of this name, for which some of the modern Speculative Masons have substituted Hiram Abif, and others Adoniram, will be hereafter discussed.

[3] This name has been a Sphinxian enigma which many a Masonic Œdipos has failed to solve.   I shall recur to it in a subsequent page.

[4] The introduction of this monarch into the Legend leads us to an inquiry into an interesting period of French Masonic history that will be hereafter discussed.

grace of God, he was elect to be Kinge of Fraunce. And when he was in his estate, he tooke Masons, and did helpe to make men Masons that were none; and set them to worke, and gave them both the charge and the manners and good paie, as he had learned of other Masons; and confirmed them a charter from yeare to yeare, to hold their semble when they would; and cherished them right much; and thus came this science into Fraunce.

" England in all this season stood voyd, as for any charge of Masonrye unto St. Albones[1] tyme. And in his days the King of England that was a Pagan, he did wall the towne about, that is called Sainct Albones. And Sainct Albones was a worthy Knight and stewart with the Kinge of his household, and had governance of the realme, and also of the makinge of the town walls; and loved well Masons and cherished them much. And he made their paie right good, standing as the realme did; for he gave them ij.*s.* vj.*d.* a weeke and iij.*d.* to their nonesynches.[2] And before that time, through all this land, a Mason tooke but a penny a day and his meate, till Sainct Albones amended it, and gave them a chartour of the Kinge and his Counsell for to hold a general councell, and gave it the name of As-semble; and thereat he was himselfe, and helped to make Masons and gave them charges as you shall heare afterward.

" Right soon after the decease of Sainct Albone, there came divers wars into the realme of England of divers Nations soe that the good rule of Masonrye was destroyed unto the tyme of Kinge Athelstone's days that was a worthy Kinge of England and brought this land into good rest and peace; and builded many great works of Abbyes and Toures, and other many divers buildings; and loved well Masons. And he had a sonne that height Edwinne, and he loved Masons much more than his father did. And he was a great practiser in Geometrie; and he drew him much to talke and to commune with Masons, and to learn of them science; and afterwards for love that he had to Masons, and to the science, he was made Mason, and he gatt of the Kinge his father, a Chartour and Commission to hold every yeare

---

[1] St. Alban, the protomartyr of England. Of his connection with the Legend, more hereafter.

[2] A corruption of the old English word *noonshun*, from which comes our modern *luncheon*. It meant the refreshment taken at noon, when laborers desist from work to *shun* the heat. It may here mean food or subsistence in general. St. Alban gave his Masons two shillings a week and three pence for their daily food. (See *Nonesynches* in Mackey's " Encyclopædia of Freemasonry.")

once an Assemble, wher that ever they would, within the realme of England; and to correct within themselves defaults and trespasses that were done within the science. And he held himselfe an Assemble at Yorke,[1] and these he made Masons, and gave them charges, and taught them the manners, and commanded that rule to be kept ever after, and tooke then the chartour and commission to keepe, and made ordinance that it should be renewed from kinge to kinge.

"And when the Assemble was gathered he made a cry that all old Masons and young that had any writeinge or understanding of the charges and the manners that were made before in this land, or in any other, that they should show them forth. And when it was proved, there were founden some in French, and some in Greek, and some in English and some in other languages; and the intent of them all was founden all one. And he did make a booke thereof, and how the science was founded. And he himselfe bad and commanded that it should be readd or tould, when that any Mason should be made for to give him his charge. And fro that day into this tyme manners of Masons have been kept in that form as well as men might governe it. And furthermore divers Assembles have beene put and ordayned certain charges by the best advice of Masters and fellows."

Then follow the charges that are thus said to have been enacted at York and at other General Assemblies, but which properly constitute no part of the Legend, at least no part connected with the legendary details of the rise and progress of the Institution. The Legend ends with the account of the holding of an Assembly at York, and other subsequent ones, for the purpose of enacting laws for the government of the Order.

---

[1] This part of the Legend which refers to Prince Edwin and the Assembly at York is so important that it demands and will receive a future comprehensive examination.

CHAPTER V

THE HALLIWELL POEM AND THE LEGEND

HERE is one manuscript which differs so much from all the others in its form and in its contents as to afford the strongest internal evidence that it is derived from a source entirely different from that which gave origin to the other and later documents.

I allude to what is known to Masonic antiquaries as the Halliwell MS. As this is admitted to be the oldest Masonic document extant, and as some very important conclusions in respect to the early history of the Craft are about to be deduced from it, a detailed account of it will not be deemed unnecessary.

This work was first published in 1840 by Mr. James Orchard Halliwell, under the title of "A Poem on the Constitutions of Masonry,"[1] from the original manuscript in the King's Library of the British Museum. Mr. Halliwell, who subsequently adopted the name of Phillips, is not a member of the Brotherhood, and Woodford appropriately remarks that "it is somewhat curious that to Grandidier and Halliwell, both non-Masons, Freemasonry owes the impetus given at separate epochs to the study of its archæology and history."[2]

Halliwell says that the manuscript formerly belonged to Charles Theyer, a well-known collector of the 17th century. It is undoubtedly the oldest Masonic MS. extant. Messrs. Bond and Egerton of the British Museum consider its date to be about the middle of the 15th century. Kloss[3] thinks that it was written between the years 1427 and 1445. Dr. Oliver[4] maintains that it is a transcript of the Book of Constitutions adopted by the General Assembly, held

---

[1] In a brochure entitled "The Early History of Freemasonry in England." A later and improved edition was published in 1844.

[2] In Kenning's "Encyclopædia," voc. *Halliwell*.

[3] "Die Freimaur in ihrer wahren Bedentung." S. 12.

[4] *American Quart. Rev. of Freemasonry*, vol. i., p. 547.

in the year 926, at the City of York. Halliwell himself places the date of the MS. at 1390. Woodford[1] concurs in this opinion. I am inclined to think that this is the true date of its transcription.

The manuscript is in rhymed verse, and consists of 794 lines. At the head of the poem is the inscription : "*Hic incipiunt constituciones artis gemetriæ secundum Euclydem.*" The language is more archaic than that of Wicliffe's version of the Bible, which was written toward the end of the 14th century, but approaches very nearly to that of the Chronicles of Robert of Gloucester, the date of which was at the beginning of the same century. Therefore, if we admit that the date of 1390, attributed by Halliwell and Woodford to the transcription in the British Museum, is correct, we may, I think, judging by the language, safely assign to the original the date of about 1300. Further back than this, philology will not permit us to go.

Lines 1–86 of this MS. contain the history of the origin of geometry, or Masonry, and the story of Euclid is given at length, much like that which is in the *Legend of the Craft.* But no other parts of that Legend are referred to, except the portion which records the introduction of Masonry into England. From the narrative of the establishment of Masonry in Egypt by Euclid, the poem passes immediately to the time when the "craft com ynto Englond." Here the legendary story of King Athelstan and the Assembly called by him is given, with this variation from the common Legend, that there is no mention of the city of York, where the Assembly is said to have been held, nor of Prince Edwin, who summoned it.

Lines 87–470 contain the regulations which were adopted at that Assembly, divided into fifteen articles and the same number of points. There is a very great resemblance, substantially, between these regulations and the charges contained in the subsequent or second set of Manuscript Constitutions. But the regulations in the Halliwell poem are given at greater length, with more particularity and generally accompanied with an explanation or reason for the law.

After an interpolation, to be referred to hereafter, the poem proceeds under the title of "*Ars quatuor coronatorum,*" *The Art of*

---

[1] Preface to Hughan's " Old Charges," p. vii.

the Four Crowned Ones, a title never applied to Masonry in the later and purely English manuscripts. We have first an invocation to God and the Virgin, and then the Legend of the Four Crowned Martyrs, which ends on line 534.

Now this Legend of the Four Crowned Martyrs[1]—*die Vier Gekrönten*—is found in none of the purely English manuscripts, but is of German origin, and peculiar to the German Steinmetzen or Stone Masons of the Middle Ages. Its introduction in this manuscript is an evidence of the German origin of the document, and, as Findel[2] says, "must be regarded as a most decided proof of the identity of the German and English Stone Masons, and of their having one common parentage."

The details of this Legend close at the 534th line, and the poem then proceeds to give a small and imperfect portion of what is known in our later manuscripts as the *Legend of the Craft.*

I am persuaded that all this part of the poem has been dislocated from its proper place, and that in the original the lines from 535 to 576 formed a portion of the *Legend of the Craft*, as it must have been inserted in the introductory part of the second manuscript. I think so, first, because in all other manuscripts the Legend forms the exordium and precedes the charges; secondly, because it has no proper connection with or sequence to the Legend of the Four Crowned Martyrs which precedes it, and which terminates on the 354th line ; and lastly, because it is evidently an interruption of the religious instructions which are taken up on line 577, and which naturally follow line 534. The writer having extolled the Christian steadfastness and piety of the four martyrs whose feast he tells us is on the eighth day after Allhalloween, proceeds on line 576 to admonish his readers to avoid pride and covetousness and to practice virtue. There is here a regular and natural connection, which, however, would be interrupted by the insertion between the two clauses of an imperfect portion of a legend which has reference to the very beginning of the history of Masonry. Hence I conclude that all that part of the Legend which described the events that were connected with Noah's flood and the Tower of Babel is an interpolation, and belongs to another manuscript and to another place.

---

[1] See the full details of this Legend in Mackey's " Encyclopædia of Freemasonry," art. *Four Crowned Martyrs.*
[2] " History of Freemasonry," Lyon's Trans., p. 31.

In fact, the copyist had two manuscripts before him, and he transcribed sometimes from one and sometimes from the other, apparently with but little judgment, or, rather, he copied the whole of one and then interpolated it with extracts from the other without respect to any congruity of subjects.

The rest of the poem is occupied with instructions as to behavior when in church, when in the company of one's superiors, and when present at the celebration of the mass. The whole ends with what we find in no other manuscript, the now familiar Masonic formula, "Amen, so mote it be."

Line 471 furnishes, I think, internal evidence that the poem was originally composed of two distinct works, written, in all probability, by two different persons, but in the copy which we now have, combined in one by the compiler or copyist. Mr. Woodford also is of the opinion that there are two distinct poems, although the fact had not attracted the attention of Halliwell. The former gentleman says that "it seems to be in truth two legends, and not only one." This is evident, from the fact that this second part is prefaced by the title, "*Alia ordinacio artis gemetriæ*," that is, "*Another* Constitution of the art of geometry." This title would indicate that what followed was a different *Ordinacio* or Constitution and taken from a different manuscript. Besides, line 471, which is the beginning of the other or second Constitution, does not fall into its proper place in following line 470, but is appropriately a continuation of line 74. To make this evident, I copy lines 70–74 from the poem, and follow them by lines 471–474, whence it will be seen that the latter lines are an appropriate and natural continuation of the former.

> Line 70. He sende about ynto the londe
>   71. After alle the masonus of the crafte,
>   72. To come to hym ful evene stragfte
>   73. For to amende these defaultys alle
>   74. By good counsel gef it hyt mytgh falle.
>
>   · · · · · · ·
>
>   471. They ordent ther a semble to be y-holde
>   472. Every yer, whersever they wolde
>   473. To amende the defautes, gef any where fonde
>   474. Amonge the craft withynne the londe.

The second manuscript seems to have been copied from line 471, as far as line 496. There, I suppose, the charges or regulations to have followed, which having been given from the first manuscript the copyist omitted, as a needless repetition, but went on immediately with the " ars quatuor coronatorum." This ended at line 534. It is now evident that he went back to a preceding part of the second manuscript and copied the early account of Masonry from line 535 to 576. The bare reading of these lines will convince the reader that they are not in their proper place, and must have formed a part of the beginning of the second poem.

Line 577 appropriately follows line 534, when the interpolation is left out, and then the transcription is correctly made to the end of the poem. The first manuscript was apparently copied correctly, with the exception of the two interpolations from the second MS. There is a doubt whether the Legend of the Crowned Martyrs belonged to the first or to the second poem. If to the first, then we have the whole of the first poem, and of the second only the interpolations. This is, however, a mere conjecture without positive proof. Yet it is very probable.

On the whole, the view I am inclined to take of this manuscript is as follows:

1. There were two original manuscripts, out of which the copyist made a careless admixture.

2. The first MS. began with line 1 and went on to the end at line 794. But this is only conjectural. It may have ended, or rather the copying ceased, at line 470.

3. If the conjecture just advanced be correct, then from a second MS. the copyist made interpolations, in the following way.

4. The beginning of the second MS. is lost. But from very near the commencement, which probably described the antediluvian tradition of Lamech, the copyist had selected a portion which begins with line 535 and ends at line 576. He had previously interpolated the lines from 471 to 496.

5. We have, then, the whole of the first manuscript, from the 1st line to the 794th, with the addition of two interpolations from the second, consisting only of 68 lines, namely: from line 471 to 496, and from line 535 to 576.

6. The first manuscript is deficient in any references to antediluvian Masonry, but begins with the foundation of Masonry in Egypt, as its title imports. This deficiency was, in part, supplied by the second interpolation (535-596). This part begins with the building

of Babel. But it is evident from the words, " many years after," that there was a preceding part to this manuscript that has not been copied. The " many years after " refer to some details that had been previously made. The account of the Seven Sciences, found in all later manuscripts, is not given in the first poem. It is inserted in this from the second.

7. So of the poem in the form we now have it, the parts copied from the second MS. consist only of 68 lines, which have been interpolated in two places into the first MS.—namely, lines 471–496, and lines 535–576; and these have been dislocated from their proper places. All the rest of the poem constitutes the original first manuscript. If I hesitate at all in coming to the positive conclusion that the first and last parts of the poem were composed by the same author, it is because the latter is written in a slightly different metre. This, therefore, leaves the question where the first poem ends and where the second begins, still open to discussion.

The variations which exist between the Halliwell poem, or, rather, poems, and other Masonic manuscripts of later date, are very important, because they indicate a difference of origin, and, by the points of difference, suggest several questions as to the early progress of Masonry in England.

1. The form of the Halliwell MS. differs entirely from that of the others. The latter are in prose, while the former is in verse. The language, too, of the Halliwell MS. is far more antiquated than that of the other manuscripts, showing that it was written in an earlier stage of the English tongue. It belongs to the Early English which succeeded the Anglo-Saxon. The other manuscripts were written at a later period of the language.

2. The Halliwell MS. is evidently a Roman Catholic production, and was written when the religion of Rome prevailed in England. The later manuscripts are all Protestant in their character, and must have been written after the middle of the 16th century, at least, when Protestantism was introduced into that country by Edward VI. and by Queen Elizabeth.[1]

The different religious character of the two sets of manuscripts

---

[1] Edward VI. reigned from 1547-1553; Elizabeth reigned from 1558-1603; the interval was occupied by the Roman Catholic reign of Mary. But the archaic style of the " Halliwell MS." forbids any theory of its having been written during that intermediate period.

is very patent.   We see ecclesiastical influence very strongly mani
fested in the Halliwell MS.   So marked is this that Mr. Halliwell
supposes that it was written by a priest, which, I think, is not impossible, although not for the reason he assigns, which is founded on his
incorrect translation of a single word.[1]

But the Roman Catholic character of the poem is proven by
lines 593–692, which are occupied in directions how the mass is to
be heard ; and, so ample are these directions as to the ritual observance of this part of the Roman Catholic worship, that it is very
probable that they were written by a priest.

In the subsequent manuscripts we find no such allusions.   Freemasonry, when these documents were written, was Christian in its
character, but it was Protestant Christianity.   The invocation with
which each one begins is to the Trinity of Father, Son, and Holy
Ghost ; but no mention is made, as in the Halliwell MS. of the
Virgin and the saints.   The only reference to the Church is in the
first charge, which is, " that you shall be a true man to God and the
holy Church, and that you use no heresy nor error by your understanding or teaching of discreet men "—a charge that would be eminently fitting for a Protestant Christian brotherhood.

On referring to the first charge adopted after the revival in 1717
by the Grand Lodge of England, we find that then, for the first
time, the sectarian character was abandoned, and the toleration of a
universal religion adopted.

Thus it is said in that charge : " Though in ancient times Ma-

---

[1] A philological note may, here, be not uninteresting.   Mr. Halliwell, in support of
his assertion that the writer of the poem was a priest, quotes line 629 : " And, when the
Gospel *me* rede schal "—where he evidently supposes that *me* was used instead of *I*, and
that the line was to be translated—" when I shall read the Gospel."   But in none of the
old manuscripts is the flagrant blunder committed of using the accusative *me* in place of
the nominative *Y* or *I*.   The fact is, that the Anglo-Saxon *man*, signifying *one*, or *they*,
like the French *on* in " on dit," as " man dyde," *one or they did*, or *it was done*, gave
way in Early English to *me*, used in the same sense.   Examples of this may be found in
the writers who lived about the time of the composition of the " Halliwell MS." A few
may suffice.   In the *Ayenbite of Inwyt* is the following line : " Ine the ydele wordes *me*
zeneyeth ine vif maneres," that is, " In the idle word *one* sinneth in five ways."   Again,
in Robert of Gloucester's Chronicle are these phrases : " By this tale *me* may yse," *i.e. :*
" By this tale *may be seen*," Story of Lear, line 183.   " And best *me* may to hem truste,"
i.e. : " And they *may be trusted* best," ib., l. 184.   " The stude that he was at yslawe *me*
cleputh yet Morgan," *i.e. :* " The place where he was slain *is called* Morgan still," ib., l.
213.   And the line in the Halliwell poem, which Mr. Halliwell supposed to mean, " And
when *I* shall read the Gospel," properly translated, is, " And when the Gospel *shall be
read*."   It furnishes, therefore, no proof that the writer was a priest.

sons were charged in every country to be of the religion of that country or nation, whatever it was, yet 'tis now thought more expedient only to oblige them to that religion in which all men agree, leaving their particular opinions to themselves." [1]

Now, comparing the religious views expressed in the oldest Masonic Constitution of the 14th century, with those set forth in the later ones of the 16th and 17th, and again with those laid down in the charge of 1717, we find an exact record of the transitions which from time to time took place in the religious aspect of Freemasonry in England and in some other countries.

At first it was Roman Catholic in its character, and under ecclesiastical domination.

Then, after the Reformation, rejecting the doctrines of Rome and the influence of the priesthood, it retained its Christian character, but became Protestant in its peculiar views.

Lastly, at the time of the so-called Revival, in the beginning of the 18th century, when Speculative Masonry assumed that form which it has ever since retained, it abandoned its sectarian character, and adopted a cosmopolitan and tolerant rule, which required of its members, as a religious test, only a belief in God.

---

[1] Anderson's " Constitutions," 1st ed., 1723, p. 50.

CHAPTER VI

LL these facts concerning the gradual changes in the religious character of the Institution, which by a collation of the old manuscripts we are enabled to derive from the *Legend of the Craft*, are corroborated by contemporaneous historical documents, as will be hereafter seen, and thus the "Legend," notwithstanding the many absurdities and anachronisms which deface it, becomes really valuable as an historical document.

But this is not all. In comparing the Halliwell poem with the later manuscripts, we not only find unmistakable internal evidence that they have a different origin, but we learn what that origin is.

The Halliwell poem comes to us from the Stonemasons of Germany. It is not, perhaps, an exact copy of any hitherto undiscovered German document, but its author must have been greatly imbued with the peculiar thoughts and principles of the German "Steinmetzen" of the Middle Ages.

The proof of this is very palpable to any one who will carefully read the Halliwell poem, and compare its idea of the rise and progress of Geometry with that exhibited in the later manuscript Constitutions.

These latter trace the science, as it is always called, from Lamech to Nimrod, who "found" or invented the Craft of Masonry at the building of the Tower of Babel, and then to Euclid, who established it in Egypt, whence it was brought by the Israelites into Judea, and there again established by David and Solomon, at the building of the Temple. Thence, by a wonderful anachronism it was brought into France by one Namus Grecus, who had been a workman at the Temple, and who organized the Science in France under the auspices of Charles Martel. From France it was carried to England in the time of St. Alban. After a long interruption in consequence of the

33

Danish and Saxon wars, it finally took permanent root at York, where Prince Edwin called an Assembly, and gave the Masons their charges under the authority of a Charter granted by King Athelstan.

It will be observed that nowhere in this later Legend is there any reference to Germany as a country in which Masonry existed. On the contrary, the Masonry of England is supposed to have been derived from France, and due honor is paid to Charles Martel as the founder of the Order in that kingdom.

Hence we may rationally conclude that the *Legend of the Craft* was modified by the influence of the French Masons, who, as history informs us, were brought over into England at an early period.

In this respect, authentic history and the Legend coincide, and the one corroborates the other.

Different from all this is the Legend of the Halliwell poem, the internal evidence clearly showing a Germanic origin, or at least a Germanic influence. The Rev. Bro. Woodford objects to this view, because, as he says, "the Legend was then common to both countries." But with all due respect, I can not but look upon this argument as a sort of *petitio principii*. The very question to be determined is, whether this community of belief, if it existed at that time, did not owe its origin to an importation from Germany. It is certain that in none of the later English manuscripts is there any allusion to the Four Crowned Martyrs, who were the recognized patrons of German Operative Masonry.

The variations of the Halliwell poem from the later manuscripts are as follows: It omits all reference to Lamech and his sons, but passing rapidly over the events at the Tower of Babel, the building of which it ascribes to Nebuchadnezzar, it begins (if we except a few lines interpolated in the middle of the poem) with the Legend of Euclid and the establishment of Masonry by him in Egypt.

There is no mention of King Solomon's Temple, whereas the history of the building of that edifice, as a Masonic labor, constitutes an important part of all the later manuscripts.

The Legend of the Four Crowned Martyrs, concerning whom all the later manuscripts are silent, is given at some length, and they are described as "gode masonus as on erthe schul go." These were the tutelar saints of the German Operative Masons of the Middle

Ages, but there is no evidence that they were ever adopted as such by the English brotherhood.

There is no allusion in the Halliwell poem to Charles Martel, and to the account of the introduction of Masonry into England from France, during his reign, which forms a prominent part of all the later manuscripts.

Neither is there any notice of the Masonry in England during the time of St. Alban, but the poem attributes its entrance into that country to King Athelstan.

Lastly, while the later manuscripts record the calling of the Assembly at the city of York by Prince Edwin, the Halliwell makes no mention of York as the place where the Assembly was called, nor of Edwin as presiding over it. This fact demolishes the theory of Dr. Oliver, that the Halliwell poem is a copy of the so-called Old York Constitutions.

From all these considerations, I think that we are justified in assigning to the Halliwell poem and to the other later manuscripts two different sources. The former is of Germanic, and the latter of French origin. They agree, however, in a general resemblance, diversified only in the details. This suggests the idea of a common belief, upon which, as a foundation, two different structures have been erected.

CHAPTER VII

THE LEGEND, THE GERM OF HISTORY

HE *Legend of the Craft,* as it has been given in the fourth chapter of this work from the exemplar in the Dowland MS., appears to have been accepted for centuries by the body of the Fraternity as a truthful history. Even at the present day, this Legend is exerting an influence in the formation of various parts of the ritual. This influence has even been extended to the adoption of historical views of the rise and progress of the Institution, which have, in reality, no other foundation than the statements which are contained in the Legend.

For these reasons, the *Legend of the Craft* is of great importance and value to the student of Masonic history, notwithstanding the absurdities, anachronisms, and unsupported theories in which it abounds.

Accepting it simply as a document which for so long a period claimed and received the implicit faith of the Fraternity whose history it professed to give—a faith not yet altogether dead—it is worthy of our consideration whether we can not, by a careful examination of its general spirit and tenor, irrespective of the bare narrative which it contains, discover some key to the true origin and character of that old and extensive brotherhood of which it is the earliest record.

I think that we shall find in it the germ of many truths, and the interpretation of several historic facts concerning which it makes important suggestions.

In the first place, it must be remarked that we have no way of determining the precise period when this Legend was first composed, nor when it was first accepted by the Craft as a history of the Institution. The earliest written record that has been discovered among English Masons bears a date which is certainly not later than about the end of the 14th century. But this by no means proves that no earlier exemplar ever existed, of which the *Constitutions*, which have so far been brought to light, may only be copies.

On the contrary, we have abundant reason to believe that all the *Old Records* which have been published are, with the exception of the Halliwell MS., in fact derived from some original text which however, has hitherto escaped the indefatigable researches of the investigators.

If, for instance, we take the Sloane MS., No. 3,848, the assumed date of which is A.D. 1646, and the Harleian MS., No. 2,054, the date of which is supposed to be A.D. 1650, and if we carefully collate the one with the other, we must come to the conclusion either that the latter was copied from the former, or that both were copied from some earlier record, for whose exhumation from the shelves of the British Museum, or from the archives of some old Lodge, we may still confidently hope.

The resemblances in language and ideas, and the similarity of arrangement that are found in both documents, very clearly indicate a common origin, while the occasional verbal discrepancies can be safely attributed to the carelessness of an inexpert copyist. Brother Hughan,[1] who is high authority, styles the Harleian, from its close resemblance," an indifferent copy " of the Sloane. The Rev. A. F. A. Woodford,[2] who assigns the earlier date of 1625 to the original Harleian, says it " is nearly a verbatim copy of Dowland's form, slightly later, and must have been transcribed either from an early, and almost contemporary, copy of Dowland's, or it is really a copy of Dowland's itself." These opinions by experts strengthen the view I have advanced, that there was a common origin for all of these manuscripts.

If we continue the collation of the manuscripts of later date, as far, even, as the Papworth, which is supposed to have been transcribed about the year 1714, the same family likeness will be found in all. It is true, that in the transcription of the later manuscripts —those, for example, that were copied toward the end of the 17th and the beginning of the 18th centuries—the language has been improved, some few archaisms have been avoided, and more recent words substituted for them. Scriptural names have been sometimes spelt with a greater respect for correct orthography, and a feeble

---

[1] " Old Charges of the Brit. Freemasons," p. 8.
[2] Preface to Hughan's " Old Charges," p. xi.

attempt has been made to give a modern complexion to the document. But in all of them there is the same misspelling of words, the same violations of the rules of grammar, the same arrangement of the narrative, and a preservation and repetition of all the statements, apocryphal and authentic, which are to be found in the earliest exemplars.

I have said that the *Legend of the Craft*, as set forth in the later manuscripts, was for centuries accepted by the Operative Masons of England, with all its absurdities of anachronism, as a veritable history of the rise and progress of Masonry from the earliest times, and that the influence of this belief is still felt among the Speculative Masons of the present day, and that it has imbued the modern rituals with its views.

This fact gives to this Legend an importance and a value irrespective of its character as a mere Legend. And its value will be greatly enhanced if we are able to show that, notwithstanding the myths with which it abounds, the *Legend of the Craft* really contains the germ of historical truth. It is, indeed, an historical myth—one of that species of myths so common in the mythology of antiquity, which has a foundation in historical truth, with the admixture of a certain amount of fiction in the introduction of personages and circumstances, that are either not historical, or are not historically treated. Indeed, it may be considered as almost rising into the higher class of historical myths, in which the historical and truthful greatly predominate over the fictitious.[1]

In the contemplation of the Legend of the Mediæval Masons from this point of view, it would be well if we should govern ourselves by the profound thought of Max Müller,[2] who says, in writing on a cognate subject, that "everything is true, natural, significant, if we enter with a reverent spirit into the meaning of ancient art and ancient language. Everything becomes false, miraculous, and unmeaning, if we interpret the deep and mighty words of the seers of old in the shallow and feeble sense of modern chroniclers."

Examined in the light of this sentiment, which teaches us to look upon the language of the myth, or Legend, as containing a deeper meaning than that which is expressed upon its face, we shall

---

[1] For a classification of myths into the historical myth and the mythical history, see the author's treatise on the " Symbolism of Freemasonry," p. 347.

[2] " Science of Language," 2d series, p. 578.

find in the *Legend of the Craft* many points of historical reference, and, where not historical, then symbolical, which will divest it of much of what has been called its absurdities.

It is to an examination of the Legend in this philosophic spirit that I now invite the reader.   Let it be understood that I direct my attention to the Legend contained in the later manuscripts, such as the Dowland, Harleian, Sloane, etc., of which a copy has been given in preceding pages of this work, and that reference is made only as occasion may require to the Halliwell MS. for comparison or ex-planation.   This is done because the Legend of the later manuscripts is undoubtedly the one which was adopted by the English Masons, while that of the Halliwell MS. appears to have been of exotic growth, which never took any extensive root in the soil of English Masonry.

In the subsequent chapters devoted to this subject, which may be viewed as Commentaries on the *Legend of the Craft*, I shall investigate the signification of the various subordinate Legends into which it is divided.

CHAPTER VIII

HE manuscript begins with an invocation to the Trinity. This invocation is almost identical with that which prefaces the Harleian, the Sloane, the Landsdowne, and, indeed, all the other manuscripts, except the Halliwell and the Cooke. From this fact we may justly infer that there was a common exemplar, an "editio princeps," whence each of these manuscripts was copied. The very slight verbal variations, such as "Father of Kings" in the Dowland, which is "Father of Heaven" in the others, will not affect this conclusion, for they may be fairly attributed to the carelessness of copyists. The reference to the Trinity in all these invocations is also a conclusive proof of the Christian character of the building corporations of the Middle Ages—a proof that is corroborated by historical evidences. As I have already shown, in the German Constitutions of the Stonemasons, the invocation is "In the name of the Father, Son, and Holy Ghost, in the name of the blessed Virgin Mary, and also in honor of the Four Crowned Martyrs"—an invocation that shows the Roman Catholic spirit of the German Regulations; while the omission of all reference to the Virgin and the Martyrs gives a Protestant character to the English manuscripts.

Next follows a descant on the seven liberal arts and sciences, the nature and intention of each of which is briefly described. In all of the manuscripts, even in the earliest—the Halliwell—will we find the same reference to them, and, almost literally, the same description. It is not surprising that these sciences should occupy so prominent a place in the Old Constitutions, as making the very foundation of Masonry, when we reflect that an equal prominence was given to them in the Middle Ages as comprehending the whole body of human knowledge. Thus Mosheim[1] tells us that in the 11th century they

---

[1] "Ecclesiast. Hist. XI. Cent.," part ii., chap. i.

were taught in the greatest part of the schools; and Holinshed, who wrote in the 16th century, says that they composed a part of the curriculum that was taught in the universities. Speculative Masonry continues to this day to pay an homage to these seven sciences, and has adopted them among its important symbols in the second degree. The connection sought to be established in the old manuscripts between them and Masonry, would seem to indicate the existence of a laudable ambition among the Operative Masons of the Middle Ages to elevate the character of their Craft above the ordinary standard of workmen—an elevation that, history informs us, was actually effected, the Freemasons of the Guild holding themselves and being held by others as of higher rank and greater acquirements than were the rough Masons who did not belong to the corporation of builders.

The manuscript continues by a declaration that Geometry and Masonry are identical. Thus, in enumerating and defining the seven liberal arts and sciences, Geometry is placed as the fifth, "the which science," says the Legend, "is called Masonrye."[1]

Now, this doctrine that Geometry and Masonry are identical sciences, has been held from the time of the earliest records to the present day by all the Operative Masons who preceded. the 18th century, as well as by the Speculative Masons after that period.

In the ritual of the Fellow Craft's degree used ever since, at least from the middle of the last century, the candidate is informed that "Masonry and Geometry are synonymous terms." The Lodge-room, wherever Speculative Masonry has extended, shows, by the presence of the hieroglyphic letter in the East, that the doctrine is still maintained.

Gadicke, the author of a German *Lexicon of Freemasonry*, says, that as Geometry is among the mathematical sciences the one which has the most especial reference to architecture, we can, therefore, under the name of Geometry, understand the whole art of Freemasonry.

Hutchinson, speaking of the letter G, says that it denotes Geometry, and declares that as a symbol it has always been used by artificers—that is, architects—and by Masons.[2]

---

[1] Dowland MS. The Halliwell poem expresses the same idea in different words:

" At these lordys prayers they counterfetyd gemetry,
And gaf hyt the name of Masonry." (Lines 23, 24.)

[2] " Spirit of Freemasonry," lect. viii., p. 92, 2d edit.

The modern ritual maintains this legendary idea of the close con‐ nection that exists between Geometry and Masonry, and tells us that the former is the basis on which the latter, as a superstructure, is erected.   Hence we find that Masonry has adopted mathematical figures, such as angles, squares, triangles, circles, and especially the 47th proposition of Euclid, as prominent symbols.

And this idea of the infusion of Geometry into Masonry as a prevailing element—the idea that is suggested in the Legend—was so thoroughly recognized, that in the 18th century a Speculative Mason was designated as a " Geometrical Mason."

We have found this idea of Geometry as the fundamental science of Masonry, set forth in the *Legend of the Craft*.   It will be well to see how it was developed in the Middle Ages, in the authentic history of the Craft.   Thus we shall have discovered another link in the chain which unites the myths of the Legend with the true his‐ tory of the Institution.

The Operative Masons of the Middle Ages, who are said to have derived the knowledge of their art as well as their organization as a Guild of Builders from the Architects of Lombardy, who were the first to assume the title of " Freemasons," were in the possession of secrets which enabled them everywhere to construct the edifices on which they were engaged according to the same principles, and to keep up, even in the most distant countries, a correspondence, so that every member was made acquainted with the most minute improvement in the art which had been discovered by any other.[1] One of these secrets was the knowledge of the science of symbolism,[2] and the other was the application of the principles of Geometry to the art of building.

" It is certain," says Mr. Paley,[3] " that Geometry lent its aid in the planning and designing of buildings"; and he adds that "prob‐ ably the equilateral triangle was the basis of most formations."

The geometrical symbols found in the ritual of modern Free‐ masonry may be considered as the débris of the geometrical secrets of the Mediæval Masons, which are now admitted to be lost.[4]   As

---

[1] Hope, " Historical Essay on Architecture."

[2] M. Maury (" Essai sur les Legendes Pieures du Moyen-Aye ") gives many instances of the application of symbolism by these builders to the construction of churches.

[3] " Manual of Gothic Architecture," p. 78.

[4] Lord Lindsay, " Sketches of the History of Christian Art," ii., 14.

these founded their operative art on the knowledge of Geometry, and as the secrets of which they boasted as distinguishing them from the "rough Masons" of the same period consisted in an application of the principles of that science to the construction of edifices, it is not surprising that in their traditional history they should have so identified architecture with Geometry, and that with their own art of building, as to speak of Geometry and Masonry as synonymous terms. "The fifth science," says the Dowland MS., is "called Geometry, . . . the which science is called Masonrye." Remembering the tendency of all men to aggrandize their own pursuits, it is not surprising that the Mediæval Masons should have believed and said that "there is no handycraft that is wrought by man's hand but it is wrought by Geometry."

In all this descant in the old manuscripts on the identity of Geometry and Masonry, the *Legend of the Craft* expresses a sentiment the existence of which is supported by the authentic evidence of contemporaneous history.

CHAPTER IX

THE LEGEND OF LAMECH'S SONS AND THE PILLARS

 HE traditional history of Masonry now begins, in the *Legend of the Craft*, with an account of the three sons of Lamech, to whom is attributed the discovery of all sciences. But the most interesting part of the Legend is that in which the story is told of two pillars erected by them, and on which they had inscribed the discoveries they had made, so that after the impending destruction of the world the knowledge which they had attained might be communicated to the post-diluvian race.

This story is not mentioned in the Bible, but is first related by Josephus in the following words:

"They also [the posterity of Seth] were the inventors of that peculiar sort of wisdom which is concerned with the heavenly bodies and their order. And that their inventions might not be lost before they were sufficiently known, upon Adam's prediction that the world was to be destroyed at one time by the force of fire, and at another time by the violence and quantity of water, they made two pillars, the one of brick, the other of stone; they inscribed their discoveries on them both, that in case the pillar of brick should be destroyed by the flood, the pillar of stone might remain and exhibit those discoveries to mankind, and also inform them that there was another pillar of brick erected by them. Now this remains in the land of Siriad to this day."[1]

Although this traditional narrative has received scarcely any estimation from scholars, and Josephus has been accused either of "incredible audacity or frivolous credulity,"[2] still it has formed the

---

[1] Josephus, "Antiquities of the Jews," B. I., ch. ii., Whiston's trans.

[2] "Incredibili audaciâ aut futili credulitate usus est," is the language of Hornius in his "*Geographia Vetus.*" But Owen ("Theologomena," lib. iv., .c. ii., 6), although inclined to doubt the story, thinks it not impossible if we suppose hieroglyphics like those of the Egyptians to have been used for the inscriptions, instead of letters.

foundation on which the Masonic Legend of the pillars has been erected. But in passing from the Jewish historian to the Legend-maker of the Craft, the form of the story has been materially altered. In Josephus the construction of the pillars is attributed to the posterity of Seth; in the Legend, to the children of Lamech. Whence was this important alteration derived?

The Dowland and all subsequent manuscripts cite the fourth chapter of Genesis as authority for the Legend. But in Genesis no mention is made of these pillars. But in the Cooke MS., which is of an earlier date, we can trace the true source of the Legend in its Masonic form, which could not be done until that manuscript was published.

To the Cooke MS. has been accorded the date of 1490. It differs materially in form and substance from the Halliwell MS., which preceded it by at least a century, and is the first of the Old Constitutions in which anything like the present form of the Legend appears.

The way in which the Legend of Lamech is treated by it, enables us to discover the true source whence this part of the *Legend of the Craft* was derived.

It must be remarked, in the first place, that the Halliwell poem, the earliest of the old manuscripts, the date of which is not later than the close of the 14th century, contains no allusion to this Legend of Lamech and his children. The Cooke MS. is the first one in which we find the details. The Cooke MS. is assigned, as has been before said, to the end of the 15th century, about the year 1490. In it the Legend of the pillars is given (from line 253 to 284) in the following words:

"And these iii brotheryn [the sons of Lamech] aforesayd, had knowlyche that God wold take vengans for synne other by fyre or watir, and they had greter care how they myght do to saue the sciens that they founde, and they toke her [their] consell to gedyr and by all her [their] witts they seyde that were ij manner of stonn of suche virtu that the one wolde neuer brenne [burn] and that stonn is called marbyll and that other stonn that woll not synke in watir, and that stone is namyd laterus,[1] and so they deuysyd to wryte all the sciens that they had Found[2] in this ij stonys if that god wolde

---

[1] From the Latin "later," a *brick*.

[2] It is to be regretted that in nearly all the recent printed copies of the old manu-

take vengeans by fyre that the marbyll scholde not brenne. And yf god sende vengeans by watir that the other scholde not droune, and so they prayed her elder brother jobell that wold make ij pillers of these ij stones, that is to sey of marbill and of laterus, and that he wolde write in the ij pylers alle the sciens and crafte that alle they had founde, and so he did."

Comparing this Legend with the passage that has been cited from Josephus, it is evident that the Legend-maker had not derived his story from the Jewish historian. The latter attributes the building of the pillars to the children of Seth, while the former assigns it to the children of Lamech. How are we to explain this change in the form of the Legend? We can only solve the problem by reference to a work almost contemporary with the legendist.

Ranulph Higden, a Benedictine monk of St. Werburg's Abbey, in Chester, who died in the latter half of the 14th century, wrote a Universal history, completed to his own times, under the title of *Polychronicon.*

The *Polychronicon* was written in the Latin language, but was translated into English by Sir John Trevisa. This translation, with several verbal alterations, was published in London by William Caxton in 1482, about ten years before the date of the Cooke MS. With this work, the compiler of the Legend in the Cooke MS. appears to have been familiar. He cites it repeatedly as authority for his statements.

Thus he says: "Ye schal understonde that amonge all the craftys of the world of mannes crafte Masonry hath the most notabilite and moste parte of this sciens Gemetry as his notid and seyd in storiall as in the bybyll and in the master of stories. And in policronico a cronycle prynted."

Now the Legend of Lamech's children is thus given in Caxton's edition of the translation of Higden's *Polychronicon :*[1]

---

scripts, the editors have substituted the double *ff* for the capital *F* which is in the original. The scribes or amanuenses of the Middle Ages were fond of employing capital letters often when there was really no use for them, but they never indulged in the folly of unnecessarily doubling initial letters. What the modern editors of the manuscripts have mistaken for a double *ff* was really the ff or ff the capital F of the scribes. This is not of much importance, but even in small things it is well to be accurate. Bro. Hughan, in his edition of the "Old Charges," is, as we might expect, generally correct in this particular. But sometimes, perhaps inadvertently, he has printed the double instead of the capital letter.

[1] Book II., ch. v.

"Caym Adams fyrste sone begate Enoch, he gate Irad, he gate Manayell, he gate Matusale, he gate Lameth.   This Lameth toke twey wyves, Ada and Sella, and gate tweyne sons on Ada.   Iabell that was fader of them that woned in tentes and in pauylons.   And Tuball that was fader of organystre and of harpers.   And Lameth gate on Sella Tubal cayn that was a smith worchyng with hamer, and his sister Noema, she found fyrst weuynge crafte.

.   .   .   .

"*Josephus.*   Jabell ordayned fyrste flockes of beestes and marks to know one from another.   And departed kyddes from lambes and yonge from the olde.   *Petrus* Tubalcayn founde fyrst smythes crafte.   Tuball had grete lykynge to here the hamers sowne.   And soo he vsed them moche in the accordé of melodye, but he was not finder of the instruments of musyke.   For they were founde longe afterwarde."

The reader will at once perceive whence the composer of the Legend in the Cooke MS. derived his information about the family of Lamech.   And it will be equally plain that the subsequent writers of the Old Constitutions took the general tone of their Legend from this manuscript.

The *Polychronicon*, after attributing the discovery of music to Pythagoras, proceeds to descant upon the wickedness of mankind immediately after the time of Seth, and repeats the biblical story of the intermarriage of the sons of God and the daughters of men, which he explains as signifying the sons of Seth and the daughters of Cain.   Then follows the following passage :

"*Josephus.*   That tyme men wyste as Adam and sayde, that they sholde be destroyed by fyre or elles by water.   Therefore bookes that they hadde made by grete trauaille and studye, he closed them in two grete pylers made of marbill and of brent tyle.   In a pyler of marbill for water and in a pyler of tyle for fyre.   For it should be sauved by that maner to helpe of mankynde.   Men sayth that the pyler of stone escaped the floode, and yet is in Syrya."

Here we find the origin of the story of the two pillars as related in the *Legend of the Craft*.   But how can we account for the change of the constructors of these pillars from the children of Seth, as stated in Josephus, and from him in the *Polychronicon*, to the children of Lamech, as it is given in the Legend ?

By the phrase "That tyme men wyste," or "at that time men

knew," with which Trevisa begins his translation of that part of Higden's work, he undoubtedly referred to the "tyme" contemporary with the children of Seth, of whom he had immediately before been speaking.   But the writer of the Legend engaged in recounting the narrative of the invention of the sciences by the children of Lamech, and thus having his attention closely directed to the doings of that family, inadvertently, as I suppose, passed over or omitted to notice the passage concerning the descendants of Seth, which had been interposed by the author of the *Polychronicon*, and his eye, catching the account of the pillars a little farther on, he applied the expression, " that tyme," not to the descendants of Seth, but to the children of Lamech, and thus gave the Masonic version of the Legend.

I have called this ascription of the pillars to the children of Lamech a " Masonic version," because it is now contained only in the *Legend of the Craft*, those who do not reject the story altogether as a myth, preferring the account given by Josephus.

But, in fact, the error of misinterpreting Josephus occurred long before the *Legend of the Craft* was written, and was committed by one of the most learned men of his age.

St. Isidore, Bishop of Seville, who died in the year 636, was the author of many works in the Latin language, on theology, philosophy, history, and philology.   Among other books written by him was a *Chronicon*, or Chronicle, in which the following passage occurs, where he is treating of Lamech:

" In the year of the world 1642, Lamech being 190 years old, begat Noah, who, in the five hundredth year of his age, is commanded by the Divine oracle to build the Ark.   In these times, as Josephus relates, those men knowing that they would be destroyed either by fire or water, inscribed their knowledge upon two columns made of brick and of stone, so that the memory of those things which they had wisely discovered might not be lost.   Of these columns the stone one is said to have escaped the Flood and to be still remaining in Syria." [1]

It is very evident that in some way the learned Bishop of Seville had misunderstood the passage of Josephus, and that to him the sons of Lamech are indebted for the honor of being considered the con-

---

[1] "Opera Isidori," ed. Matriti, 1778, tom. i., p. 125.

structors of the pillars. The phrase "his temporibus," *in these times*, clearly refers to the times of Lamech.

It is doubtful whether the author of the *Legend of the Craft* was acquainted with the works of Isidore, or had read this passage. His *Etymologies* are repeatedly cited in the Cooke manuscript, but it is through Higden, whose *Polychronicon* contains many quotations from the *Libri Etymologiarum* of the Spanish Bishop and Saint. But I prefer to assume that the Legend-maker got his ideas from the *Polychronicon* in the method that I have described.

In the last century a new Legend was introduced into Masonry, in which the building of these pillars was ascribed to Enoch. But this Legend, which is supposed to have been the invention of the Chevalier Ramsay, is altogether modern, and has no connection with the *Legend of the Craft*.

In borrowing the story of the antediluvian pillars from Josephus, through the *Polychronicon*, though they have made some confusion in narrating the incidents, the Old Operative Masons were simply incorporating into their *Legend of the Craft* a myth which had been universal among the nations of antiquity, for all of them had their memorial columns. Sesostris, the great Egyptian king and conqueror, sometimes called Sethos, or Seth, and who, Whiston thinks, has been confounded by Josephus with the Adamic Seth, erected pillars in all the countries which he conquered as monuments of his victories.

The *Polychronicon*, with which we see that the old Masons were familiar, had told them that Zoroastres, King of Bactria, had inscribed the seven liberal arts and sciences on fourteen pillars, seven of brass and seven of brick. Hercules was said to have placed at the Straits of Gades two pillars, to show to posterity how far he had extended his conquests.

In conclusion, it should be observed that the story of the pillars as inserted in the *Legend of the Craft* has exerted no influence on the modern rituals of Freemasonry, and is never referred to in any of the ceremonies of Ancient Craft Masonry. The more recent Legend of the pillars of Enoch belongs exclusively to the higher and more modern degrees. The only pillars that are alluded to in the primitive degrees are those of Solomon's temple. But these develop so important a portion of the symbolism of the Institution as to demand our future consideration in a subsequent part of this work.

CHAPTER X

HE next part of the *Legend of the Craft* which claims our attention is that which relates to Hermes, who is said to have discovered one of the pillars erected by the sons of Lamech, and to have communicated the sciences inscribed on it to mankind. This may, for distinction, be called "*The Legend of Hermes.*"

The name has suffered cruel distortion from the hands of the copyists in the different manuscripts. In the Dowland MS. it is *Hermarynes ;* in the Landsdowne, *Herminerus ;* in the York, *Hermarines ;* in the Sloane, 3,848, *Hermines* and *Hermenes*, who " was afterwards called Hermes"; and worst and most intolerable of all, it is in the Harleian, *Hermaxmes*. But they all evidently refer to the celebrated Hermes Trismegistus, or the thrice great Hermes. The Cooke MS., from which the story in the later manuscripts is derived, spells the name correctly, and adds, on the authority of the *Polychronicon*, that while Hermes found one of the pillars, Pythagoras discovered the other. Pythagoras is not mentioned in any of the later manuscripts, and we first find him referred to as a founder in Masonry in the questionable manuscript of Leland, which fact will, perhaps, furnish another argument against the genuineness of that document.

As to Hermes, the Legend is not altogether without some historical support, although the story is in the Legend mythical, but of that character which pertains to the historical myth.

He was reputed to be the son of Taut or Thoth, whom the Egyptians deified, and placed his image beside those of Osiris and Isis. To him they attributed the invention of letters, as well as of all the sciences, and they esteemed him as the founder of their religious rites.

Hodges says, in a note on a passage of Sanchoniathon,[1] that "Thoth was an Egyptian deity of the second order. The Græco-Roman mythology identified him with Hermes or Mercury. He was reputed to be the inventor of writing, the patron deity of learning, the scribe of the gods, in which capacity he is represented signing the sentences on the souls of the dead." Some recent writers have supposed that Hermes was the symbol of Divine Intelligence and the primitive type of Plato's " Logos."

Manetho, the Egyptian priest, as quoted by Syncellus, distinguishes three beings who were called Hermes by the Egyptians. The first, or Hermes Trismegistus, had, before the deluge, inscribed the history of all the sciences on pillars; the second, the son of Agathodemon, translated the precepts of the first ; and the third, who is supposed to be synonymous with Thoth, was the counsellor of Osiris and Isis. But these three were in later ages confounded and fused into one, known as Hermes Trismegistus. He was always understood by the philosophers to symbolize the birth, the progress, and the perfection of human sciences. He was thus considered as a type of the Supreme Being. Through him man was elevated and put into communication with the gods.

The Egyptians attributed to him the composition of 36,525 books on all kinds of knowledge.[2] But this mythical fecundity of authorship has been explained as referring to the whole scientific and religious encyclopædia collected by the Egyptian priests and preserved in their temples.

Under the title of Hermetic books, several works falsely attributed to Hermes, but written, most probably, by the Neo-Platonists, are still extant, and were deemed to be of great authority up to the 16th century.[3]

It was a tradition very generally accepted in former times that this Hermes engraved his knowledge of the sciences on tables or pillars of stone, which were afterward copied into books.

Manetho attributes to him the invention of *stylæ*, or pillars, on which were inscribed the principles of the sciences. And Jamblichus

---

[1] Cory's " Ancient Fragments," edited by E. Richmond Hodges, Lond., 1876, p. 3.

[2] Jamblichus, citing Selencos, " de Mysteriis," segm. viii., c. 1.

[3] Rousse, Dictionnaire *in voc.* The principal of these is the " Pœmander," or of the Divine Power and Wisdom.

says that when Plato and Pythagoras had read the inscriptions on these columns they formed their philosophy.[1]

Hermes was, in fact, an Egyptian legislator and priest. Thirty-six books on philosophy and theology, and six on medicine, are said to have been written by him, but they are all lost, if they ever existed. The question, indeed, of his own existence has been regarded by modern scholars as extremely mythical. The Alchemists, however, adopted him as their patron. Hence Alchemy is called the Hermetic science, and hence we get Hermetic Masonry and Hermetic Rites.

At the time of the composition of the *Legend of the Craft*, the opinion that Hermes was the inventor of all the sciences, and among them, of course, Geometry and Architecture, was universally accepted as true, even by the learned. It is not, therefore, singular that the old Masons, who must have been familiar with the Hermetic myth, received it as something worthy to be incorporated into the early history of the Craft, nor that they should have adopted him, as they did Euclid, as one of the founders of the science of Masonry.

The idea must, however, have sprung up in the 15th century, as it is first broached in the Cook MS. And it was, in all probability, of English origin, since there is no allusion to it in the Halliwell poem.

The next important point that occurs in the *Legend of the Craft* is its reference to the Tower of Babel, and this will, therefore, be the subject of the next chapter.

---

[1] Juxta antiquas Mercurii columnas, quas Plato quondam, et Pythagoras cum lectitassent, philosophiam constituerunt. Jamblichus, "de Mysteriis," segm. i., c. 2.

CHAPTER XI

THE TOWER OF BABEL

NLIKE the legend of Hermes, the story of the Tower of Babel appears in the Halliwell poem, which shows, if my theory of the origin of that poem be correct, that the Legend was not confined at an early period to the English Masons. In the second of the two poems, which I have heretofore said are united in one manuscript, the legend of Babel, or Babylon, is thus given :[1]

> "Ye mow here as y do rede,
> That many years after, for gret drede,
> That Noee's flod was alle y-ronne,[2]
> The tower of Bebyloine was begonne,
> Also playne werk of lyme and ston,
> As any mon schulde toke uppon,
> Seven myle the heyghte shadweth the sonne.
> King Nabugodonosor let hyt make
> To gret strenthe for monus[3] sake
> Thaygh such a flod agayne schulde come,
> Over the werke hyt schulde not nome,[4]
> For they hadde so hye pride, with strange bost,
> Alle that werke therfore was y-lost ;
> An angele smot hem so with dyveres speeche,
> That never won wyste what other schuld reche."[5]

The statements of this Halliwell Legend are very meagre, nor is it possible to say with any certainty whence the writer derived his details. From neither the Book of Genesis, nor Berosus, nor Josephus could he have derived the information which has given its peculiar form to the legend. The anachronism of making Nebuchadnezzar, who lived about sixteen centuries after the event, the builder of the

---

[1] Lines 535–550.
[2] Rain—Ang.-Sax. *rinan*, to rain—That Noah's flood would still rain.
[3] Men's sake.　　[4] Get—should not get over the work—cover it.　　[5] Say.

tower is worthy of notice. It would appear that the writer of the poem had a general acquaintance with the well-known tradition of Babel, and that in loosely giving an account of it, he had confused the time and place of the erection and the supposed name of the builder. At all events, the subsequent Masonic legendists did not accept the Halliwell writer as authority, or, more probably, were wholly unacquainted with his poem. It did not exert any influence over the subsequent manuscripts.

The next time that the Babel legend appears is in the Cooke MS., written at least a century after the Halliwell. The legend, as there given, is in the following words:

"Hit is writen in the bibull Genesis, Cap. 1mo, wo [how] that Cam, Noe's sone, gate Nembrothe, and he wax a myghty man apon the erthe, and he wax a stronge man, like a Gyant, and he was a grete kyng, and the bygynyng of his kyngdom was [the] trew kyngdom of Babilon and Arach and Archad and Calan[1] and the lond of Sennare. And this same Cam[2] he gan the towre of babilon, and he taught to his werkemen the craft of mesurie,[3] and he had with him mony masonys mo than xl. thousand, and he louyd and chereshed them well, and hit is wryten in Policronicon and in the master of stories and in other stories mo, and this a part wytnes [the] bybull in the same x. chapter where he seyth that asure [Assur] was nye kynne to Nembrothe[4] gede [went] owt of the londe of Senare, and he bylded the City Nunyve and Plateas and other mo. Thus he seyeth, ' De terra illa et de Sennare egressus est Asure et edifiiavit Nunyven et Plateas civitates et Cale et Iesu quoque inter Nunyven et hæc est Civitas Magna.'

"Reson wolde [requires] that we schold telle opunly how and in what manner that the charges of masoncraft was fyrst foundyd and ho gaf [who gave] fyrste the name to hit of masonri. And ye schyll knaw well that hit [is] told and writen in Policronicon and in Methodus episcopus and Martyrus that Asur that was a worthy lord

---

[1] The names of cities.

[2] The word *Nembroth* had been first written in the manuscript, then erased, and the "Cam" (for Ham) inserted. But this correction is itself incorrect and incongruous with the rest of the legend.

[3] Mesuri—measure. The author of the manuscript had previously maintained that *measure* and geometry were identical. So here "the craft of mesuri" means the craft of geometry, and geometry was always supposed to be the same as Masonry.

[4] *Cam* originally written, then erased and *Nembrothe* inserted.

of Sennare, sende to Nembroth the kyng to sende hym masons and workemen of crafte that myght helpe hym to make his Cite that he was in wyll to make. And Nembroth sende hym xxx C. (3,000) of masons. And whan they scholde go and [he] sende hem forth he callyd hem by for hym [before him] and seyd to hem, ye must go to my cosyn Asure to helpe hym to bilde a cyte, but loke that ye be well governyd, and I shall give you a charge profitable for you and me. . . .

"And they resceyved the charge of him that was here [their] maister and here lorde, and went forth to Asure and bilde the cite of Nunyve in the country of Plateas and other cites mo, that men call Cale and Iesen that is a gret cite bi twene Cale and Nunyve. And in this manner the craft of masonry was fyrst preferryd [brought forward] and chargyd for a sciens."

We next meet with the Legend in the later manuscripts, in a form differing but little from that of the Cooke MS. The Dowland, which is the earliest of these manuscript Constitutions, and the date of which is supposed to be about the year 1550, has already been printed in this work. But for the convenience of the reader, in comparing the three forms of the Legend, so much of it as refers to the Babel legend is again inserted. It is in these words, which, it may be remarked, are very closely followed by all the subsequent manuscripts up to the beginning of the 18th century :

"At the makinge of the Tower of Babylon, there was Masonrye first made much of. And the Kinge of Babylon that height Nemrothe was a mason himselfe, and loved well the science as it is said with masters of histories. And when the City of Ninyve and other citties of the East should be made, Nemrothe the Kinge of Babylon sent thither three score masons at the rogation of the Kinge of Nyneve, his cosen. And when he sent them forth he gave them a charge in this manner. . . . And this was the first tyme that ever Masons had any charge of his science."

In comparing the three forms of the Babylonish legend, which have here been cited, namely, as given in the Halliwell, the Cooke, and the Dowland MSS., we shall readily detect that there was a gradual growth of the details until the legend eventually took the shape which for a long time was accepted by the Craft.

In the Halliwell poem the legend is very brief, and by its abrupt termination would impress the opinion upon the reader that Masonry had no part in the building of the Tower of Babel, the only effect of which was to produce a confusion of languages and the dispersion of mankind. It was only "many years after" that the "craft of geometry," or Masonry, was taught by Euclid. In fact, the whole tendency of the Halliwell legend is to trace the origin of Masonry to Euclid and the Egyptians. In his account of the Tower of Babel, the writer of the Halliwell poem seems to have been indebted only to the Scriptural narrative, although he has confounded Nebuchadnezzar, the repairer of Babylon, with Nimrod, its original founder.

But the writer of the Cooke MS. took his details of the legend from another source. Only a few years before the composition of this manuscript, Caxton had published, and thus placed in the hands of the English Masons, Trevisa's translation of Ranulph Higden's *Polychronicon*, or Universal History. Of this book, rich in materials for legendary composition, the writer of the Cooke MS. readily availed himself. This he honestly acknowledges in several places. And although he quotes as other authorities Herodotus, Josephus, and Methodius, it is very evident that he knows nothing of these historians except from the citations from them made by the monk Higden in the *Polychronicon.*

The English Masons were probably already acquainted with the legend in the imperfect form in which it is given in the Halliwell poem. But for the shape which it assumed from the time of the composition of the Cooke MS., and which was adopted in the Dowland and all the later manuscripts, the Craft were, I think, undoubtedly indebted to the *Polychronicon* of the Monk of Chester, through its translation by Trevisa and its publication by Caxton.

There are two other forms of the Babylonian legend, of later date, which must be read before we can thoroughly understand the growth of that legend.

In 1723 Anderson published, by authority of the Grand Lodge of England, the *Constitutions of the Free-Masons.* Dr. Anderson was, no doubt, in possession of, or had access to, many sources of information in the way of old manuscripts which have since been lost, and with these, assisted in some measure by his own inventive genius, he has extended the brief *Legend of the Craft* to 34 quarto pages. But as this work was of an official character, and was written and published under the sanction of the Grand Lodge, and freely distributed among the Lodges and Masons of the time, the form of the Legend adopted by him was accepted by the Fraternity for a very long period as authentic. The Andersonian legend of the Tower of Babel molded, therefore, the belief of the English Craft for at least the whole of the 18th century.

Before giving any citations from the Andersonian version of the legend, it will be necessary to refer to another copy of the Old Constitutions.

Dr. Krause, the author of a learned Masonic work, entitled *The Three Oldest Documents of the Brotherhood of Freemasons*, published in that work in 1810 a German translation of a document which he calls the *York Constitutions*.[1]

Of this document Krause gives the following account. He says that Bro. Schneider, of Altenberg, had written communication from Bro. Böttger, who stated that in the year 1799 he had seen at London a copy of the York Constitutions in a very old manuscript, consisting of 107 leaves in large folio, almost one-third of which he had been unable to read, because it was written in the early English language, and hence he was forced to employ a learned Englishman as an interpreter. Schneider made diligent inquiries after this manuscript, and eventually received a certified Latin translation, made in 1806, from which, in 1808, he composed a German version.

This document Krause supposes to be a genuine exemplar of the Constitutions enacted at York in 926. The original manuscript has, however, never been found; it is not referred to in any of the records of the old Grand Lodge of York, and seems to have remained in mysterious obscurity until seen in 1799 by this Bro. Böttger while on a visit to London.

For these reasons, Findel deems it a spurious document. Bro. Woodford, than whom there is none more competent to judge of questions of this kind, does not assent to this opinion, but, having his doubts, thinks the matter should remain in abeyance for the present. Bro. Hughan, another accomplished critic, believes that it is probably a compilation of the early part of the last century.

When the reader shall have collated the extracts about to be given from Anderson's *Constitutions* and the Krause MS., he will, I think, concur with me, that either Anderson had seen the latter

---

[1] " Die drei ältesten Kunsturkunden der Freimaurerbrüderschaft," vol. iii., p. 5.

manuscript, or that the author of it had been familiar with the work of Anderson. The general similarity of ideas, the collocation of certain words, and the use of particular phrases, must lead to the conclusion that one of the two writers was acquainted with the production of the other. Which was the earlier one is not easily determined, nor is it important, since they were almost contemporaneous documents, and, therefore, they both show what was the form assumed by the legend in the early part of the 18th century.[1]

The Anderson version of the Babylon legend is as follows:[2]

"About 101 years after the Flood we find a vast number of 'em [the offspring of the sons of Noah], if not the whole race of Noah, in the vale of Shinar, employed in building a city and large tower, in order to make themselves a name and to prevent their dispersion. And tho' they carried on the work to a monstrous height, and by their vanity provoked God to confound their devices, by confounding their speech, which occasioned their dispersion; yet their skill in Masonry is not the less to be celebrated, having spent above 53 years in that prodigious work, and upon their dispersion carried the mighty knowledge with them into distant parts, where they found the good use of it in the settlement of their kingdoms, commonwealths, and dynasties. And tho' afterwards it was lost in most parts of the earth it was especially preserved in Shinar and Assyria, where Nimrod, the founder of that monarchy, after the dispersion built many splendid cities, as Ereck, Accad, and Calneh in Shinar, from whence afterwards he went forth into Assyria and built Nineveh, Rehoboth, Caleh, and Rhesin.

"In these parts, upon the Tigris and the Euphrates, afterwards flourished many learned Priests and Mathematicians, known by the names of Chaldees and Magi, who preserved the good science, Geometry, as the kings and great men encouraged the Royal Art."

The Krause MS., or the reputed *York Constitutions*, gives the Babylonian legend as follows:[3]

---

[1] The oftener I read this document, and the more I reflect on its internal evidence, the more I become convinced that it was written after the first edition of Anderson's "Constitutions," and, perhaps, after the second. Indeed, I am almost prepared to assign any part of the 18th century for the date of its composition.

[2] "Constitutions," 1st edition, p. 3.

[3] See it in Hughan's "Old Charges of the British Freemasons," p. 80. It must be remembered that it is there an English version of the German which had been translated from a Latin translation of the original old English—*ut dicitur*. I have corrected a few errors in the translation in the "Old Charges" by a collation with the German of Krause.

"Two generations after Noah, his descendants, proud of their knowledge, built on a plain, in the land of Shinar, a great city and a high tower of lime, stones, and wood, in order that they might dwell together, under the laws which their ancestor, Noah, had made known, and that the names of Noah's descendants might be preserved for all time. This arrogance, however, did not please the Lord in heaven, the lover of humility, therefore he caused a confusion of their speech before the tower was finished, and scattered them in many uninhabited lands, whither they brought with them their laws and arts, and then founded kingdoms and principalities, as the Holy Books often testify. Nimrod, in particular, built a town of considerable size; but Noah's son, Shem, remained in Ur, in the land of the Chaldeans, and propagated a knowledge of all the arts and sciences abroad, and taught also Peleg, Serug, Nahor, Terah, and Abraham, the last of whom knew all the sciences, and had knowledge, and continued to instruct the sons of freeborn men, whence afterwards the numerous learned priests and mathematicians who have been known under the name of the wise Chaldeans."

We have now five different documents presenting three different forms of the Legend of the Tower of Babel:

1. *The Halliwell poem.* This Legend briefly recounts the facts of the building of the tower and the subsequent interruption of the work by the confusion of tongues and the dispersion of the builders. By an anachronism, Nebuchadnezzar is designated as the monarch who directed the construction. Not a word is said about the Institution of Masonry at that time. In fact, the theory of the Halliwell MS. seems rather to be that Masonry was, "many years after," taught for the first time in Egypt by Euclid.

The form of the Legend was never accepted by the Operative Masons of the Guild, certainly not after the end of the 15th century.

2. *The Cooke and later manuscripts.* This form of the Legend ascribes the origin of Masonry to the era of the building of the tower. Nimrod is made the Grand Master and makes the first charge—that is, frames the first Constitution that the Masons ever had. Asshur, the son of Shem, is also represented as a great Mason, the builder of the city of Nineveh, and to whom Nimrod sent workmen to assist him. From Babylon, Masonry was carried next into Egypt.

This form of the Legend, first presented in the Cooke MS., and followed almost literally in the Dowland and all the succeeding manuscript Constitutions, seems to have embodied the prevailing belief of the Fraternity until about the end of the 17th or the beginning of the 18th century.

3. *The Andersonian* and the *York Constitutions.* In these the form of the Legend is greatly improved. The idea that Masonry was first established with appropriate laws at the Tower of Babel under the superintendence of Nimrod is still preserved. But Asshur no longer appears as a builder of cities, assisted by "his cosen," but is transformed, and correctly too, into the kingdom of Assyria, where Nimrod himself built Nineveh and other cities. And the next appearance of Masonry is said to be, not in Egypt, as in the preceding manuscripts, but is said to have been propagated after the dispersion by the Magi in the land of the Chaldeans.

This form of the Legend prevailed during perhaps the whole of the 18th century. It became the settled conviction of the Masons of that period that Masonry was instituted at the Tower of Babel by Nimrod and thence propagated to the Chaldeans.

Thus, in Smith's *Use and Abuse of Freemasonry*,[1] published in 1783, it is said that after the Flood the Masons were first called Noachidæ, and afterwards sages or wise men, Chaldeans, etc. And Northouck, who, in 1784, by order of the Grand Lodge, published an edition of the *Constitutions* far superior to that of Anderson, says[2] that Nimrod founded the empire of Babylon, and that "under him flourished those learned mathematicians whose successors were styled *Magi*, or wise men."

But about the end of the last century, or, perhaps, still later, about the beginning of the present, this legendary account of the origin of Freemasonry began to be repudiated, and another one, in contradiction of the old manuscripts, was substituted for it.

Masonry was no longer believed to have originated at the Tower of Babel; the Temple of Jerusalem was considered as the place of its birth; and Solomon and not Nimrod was called the "first Grand Master."

Accepting this Legend, as we do the other Legends of Masonry, which, in the language of Oliver,[3] "are entitled to consideration, though their authenticity may be denied and their aid rejected," we

---

[1] *Op. cit.*, p. 29.   [2] *Op. cit.*, p. 11.

[3] "Historical Landmarks," vol. i., lect. i., p. 53.

say that at the present day the Babylonish legend has assumed the present form.

Before the Flood there was a system of religious instruction which, from the resemblance of its legendary and symbolic character to that of Freemasonry, has been called by some authors "antediluvian Masonry." This system was preserved by Noah, and after the deluge was communicated by him to his immediate descendants. This system was lost at the time of the dispersion of mankind, and corrupted by the pagans in their Mysteries. But subsequently it was purified, and Freemasonry, as we now have it, was organized by the King of Israel at the time of the building of the temple.

This idea is well exemplified in the American ritual, which was, we have every reason to believe, invented about the end of the last century.

In this ritual, much of which is, however, being lost or becoming obsolete, from the necessary imperfections of oral transmission, the aspirant is supposed to represent one who is travelling from the intellectual blindness of the profane world into the brightness of Masonry, in whose arena he expects to find the light and truth, the search for which is represented by his initiation. This symbolic journey is supposed to begin at the Tower of Babel, where, in the language of the ritual, "language was confounded and Masonry lost," and to terminate at the Temple of Solomon, where "language was restored and Masonry found."

Hence, according to this latest form of the Legend, the Tower of Babel is degraded from the prominent place which was given to it in the older forms as the birth-place of Masonry, and becomes simply the symbol of the darkness and ignorance of the profane world as contradistinguished from the light and knowledge to be derived from an initiation into the system of Speculative Masonry.

But the old Masons who framed the *Legend of the Craft* were conforming more than these modern ritualists to the truth of history when they assigned to Babylon the glory of being the original source of the sciences. So far from its being a place of intellectual darkness, we learn from the cuneiform inscriptions that the Ancient Babylonians and their copyists, the Assyrians, were in possession of a wonderful literature. From the ruins of Babylon, Nineveh, and other ancient cities of the plain of Shinar tablets of terra cotta have been excavated, inscribed with legends in cuneiform characters. The interpretation of this once unknown alphabet and language has yielded to the genius and the labors of such scholars as Grotefend, Botta, Layard, and Rawlinson.

From the fragments found at Kouyunjik, the modern Arabic name for the site of Nineveh, the late Mr. George Smith conjectured that there were in the Royal Library at Nineveh over ten thousand inscribed tablets, including almost every subject in ancient literature, all of which literature was borrowed by the Assyrians from Babylonian sources.[1]

Speaking of this literature, Smith says that "at an early period in Babylonian history a great literary development took place, and numerous works were produced which embodied the prevailing myths, religion, and science of that day. Written, many of them, in a noble style of poetry, and appealing to the strongest feelings of the people on one side, or registering the highest efforts of their science on the other, these texts became the standards for Babylonian literature, and later generations were content to copy these writings instead of making new works for themselves."[2]

We see, therefore, that the Masons of the present day are wrong when they make Babel or Babylon the symbol of intellectual darkness, and suppose that there the light of Masonry was for a time extinguished, to be re-illumined only at the Temple of Solomon.

And, again, the *Legend of the Craft* vindicates its character, and correctly clothes an historical fact in symbolic language, when it portrays Babylonia, which was undoubtedly the fountain of all Semitic science and architecture, as also the birth-place of Operative Masonry.

---

[1] " Chaldean Account of Genesis," p. 21.   [2] Ibid., p. 22.

CHAPTER XII

HE universal sentiment of the Masons of the present day is to confer upon Solomon, King of Israel, the honor of being their "first Grand Master." But the *Legend of the Craft* had long before, though there was a tradition of the temple extant, bestowed, at least by implication, that title upon Nimrod, the King of Babylonia and Assyria. It had attributed the first organization of a fraternity of craftsmen to him, in saying that he gave a charge to the workmen whom he sent to assist the King of Nineveh in building his cities. That is to say, he framed for them a Constitution, and, in the words of the Legend, "this was the first tyme that ever Masons had any charge of his science." It was the first time that the Craft were organized into a fraternity working under a Constitution or body of laws; and as Nimrod was the autocratic maker of these laws, it results as a necessary consequence, that their first legislator, legislating with dictatorial and unrestricted sovereign power, was also their first Grand Master.

This view of the early history of Masonry, presented to us by the *Legend of the Craft*, which differs so much from the modern opinion, although it has almost become obsolete, is worthy of at least a passing consideration.

Who was this Nimrod, who held so exalted a position in the eyes of the old legendists, and why had they assigned to him a rank and power which modern Craftsmen have thought to belong more justly to the King of Israel?

The answers to these questions will be an appropriate commentary on that part of the *Legend of the Craft* which contains the story of this old Assyrian monarch.

The estimation of the character of Nimrod which has been almost universally entertained by the ancients as well as the moderns, obtains no support from the brief account of him contained in the Book of Genesis.

Josephus portrays him as a tyrant in his government of his people, vainglorious of his great power, a despiser and hater of God, and instigated by this feeling, the builder of a tower through which he would avenge himself on God for having destroyed the world.

For this view of the character of Nimrod, Josephus was in all probability indebted to the legends of the orientalists, which had clustered around the name of Nimrod, just as in ancient times legends always did cluster around great and mighty men.

Thus in the ancient chronicles he was represented as of gigantic stature, ten or twelve cubits in height. To him was attributed the invention of idolatry, and he is said to have returned to Chaldea after the destruction of the Tower of Babel, and to have persuaded the inhabitants to become fire-worshippers. He built a large furnace and commanded that all who refused the idolatrous worship should be cast into it. Among his victims were Abraham or Abram, the patriarch, and his father Terah. The latter was consumed, but the former by the interposition of a miracle came out unhurt. It is hardly necessary to say that such legends are altogether mythical and of no historical value.

The Scriptural account of Nimrod is a very brief and unsatisfactory one. It is merely that:

" Cush begat Nimrod ; he began to be a mighty one in the earth. He was a mighty hunter before the Lord ; wherefore it is said, Even as Nimrod the mighty hunter before the Lord. And the beginning of his kingdom was Babel, and Erech, and Accad, and Calneh, in the land of Shinar. Out of that land went forth Ashur and builded Nineveh, and the city Rehoboth, and Calah, and Resen between Nineveh and Calah : the same is a great city." [1]

The most learned commentators have differed as regards the translation of the 11th verse. The Septuagint, the Vulgate, Luther's and our own recognized version say—" Out of that land went forth Ashur, and builded Nineveh." Higden, in the *Polychronicon*, which I have already said was the source of the Masonic Legend, adopts the same version. And the Cooke and the later manuscripts assign the building of Nineveh and the other cities of Assyria to Ashur, the son of Shem, and the kinsman of Nimrod, who assisted

---

[1] Genesis x. 8–12.

him with workmen. Such was the legend until the beginning of the 18th century.

But the best modern Hebrew scholars, such as Borhart, Le Clerc, Gesenius, and a great many others, insist that *Ashur* is not the name of a person, but of a country, and that the passage should be rendered : "Out of that land he (Nimrod) went forth to Assyria and builded Nineveh, and the city Rehoboth, and Calah, and Resen, between Nineveh and Calah." This is the form of the legend that was adopted by Dr. Anderson and by the author of the Krause document, and after the publication of Anderson's work it took the place of the older form.

The Craft have in both forms of the legend recognized Nimrod as a great Mason, nor have the vituperations of Josephus and the scandalous legends of the orientalists had the slightest effect on their apparent estimation of that mighty monarch, the founder of nations and the builder of cities.

And now, in the latter part of the 19th century, comes a learned scholar,[1] well acquainted with the language of the ancient Babylonians and Assyrians, and with the complicated cuneiform alphabet in which it is clothed, and visiting the remains of the ruined cities which Nimrod had built, finds the fragments of twelve tablets which contain the history of a Babylonian monarch to whom he gave the provisional name of Izdubar and whom he identified with Nimrod. If this identification be correct, and there is certainly strong internal evidence in favor of it, we have in these tablets a somewhat connected narrative of the exploits of the proto-monarch of Babylon, which places his character in a more favorable light than that which had hitherto been received as the popular belief founded on the statement of Josephus and the oriental traditions.

The Izdubar legends, as Mr. Smith has called the inscriptions on these tablets, represent Nimrod as a mighty leader, a man of great prowess in war and in hunting, and who by his ability and valor had united many of the petty kingdoms into which the whole of the valley of the Euphrates was at that time divided, and thus established the first empire in Asia.[2] He was, in fact, the hero of the ancient

---

[1] The late George Smith, of the British Museum, the author of " Assyrian Discoveries," of the "Chaldean Account of Genesis," and many other writings in which he has given the learned result of his investigations of the cuneiform inscriptions.

[2] Smith, " Chaldean Account of Genesis," p. 174.

Babylonians, and therefore it was only natural that they should con-
secrate the memory of him who as a powerful and beneficent king had
first given them that unity which secured their prosperity as a nation.[1]

If we now refer to the *Legend of the Craft*, we shall find that
the old Masonic legendist, although of course he had never seen
nor heard of the discoveries contained in the cuneiform inscriptions,
had rejected the traditional estimate of Nimrod's character, as well
as the supposed results of the destruction of the Tower of Babel,
and had wisely selected Babylon as the first seat and Nimrod (whoever may have been meant by that name) as the founder of the
sciences, and especially of architecture.

In this there is a conformity of the legendary account with the
facts of history, not usual with legendists.

"We must give," says Canon Rawlinson,[2] "the Babylonians credit
for a genius and a grandeur of conception rarely surpassed, which led
them to employ the labor whereof they had the command, in works
of so imposing a character. With only 'brick for stone,' and at
first only 'slime for mortar,' they constructed edifices of so vast a
size that they still remain, at the present day, among the most enor-
mous ruins in the world, impressing the beholder at once with awe
and admiration."

The *Legend of the Craft* continually confounds Masonry, Geometry, and Architecture, or rather uses them as synonymous and
convertible terms. It is not, therefore, surprising that it should
have selected Babylon as the birth-place, and Nimrod as the founder
of what they called "the science." The introduction of his name
into the Legend, may be attributed, says the Rev. Bro. Woodford,[3]
"to an old assumption that rulers were patrons of the building sodalities." I rather imagine that the idea may be traced to the fact
that Nimrod was supposed to be a patron of architecture and the
builder of a great number of cities. The mediæval Operative
Masons were always ready to accept any distinguished architect or
builder as a patron and member of the Craft. Thus the history of
Masonry compiled by Dr. Anderson, out of the *Old Records*, is
nothing but a history of architecture, and almost every king, prelate,
or nobleman who had erected a palace, a church, or a castle, is
called a distinguished Freemason and a patron of the Institution.

---

[1] Smith, *ib.*, p. 294.   [2] In Smith's "Dict. of the Bible," *voce*, Babel.
[3] Kenning's "Encyclopædia," in *voce* Nimrod.

CHAPTER XIII

AVING disposed of the establishment of Masonry in Babylon, the *Legend of the Craft* next proceeds by a rapid transition to narrate the history of its introduction into Egypt. This Egyptian episode, which in reference to the principal action in it has been called the "Legend of Euclid," is found in all the old manuscripts.

It forms the opening feature of the Halliwell poem, being in that document the beginning of the history of Masonry; it is told with circumstantial minuteness in the Cooke MS., and is apparently copied from that into all the later manuscripts, where the important details are essentially the same, although we find a few circumstances related in some which are omitted in others.

Divesting the narrative of the archaic language of the manuscripts, the legend may be given as follows:

Once on a time, to use the story-teller's style, Abraham and his wife went to Egypt. Now Abraham was very learned in all the seven arts and sciences, and was accompanied by Euclid, who was his scholar, and to whom he had imparted his knowledge. At that time the lords or rich men of Egypt were in sore distress, because having a very numerous progeny of sons, for whom they could find no occupation, they knew not how they could obtain for them a livelihood.

In this strait they held a council and made proclamation that if any one could suggest a remedy, he should lay his plans before them, when he should be suitably rewarded.

Upon this Euclid presented himself and offered to supply these sons with an honest means of living, by teaching them the science of Geometry, provided they should be placed by their fathers under his exclusive control, so that he might have the power of ruling them according to the laws of the Craft.

To this proposition the Egyptian nobles gladly consented, and granted Euclid all the power that he had asked, and secured the grant to him by a sealed commission.

Euclid then instructed them in the practical part of Geometry, and taught them how to erect churches, castles, towers, and all other kinds of buildings in stone. He also gave them a code of laws for their government.

Thus did Euclid found in the land of Egypt the science which he named Geometry, but which has ever since been called Masonry.

I have said that while all the manuscripts agree in the prominent circumstances of this legend, there are in some of them a few discrepancies as to some of the minor details.

Thus the Halliwell poem makes no allusion to Abraham, but imputes the founding of Masonry to Euclid alone, and it will be remembered that the title of that poem is, " The Constitutions of the art of Geometry according to Euclid."

The Cooke MS. is far more full in details than either the Halliwell poem or the manuscripts that succeeded it. It says that Abraham taught Geometry to the Egyptians, and that Euclid was his scholar. But a few lines after, quoting St. Isidore as its authority, it says that Euclid was one of the first founders of Geometry, and that in his time there was an inundation of the Nile, and he taught them to make dykes and walls to restrain the water, and measured the land by means of Geometry, and divided it among the inhabitants, so that every man could enclose his own property with ditches and walls. In consequence of this the land became fertile, and the population increased to such a degree, that there was found a difficulty in finding for all employment that would enable them to live. Whereupon the nobles gave the government of their children to Euclid, who taught them the art of Geometry, so called because he had with its aid measured the land,[1] when he built the walls and ditches to separate each one's possession.

The needless repetitions and confusion of details in the Cooke MS. show that the author had derived the information on which he constructed his legend from various sources—partly from the authority of St. Isidore, as he is quoted in Higden's *Polychronicon*, and partly from the tradition of the Craft.

---

[1] Geometry from the Greek γη (ge) *land* and μετρον (metron) *measure*.

The later manuscripts have copied the details of the Legend as contained in the Cooke codex, but with many omissions, so as to give it the form in which it was known to the Craft in the 16th and 17th centuries.

Thus the Dowland MS., whose date is supposed to be about 1550, gives the story almost exactly as it is in the Halliwell poem, except that it adds Abraham and Sarah as *dramatis personæ*, making it in this respect coincide with the Cooke MS., and probably with the form of the original Legend.

In this it is followed by the York, No. 1 (1600), the Grand Lodge (1632), the Sloane (1646), the Lodge of Hope (1680), the Alnwick (1701), and even the Papworth MS., as late as 1714.

The Landsdowne MS. (1560), and the Antiquity (1686), have the Legend in a very imperfect form, and either did not copy or greatly curtailed the Dowland MS., as they but slightly refer to Egypt and to Euclid, and not at all to Abraham.

As to the reputation for great learning which the legendists have given to Abraham, although the Bible dwells only on his piety, they found their authority in Josephus, as well as in Isidore.

Josephus says that among the Egyptians he was esteemed as a very wise man, and that besides reforming their customs, he taught them arithmetic and astronomy.

It is evident, as has been already noticed, that the *Legend of the Craft* has been indebted for much of its materials to the *Antiquities* of Josephus, and the *Etymologies* of St. Isidore, and the *Polychronicon* of Ranulph Higden—the first two at second hand, in all probability through the citations of those works which are made in the third.

The Krause MS., which is said to have been translated from the English into the Latin, and afterward into German, and published by Dr. Krause,[1] gives the Legend in an entirely different form.

Notwithstanding that I have declared my belief that this document is spurious with a date of not earlier than the second decade, or more probably toward the middle of the 18th century, yet, as an indication of the growth and the change of the Legend at that period, it will be worth while to compare its form with that in the

---

[1] " Die drei ältesten Kunsturkunden," iii., 59–113.

older manuscripts, at least so far as relates to the Egyptian episode, which is in the following words :

"Abraham was skilled in all the sciences and continued to teach them to the sons of the freeborn, whence afterwards came the many learned priests and mathematicians who were known by the name of the Chaldean Magi.   Afterwards, Abraham continued to propagate these sciences and arts when he came to Egypt, and found there, especially in Hermes, so apt a scholar, that the latter was at length called the Trismegistus of the sciences, for he was at the same time priest and natural philosopher in Egypt ; and through him and a scholar of his the Egyptians received the first good laws and all the sciences in which Abraham had instructed him.   Afterwards Euclid collected the principal sciences and called them Geometry.   But the Greeks and Romans called them altogether Architecture.

"But in consequence of the confusion of languages, the laws and arts and sciences could not formerly be propagated until the people had learned to make comprehensible by signs that which they could not understand by words.   Wherefore, Mizraim, the son of Cham, brought the custom of making himself understood by signs with him into Egypt, when he colonized a valley of the Nile.   This art was afterwards extended into all distant lands, but only the signs that are given by the hands have remained in architecture ; for the signs by figures are as yet known to but few.

"In Egypt the overflowings of the Nile afforded an opportunity to use the art of measurement, which had been introduced by Mizraim, and to build bridges and walls as a protection against the water. They used burnt stone and wood and earth for these purposes. Therefore when the heathen kings had become acquainted with this, they were compelled to prepare stone and lime and bricks and therewith to erect buildings, by which, through God's will, however, they became only the more experienced artists and were so celebrated that their art spread as far as Persia."

If the reader compares this legend of the Krause manuscript with that which is given by Dr. Anderson in the first edition of his *Constitutions*, he will be constrained to admit that both documents are derived from the same source, or that one of them is an abridged or an expository copy of the other.   It is evident that the statement in Anderson is merely a synopsis of that more detailed narrative contained in the Krause Legend, or that it is an expansion of the statement in the first edition of the *Constitutions*.

If the Krause MS. was written before Anderson compiled his history, it could not have been long anterior, and must have been composed between 1714, the date of the Papworth MS., which contains the Legend in its mediæval form, and 1723, when Anderson published his work. Within this period the Masons sought to modify the old *Legend of the Craft*, so as to deprive it of its apparent absurdities, and to omit its anachronisms so as to give it the appearance of an authentic historical narrative.

Instead, therefore, of having the date of 926, which has been ascribed to it by Dr. Krause, his manuscript is, as Bro. Hughan thinks it, "a compilation of the early part of the last century." It is, however, important, as I have said, because it shows how the old Legend was improved and divested of its anachronisms.

It is certainly a very absurd anachronism to make Euclid the contemporary of Abraham, who lived more than two thousand years before him. Nor is it less absurd to suppose that Euclid invented Masonry in Egypt, whence it was carried to India, and practiced by King Solomon, since the great geometrician did not flourish until six centuries and a half after the construction of the Temple.

Considered, then, as an historical narrative, the Legend of Euclid is a failure. And yet it has its value as the symbolical development of certain historical facts.

The prominent points in this Legend being, of course, those on which the old believers of it most strenuously dwelt, are:

1. That Geometry is the groundwork of Masonry;

2. That Euclid was the most distinguished of all geometricians; and,

3. That the esoteric method of teaching this as well as all the other sciences which was pursued by the priests of Egypt, was very analogous to that which was adopted by the Operative Masons of the Middle Ages, in imparting to their disciples the geometric and architectural secrets, which constituted what they called the Mystery of the Craft.

The Legend, in fact, symbolizes the well-recognized fact, that in Egypt, in early times—of which there is no historical objection to make Abraham the contemporary—there was a very intimate connection between the science of Geometry and the religious system of the

Egyptians; that this religious system embraced also all scientific instruction; that this instruction was secret, and communicated only after an initiation,[1] and that in that way there was a striking analogy between the Egyptian system and that of the mediæval Masons. And this fact of an analogy, the latter sought to embody in the apparent form of an historical narrative, but really in the spirit of a symbolic picture.

Thus considered, the *Legend of the Craft*, in its episode of Euclid and his marvelous doings in the land of Egypt, is divested of its absurdity, and it is brought somewhat nearer to the limits of historical verity than the too literal reader would be disposed to admit.

---

[1] Kendrick confirms this statement in his " Ancient Egypt," where he says: " When we read of foreigners (in Egypt) being obliged to submit to painful and tedious ceremonies of initiation, it was not that they might learn the secret meaning of the rites of Osiris, or Isis, but that they might partake of the knowledge of astronomy, physick, *geometry*, and theology."—(Vol. i., p. 383.)

CHAPTER XIV

THE LEGEND OF THE TEMPLE

ROM this account of the exploits of Abraham and his scholar Euclid, and of the invention of Geometry, or Masonry in Egypt, the *Legend of the Craft* proceeds, by a rapid stride, to the narrative of the introduction of the art into Judea, or as it is called in all of them, "the land of behest," or the land of promise.

Here it is said to have been principally used by King Solomon, in the construction of the temple at Jerusalem. The general details connected with the building of this edifice, and the assistance given to the King of Israel, by Hiram, King of Tyre, are related with sufficient historical accuracy, and were probably derived either directly or at second hand, through the *Polychronicon*, from the first Book of Kings, which, in fact, is referred to in all the manuscripts as a source of information.[1]

The assumption that Freemasonry, as it now exists, was organized at the Temple of Solomon, although almost universally accepted by Masons who have not made Masonry a historical study, but who derive their ideas of the Institution from the mythical teachings of the ritual, has been utterly rejected by the greater part of the recent school of iconoclasts, who investigate the history of Freemasonry by the same methods which they would pursue in the examination of any other historical subject.

The fact, however, remains, that in the *Legend of the Craft* the Temple is prominently and definitely referred to as a place where Masons congregated in great numbers, and where Masonry was confirmed or established, and whence it traveled into other countries.[2]

---

[1] "As it is said in the Bible, in the third book of Kings," are the words of the Cooke MS. In the canon of Scripture as then used, the two books of Samuel were called the first and second of Kings. The third book of Kings was then the first according to the present canon.

[2] "And thus was that worthy Science of Masonry confirmed in the country of Jerusalem, and in many other kingdoms."—*Dowland MS.*

Considering the *Legend of the Craft* as merely a narrative of the rise and progress of architecture in its connection with a peculiar architectural association, it was natural that in such a narrative some reference should be made to one of the most splendid specimens of ancient architectural art that the ancient world had exhibited. And since this Temple was, by its prominence in the ritual of Jewish worship, intimately connected with both the Jewish and Christian religions, we shall be still less surprised that an association not only so religious, but even ecclesiastical as mediæval Masonry was, should have considered this sacred edifice as one of the cradles of its Institution.

Hence we find the Temple of Jerusalem occupying a place in the *Legend of the Craft* which it has retained, with many enlargements, to the present day.

But there is a difference in the aspect in which this subject of the Temple is to be viewed, as we follow the progress of the Order in its transition from an Operative to a Speculative Institution.

Originally referred to by the legendists as a purely historical fact, whose details were derived from Scripture, and connected by a sort of *esprit du corps*, with the progress of their own association, it was retained during and after the development of the Order into a Speculative character, because it seemed to be the very best foundation on which the religious symbolism of that Order could be erected.

But notwithstanding that the masses of the Institution, learned as well as unlearned, continue to accept the historical character of this part of the Legend, the Temple is chiefly to be considered in a symbolic point of view. It is in this aspect that we must regard it, and in so doing we shall relieve the Legend of another charge of absurdity. It is true that we are unable now to determine how much of true history and how much of symbolism were contemplated by the authors of the Legend, when they introduced the Temple of Jerusalem into that document as a part of their traditional narrative. But there is a doubt, and we can not now positively assert that the mediæval Freemasons had not some impression of a symbolic idea when they incorporated it into their history.

The Temple might, indeed, from its prominence in the ritual, be almost called the characteristic symbol of Speculative Masonry. The whole system of Masonic Symbolism is not only founded on the Temple of Jerusalem, but the Temple idea so thoroughly permeates it that an inseparable connection is firmly established, so that if the Temple symbol were obliterated and eliminated from the system of Freemasonry—if that system were purged of all the legends and myths that refer to the building of the Solomonic Temple, and to the events that are supposed to have then and there occurred, we should have nothing remaining by which to recognize and identify Speculative Masonry, as the successor of the Operative System of the Middle Ages. The history of the Roman Empire with no account of Julius Cæsar, or of Pompey, or that of the French Revolution, with no allusion to Louis XVI., or to Robespierre, would present just as mutilated a narrative as Freemasonry would, were all reference to the Temple of Solomon omitted.

Seeing, then, the importance of this symbol, it is proper and will be interesting to trace it back through the various exemplars of the *Legend of the Craft* contained in the Old Constitutions, because it is to that Legend that modern Freemasonry owes the suggestion at least, if not the present arrangement and formulæ of this important symbol.

In the oldest Constitution that we have, the one known as the Halliwell MS., whose date is supposed not to be later than the end of the 14th century, there is not the least allusion to the Temple of Solomon, which is another reason why I ascribe to that document, as I have before said, an origin different from that of the other and later manuscripts.

The word *temple* occurs but once in the entire poem, and then it is used to designate a Christian church or place of worship.[1] But in the Cooke MS., written, as it is estimated, about a century afterward, there are ample references to the Solomonic Temple, and the statement made in the *Legend of the Craft* is for the first time enunciated.

After this, there is not a Constitution written in which the same narrative is not repeated. There does not appear in any of them, from the Landsdowne MS. in 1560 to the Papworth in 1701, any enlargement of the narrative or any development of new occur-

---

[1] " He made the bothe halle and eke bowre,
And hye *tempuls* of gret honoure,
To sport hym yn bothe day and nighth,
And to worschepe hys God with all hys myght."
(Lines 63–66).

rences. Each of them dilates, in almost the same words, upon the
Temple of Solomon as connected with Masonry in many words, and
gives elaborate details of the construction of the edifice, of the number of Masons employed, how they were occupied in performing
other works of Masonry, and, finally, how one of them left Jerusalem and extended the art into other countries. We thus see that
up to the end of the 17th century the *Legend of the Craft* in all
its essential details continued to be accepted as traditional history.

In the beginning of the 18th century the Legend began to assume
a nearer resemblance to its present form. The document already
referred to as the Krause MS., and which Dr. Krause too hastily
supposed was a copy of the original *York Constitutions* of 926, is
really, as I have heretofore shown, a production of the early part
of the 18th century. In this document the Legend is given in the
following words:

" Although, by architecture great and excellent buildings had already been everywhere constructed, they all remained far behind the
holy Temple, which the wise King Solomon caused to be erected
in Jerusalem, to the honor of the true God, where he employed an
uncommonly large number of workmen, as we find in the Holy
Scriptures ; and King Hiram of Tyre also added a number to them.
Among these assistants who were sent was King Hiram's most skil-
ful architect, a widow's son, whose name was Hiram Abif, and who
afterwards made the most exquisite arrangements and furnished the
most costly works, all of which are described in the Holy Scriptures.
The whole of these workmen were, with King Solomon's approval,
divided into certain classes, and thus at this great building was first
founded a worthy Society of Architects."

Whether the author of the Krause MS. had copied from Anderson, or Anderson from him, or both from some other document which
is no longer extant, is a question that has already been discussed.
But the description of the Temple and its connection with the history of Masonry, are given by Dr. Anderson with much of the features of the Krause form of the Legend, except that the details are
more copious. Now, what was taught concerning the Temple by
Anderson in his History contained in the first edition of the *Constitutions*, although afterward polished and perfected by Preston and
other ritual makers, is substantially the same as that which is taught
at the present day in all the Lodges.

Therefore, notwithstanding that Dr. Krause asserts,[1] that "the Temple of Solomon is no symbol, certainly not a prominent one of the English system," I am constrained to believe that it was one of the prominent symbols alluded to in the Mediæval Legend, and that the symbol of the Temple upon which so much of the symbolism of Modern Speculative Masonry depends, was, in fact, suggested to the revivalists by the narrative contained in the *Legend of the Craft*.

Whether the Operative Masons of the Middle Ages, who seem to have accepted this Legend as authentic history, had also, underlying the narrative, a symbolic interpretation of the Temple and of certain incidents that are said to have occurred in the course of its erection, as referring to this life and the resurrection to a future one, or whether that interpretation was in existence at the time when the *Legend of the Craft* was invented, and was subsequently lost sight of, only to be recovered in the beginning of the 18th century, are questions that will be more appropriately discussed in succeeding pages of this work, when the subject of the myths and symbols of Freemasonry is under consideration.

But it is evident that between the narrative in the Legend concerning the Temple, with its three builders, the Kings of Israel and Tyre, and Solomon's Master of the Works, and the symbolism of Modern Speculative Masonry in allusion to the same building and the same personages, there has been a close, consecutive connection.

Hence, again, we find that the *Legend of the Craft* is of value in reference to the light which it throws on the progress of Masonic science and symbolism, which otherwise it would not possess, if it were to be considered as a mere mythical narrative without any influence on history.

Before concluding this subject, it will be necessary to refer to the name of the chief builder of the Temple, and whose name has undergone that corruption in all the manuscripts to which all proper names have been subjected in those documents.

Of course, it is known, from the testimony of Scripture, that the real name and title of this person, as used in reference to King Solomon and himself, was *Hiram Abif*, that is, "his father Hiram."[2]

---

[1] "Die drei altesten Kunsturkunden," vol. i., p. 155, note 41.

[2] When the King of Tyre speaks of him, it is as *Hiram Abi*, that is, "My father Hiram," 2 Chron. ii. 13.

This Hebrew appellative is found for the first time in Masonic doc-uments in Anderson's *Constitutions*, and in the Krause MS., both being of the date of the early part of the 18th century. Previous to that period we find him variously called in all the Old Manuscripts, from the Dowland in 1550 to the Alnwick in 1701, Aman, Amon, Aynone, Aynon, Anon, and Ajuon. Now, of what word are these a corruption?[1]

The Cooke MS. does not give any name, but only says, that "the King's son of Tyre was Solomon's Master Mason." All the other and succeeding manuscripts, without exception, admit this relation. Thus the Dowland, in which it is followed by all the others, says that King Hiram "had a son that was called AYNON, and he was a Master of Geometry, and was chief Master of all Solomon's Masons."

The idea was thus established that this man was of royal dignity, the son of a King, and that he was also a ruler of the Craft.

Now, the Hebrew word *Adon* denotes a lord, a prince, a ruler or master. It is, in short, a title of dignity. In the Book of Kings we meet with Adoniram, who was one of the principal officers of King Solomon, and who, during the construction of the Temple, performed an important part as the chief or superintendent of the levy of thirty thousand laborers who worked on Mount Lebanon.

The old Masons may have confounded this person with Hiram from the similarity of the terminational syllables. The modern Con-tinental Masons committed the same error when they established the Rite of Adonhiram or Adoniram, and gave to Hiram Abif the title of Adon Hiram, or the Lord or Master Hiram. If the Old Masons did this, then it is evident that they abbreviated the full name and called him *Adon*.

But I am more inclined to believe that the author of the first or original old manuscript, of which all the rest are copies, called the chief builder of Solomon *Adon*, Lord and Master, in allusion to his supposed princely rank and his high position as the chief builder or Master of the Works at the Temple.

---

[1] The Papworth MS., whose supposed date is 1714, rejects all these words and calls him *Benaim*, which is a misspelling of *Bonaim, builders*, and that a grammatical error for *Boneh*, the Builder. The writer had evidently got an inkling of the new form which the Legend was beginning to assume. Anderson, it will be recollected, speaks of the "Bonai, or builders in stone."

The corruption from *Adon* to *Aynon*, or *Amon*, or even *Ajuon*, is not greater than what occurs in other names in these manuscripts, as where *Hermes* is transmuted into *Hermarines*, and *Euclid* into *Englet*. Indeed the copyists of these mediæval documents appear to have had a Gallic facility in corrupting the orthography of all foreign names, very often almost totally destroying their identity.

As to the real meaning of Hiram Abif, either as a historic or symbolic character, that topic will be thoroughly considered in another part of this work, when the subject of Masonic Symbols comes to be considered. The topic of the corruption of the name in the old manuscripts, and its true signification, will again be treated when I come to investigate the "Legend of Hiram Abif."

The Legend of the Temple could not be appropriately completed without a reference to Solomon, King of Israel, and some inquiry as to how he became indebted for the important place he has held in mediæval Freemasonry.

The popularity of King Solomon among the Eastern nations is a familiar fact, known not only to Oriental scholars, but even to those whose knowledge on the subject is confined to what they have learned from their youthful reading of the *Arabian Nights' Entertainments*. Among the Arabians and the Persians, the King of Israel was esteemed as a great magician, whose power over the genii and other supernatural beings was derived from his possession of the Omnific Name, by the use of which he accomplished all his wonderful works, the said name being inscribed on his signet-ring.

It is not singular, seeing the communication which took place before and after the Crusades between the East and the West, that the wise son of David should have enjoyed an equal popularity among the poets and romancers of the Middle Ages.

But among them the character that he sustains is not that of a great magician, so much as that of a learned philosopher. Whenever a Norman romancer or a Provençal minstrel composed a religious morality, a pious declamation, or a popular proverb, it was the name of Solomon that was often selected to "point the moral or adorn the tale."

Unlike the Orientalists, whose tendencies were always toward the mystical, the mediæval writers most probably derived their opinion of the King of Israel, from the account of him and of his writings in the Bible.   Now, there he is peculiarly distinguished as a proverbialist.

Proverbs are the earliest outspoken thought of the people, and they precede, in every nation, all other forms of literature.   It was therefore to be expected, that at the awakening of learning in the Middle Ages, the romancers would be fascinated by the proverbial philosophy of King Solomon, rather than by his magical science, on which the Eastern fabulists had more fondly dwelt.

Legrand D'Aussy, in his valuable work *On the Fables and Romances of the 12th and 13th Centuries*, gives two interesting specimens from old manuscripts, of the use made by their writers of the traditional reputation of King Solomon.

The first of these is a romance called " The Judgment of Solomon."   It is something like the Jewish story of the two mothers. But here the persons upon whom the judgment is to be passed are two sons of the Prince of Soissons.   The claim advanced was for a partition of the property.   To determine who was better entitled to be the heir, by the reverence he might exhibit for the memory of his father, Solomon required each to prove his knightly dexterity by transfixing a mark with his lance, and that mark was to be the body of his dead father.   The elder readily complied with the odious condition.   The younger indignantly refused.   To him Solomon decreed the heritage.

We see here how ready these romancers of the Middle Ages were to invent a narrative and fit it into the life of their favorite Solomon.   The makers of the Masonic *Legend of the Craft*, who were their contemporaries, promptly followed their example. There is in that Legend, as we have seen, some anachronisms, but none more absurd than that which makes a Prince of Soissons, who could not have been earlier than the time of Clovis, in the 6th century, the contemporary of a Jewish monarch who lived at least sixteen centuries before Soissons was known as a kingdom.

But it shows us the spirit of the age and how Legends were fabricated.   We are thus prepared to form a judgment of the Masonic myths.

The Middle Ages also attributed to King Solomon a very familiar acquaintance with the science of astrology.   In so doing they by no means borrowed the Oriental idea that he was a great magician ; for astrology formed no part of Eastern occult magic.   The

King Solomon

mediæval astrologer was deemed a man of learning, just as at this day is the astronomer. Astrology was, in fact, the astronomy of the Middle Ages. Solomon's astrological knowledge was therefore only a part of that great learning for which he had the reputation.

In the collection of unpublished *Fabliaux et Contes*, edited by M. Meon, is a poem entitled, " Le Lunaire que Salemon fist"; that is, " The Lunary which Solomon made."

The lunary or lunarium was a table made by astrologers to indicate the influence exerted by the moon on human affairs.

The poem, which consists of 910 lines, written in the old French or Norman language, contains directions for the conduct of life, telling what is to be done or what omitted on every day of the month. The concluding lines assign, without hesitation, the authorship to Solomon, while it pays the mediæval tribute to his character :

> " Here is ended the lesson
> Made by the good King Solomon,
> To whom in his life God gave
> Riches and honor and learning,
> More than to any other born
> Or begotten of woman."

The canonical book of Proverbs gave the writers of the Middle Ages occasion to have an exalted opinion of Solomon as a maker of those pithy sayings—a characteristic of his genius of which the Orientals seem to have been unmindful.

One of the most remarkable works of mediæval literature is a poem by the Comte de Bretagne, entitled " Proverbs of Marcol and Solomon."

This Marcol is represented as a commentator, or rather, perhaps, a rival of King Solomon. The work is a poem divided into stanzas of six lines each. The first three lines contain a proverb of Solomon ; the next three another proverb on the same subject, and in response, by Marcol.

There is another mediæval poem in the collection of M. Meon, entitled " Of Marco and Solomon." The responsive style is the same as that of the Comte de Bretagne, but the one hundred and thirty-seven proverbs which it contains are all new.

But still more apposite to the present inquiry is the fact that among the mediæval writers Solomon bore the reputation of an artisan of consummate skill. He was like the Volund or Wieland of the Scandinavian and Teutonic myths—the traditional smith who fabricated the decorations of chambers, the caparison of war-horses, and the swords and lances of cavaliers. In the poems of the Middle Ages, whenever it becomes necessary to speak of any of these things as having been made with exquisite and surpassing skill, it is said to be "the work of Solomon"—*l'uevre Salemon.*

But enough has been said to show that King Solomon was as familiar to the romancers of the Middle Ages as he was to the Jews of Palestine or to the Orientalists of Arabia and Persia. Philip de Thuan, who, in the 12th century, wrote his *Bestiary*, a sort of natural history spiritualized, says that by Solomon was signified any wise man—*Sacez par Salemuon sage gent entendum.*

Now, about the same time that these fable-makers and song-writers of the 12th, 13th, and 14th centuries were composing these stories about King Solomon, the makers of the Masonic *Legend of the Craft* were inventing their myths about the same monarch and the Temple which he erected.

This is a concurrence of time which suggests that possibly the popularity of King Solomon with the romancers of the Middle Ages made the incorporation of his name in the Masonic Legend less difficult to those who framed that mythical story.

We might, indeed, be led to suspect that the use of Solomon in their Legends and traditions was first suggested to the Stonemasons and to the cognate associations, such as the "Compagnons de la Tour" of France, from the frequent references to it by the contemporary romancers.

But the subsequent myths connected with Solomon as the head of the association of Masons at the Temple were, at a much later period, borrowed, in great part, from the Talmudists, and have no place among the song-writers and fabulists of the Middle Ages.

CHAPTER XV

THE EXTENSION OF THE ART INTO OTHER COUNTRIES

THE *Legend of the Craft* next proceeds to narrate how Masonry was extended "into divers countryes," some of the Masons traveling to increase their knowledge of their art, and others to extend that which they already possessed.

This subject is very briefly treated in the different manuscripts. The Halliwell poem says nothing of the progressive march of Masonry, except that it details almost as an episode the persecution of the "Four Crowned Martyrs" as Christian Masons, in the reign of the Roman Emperor Diocletian, and we should almost be led to infer from the tenor of the poem that Masonry was introduced directly into England from Egypt.

The Cooke MS. simply says that from Egypt Masonry "went from land to land and from kingdom to kingdom," until it got to England.

The later manuscripts are a little more definite, although still brief. They merely tell us that skillful craftsmen largely traveled into various countries, some that they might acquire more knowledge and skill, and others to teach those who had but little skill.

There is certainly nothing that is mythical or fabulous in this statement. Every authentic history of architecture concurs in the statement that at an early period the various countries of Europe were perambulated by bodies of builders in search of employment in the construction of religious and other edifices. The name, indeed, of "Traveling Freemasons" which was bestowed upon them, is familiar in architectural historical works.[1]

Indeed, as Mr. George Godwin says, "There are few points in the Middle Ages more pleasing to look back upon than the existence

---

[1] See Hope's " Historical Essay on Architecture."

of the associated Masons; they are the bright spot in the general darkness of that period, the patch of verdure when all around is barren."[1]   But this interesting subject will be more fully discussed in another part of this work, when we come to treat of the authentic history of Masonry.   This portion of the Legend can not be said to belong to the prehistoric period.

It is sufficient, for the present, to have shown that in this part, as elsewhere, the *Legend of the Craft* is not a merely fictitious narrative, but that the general statement of the extension of Freemasonry throughout Europe at an early period is confirmed by historical evidence.

On examining the *Legend of the Craft*, it will be found to trace the extension of Masonry through its successive stages of progress from Babylon and Assyria to Egypt, from Egypt to Judea, from Judea to France, and from France to England.   Accepting Masonry and the art of building as synonymous terms, this line of progress will not be very adverse, with some necessary modifications, to that assumed to be correct by writers on architecture.   But, as I have just said, the consideration of this subject belongs not to the prehistoric, but to the historic period of the Society.

---

[1] " The Builder," vol. ix., p. 463.

CHAPTER XVI

THE LEGEND OF CHARLES MARTEL AND NAMUS GRECUS

T HE Legend, now approaching the domain of authentic history, but still retaining its traditional character, proceeds to narrate, but in a very few words, the entrance of Masonry into France.

This account is given in the following language in the Dowland manuscript:

" And soe it befell that there was one curious Mason that height MAYMUS GRECUS, that had been at the making of Solomon's temple, and he came into France, and there he taught the science of Masonrye to men of France. And there was one of the Regal lyne of Fraunce, that height CHARLES MARTELL; and he was a man that loved well such a science, and drew to this MAYMUS GRECUS that is above said, and learned of him the science, and tooke upon him the charges and manners; and afterwards, by the grace of God, he was elect to be Kinge of France. And whan he was in his estate, he tooke Masons and did helpe to make men Masons that were none; and he set them to worke, and gave them both the charge and the manners and good paie, as he had learned of other Masons; and confirmed them a Charter from yeare to yeare, to holde their semble wher they would; and cherished them right much; and thus came the science into France."

This Legend is repeated, almost word for word, in all the later manuscripts up to the year 1714.

It is not even alluded to in the earliest of all the manuscripts— the Halliwell poem—which is another proof that that document is of German origin.

The Cooke MS. has the Legend in the following words:

" Sumtyme ther was a worthye kyng in Frauns, that was clepyd Carolus secundus that ys to sey Charlys the secunde. And this Charlys was elyte [elected] kyng of Frauns by the grace of God and by lynage [lineage] also. And sume men sey that he was elite [elected] by fortune the whiche is fals as by cronycle he was of the kynges blode Royal. And this same kyng Charlys was a mason bifor that he was kyng. And after that he was kyng he lovyd masons and cherschid them and gaf them chargys and mannerys at his devise the whiche sum ben yet used in fraunce and he ordeynyd that they scholde have a semly [assembly] onys in the yere and come and speke togedyr and for to be reuled by masters and felows of thynges amysse." [1]

The absence of all allusion to Namus Grecus (a personage who will directly occupy our attention) in the Cooke document is worthy of notice.

When Dr. Anderson was putting the *Legend of the Craft* into a modern shape, he also omitted any reference to Namus Grecus but he preserved the spirit of the Legend, so far as to say, that according to the old records of Masons, Charles Martel " sent over several expert craftsmen and learned architects into England at the desire of the Saxon kings." [2]

I think it will be proved, when in the course of this work the authentic history of Masonry comes to be treated, that the statement in the *Legend of the Craft* in relation to the condition of the art in France during the administration of Charles Martel is simply a historical fact. In claiming for the " Hammerer" the title of King of France, while he assumed only the humble rank of Duke of the Franks and Mayor of the Palace, the legendists have only committed a historical error of which more experienced writers might be guilty.

The introduction of the name of Namus Grecus, an unknown Mason, who is described as being the contemporary of both Solomon and of Charles Martel, is certainly an apparent anachronism that requires explanation.

This Namus Grecus has been a veritable sphinx to Masonic antiquaries, and no Œdipus has yet appeared who could resolve the riddle. Without assuming the sagacity of the ancient expounder of enigmas, I can only offer a suggestion for what it may be considered worth.

I suppose *Grecus* to be merely an appellative indicating the fact that this personage was a Greek. Now, the knowledge of his exist-

---

[1] Cooke MS., lines 576–601.   [2] " Constitutions," ed. 1723, p. 30.

ence at the court of Charles Martel was most probably derived by
the English legendist from a German or French source, because the
Legend of the Craft is candid in admitting that the English Masons had collected the writings and charges from other countries.
Prince Edwin is said to have made a proclamation that any Masons
who "had any writing or understanding of the charges and the manners that were made before in this land [England] or in any other,
that they should shew them forth." And there were found "some
in French, some in Greek, some in English, and some in other languages."

Now, if the account and the name of this Greek architect had
been taken from the German, the text would most probably have
been "ein Maurer *Namens Grecus*"; or, if from the French, it would
have been "un Maçon *nommé Grecus*." The English legendist
would, probably, mistake the words *Namens Grecus*, or *nommé
Grecus*, each of which means "he was named Grecus," or, literally,
"a Mason by the name of Grecus," for the full name, and write him
down as *Namus Grecus*. The *Maymus* in the Dowland MS. is
evidently a clerical error. In the other manuscripts it is *Namus*.
The corrected reading, then, would be—"there was a Mason named
(or called) a Greek."

It can not be said that it is not probable that any legendist would
have fallen into such an error when we remember how many others
as great, if not greater, have been perpetrated in these *Old Records*.
See, for instance, in these manuscripts such orthographical mistakes
as *Hermarines* for *Hermes*, and *Englet* for *Euclid*; to say nothing
of the rather ridiculous blunder in the Leland MS., where *Pythagore*, the French form of *Pythagoras*, has suffered transmutation into
Peter Gower. So it is not at all unlikely that *Namens Grecus*, or
nommé Grecus, should be changed into *Namus Grecus*.

The original Legend, in all probability meant to say merely that
in the time of Charles Martel, a Greek artist, who had been to Jerusalem, introduced the principles of Byzantine architecture into France.

Now, history attests that in the 8th century there was an influx
of Grecian architects and artificers into Southern and Western Europe, in consequence of persecutions that were inflicted on them by
the Byzantine Emperors. The Legend, therefore, indulges in no
spirit of fiction in referring to the advent in France, at that period,
of one of these architects.

It is also a historical fact that Charles the Great of France was a liberal encourager of the arts and sciences, and that he especially promoted the cultivation of architecture on the Byzantine or Greek model in his dominions.

Dr. Oliver, in the second edition of the *Constitutions*, repeats the Legend with a slight variation. He says that " Ethelbert, King of Mercia, and general monarch, sent to Charles Martel, the Right Worshipful Grand Master of France (father of King Pippin), who had been educated by Brother *Mimus Grœcus;* he sent over from France (about A.D. 710) some expert Masons to teach the Saxons those laws and usages of the ancient fraternity, that had been happily preserved from the havock of the Goths."

Pritchard, in his *Masonry Dissected*, gives, upon what authority I know not, the Legend in the following form :

Euclid "communicated the art and mystery of Masonry to Hiram, the Master Mason concerned in the building of Solomon's Temple in Jerusalem, where was an excellent and curious Mason, whose name was *Mannon Grecus*, who taught the art of Masonry to one Carolus Marcil in France, who was afterwards elected King of France."

Upon this change of the name to *Mannon Grecus*, Krause suggests a derivation as follows : In using this name he thinks that Pritchard intended to refer to the celebrated scholastic philosopher Mannon, or Nannon, who was probably celebrated in his time for his proficiency in the language and literature of Greece. Nannon lived in the reign of Charles the Bold, and was the successor of Erigena in the direction of the schools of France.

I think the derivation of the name offered by Dr. Krause is wholly untenable though ingenious, for it depends upon a name not found in any of the old manuscripts, and besides, the philosopher did not live in the time of Charles Martel, but long afterward.

Between his derivation and mine, the reader may select, and probably will be inclined to reject both.

As far as the Legend regards Charles Martel as the patron of architecture or Masonry in France, one observation remains to be made.

If there has been an error of the legendists in attributing to Charles Martel the honor that really belonged to his successor, Charles the Great, it is not surprising when we consider how great was the ignorance of the science of chronology that prevailed in those days. However, it must be remarked, that at the present day the French Masonic writers speak of Charles Martel as the founder of Masonry in France.

The error of making the Greek architect a contemporary both of Solomon and of Charles Martel, is one which may be explained, either as the expression of a symbolic idea, alluding to the close connection that had existed between Oriental and Byzantine architecture, or may be excused as an instance of blundering chronology for which the spirit of the age, more than the writer of the Legend, is to be blamed. This objection will not, however, lie if we assume that Namus Grecus meant simply a Greek architect.

But this whole subject is so closely connected with the authentic history of Masonry, having really passed out of the prehistoric period, that it claims a future and more elaborate consideration in its proper place.

CHAPTER XVII

THE LEGEND OF ST. ALBAN

HE *Legend of the Craft* now proceeds to narrate the history of the introduction of Masonry into England, in the time of St. Alban, who lived in the 3d century.

The Legend referring to the protomartyr of England is not mentioned in the Halliwell poem, but is first found in the Cooke MS., in the following words: "And sone after that come seynt Adhabell into Englond, and he convertyd seynt Albon to cristendome. And seynt Albon lovyd well masons, and he gaf hem fyrst her charges and maners fyrst in Englond. And he ordeyned convenyent[1] to pay for their travayle."[2]

The later manuscripts say nothing of St. Adhabell, and it is not until we get to the Krause MS. in the beginning of the 18th century, that we find any mention of St. Amphibalus, who is described in that document as having been the teacher of St. Alban. But St. Amphibalus, of which the Adhabell of the Cooke MS. is undoubtedly a corruption, is so apocryphal a personage, that I am rejoiced that the later legendists have not thought proper to follow the Cooke document and give him a place in the Legend.

In fact, *amphibalum* was the ecclesiastical name of a cloak, worn by priests of the Romish Church over their other vestments.[3] It was a vestment ecclesiastically transmuted into a saint, as the hand-

---

[1] Cooke translates this " convenient times," supplying the second word. But a more correct word is *suitable* or *proper*, which is an old meaning of *convenient*. " He ordained suitable pay for their labor," and this agrees with the later manuscripts which impress the fact that St. Alban " made their pay right good."

[2] Cooke MS., lines 602–611.

[3] It is significant that among the spurious relics sent, when fearing the Danish invasion, in the reign of Edward the Confessor, by the Abbot of St. Albans, to the monks of Ely, was a very rough, shagged old *coat*, which it was said had been usually worn by St. Amphibalus.

kerchief on which Christ left the image of His face when, as it is said, it was handed to Him on His way to Calvary, by a pious Jewess, became from the Greco-Latin *vera icon*, "the true image," converted into St. Veronica. The Masonic are not the only legendists who draw deeply on our credulity.

Of St. Alban, ecclesiastical history furnishes only the following meager details, and even of these some are apocryphal, or at least lack the stamp of authenticity.

He was born (so runs the tradition) in the 3d century, in Hertfordshire, England, near the town of Verulanium. Going to Rome, he served for seven years as a soldier under the Emperor Diocletian. He then returned with a companion and preceptor Amphibalus, to Britain, and betook himself to Verulanium. When the persecutions of the Christians commenced in Britain, Amphibalus was sought for, as one who had apostatized to the new religion; but as he could not be found, St. Alban voluntarily presented himself to the judge, and after undergoing torture was imprisoned. Soon after this, the retreat of Amphibalus having been discovered, both he and St. Alban suffered death for being Christians. Four centuries after his martyrdom, Offa, King of the Mercians, erected a monastery at Holmehurst, the hill where he was buried, and soon after the town of St. Albans arose in its vicinity.

When the Christian religion became predominant in England, the Church paid great honors to the memory of the protomartyr. A chapel was erected over his grave, which, according to the Venerable Bede, was of admirable workmanship.

The Masonic Legend contains details which are not furnished by the religious one. According to it, St. Alban was the steward of the household of Carausius, he who had revolted from the Emperor Maximilian, and usurped the sovereignty of England. Carausius employed him in building the town walls. St. Alban, thus receiving the superintendence of the Craft, treated them with great kindness, increased their pay, and gave them a charter to hold a general assembly. He assisted them in making Masons, and framed for them a constitution—for such is the meaning of the phrase, "gave them charges."

Now, there is sufficient historical evidence to show that architecture was introduced into England by the Roman artificers, who followed, as was their usage, the Roman legions, habilitated themselves in the conquered colonies, and engaged in the construction not only of camps and fortifications, but also when peace was restored in the building of temples and even private edifices.   Architectural ruins and Latin inscriptions, which still remain in many parts of Britain, attest the labors and the skill of these Roman artists, and sustain the statement of the Legend, that Masonry, which, it must be remembered, is, in the *Old Records*, only a synonym of architecture, was introduced into England during the period of its Roman colonization.

As to the specific statement that St. Alban was the patron of Masons, that he exercised the government of a chief over the Craft, and improved their condition by augmenting their wages, we may explain this as the expression of a symbolical idea, in which history is not altogether falsified, but only its dates and personages confused.

Carausius, the Legend does not mention by name.   It simply refers to some King of England, of whose household St. Alban was the steward.   Carausius assumed the imperial purple in the year in which St. Alban suffered martyrdom.   The error of making him the patron of St. Alban is not, therefore, to be attributed to the legendist, but to Dr. Anderson, who first perpetrated this chronological blunder in the second edition of his *Constitutions*.   And though he states that "this is asserted by all the old copies of the *Constitutions*,"[1] we fail to find it in any that are now extant.

This "Legend of St. Alban," as it has been called, is worthy of a farther consideration.

The foundation of this symbolical narrative was first laid by the writer of the Cooke MS., or, rather, copied by him from the tradition existing among the Craft at that time.   Its form was subsequently modified and the details extended in the Dowland MS., for tradition always grows in the progress of time.   This form and these details were preserved in all the succeeding manuscript Constitutions, until they were still further altered and enlarged by Anderson, Preston, and other Masonic historians of the last century.

With the gratuitous accretions of these later writers we have no concern in any attempted explanation of the actual signification of the Legend.   Its true form and spirit are to be found only in the Dowland MS. of the middle of the 16th century, and in those which

---

[1] Anderson, " Constitutions," 2d edit., p. 57.

were copied from it, up to the Papworth, at the beginning of the 18th. To these, and not to anything written after the period of the Revival, we must direct our attention.

Admitting that on the conquest of England by the Roman power, the architects who had accompanied the victorious legions introduced into the conquered colony their architectural skill, it is very likely that some master workmen among them had been more celebrated than others for their skill, and, indeed, it is naturally to be supposed that to such skillful builders the control of the Craft must have been confided. Whether there were one or more of these chief architects, St. Alban, if not actually one of them, was, by the lapse of time and the not unusual process by which legendary or oral accretions are superimposed on a plain historical fact, adopted by the legendists as their representative. Who was the principal patron of the Architects or Masons during the time of the colonization of England by the Romans, is not so material as is the fact that architecture, with other branches of civilization, was introduced at that era into the island by its conquerors.

This is an historical fact, and in this point the *Legend of the Craft* agrees with authentic history.

But it is also an historical fact that when, by the pressure of the Northern hordes of barbarians upon Rome, it was found necessary to withdraw all the legions from the various colonies which they protected from exterior enemies and restrained from interior insurrection, the arts and sciences, and among them architecture, began to decline in England. The natives, with the few Roman colonists who had permanently settled among them, were left to defend themselves from the incursions of the Picts on the north, and the Danish and Saxon pirates in the east and south. The arts of civilization suffered a depression in the tumult of war. Science can not flourish amid the clang and clash of arms. This depression and suspension of all architectural progress in England, which continued for some centuries, is thus expressed in the quaint language of the Legend :

" Right soone after the decease of Saint Albone, there came divers wars into the realme of England of divers Nations, soe that the good rule of Masonrye was destroyed unto the tyme of Kinge Athelstone's days."

There is far more of history than of fiction in this part of the Legend.

The next point of the *Legend of the Craft* to which our attention is to be directed, is that which relates to the organization of
Masonry at the city of York, in the 10th century.   This part of the
Legend is of far more importance than any of those which have
been considered.   The prehistoric here verges so closely upon the
historic period, that the true narrative of the rise and progress of
Masonry can not be justly understood until each of these prehistoric and historic elements has been carefully relegated to its appropriate period.   This will constitute the subject matter of the
next chapter.

CHAPTER XVIII

HE suppression of all architectural art and enterprise having lasted for so long a period in Britain, the *Legend of the Craft* next proceeds to account for its revival in the 10th century and in the reign of Athelstan, whose son Edwin called a meeting, or General Assembly, of the Masons at York in the year 926, and there revived the Institution, giving to the Craft a new code of laws.

Now, it is impossible to attach to this portion of the Legend, absolutely and without any reservation, the taint of fiction. The convocation of the Craft of England at the city of York, in the year 926, has been accepted by both the Operative Masons who preceded the Revival, and by the Speculatives who succeeded them, up to the present day, as a historical fact that did not admit of dispute. The two classes of Legends—the one represented by the Halliwell poem, and the other by the later manuscripts—concur in giving the same statement. The Cooke MS., which holds an intermediate place between the two, also contains it. But the Halliwell and the Cooke MSS., which are of older date, give more fully the details of what may be called this revival of English Masonry. Thoroughly to understand the subject, it will be necessary to collate the three accounts given in the three different sets of manuscripts.

The Halliwell poem, whose conjectural date is about 1390, contains the account in the following words. I will first give it, relieved of its archaisms, for the convenience of the reader inexpert in early English, and then follow with a quotation of the original language:

"This craft came into England, as I tell you, in the time of good King Athelstane's reign. He made them both hall and also chamber, and lofty churches of great honour, to recreate him in both day and night and to worship his God with all his strength. This good lord loved this craft full well, and purposed to strengthen it in every part, on account of several defects which he discovered in the craft. He sent about into the land after all the masons of the craft to come straight to him, to amend all these defects by good counsel, if it could be done. Then he permitted an assembly to be made of various lords according to their rank, dukes, earls, and barons also, knights, squires, and many more, and the great burgesses of that city, they were all there in their degree; these were there, each one in every way to make laws for the society of these masons. There they sought by their wisdom how they might govern it. There they invented fifteen articles, and there they made fifteen points." [1]

The original is as follows:

> "Thys craft com ynto England as y you say,
> Yn tyme of good kynge Athelston's day;
> He made the both halle and eke boure,
> And hye templus of gret honoure,
> To sportyn hym yn bothe day and nyghth,
> And to worschepe his God with alle hys myghth.
> Thys goode lorde loved thys craft ful wel,
> And purposud to strenthyn hyt ever del,
> For dyvers defautys that yn the craft he fonde;
> He sende aboute ynto the londe
> After alle the masonus of the crafte
> To come to hym ful evene strayfte,
> For to amende these defaultys alle
> By good counsel gef hyt mygth falle.
> A semblé thenne he cowthe let make
> Of dyvers lordis in here state
> Dukys, erlys and barnes also,
> Knygthys, sqwyers and mony mo,
> And the grete burges of that syté,
> They were ther alle yn here degré;
> These were there uchon algate,
> To ordeyne for these masonus estate,
> Ther they sowgton ly here wytte
> How they mygthyn governe hytte:
> Fyftene artyculus they there sowgton,
> And fyftene poyntys ther they wrogton."

One hundred years afterward we find the Legend, in the Cooke MS., as follows:

" And after that was a worthy kynge in Englond that was callyd

---

Athelstone, and his yongest sone lovyd well the sciens of Gemetry, and he wyst well that handcraft had the practyke of Gemetry so well as masons, wherefore he drew him to consell and lernyd [the] practyke of that sciens to his speculatyfe.[1] For of speculatyfe he was a master, and he lovyd well masonry and masons. And he bicome a mason hymselfe. And he gaf hem [gave them] charges and names[2] as it is now usyd in Englond and in other countries. And he ordeyned that they schulde have resonabull pay. And purchesed [obtained] a fre patent of the kyng that they schulde make a sembly when they saw resonably tyme a [to] cume togedir to her [their] counsell of the whiche charges, manors & semble as is write and taught in the boke of our charges wherefor I leve it at this tyme."[3]

In a subsequent part of the manuscript, which appears to have been taken from the aforesaid "boke of charges," with some additional details, are the following words:

"After that, many yeris, in the tyme of Kyng Adhelstane, wiche was sum tyme kynge of Englonde, bi his counsell and other gret lordys of the lond by comyn [common] assent for grete defaut y-fennde [found] among masons thei ordeyend a certayne reule amongys hem [them]. On [one] tyme of the yere or in iii yere as nede were to the kyng and gret lordys of the londe and all the comente [community], fro provynce to provynce and fro countre to countre congregacions schulde be made by maisters, of all maisters masons and felaus in the forsayd art. And so at such congregacions, they that be made masters schold be examined of the articuls after written & be ransacked [examined] whether they be abull and kunnyng to the profyte of the lordys hem to serve [to serve them] and to the honour of the forsayd art."[4]

Sixty years afterward we find this Legend repeated in the Dowland MS., but with some important variations. This Legend has already been given in the *Legend of the Craft*, but for the convenience of immediate comparison with the preceding documents it will be well to repeat it here. It is in the following words:

" Right soone after the decease of Saint Albone there came divers

---

[1] Cooke calls particular attention to this word as of much significative import. I think it simply means that the king added a practical knowledge of Masonry or architecture to his former merely speculative or theoretical acquaintance with the art.

[2] This is evidently an error of the pen for *maners*, i.e., *usages*.

[3] Cooke MS., lines 611–642. [4] Cooke MS., lines 693–719.

warrs into the realme of England of divers Nations, soe that the good rule of Masonrye was destroyed unto the tyme of Kinge Athelstones days that was a worthy Kinge of England, and brought this land into good rest and peace and builded many great works of Abbyes and Towres and other many divers buildings and loved well Masons. And he had a Sonn that height Edwinne, and he loved Masons much more than his father did. And he was a great practiser in Geometry, and he drew him much to talke and to commune with Masons and to learne of them science, and afterwards for love that he had to Masons and to the science he was made Mason,[1] and he gatt of the Kinge his father a Chartour and Commission to hold every yeare once an Assemble wher that ever they would within the realme of England, and to correct within themselves defaults and trespasses that were done within the science. And he held himselfe an Assemble at Yorke, and there he made Masons and gave them charges and taught them the manners, and commanded that rule to be kept ever after. And tooke them the Chartour and Commission to keepe and made ordinance that it should be renewed from kinge to kinge.

"And when the Assemble was gathered he made a cry that all old Masons and young, that had any writeings or understanding of the charges and the manners that were made before in this land, or in any other, that they should shew them forth. And when it was proved there was founden some in Frenche and some in Greek and some in English and some in other languages; and the intent of them all was founden all one. And he did make a booke thereof, and how the science was founded. And he himselfe bad and commanded that it should be readd or tould, when that any Mason should be made, for to give him his Charge. And fro that day into this tyme manners of Masons have beene kept in that forme as well as men might governe it. And furthermore divers Assembles have beene put and ordayned certain charges by the best advice of Masters and Fellowes."

It will be remarked that in neither of the two oldest manuscripts,

---

[1] The next MS. in date, the Landsdowne, names the place where he was made as Windsor. This statement is not found in any of the other manuscripts except the Antiquity MS. It may here be observed that nothing more clearly proves the great carelessness of the transcribers of these manuscripts than the fact that although they must have all been familiar with the name of Edwin, one of them spells it *Ladrian* and another *Hoderine.*

the Halliwell and the Cooke, is there any mention of Prince Edwin, or of the city of York. For the omission I shall hereafter attempt to account. As to that of the latter I agree with Bro. Woodford, that as the fact of the Assembly is stated in all the later traditions, and as a city is mentioned whose burgesses were present, we may fairly understand both of the oldest manuscripts also to refer to York.[1] At all events, their silence as to the place affords no sufficient evidence that it was not York, as opposed to the positive declaration of the later manuscripts that it was.

We see, then, that all the old Legends assert expressly, or by implication, that York was the city where the first General Masonic Assembly was held in England, and that it was summoned under the authority of King Athelstan.

The next point in which all the later manuscripts, except the Harleian,[2] agree is, that the Assembly was called by Prince Edwin, the King's son.

The Legend does not here most certainly agree with history, for there is no record that Athelstan had any son. He had, however, a brother of that name, who died two years before him.

Edward the Elder, the son of Alfred the Great, died in the year 925, leaving several legitimate sons and one natural one, Athelstan. The latter, who was the eldest of the sons of Edward, obtained the throne, notwithstanding the stain on his birth, in consequence of his age, which better fitted him to govern at a time when the kingdom was engaged in foreign and domestic wars.

All historians concur in attributing to Athelstan the character of a just and wise sovereign, and of a sagacious statesman. It has been said of him that he was the most able and active of the ancient princes of England. What his grandfather, the great Alfred, commenced in his efforts to consolidate the petty monarchies into which the land was divided, into one powerful kingdom, Athelstan, by his energy, his political wisdom, and his military prowess, was enabled to perfect, so that he has been justly called the first monarch of all England.

Although engaged during his whole reign in numerous wars, he

---

[1] " On the Connection of York with the History of Freemasonry in England." By A. F. Woodford, A.M., in Hughan's " Masonic Sketches and Reprints," p. 168.

[2] The Harleian MS. makes no mention of Prince Edwin, but attributes the organization of Masonry at York to King Athelstan himself.

did not neglect a cultivation of the employments of peace, and encouraged by a liberal patronage the arts and especially architecture.

The only stain upon his character is the charge that having suspected his brother Edwin of being engaged in a conspiracy against his throne, he caused that prince to be drowned. Notwithstanding the efforts of Preston to disprove this charge, the concurrent testimony of all the old chroniclers afford no room to doubt its truth. But if anything could atone for this cruel act of state policy, it would be the bitter anguish and remorse of conscience which led the perpetrator to endure a severe penance of seven years.

Of Edwin, the Saxon historians make no mention, except when they speak of his untimely death. If we may judge of his character from this silence, we must believe that he was not endued with any brilliant qualities of mind, nor distinguished by the performance of any important act.

Of all the half-brothers of Athelstan, the legitimate children of Edward the Elder, Edmund seems to have been his favorite. He kept him by his side on battle-fields, lived single for his sake, and when he died in 941, left to him the succession to the throne.

But there is another Edwin of prominent character in the annals of Saxon England, to whom attention has been directed in connection with this Legend, as having the best claim to be called the founder or reviver of English Masonry.

Of Edwin, King of Northumbria, it may be said, that in his narrow sphere, as the monarch of a kingdom of narrow dimensions, he was but little inferior in abilities or virtues to Athelstan.

At the time of his birth, in 590, Northumbria was divided into two kingdoms, that of Bernicia, north of the Humber, and that of the Deira, on the south of the same river. Of the former, Ethelfrith was King, and of the latter, Ella, the father of Edwin.

Ella died in 593, and was succeeded by Edwin, an infant of three years of age.

Soon after, Ethelfrith invaded the possessions of Edwin, and attached them by usurpation to his own domains.

Edwin was sent to Wales, whence when he grew older he was obliged to flee, and passed many years in exile, principally at the Court of Redwald, King of East Anglia. By the assistance of this monarch he was enabled to make war upon his old enemy, Ethelfrith, who, having been slain in battle, and his sons having fled into

Scotland, Edwin not only regained his own throne, but that of the usurper also, and in the year 617 became the King of Northumbria, of which the city of York was made the capital.

Edwin was originally a pagan, but his mind was of a contemplative turn, and this made him, says Turner, more intellectual than any of the Saxon Kings who had preceded him. He was thus led to a rational consideration of the doctrines of Christianity, which he finally accepted, and was publicly baptized at York, on Easter day, in the year 627. The ceremony was publicly performed in the Church of St. Peter the Apostle, which he had caused to be hastily constructed of wood, for the purposes of divine service, during the time that he was undergoing the religious instructions preliminary to his receiving the sacrament.

But as soon as he was baptized, he built, says Bede, under the direction of Paulinus, his religious instructor and bishop, in the same place, a much larger and nobler church of stone.

During the reign of Edwin, and of his successors in the same century, ecclesiastical architecture greatly flourished, and many large churches were built. Edwin was slain in battle in 633, having reigned for seventeen years.

The Venerable Bede gives us the best testimony we could desire as to the character of Edwin as ruler, when he tells us that in all of his dominions there was such perfect peace that a woman with a new-born babe might walk from sea to sea without receiving any harm. Another incident that he relates is significant of Edwin's care and consideration for the comforts of his people. Where there were springs of water near the highways, he caused posts to be fixed with drinking vessels attached to them for the convenience of travelers. By such acts, and others of a higher character, by his encouragement of the arts, and his strict administration of justice, he secured the love of his subjects.

So much of history was necessary that the reader might understand the argument in reference to the true meaning of *the York Legend*, now to be discussed.

In the versions of the Legend given by Anderson and Preston, the honor of organizing Masonry and calling a General Assembly is attributed to Edwin the brother, and not to Edwin the son of Athelstan. These versions are, however, of no value as historical documents, because they are merely enlarged copies of the original Legend.

But in the Roberts *Constitutions*, printed in 1722, and which was claimed to have been copied from a manuscript about five hundred years old, but without any proof (as the original has never been recovered), the name of Edwin is altogether omitted, and Athelstan himself is said to have been the reviver of the institution. The language of this manuscript, as published by J. Roberts, is as follows:[1]

" He [Athelstan] began to build many Abbies, Monasteries, and other religious houses, as also Castles and divers Fortresses for defence of his realm. He loved *Masons* more than his father; he greatly study'd *Geometry*, and sent into many lands for men expert in the science. He gave them a very large charter to hold a yearly assembly, and power to correct offenders in the said science; and the king himself caused a General Assembly of all *Masons* in his realm, at *York*, and there were made many *Masons*, and gave them a deep charge for observation of all such articles as belonged unto *Masonry* and delivered them the said Charter to keep."

In the omission of all reference to Prince Edwin, the Harleian and Roberts manuscripts agree with that of Halliwell.

There is a passage in the Harleian and Roberts MSS. that is worthy of notice. All the recent manuscripts which speak of Edwin as the procurer of the Charter, say that " he loved Masons much more than his father did "—meaning Athelstan. But the Harleian and Roberts MSS., speaking of King Athelstan, use the same language, but with a different reference, and say of King Athelstan, that " he loved Masons more than his father "—meaning King Edward, whose son Athelstan was.

Now, of the two statements, that of the Harleian and Roberts MSS. is much more conformable to history than the other. Athelstan was a lover of Masons, for he was a great patron of architecture, and many public buildings were erected during his reign. But it is not recorded in history that Prince Edwin exhibited any such attachment to Masonry or Architecture as is attributed to him in the old records, certainly not an attachment equal to that of Athelstan. On the contrary, Edward, the son of Alfred and the father of Athelstan, was not distinguished during his reign for any marked patronage of

---

[1] The book was republished by Spencer in 1870. The Roberts " Constitutions " and the Harleian MS. No. 1942, are evidently copies from the same original, if not one from the other. The story of Athelstan is, of course, identical in both, and the citation might as well have been made from either.

the arts, and especially of architecture; and it is, therefore, certain that his son Athelstan exhibited a greater love to Masons or Architects than he did.

Hence there arises a suspicion that the Legend was originally framed in the form presented to us by the Halliwell poem, and copied apparently by the writers of the Harleian and Roberts MSS., and that the insertion of the name of Prince Edwin was an after-thought of the copiers of the more recent manuscripts, and that this insertion of Edwin's name, and the error of making him a son of Athelstan, arose from a confusion of the mythical Edwin with a different personage, the earlier Edwin, who was King of Northumbria.

It may also be added that the son of Athelstan is not called Edwin in all of the recent manuscripts. In one Sloane MS. he is called *Ladrian*, in another *Hegme*, and in the Lodge of Hope MS. *Hoderine*. This fact might indicate that there was some confusion and disagreement in putting the name of Prince Edwin into the Legend. But I will not press this point, because I am rather inclined to attribute these discrepancies to the proverbial carelessness of the transcribers of these manuscripts.

How, then, are we to account for this introduction of an apparently mythical personage into the narrative, by which the plausibility of the Legend is seriously affected?

Anderson, and after him Preston, attempts to get out of the difficulty by calling Edwin the brother, and not the son, of Athelstan. It is true that Athelstan did have a younger brother named Edwin, whom some historians have charged him with putting to death. And in so far the Legend might not be considered as incompatible with history. But as all the manuscripts which have to this day been recovered which speak of Edwin call him the king's son and not his brother, notwithstanding the contrary statement of Anderson,[1] I prefer another explanation, although it involves the charge of anachronism.

The annals of English history record a royal Edwin, whose de-

---

[1] Anderson says in the second edition of the " Book of Constitutions " that in all the Old Constitutions it is written Prince Edwin, the king's brother—a statement that is at once refuted by a reference to all the manuscripts from the Dowland to the Papworth, where the word is always *son*. So much for the authority of the old writers on Masonic history.

votion to the arts and sciences, whose wise statesmanship, and whose patronage of architecture, must have entitled him to the respect and the affection of the early English Masons.   Edwin, King of Northumbria, one of the seven kingdoms into which England was divided during the Anglo-Saxon heptarchy, died in 633, after a reign of sixteen years, which was distinguished for the reforms which he accomplished, for the wise laws which he enacted and enforced, for the introduction of Christianity into his kingdom, and for the improvement which he effected in the moral, social, and intellectual condition of his subjects.   When he ascended the throne the north ern metropolis of the Anglican Church had been placed at York, where it still remains.   The king patronized Paulinus, the bishop, and presented him with a residence and with other possessions in that city.   Much of this has already been said, but it will bear repetition.

To this Edwin, and not to the brother of Athelstan, modern Masonic archæologists have supposed that the *Legend of the Craft* refers.

Yet this opinion is not altogether a new one.   More than a century and a half ago it seems to have prevailed as a tradition among the Masons of the northern part of England.   For in 1726, in an address delivered before the Grand Lodge of York by its Junior Grand Warden, Francis Drake, he speaks of it as being well known and recognized, in the following words:

"You know we can boast that the first Grand Lodge ever held in England was held in this city [York]; where Edwin, the first Christian King of the Northumbers, about the six hundredth year after Christ, and who laid the foundation of our Cathedral,[1] sat as Grand Master."

Bro. A. F. A. Woodford, a profound Masonic archæologist, accepts this explanation, and finds a confirmation in the facts that the town of Derventio, now Auldby, six miles from York, the supposed seat of the pseudo-Edwin, was also the chief seat and residence of Edwin, King of Northumbria, and that the buildings, said in one of the manuscripts to have been erected by the false Edwin, were really erected, as is known from history, by the Northumbrian Edwin.

I think that with these proofs, the inquirer will have little or no

---

[1] Bede (L. 2., c. 13) and Rapin (p. 246) both confirm this statement that the founda-tions of the York Cathedral, or Minster, were laid in the reign of Edwin.

hesitation in accepting this version of the Legend, and will recognize the fact that the writers of the later manuscripts fell into an error in substituting Edwin, the son (as they called him, but really the brother) of Athelstan, for Edwin, the King of Northumbria.

It is true that the difference of dates presents a difficulty, there being about three hundred years between the reigns of Edwin of Northumbria, and Athelstan of England. But that difficulty, I think, may be overcome by the following theory which I advance on the subject:

The earlier series of manuscripts, of which the Halliwell poem is an exemplar, and, perhaps, also the Harleian and the Roberts MSS.,[1] make no mention of Edwin, but assign the revival of Masonry in the 10th century to King Athelstan.

The more recent manuscripts, of which the Dowland is the earliest, introduce Prince Edwin into the Legend and ascribe to him the honor of having obtained from Athelstan a charter, and of having held an Assembly at York.

There are, then, two forms of the Legend, which, for the sake of distinction, may be designated as the older and the later. The older Legend makes Athelstan the reviver of Masonry in England, and says nothing at all of Edwin. The later takes this honor from Athelstan and gives it to Prince Edwin, who is called his son.

The part about Edwin is, then, an addition to the older legend, and was interpolated into it by the later legendists, as will be evidently seen if the following extract from the Dowland MS. be read, and all the words there printed in italics be omitted. So read, the passage will conform very substantially with the corresponding one in the Roberts MS., which was undoubtedly a copy from some older manuscript which contained the legend in its primitive form, wherein there is no mention of Prince Edwin. Here is the extract to be amended by the omission of words in italics:

" The good rule of Masonry was destroyed unto the tyme of Kinge Athelstone dayes that was a worthy Kinge of England, and brought this land into good rest and peace ; and builded many great works of Abbyes and Towres, and other many divers buildings and loved well Masons. *And he had a sonn that height Edwinne,* and

---

[1] The fact that the Legend in the Roberts " Constitutions " agrees in this respect with the older legend, and differs from that in all the recent manuscripts, gives some color to the claim that it was copied from a manuscript five hundred years old.

he loved Masons much more than his father did. And he was a
great practiser in Geometry; and he drew him much to talke and
to commune with Masons, and to learne of them science; and afterward for love that he had to Masons and to the science he was made
a Mason and he gatt [1] [*i.e.*, he gave] *of the Kinge his father* a
Charter and commission to hold every year once an Assemble, wher
that ever they would, within the realme of England; and to correct
within themselves defaults and trespasses that were done within the
science. And he held himselfe an Assemble at Yorke, and there he
made Masons, and gave them charges, and taught them the manners,
and commanded that rule to be kept ever after, and tooke then the
Chartour and Commission to keepe, and made ordinance that it
should be renewed from Kinge to Kinge."

The elimination of only thirteen words relieves us at once of all
difficulty, and brings the Legend into precise accord with the tradition of the older manuscripts.

Thus eliminated it asserts:

1. That King Athelstan was a great patron of the arts of civilization—"he brought the land into rest and peace." This statement
is sustained by the facts of history.

2. He paid especial attention to architecture and the art of building, and adorned his country with abbeys, towns (*towers* is a clerical
error), and many other edifices. History confirms this also.

3. He was more interested in, and gave a greater patronage to,
architecture than his father and predecessor, Edward—another historical fact.

4. He gave to the Masons or Architects a charter as a guild, and
called an assembly of the Craft at York. This last statement is altogether traditional. Historians are silent on the subject, just as they
are on the organization of a Grand Lodge in 1717. The mere silence
of historians as to the formation of a guild of craftsmen or a private
society is no proof that such guild or society was not formed. The
truth of the statement that King Athelstan caused an assembly of
Masons to be held in the year 926 at the city of York, depends

---

[1] This word is used in the sense of *given* or *granted*, in an undoubted historical document, Athelstan's charter to the town of Beverly.

" Yat I, the Kynge Adelston,
Has *gaten* and given to St. John
Of Beverlae, etc."

solely on a tradition, which has, however, until recently, been accepted by the whole Masonic world as an undoubted truth.

But that the city of York was the place where an assembly was convened by Athelstan in the year 926 is rendered very improbable when we refer to the concurrent events of history at that period of time.

In 925 Athelstan ascended the throne. At that time Sigtryg was the reigning King of Northumbria, which formed no part of the dominions of Athelstan. To Sigtryg, who had but very recently been converted from Paganism to Christianity, Athelstan gave his sister in marriage. But the Northumbrian king having apostatized, his brother-in-law resolved to dethrone him, and prepared to invade his kingdom. Sigtryg having died in the meantime, his sons fled, one into Ireland and the other into Scotland, and Athelstan annexed Northumbria to his own dominions.

This occurred in the year 926, and it is not likely that while pursuing the sons of Sigtryg, one of whom had escaped from his captors and taken refuge in the city of York, whose citizens he vainly sought to enlist in his favor, Athelstan would have selected that period of conflict, and a city within his newly-acquired territory, instead of his own capital, for the time and place of holding an assembly of Masons.

It is highly improbable that he did, but yet it is not absolutely impossible. The tradition may be correct as to York, but, if so, then the time should be advanced, by a few years, to that happy period when Athelstan had restored the land "into good rest and peace."

But the important question is, whether this tradition is mythical or historical, whether it is a fiction or a truth. Conjectural criticism applied to the theory of probabilities alone can aid us in solving this problem.

I say, therefore, that there is nothing in the personal character of Athelstan, nothing in the recorded history of his reign, nothing in the well-known manner in which he exercised his royal authority and governed his realm, that forbids the probability that the actions attributed to him in the *Legend of the Craft* actually took place.

Taking his grandfather, the great Alfred, as his pattern, he was liberal in all his ideas, patronized learning, erected many churches, monasteries, and other edifices of importance throughout his dominions, encouraged the translation of the Scriptures into Anglo-Saxon, and, what is of great value to the present question, gave charters to many guilds or operative companies as well as to several municipalities.

Especially is it known from historical records that in the reign of Athelstan the *frith-gildan*, free guilds or sodalities, were incorporated by law. From these subsequently arose the craft-guilds or associations for the establishment of fraternal relations and mutual aid, into which, at the present day, the trade companies of England are divided.

There would be nothing improbable in any narrative which should assert that he extended his protection to the operative Masons, of whose art we know that he availed himself in the construction of the numerous public and religious edifices which he was engaged in erecting. It is even more than plausible to suppose that the Masons were among the sodalities to whom he granted charters or acts of incorporation.

Like the Rev. Bro. Woodford, whose opinion as a Masonic archæologist is of great value, I am disposed to accept a tradition venerable for its antiquity and for so long a period believed in by the craft as an historical record in so far as relates to the obtaining of a charter from Athelstan and the holding of an assembly. " I see no reason, therefore," he says, " to reject so old a tradition that under Athelstan the operative Masons obtained his patronage and met in General Assembly." [1]

Admitting the fact of Athelstan's patronage and of the Assembly at some place, we next encounter the difficulty of explaining the interpolation of what may be called the episode of Prince Edwin.

I have already shown that there can be no doubt that the framers of the later legend had confounded the brother, whom they, by a mistake, had called the son of Athelstan, with a preceding king of the same name, that is, with Edwin, King of Northumbria, who, in the 7th century, did what the pseudo-Edwin is supposed to have done in the 10th. That is to say, he patronized the Masons of his time, introduced the art of building into his kingdom, and probably held an Assembly at York, which was his capital city.

Now, I suppose that the earlier Masons of the south of England, who framed the first *Legend of the Craft*, such as is presented to

<hr/>

[1] " The Connection of York with the History of Freemasonry in England," inserted in Hughan's " Unpublished Records of the Craft," p. 168.

us in the old poem, first published by Mr. Halliwell in 1840, and also in the Harleian manuscript and in the one printed by Roberts in 1722, were unacquainted with the legend of Edwin of Northumbria, although, if we may believe Bro. Drake, it was a well-known tradition in the north of England. The earlier legends of the south, therefore, gave the honor of patronizing the Masons and holding an Assembly at York in 926 to Athelstan alone. This was, therefore, the primitive *Legend of the Craft* among the Masons of London and the southern part of the kingdom.

But in time these southern Masons became, in consequence of increased intercourse, cognizant of the tradition that King Edwin of Northumbria had also patronized the Masons of his kingdom, but at an earlier period. The two traditions were, of course, at first kept distinct. There was, perhaps, a reluctance among the Masons of the south to diminish the claims of Athelstan as tne first reviver, after St. Alban, of Masonry in England, and to give the precedence to a monarch who lived three hundred years before in the northern part of the island.

This reluctance, added to the confusion to which all oral tradition is obnoxious, coupled with the' fact that there was an Edwin, who was a near relation of Athelstan, resulted in the substitution of this later Edwin for the true one.

It took years to do this—the reluctance continuing, the confusion of the traditions increasing, until at last the southern Masons, altogether losing sight of the Northumbrian tradition as distinct from that of Athelstan, combined the two traditions into one, and, with the carelessness or ignorance of chronology so common in that age, and especially among uncultured craftsmen, substituted Edwin, the brother of Athelstan,[1] for Edwin, the King of Northumbria, and thus formed a new *Legend of the Craft* such as it was perpetuated by Anderson, and after him by Preston, and which has lasted to the present day.

Therefore, eliminating from the narrative the story of Edwin, as it is told in the recent Legend, and accepting it as referring to Edwin of Northumbria, and as told in the tradition peculiar to the Masons of the northern part of England, we reach the conclusion that there were originally two traditions, one extant in the northern

---

[1] To the same carelessness or ignorance are we to attribute the legendary error of making Edwin the son of Athelstan.

part of England and the other in the southern part. The former
Legend ascribed the revival of Masonry in England to Edwin, King
of Northumbria in the 7th century, and the latter to Athelstan,
King of England in the 10th. There being little communication in those days between the two parts of the kingdom, the
traditions remained distinct. But at some subsequent period, not
earlier than the middle of the 16th century, or the era of the
Reformation,[1] the southern Masons became acquainted with the
true Legend of the York Masons, and incorporated it into their own
Legend, confounding, however, the two Edwins, either from ignorance, or more probably, from a reluctance to surrender the pre-
eminence they had hitherto given to Athelstan as the first reviver of
Masonry in England.

We arrive, then, at the conclusion, that if there was an Assembly at York it was convened by Edwin, King of Northumbria,
who revived Masonry in the northern part of England in the 7th
century ; and that its decayed prosperity was restored by Athelstan
in the 10th century, not by the holding of an Assembly at the city
of York, but by his general patronage of the arts, and especially
architecture, and by the charters of incorporation which he freely
granted to various guilds or sodalities of workmen.

With these explanations, we are now prepared to review and to
summarize the *Legend of the Craft*, not in the light of a series
of absurd fictions, as too many have been inclined to consider it,
but as an historical narrative, related in quaint language, not always
grammatical, and containing several errors of chronology, misspelling of names, and confusion of persons, such as were common and
might be expected in manuscripts written in that uncultured age,
and by the uneducated craftsmen to whom we owe these old manuscripts.

---

[1] I assign this era because the Halliwell poem, which is the exemplar of the older
Legend, is evidently Roman Catholic in character, while the Dowland, and all subsequent
manuscripts which contain the later Legend, are Protestant, all allusions to the Virgin,
the saints, and crowned martyrs being omitted.

CHAPTER XIX

HE *Legend of the Craft*, as it is presented to us in what I have called the later manuscripts, that is to say, the Dowland and those that follow it up to the Papworth, begins with a descant on the seven liberal arts and sciences.[1] I have already shown that among the schoolmen contemporary with the legendists these seven arts and sciences were considered, in the curriculum of education, not so much as the foundation, but as the finished edifice of all human learning. The *Legend* naturally partook of the spirit of the age in which it was invented. But especially did the Masons refer to these sciences, and make a description of them, the preface, as it were, to the story that they were about to relate, because the principal of these sciences was geometry, and this they held to be synonymous with Masonry.

Now, the intimate connection between geometry and architecture, as practiced by the Operative Freemasons of the Middle Ages, is well known, since the secrets, of which these Freemasons were supposed to be in possession, consisted almost solely in an application of the principles of the science of geometry to the art of building.

The Legend next proceeds to narrate certain circumstances connected with the children of Lamech. These details are said in the Legend to have been derived from the Book of Genesis, but were probably taken at second-hand from the *Polychronicon*, or universal history of the monk Higden, of Chester. This part of the Legend, which is not otherwise connected with the Masonic narrative, appears to have been introduced for the sake of an allusion to the pillars on which the sons of Lamech are said to have inscribed an account of the sciences which they had discovered, so that the

---

[1] The Halliwell poem, although it differs from the later manuscripts in so many particulars, agrees with them in giving a descant on the arts and sciences.

knowledge of them might not be lost in consequence of the destruction of the world which they apprehended.

The story of the inscribed pillars was a tradition of every people, narrated, with variations, by every historian and implicitly believed by the multitude. The legendists of Masonry got the account from Josephus, perhaps through Higden, but altered it to suit the spirit of their own narrative.

We are next told that Hermes discovered one of these pillars and was, from the information that it contained, enabled to restore the knowledge of the sciences, and especially of Masonry, to the post-diluvian world. This was a tribute of the legendists to the universally accepted opinion of the ancients, who venerated the "thrice great Hermes" as the mythical founder of all science and philosophy. We are next told that Nimrod, "the mighty hunter before the Lord," availed himself of the wisdom that had been recovered by Hermes. He was distinguished for his architectural works and first gave importance to the art of Masonry at the building of the Tower of Babel. The Legend attributes to Nimrod the creation of the Masons into an organized body and he was the first who gave them a constitution or laws for their government. Masonry, according to the legendary account, was founded in Babylon, whence it passed over to the rest of the world.

In all this we find simply a recognition of the historical opinion that Chaldea was the birthplace of knowledge and that the Chaldean sages were the primitive teachers of Asia and Europe. The modern discoveries of the cuneiform inscriptions show that the Masonic legendists had, at a venture, obtained a more correct idea of the true character of Nimrod than that which had been hitherto entertained, founded on the brief allusion to him in Genesis and the disparaging account of him in the *Antiquities* of Josephus.

The monastic legends had made Abraham a contemporary of Nimrod, and the Book of Genesis had described the visit of the patriarch and his wife to the land of Egypt. Combining these two statements, the idea was suggested to the legendists that Abraham had carried into Egypt the knowledge which he had acquired from the Chaldeans and taught it to the inhabitants.

Thus it is stated that Egypt was, after Babylonia, the place where the arts and sciences were first cultivated and thence disseminated to other countries. Among these arts and sciences, geometry, which we have seen was always connected in the Masonic mind with architecture, held a prominent place.   He who taught it to the Egyptians was typically represented by the name of Euclid, because the old Masons were familiar with the fact that he was then esteemed, as he still is, as the greatest of geometricians and almost the inventor of the science.

Accepting the allusion to Euclid, not as an historical anachronism, but rather as the expression of a symbolic idea, we can scarcely class the legendary statement of the condition of learning in Egypt as a pure and unadulterated fiction.   It is an undoubted fact that Egypt was the primeval land whence science and learning flowed into Southern Europe and Western Asia.   Neither can it be disputed that civilization had there ripened into maturity long before Greece or Rome were known.   It is moreover conceded that the ancient Mysteries whence Masonry has derived, not its organization, but a portion of its science of symbolism, received its birth in the land of the Nile, and that the Mysteries of Osiris and Isis were the proto-types of all the mystical initiations which were celebrated in Asia and in Southern Europe.   They have even been claimed, though I think incorrectly, as the origin of those in Gaul, in Britain, and in Scandinavia.   By a rapid transition, the Legend passes from the establishment of Masonry or architecture (for it must be remem-bered that in legendary acceptation the two words are synonymous) to its appearance in Judea, the " Land of Behest," where, under the patronage and direction of King Solomon the Temple of Jerusalem was constructed.   All that is said in this portion of the Legend pur-ports to be taken from the scriptural account of the same transac-tion and must have the same historical value.

As to the error committed in the name and designation of him who is now familiarly known to Freemasons as Hiram Abif, a suffi-cient explanation has been given in a preceding chapter.

We next have an account of the travels of these Masons or archi-tects who built the Temple into various countries, to acquire addi-tional knowledge and experience, and to disseminate the principles of their art.   The carelessness of chronology, to which I have already adverted, so peculiar to the general illiteracy of the age, has led the legendists to connect this diffusion of architecture among the various civilized countries of the world with the Tyrian and Jewish Masons ; but the wanderings of that body of builders known as the "Traveling Freemasons" of the Middle Ages, through all the kingdoms of Europe, and their labors in the construction of cathedrals, monasteries, and other public edifices are matters of historical record. Thus the historical idea is well preserved in the Legend of a body of artists who wandered over Europe, and were employed in the construction of cathedrals, monasteries, and other public edifices.

The Legend next recounts the introduction of architecture into France, and the influence exerted upon it by Grecian architects, who brought with them into that kingdom the principles of Byzantine art. These are facts which are sustained by history. The prominence given to France above Spain or Italy or Germany is, I think, merely another proof that the Legend was of French origin or was constructed under French influence.

The account of the condition of Masonry or architecture among the Britains in the time of St. Alban, or the 4th century, is simply a legendary version of the history of the introduction of the art of building into England during the Roman domination by the " Collegia Artificum " or Roman Colleges of Artificers, who accompanied the victorious legions when they vanquished Hesperia, Gaul, and Britain, and colonized as they vanquished them.

The decay of architecture in Britain after the Roman armies had abandoned that country to protect the Empire from the incursions of the northern hordes of barbarians, in consequence of which Britain was left in an unprotected state, and was speedily involved in wars with the Picts, the Danes, and other enemies, is next narrated in the Legend, and is its version of an historical fact.

It is also historically true that in the 7th century peace was restored to the northern parts of the island, and that Edwin, King of Northumbria, of which the city of York was the capital, revived the arts of civilization, gave his patronage to architecture, and caused many public buildings, among others the Cathedral of York, to be built. All of this is told in the Legend, although, by an error for which I have already accounted, Edwin, the Northumbrian king, was in the later Legend confounded with the brother of Athelstan.

The second decay of architecture in England, in consequence of the invasions of the Danes, and the intestine as well as foreign wars which desolated the kingdom until the reign of Athelstan, in the early part of the 10th century, when entire peace was restored, is

briefly alluded to in the Legend, therein conforming to the history of that troublous period.

As a consequence of the restoration of peace, the Legend records the revival of Masonry or architecture in the 10th century, under the reign of Athelstan, who called the Craft together and gave them a charter. I have already discussed this point and shown that the narrative of the Legend presents nothing improbable or incredible but that it is easily to be reconciled with the facts of contemporary history. We have only to reconcile the two forms of the Legend by asserting that Edwin of Northumbria revived Masonry in an Assembly convened by him at York, and that Athelstan restored its decayed prosperity by his general patronage, and by charters which he gave to the Guilds or corporations of handicraftsmen.

Passing in this summary method over the principal occurrences related in this *Legend of the Craft*, we relieve it from the charge of gross puerility, which has been urged against it, even by some Masonic writers who have viewed it in a spirit of immature criticism. We find that its statements are not the offspring of a fertile imagination or the crude inventions of sheer ignorance, but that, on the contrary, they really have a support in what was at the time accepted as authentic history, and whose authenticity can not, even now, be disproved or denied.

Dissected as it has here been by the canons of philosophical criticism, the *Legend of the Craft* is no longer to be deemed a fable or myth, but an historical narrative related in the quaint language and in the quainter spirit of the age in which it was written.

But after the revival of Freemasonry in the beginning of the 18th century, this Legend, for the most part misunderstood, served as a fundamental basis on which were erected, first by Anderson and then by other writers who followed him, expanded narratives of the rise and progress of Masonry, in which the symbolic ideas or the mythical suggestions of the ancient "Legend" were often developed and enlarged into statements for the most part entirely fabulous.

In this way, these writers, who were educated and even learned men, have introduced not so much any new legends, but rather theories founded on a legend, by which they have traced the origin and the progress of the institution in narratives without historic authenticity and sometimes contradictory to historic truth.

The mode in which these theories have been attempted to be supported by the citation of assumed facts have caused them to take, to some extent, the form of legends. But to distinguish them from the pure Legends which existed before the 18th century, I have preferred to call them theories.

Their chief tendency has been, by the use of unauthenticated statements, to confuse the true history of the Order. And yet they have secured so prominent a place in its literature and have exerted so much influence on modern Masonic ideas, that they must be reviewed and analyzed at length, in order that the reader may have a complete understanding of the legendary history of the institution. For of that legendary history, these theories, founded as they are on assumed traditions, constitute a part.

As having priority in date, the theory of Dr. Anderson will be the first to claim our attention.

CHAPTER XX

THE Legend or theory of Dr. Anderson is detailed first in the edition of the *Book of Constitutions* which was edited by him and published in the year 1723, and was then more extensively developed in the subsequent edition of the same work published in 1738.

Anderson was acquainted with the more recent *Legend of the Craft*, and very fully cites it from a manuscript or *Record of Freemasons, written in the reign of Edward IV.*, that is, toward the end of the 15th century. If Anderson's quotations from this manuscript are correct, it must be one of those that has been lost and not yet recovered. For among some other events not mentioned in the manuscripts that are now extant, he states that the charges and laws of the Freemasons had been seen and perused by Henry VI. and his council, and had been approved by them.

He does not appear to have met with any of the earlier manuscripts, such as those of Halliwell and Roberts, which contain the Legend in its older form, for he makes no use of the Legend of Euclid, passing over the services of that geometrician lightly, as the later manuscripts do,[1] and not ascribing to him the origin of the Order in Egypt, which theory is the peculiar characteristic of the older Legend.

But out of the later Legend and from whatever manuscripts containing it to which he had access, Anderson has formed a Legend of his own. In this he has added many things of his own creation and given a more detailed narrative, if not a more correct one, than that contained in the *Legend of the Craft*.

Anderson's Legend, or theory, of the rise and progress of Ma-

---

[1] In the slight mention that he makes of Euclid, Anderson has observed the true chronology and placed him in the era of Ptolemy Lagus, 300 years B.C.

sonry, as it is contained in the first edition of the *Book of Constitutions*, was for a long time accepted by the Craft as a true history of the Order, and it has exercised a very remarkable influence in the framing of other theories on this subject which from time to time have been produced by subsequent writers.

To the student, therefore, who is engaged in the investigation of the legendary history of Masonry, this Andersonian Legend is of great importance. While the *Legend of the Craft* in its pure form was very little known to the great body of Masonic writers and students until the manuscripts containing this Legend in its various forms were made common to the Masonic public by the labors of Halliwell, Cooke, and, above all, by Hughan and his earnest collaborators in Masonic archæology, the Legend of Anderson was accessible and familiar to all, and for a century and a half was deemed an authentic history, and even at the present day is accepted by some over-credulous and not well-informed Masons as a real narrative of the rise and progress of Masonry.

Anderson, in his history of the origin of Masonry, mindful of the French proverb, to "*commencer par la commencement*," begins by attributing to Adam a knowledge of Geometry as the foundation of Masonry and Architecture, words which throughout his Legend he uses as synonymous terms.

These arts he taught to his sons, and Cain especially practiced them by building a city. Seth also was equally acquainted with them and taught them to his offspring. Hence the antediluvian world was well acquainted with Masonry,[1] and erected many curious works until the time of Noah, who built the Ark by the principles of Geometry and the rules of Masonry.

Noah and his three sons, who were all Masons, brought with them to the new world the traditions and arts of the antediluvians. Noah is therefore deemed the founder of Masonry in the post-diluvian world, and hence Anderson called a Mason a "true Noachida" or Noachite, a term used to the present day.

The descendants of Noah exercised their skill in Masonry in the attempted erection of the Tower of Babel, but were confounded in their speech and dispersed into various countries, whereby the

---

[1] Oliver has readily accepted this theory of an antediluvian Masonry and written several very learned and indeed interesting works on the subject.

knowledge of Masonry was lost.[1] It was, however, preserved in Shinar and Assyria, where Nimrod built many cities.

In those parts afterward flourished many priests and mathematicians under the name of Chaldees and Magi, who preserved the science of Geometry or Masonry, and thence the science and the art[2] were transmitted to later ages and distant climes. Mitzraim, the second son of Ham, carried Masonry into Egypt, where the overflowing of the banks of the Nile caused an improvement in Geometry, and consequently brought Masonry much into request.

Masonry was introduced into the Land of Canaan by the descendants of the youngest son of Ham, and into Europe, as he supposes, by the posterity of Japhet, although we know nothing of their works.

The posterity of Shem also cultivated the art of Masonry, and Abraham, the head of one branch of that family, having thus obtained his knowledge of Geometry and the kindred sciences, communicated that knowledge to the Egyptians and transmitted it to his descendants, the Israelites. When, therefore, they made their exodus from Egypt the Israelites were "a whole kingdom of Masons," and while in the wilderness were often assembled by their Grand Master Moses into "a regular and general Lodge."

On taking possession of Canaan, the Israelites found the old inhabitants were versed in Masonry, which, however, their conquerors greatly improved, for the splendor of the finest structures in Tyre and Sidon was greatly surpassed by the magnificence of the Temple erected by King Solomon in Jerusalem. In the construction of this edifice, Solomon was assisted by the Masons and carpenters of Hiram, King of Tyre, and especially by the King of Tyre's namesake Hiram or Huram, to whom, in a note, Anderson gives the name of Hiram Abif, which name he has ever since retained among the Craft.[3]

---

[1] This part of the Legend has been preserved in the American rituals, wherein the candidate is said to come "from the lofty Tower of Babel, where language was confounded and Masonry lost," and to be proceeding "to the threshing-floor of Orneu the Jebusite (the Temple of Solomon) where language was restored and Masonry found."

[2] By the science is meant geometry, and by the art architecture—a distinction preserved in the Middle Ages; and the combination of them into "Geometrical Masonry," constitute the Mystery of the Freemasons of that period.

[3] In the first edition of this Legend, Anderson makes no allusion to the death of Hiram Abif during the building of the Temple. He mentions it, however, in the second edition of the "Constitutions" published fifteen years afterward. But this does not absolutely prove

Anderson gives in this Legend the first detailed account of the Temple of Solomon that is to be found in any Masonic work. It is, however, only an appropriation of that contained in the Books of Kings and Chronicles, with some statements for which he was probably indebted to his own invention. It has exerted a considerable influence upon other Legends subsequently framed, and especially upon all the rituals, and indeed upon all the modern ideas of speculative Masons.[1]

After the construction of the Temple, the Masons who had been engaged in it dispersed into Syria, Mesopotamia, Assyria, Chaldea, Babylonia, Media, Persia, Arabia, Africa, Lesser Asia, Greece, and other parts of Europe, where they taught the art to many eminent persons, and kings, princes, and potentates became Grand Masters, each in his own territory.

The Legend then passes on to Nebuchadnezzar, whom it calls a Grand Master, and asserts that he received much improvement in Masonry from the Jewish captives whom he brought to Babylon after he had destroyed that city and its Temple.

Afterward Cyrus constituted Zerubbabel the leader of the Jews, who, being released from their captivity, returned to Jerusalem and built the second Temple.

From Palestine, and after the erection of the Temple, Masonry was carried into Greece, and arrived at its height during the Jewish captivity, and in the time of Thales Milesius, the philosopher, and his pupil, Pythagoras, who was the author of the 47th Proposition of Euclid, which "is the foundation of all Masonry," Pythagoras traveled into Egypt and Babylon, and acquired much knowledge from the priests and the Magi, which he dispensed in Greece and Italy on his return.[2]

The Legend now speaks, parenthetically as it were, of the prog-

---

that he was at the time unacquainted with the tradition, but he may have thought it too esoteric for public record, for he says, in the very place where he should have referred to it, that he has left "what must not and cannot be communicated in writing."

[1] The peculiar details of the doctrine of Anderson have not been always respected. For instance, it is a very prevalent opinion among the Craft at this day, that there was a Master Mason's Lodge at the Temple, over which Solomon presided as Master and the two Hirams as Wardens, a theory which is not supported by Anderson, who says that King Solomon was Grand Master of the Lodge at Jerusalem, King Hiram Grand Master of that at Tyre, and Hiram Abif Master of Work. Const., 1st ed., p. 14.

[2] It was probably this part of the Andersonian Legend which gave rise to a similar statement made in the spurious production known as the Leland MS.

ress of Masonry in Asia Minor, and of the labors of Euclid in Egypt, in the reign of Ptolemy Lagus, in the methodical digestion of Geometry into a science.

It next dwells upon the great improvement of Masonry in Greece, whose Masons arrived at the same degree of skill and magnificence as their teachers the Asiatics and Egyptians.

From Sicily, from Greece, from Egypt and Asia, Masonry was introduced into Rome, which soon became the center of learning, and disseminated the knowledge of Masonry among the nations which it conquered.

The Emperor Augustus became the Grand Master of the Lodge at Rome, and established the Augustan style of architecture. During the prosperous condition of the Roman Empire, Masonry was carefully propagated to the remotest regions of the world, and a Lodge erected in almost every Roman garrison.

But upon the declension of the empire, when the Roman garrisons were drawn away from Britain, the Angles and lower Saxons, who had been invited by the ancient Britons to come over and help them against the Scots and Picts, at length subdued the southern part of England, where Masonry had been introduced by the Romans, and the art then fell into decay.

When the Anglo-Saxons recovered their freedom in the 8th century Masonry was revived, and at the desire of the Saxon kings, Charles Martel, King of France, sent over several expert craftsmen, so that Gothic architecture was again encouraged during the Heptarchy.

The many invasions of the Danes caused the destruction of numerous records, but did not, to any great extent, interrupt the work, although the methods introduced by the Roman builders were lost.

But when war ceased and peace was proclaimed by the Norman conquest, Gothic Masonry was restored and encouraged by William the Conqueror and his son William Rufus, who built Westminster Hall. And notwithstanding the wars that subsequently occurred, and the contentions of the Barons, Masonry never ceased to maintain its position in England. In the year 1362, Edward III. had an officer called the King's Freemason, or General Surveyor of his buildings, whose name was Henry Yvele, and who erected many public buildings.

Anderson now repeats the *Legend of the Craft*, with the story

of Athelstan and his son Edwin, taking it, with an evident modification of the language, from a record of Freemasons, which he says
was written in the reign of Edward IV. This record adds, as he
says, that the charges and laws therein contained had been seen and
approved by Henry VI. and the lords of his council, who must
therefore, to enable them to make such a review, have been incorporated with the Freemasons. In consequence of this, the act passed
by Parliament when the King was in his infancy, forbidding the
yearly congregations of Masons in their General Assemblies, was
never enforced after the King had arrived at manhood, and had
perused the regulations contained in that old record.

The Kings of Scotland also encouraged Masonry from the earliest times down to the union of the crowns, and granted to the Scottish Masons the prerogative of having a fixed Grand Master and
Grand Warden.[1]

Queen Elizabeth discouraged Masonry, and neglected it during
her whole reign. She sent a commission to York to break up the
Annual Assembly, but the members of the commission, having been
admitted into the Lodge, made so favorable a report to the Queen,
of the Fraternity, that she no longer opposed the Masons, but tolerated them, although she gave them no encouragement.

Her successor, James I., was, however, a patron of Masonry,
and greatly revived the art and restored the Roman architecture,
employing Inigo Jones as his architect, under whom was Nicholas
Stone as his Master Mason.

Charles I. was also a Mason, and patronized the art whose successful progress was unhappily diverted by the civil wars and the
death of the king.

But after the restoration of the royal family, Masonry was again
revived by Charles II., who was a great encourager of the craftsmen,
and hence is supposed to have been a Freemason.

In the reign of James II., Masonry not being duly cultivated,
the London Lodges " much dwindled into ignorance."

But on the accession of William, that monarch "who by most is
reckoned as a Freemason," greatly revived the art, and showed himself a patron of Masonry.

---

[1] From this it appears that Anderson was acquainted with the claim of the St. Clairs
of Roslin to the hereditary Grand Mastership of Scotland, a point that has recently been
disputed.

His good example was followed by Queen Anne, who ordered fifty new churches to be erected in London and its suburbs, and also by George I., her successor.

With an allusion to the opinion that the religious and military Orders of knighthood in the Middle Ages had borrowed many of their solemn usages from the Freemasons,[1] the Legend here ends.

Upon a perusal of this Legend, it will be found that it is in fact, except in the latter portions, which are semi-historical, only a running commentary on the later *Legend of the Craft*, embracing all that is said therein and adding other statements, partly derived from history and partly, perhaps, from the author's invention.

The second edition of the *Constitutions* goes more fully over the same ground, but is written in the form rather of a history than of a legend, and a review of it is not, therefore, necessary or appropriate in this part of the present work, which is solely devoted to the Legends of the Order.

In this second edition of Anderson's work, there are undoubtedly many things which will be repudiated by the skeptical student of Masonic history, and many which, if not at once denied, require proof to substantiate them. But with all its errors, this work of Anderson is replete with facts that make it interesting and instructive, and it earns for the author a grateful tribute for his labors in behalf of the literature of Masonry at so early a period after its revival.

---

[1] It will be seen hereafter that the Chevalier Ramsay greatly developed this brief allusion of Anderson, and out of it worked his theory of the Templar origin of Freemasonry.

CHAPTER XXI

HE Legend given by Preston in his *Illustrations of Masonry*, which details the origin and early progress of the Institution, is more valuable and more interesting than that of Anderson, because it is more succinct, and although founded like it on the *Legend of the Craft*, it treats each detail with an appearance of historical accuracy that almost removes from the narrative the legendary character which, after all, really attaches to it.

In accepting the *Legend of the Craft* as the basis of his story, Preston rejects, or at least omits to mention, all the earlier part of it, and begins his story with the supposed introduction of Masonry into England.

Commencing with a reference to the Druids, who, he says, it has been suggested, derived their system of government from Pythagoras, he thinks that there is no doubt that the science of Masonry was not unknown to them. Yet he does not say that there was an affinity between their rites and those of the Freemasons, which, as an open question, he leaves everyone to determine for himself.

Masonry, according to this theory, was certainly first introduced into England at the time of its conquest by Julius Cæsar, who, with several of the Roman generals that succeeded him, were patrons and protectors of the Craft.

The fraternity were engaged in the creation of walls, forts, bridges, cities, temples, and other stately edifices, and their Lodges or Conventions were regularly held.

Obstructed by the wars which broke out between the Romans and the natives, Masonry was at length revived in the time of the Emperor Carausius. He, having shaken off the Roman yoke, sought to improve his country in the civil arts, and brought into his dominions the best workmen and artificers from all parts. Among the first class of his favorites he enrolled the Masons, for whose tenets he professed the highest veneration, and appointed his steward, Albanus, the superintendent of their Assemblies. He gave them a charter, and commanded Albanus to preside over them in person as Grand Master. He assisted in the initiation of many persons into the mysteries of the Order.

In 680 some expert brethren arrived from France and formed a Lodge under the direction of Bennet, Abbot of Wirral, who was soon afterward appointed by Kenred, King of Mercia, inspector of the Lodges and general superintendent of the Masons.

Masonry was in a low state during the Heptarchy, but in 856 it was revived under St. Swithin, who was employed by Ethelwolf, the Saxon king, to repair some pious houses; and it gradually improved until the reign of Alfred, who was its zealous protector and who maintained a number of workmen in repairing the desolations of the Danes.

In the reign of Edward, his successor, the Masons continued to hold their Lodges under the sanction of Ethred, his sister's husband, and Ethelward, his brother.

Athelstan succeeded his father in 924 and appointed his brother Edwin, patron of Masons. The latter procured a charter from Athelstan for the Masons to meet annually in communication at York, where the first Grand Lodge of England was formed in 926, at which Edwin presided as Grand Master. The *Legend of the Craft*, in reference to the collection of old writings, is here repeated.

On the death of Edwin, Athelstan undertook in person the direction of the Lodges, and under his sanction the art of Masonry was propagated in peace and security.

On the death of Athelstan, the Masons dispersed and continued in a very unsettled state until the reign of Edgar, in 960, when they were again collected by St. Dunstan, but did not meet with permanent encouragement.

For fifty years after Edgar's death Masonry remained in a low condition, but was revived in 1041 under the patronage of Edward the Confessor, who appointed Leofric, Earl of Coventry, to superintend the Craft.

William the Conqueror, who acquired the crown in 1066, appointed Gundulph Bishop of Rochester, and Roger de Montgomery,

Earl of Shrewsbury, joint patrons of the Masons. The labors of the fraternity were employed, during the reign of William Rufus, in the construction of various edifices.

The Lodges continued to assemble under Henry I. and Stephen. In the reign of the latter, Gilbert de Clare, Marquis of Pembroke, presided over the Lodges.

In the reign of Henry II., the Grand Master of the Knights Templars employed the Craft in 1135 in building their Temple. Masonry continued under the patronage of this Order until 1199, when John succeeded to the throne and Peter de Colechurch was appointed Grand Master. Peter de Rupibus succeeded him, and Masonry continued to flourish during this and the following reign.

Preston's traditionary narrative, or his theory founded on Legends, may be considered as ending here.

The rest of his work assumes a purely historical form, although many of his statements need for authenticity the support of other authorities. These will be subjects of consideration when we come to the next part of this work.

At present, before dismissing the theory of Preston, a few comments are required which have been suggested by portions of the narrative.

As to the Legend of Carausius, to whom Preston ascribes the patronage of the British craft in the latter part of the 3d century, it must be remarked that it was first made known to the fraternity by Dr. Anderson in the 2d edition of his *Constitutions*. He says that the tradition is contained in all the old Constitutions and was firmly believed by the old English Masons. But the fact is that it is to be found in none of the old records that have as yet been discovered. They speak only of a king who patronized St. Alban and who made him the steward of his household and his Master of Works. Anderson designated this until then unnamed king as Carausius, forgetting that the Saint was martyred in the same year that the monarch assumed the throne. This was a strange error to be committed by one who had made genealogy his special study and had written a voluminous work on the subject of royal successions.

From Anderson, Preston appears to have borrowed the Legend, developing it into a minuter narrative, by the insertion of several additional circumstances, a prerogative which the compilers of Masonic as well as monastic Legends have always thought proper to exercise.

The advent of French Masons into England toward the end of the 7th century, brought thither by the Abbot Bennet or Benedict, which is recorded by Preston, is undoubtedly an historical fact. Lacroix says that England from the 7th century had called to it the best workmen among the French Masons, the *Maîtres de pierre*.

The Venerable Bede, who was contemporary with that period, says that the famous Abbot Benedictus Biscopius (the Bennet of Preston) went over to France in 675 to engage workmen to build his church, and brought them over to England for that purpose.

Richard of Cirencester makes the same statement. He says that " Bennet collected Masons (coementarios) and all kinds of industrious artisans from Rome, Italy, France, and other countries where he could find them, and, bringing them to England, employed them in his works."

Preston is, however, in error as to the reign in which this event occurred. Kenred, or rather Coenred, did not succeed as King of Mercia until 704, and the Abbot Benedict had died the year before. Our Masonic writers of the last century, like their predecessors, the Legendists, when giving the substance of a statement, were very apt to get confused in their dates.

Of the Legend of the " weeping St. Swithin," to whom Preston ascribes the revival of Masonry in the middle of the 9th century, it may be remarked that as to the character of the Saint as a celebrated architect, the Legend is supported by the testimony of the Anglo-Saxon chroniclers.

Roger of Wendover, who is followed by Matthew of Westminster, records his custom of personally superintending the workmen when engaged in the construction of any building, "that his presence might stimulate them to diligence in their labors."

But the consideration of the condition of Masonry at that period, in England, belongs rather to the historical than to the legendary portion of this work.

On the whole, it may be said of Preston that he has made a considerable improvement on Anderson in his method of treating the early progress of Masonry. Still his narrative contains so many assumptions which are not proved to be facts, that his theory must, like that of his predecessor, be still considered as founded on legends rather than on authentic history.

CHAPTER XXII

THE HUTCHINSONIAN THEORY

HE theory advanced by Bro. William Hutchinson as to the origin and the progress of Freemasonry, in his treatise, first published in the year 1775 and entitled *The Spirit of Masonry*, is so complicated and sometimes apparently so contradictory in its statements, as to require, for a due comprehension of his views, not only a careful perusal, but even an exhaustive study of the work alluded to. After such a study I think that I am able to present to the reader a correct summary of the opinions on the rise and progress of the Order which were entertained by this learned scholar.

Let it be said, by way of preface to this review, that however we may dissent from the conclusions of Hutchinson, he is entitled to our utmost respect for his scholarly attainments. To the study of the history and the philosophy of Masonry he brought a fund of antiquarian research, in which he had previously been engaged in the examination of the ecclesiastical antiquities of the province of Durham. Of all the Masonic writers of the 18th century, Hutchinson was undoubtedly the most learned. And yet the theory that he has propounded as to the origin of the Masonic Institution is altogether untenable and indeed, in many of its details, absurd.

Of all the opinions entertained by Hutchinson concerning the origin of Freemasonry, the most heterodox is that which denies its descent from and its connection, at any period, with an operative society. " It is our opinion," he says, "that Masons in the present state of Masonry were never a body of architects. . . . We ground a judgment of the nature of our profession on our ceremonials and flatter ourselves every Mason will be convinced that they have not relation to building and architecture, but are emblematical and imply moral and spiritual and religious tenets." [1]

---

[1] " Spirit of Masonry," lect. xiii., p. 131.

In another place, while admitting that there were in former times builders of cities, towers, temples, and fortifications, he doubts "that the artificers were formed into bodies ruled by their own proper laws and knowing mysteries and secrets which were kept from the world."[1]

Since he admits, as we will see hereafter, that Masonry existed at the Temple of Solomon, that it was there organized in what he calls the second stage of its progress, and that the builders of the edifice were Masons, one would naturally imagine that Hutchinson would here encounter an insuperable objection to his theory, which entirely disconnects Masonry and architecture. But he attempts to obviate this difficulty by supposing that the principles of Freemasonry had, before the commencement of the undertaking, been communicated by King Solomon to "the sages and religious men amongst his people,"[2] and that these "chosen ones of Solomon, as a pious and holy duty conducted the work." Their labors as builders were simply incidental and they were no more to be regarded by reason of this duty as architects by profession, than were Abel, Noah, Abraham, Jacob, Moses, and David by reason of the building of their altars, which were, like the Temple, works of piety and devotion.[3]

This theory, in which all connection between operative and speculative Masonry is completely dissevered, and in which, in fact, the former is entirely ignored, is peculiar to Hutchinson. No other writer, no matter to what source he may have attributed the original rise of speculative Masonry, has denied that there was some period in the history of its progress when it was more or less intimately connected with the operative art. While, therefore, it is plain that the opinion of Hutchinson is in opposition to that of all other Masonic writers, it is equally evident that it contradicts all the well-established facts of history.

But besides these opinions concerning the non-operative character of the Institution, Hutchinson has been scarcely less peculiar in his other views in respect to the rise and progress of Freemasonry and its relations to other associations of antiquity.

---

[1] "Spirit of Masonry," lect. x., p. 107.

[2] Hutchinson's language is here somewhat confused, but it seems that this is the only rational interpretation that can be given to it.

[3] "Spirit of Masonry," lect. x., p. 108.

The Hutchinsonian theory may indeed be regarded as especially and exclusively his own. It is therefore worthy of consideration and review, rather in reference to the novelty of his ideas than in respect to anything of great value in the pseudo-historical statements that he has advanced.

The prominent thought of Hutchinson in developing his theory is that Masonry in its progress from the earliest times of antiquity to the present day has been divided into three stages, respectively represented by the three ancient Craft degrees.[1]

He does not give a very lucid or satisfactory explanation of the reasons which induced him to connect each of these " stages of progress " with one of the symbolical degrees, and indeed the connection appears to be based upon a rather fanciful hypothesis.

The three stages into which he divides the progress of Masonry from its birth onwards to modern times are distinguished from each other, and distinctively marked by the code of religious ethics professed and taught by each. The first stage, which is represented by the Entered Apprentice degree, commences with Adam and the Garden of Eden and extends to the time of Moses.

The religious code taught in this first stage of Masonry was confined to a " knowledge of the God of Nature and that acceptable service wherewith He was well pleased."[2]

To Adam, while in a state of innocence, this knowledge was imparted, as well as that of all the science and learning which existed in the earliest ages of the world.

When our first parent fell, although he lost his innocence, he still retained the memory of all that he had been taught while in the Garden of Eden. This very retention was, indeed, a portion of the punishment incurred for his disobedience.

It, however, enabled him to communicate to his children the sciences which he had comprehended in Eden, and the knowledge that he had acquired of Nature and the God of Nature. By them these lessons were transmitted to their descendants as the cornerstone and foundation of Masonry, whose teachings at that early

---

[1] " It is known to the world, but more particularly to the brethren, that there are three degrees of Masons—Apprentices, Craftsmen, and Masters ; their initiation, and the several advancements from the order of Apprentices, will necessarily lead us to observations in these distinct channels."—" Spirit of Masonry," lect. i., p. 1.

[2] " Spirit of Masonry," lect. i., p. 6.

period consisted of a belief in the God of Nature and a knowledge of the sciences as they had been transmitted by Adam to his posterity. This system appears to have been very nearly the same as that afterward called by Dr. Oliver the "Pure Freemasonry of Antiquity."

All of the descendants of Adam did not, however, retain this purity and simplicity of dogma. After the deluge, when mankind became separated, the lessons which had been taught by the antediluvians fell into confusion and oblivion and were corrupted by many peoples, so that the service of the true God, which had been taught in the pure Masonry of the first men, was defiled by idolatry. These seceders from the pure Adamic Masonry formed institutions of their own, and degenerated, as the first deviation from the simple worship of the God of Nature, into the errors of Sabaism, or the adoration of the Sun, Moon, and Stars. They adopted symbols and allegories with which to teach esoterically their false doctrines. The earliest of these seceders were the Egyptians, whose priests secreted the mysteries of their religion from the multitude by symbols and hieroglyphics that were comprehensible to the members of their own order only. A similar system was adopted by the priests of Greece and Rome when they established their peculiar Mysteries. These examples of conveying truth by symbolic methods of teaching were wisely followed by the Masons for the purpose of concealing their own mysteries.

From this we naturally make the deduction, although Hutchinson does not expressly say so, that, according to his theory, Masonry was at that early period merely a religious profession "whose principles, maxims, language, learning, and religion were derived from Eden, from the patriarchs, and from the sages of the East," and that the symbolism which now forms so essential an element of the system was not an original characteristic of it, but was borrowed, at a later period, from the mystical and religious associations of the pagans.[1]

---

[1] Long after, Mr. Grote, in his "History of Greece," spoke of an hypothesis of an ancient and highly instructed body of priests having their origin either in Egypt or the East, who communicated to the rude and barbarous Greeks religious, physical, and historical knowledge under the veil of symbols. The same current of thought appears to have been suggested to the Masonic writer and to the historian of Greece, but each has directed it in a different way—one to the history of the Pagan nations, the other to that of Masonry.

Such, according to the theory of Hutchinson, was the "first stage" in the progress of Masonry represented by the Entered Apprentice degree, and which consisted simply of a belief in and a worship of the true God as the doctrine was taught by Adam and the patriarchs. It was a system of religious principles, with few rites and ceremonies and fewer symbols. The second stage in the progress of Masonry, which Hutchinson supposes to be represented by the Fellow Craft degree, commences at the era of Moses and extends through the whole period of the Jewish history to the advent of Christianity. According to the theory of Hutchinson, the Jewish lawgiver was, of course, in possession of the pure Masonry of the patriarchs which constituted the first stage of the institution, but was enabled to extend its ethical and religious principles in consequence of the instructions in relation to God and the duties of man which he had himself received by an immediate revelation. In other words, Masonry in its first stage was cosmopolitan in its religious teachings, requiring only a belief in the God of Nature as he had been revealed to Adam and his immediate descendants, but in the second stage, as inaugurated by Moses, that universal belief was exchanged for one in the Deity as He had made himself known on Mount Sinai. That is to say, the second or Mosaic stage of Masonry became Judaic in its profession.

But in another respect Masonry in its second stage assumed a different form from that which had marked its primitive state. Moses, from his peculiar education, was well acquainted with the rites, the ceremonies, the hieroglyphs, and the symbols used by the Egyptian priesthood. Many of these he introduced into Masonry, and thus began that system which, coming originally from the Egyptians and subsequently augmented by derivations from the Druids, the Essenes, the Pythagoreans, and other mystical associations, at last was developed into that science of symbolism which now constitutes so important and essential a characteristic of modern Freemasonry.

A third change in the form of Masonry, which took place in its Mosaic or Judaic stage, was the introduction of the operative art of building among its disciples. Instances of this occurred in the days of Moses, when Aholiab, Bezaleel, and other Masons were engaged in the construction of the Tabernacle, and subsequently in the time of Solomon, when that monarch occupied his Masons in the erection of the Temple.

Moses and the Burning Bush

The Ark of the Covenant, and the Tabernacle

But, as has already been shown in a preceding part of this chapter, Hutchinson does not conclude from these facts that Masonry was ever connected in its origin with "builders, architects, or mechanics." The occupation of these Masons as builders was entirely accidental, and did not at all interfere with or supersede their character as members of a purely speculative association.

But it may be as well to give, at this point, in his own words, his explanation of the manner in which the Masons became, on certain occasions, builders, and whence arose in modern times the erroneous idea that the Masonic profession consisted of architects.[1]

" I presume," he says, "that the name of Mason in this society doth not denote that the rise or origin of such society was solely from builders, architects, or mechanics; at the times in which Moses ordained the setting up of the sanctuary, and when Solomon was about to build the Temple at Jerusalem, they selected from out of the people those men who were enlightened with the true faith, and, being full of wisdom and religious fervor, were found proper to conduct these works of piety. It was on those occasions that our predecessors appeared to the world as architects and were formed into a body, under salutary rules, for the government of those who were employed in these great works, since which period builders have adopted the name of Masons, as an honorary distinction and title to their profession. I am induced to believe the name of Mason has its derivation from a language in which it implies some indication or distinction of the nature of the society, and that it has not its relation to architects." [2]

Masonry was not organized at the Temple of Solomon, as is believed by those who adopt the Temple theory, but yet that building occupies, according to the views of Hutchinson, an important place in the history of the institution. It was erected during the second stage of the progress of Masonry, not, as we must infer from the language of our author, by the heathen operatives of Tyre, but solely by Israelitish Masons; or, if assisted by any, it was only by proselytes who on or before their initiation had accepted the Jewish faith.

---

[1] In a subsequent lecture (xiii.) he attempts, in an historical argument, to show that the guild of Masons incorporated in the reign of Henry V., and the laws concerning " congregations and confederacies of Masons," passed in the succeeding reign, had no reference whatever to the speculative society.

[2] " Spirit of Masonry," lect. i., p. 2. In another place in this work the etymological ideas of Hutchinson and other writers will be duly investigated.

The language of Hutchinson is on this point somewhat obscure, yet I think that it admits only of the interpretation which has been given. He says: " As the sons of Aaron alone were admitted to the holy office and to the sacrificial rites, so none but devotees were admitted to this labour (on the temple). On this stage we see those religious who had received the truth and the light of understanding as possessed by the first men, embodied as artificers and engaged in this holy work as architects." [1]

Still more explicit is the following statement, made in a subsequent part of the work: " Solomon was truly the executor of that plan which was revealed to him from above; he called forth the sages and religious men amongst his people to perform the work; he classed them according to their rank in their religious profession, as the priests of the Temple were stationed in the solemn rites and ceremonies instituted there. . . . The chosen ones of Solomon, as a pious and holy duty, conducted the work." [2]

Solomon did not, therefore, organize, as has very commonly been believed, a system of Masonry by the aid of his Tyrian workmen, and especially Hiram Abif, who has always been designated by the Craft as his " Chief Builder," but he practiced and transmitted to his descendants the primitive Masonry derived from Adam and modified into its sectarian Jewish form by Moses. The Masonry of Solomon, like that of the great lawgiver of the Israelites, was essentially Judaic in its religious ethics. It was but a continuation of that second stage of Masonry which, as I have already said, lasted, according to the Hutchinsonian theory, until the era of Christianity.

But the wisdom and power of Solomon had attracted to him the attention of the neighboring nations, and the splendor of the edifice which he had erected extended his fame and won the admiration of the most distant parts of the world, so that his name and his artif. icers became the wonder of mankind, and the works of the latter excited their emulation. Hence the Masons of Solomon were dispersed from Jerusalem into various lands, where they superintended the architectural labors of other princes, converted infidels, initiated foreign brethren into their mysteries, and thus extended the order over the distant quarters of the known world. [3]

---

[1] " Spirit of Masonry," lect. vii., p. 86. [2] Ibid., lect. x., p. 108.

[3] I have employed in this paragraph the very language of Hutchinson. However mythical the statements therein contained may be deemed by the iconoclasts, there

Hence we see that, according to the theory of Hutchinson, King Solomon, although not the founder of Masonry at the Temple and not our first Grand Master, as he has been called, was the first to propagate the association into foreign countries. Until his time, it had been confined to the Jewish descendants of the patriarchs.

The next or third stage of the progress of Masonry, represented by the Master's degree, commenced at the advent of Christianity. As Hutchinson in his description of the two preceding progressive classes of Masons had assigned to the first, as represented by the Apprentices, only the knowledge of the God of Nature as it prevailed in the earliest ages of the world, and to the second, as represented by the Fellow Crafts, the further knowledge of God as revealed in the Mosaic Legation, so to this third stage, as represented by Master Masons, he had assigned the complete and perfect knowledge of God as revealed in the Christian dispensation.

Masonry is thus made by him to assume in this third stage of its progressive growth a purely Christian character.

The introduction of rites and ceremonies under the Jewish law, which had been derived from the neighboring heathen nations, had clouded and obscured the service of God, and consequently corrupted the second stage of Masonry as established by Moses and followed by Solomon. God, perceiving the ruin which was overwhelming mankind by this pollution of His ordinances and laws, devised a new scheme for redeeming His creatures from the errors into which they had fallen. And this scheme was typified in the Third or Master's stage in the progressive course of Masonry.

Hence the Master's degree is, in this theory, exclusively a Christian invention; the legend receives a purely Christian interpretation, and the allegory of Hiram Abif is made to refer to the death or abolition of the Jewish law and the establishment of the new dispensation under Jesus Christ.

A few citations from the language of Hutchinson will place this theory very clearly before the reader.[1]

The death and burial of the Master Builder, and the consequent loss of the true Word, are thus applied to the Christian dispensation. " Piety, which had planned the Temple at Jerusalem, was expunged.[2]

---

can be no doubt that they were accepted by the learned author as undeniably historical.

[1] They are taken from " Spirit of Masonry," lect. ix.   [2] The Master is slain.

The reverence and adoration due to the Divinity *was buried in the filth and rubbish* of the world.[1]   Persecution had dispersed the few who retained their obedience,[2] and the name of the true God was almost lost and forgotten among men.[3]

"In this situation it might well be said 'That the guide to Heaven was lost and the Master of the works of righteousness was smitten.'"[4]

Again, "True religion was fled.   'Those who sought her through the wisdom of the ancients *were not able to raise her ; she eluded the grasp, and their polluted hands were stretched forth in vain for her restoration.'*"[5]

Finally he explains the allegory of the Third degree as directly referring to Christ, in the following words : "The great Father of All, commiserating the miseries of the world, sent His only Son, who was innocence[6] itself, to teach the doctrine of salvation, by whom *man was raised* from the death of sin unto the life of righteousness ; from the tomb of corruption unto the chambers of hope ; from the darkness of despair to the celestial beams of faith."   And finally, that there may be no doubt of his theory that the third degree was altogether Christian in its origin and design, he explicitly says: "Thus the Master Mason represents a man under the Christian doctrine saved from the grave of iniquity and raised to the faith of salvation.   As the great testimonial that we are risen from the state of corruption, we bear the emblem of the Holy Trinity as the insignia of our vows and of the origin of the Master's order."[7]

The christianization of the Third or Master's degree, that is, the interpretation of its symbols as referring to Christ and to Christian

---

[1] Burial and concealment in the rubbish of the Temple first, and then in an obscure grave.

[2] The confusion and consternation of the Craft.

[3] The Master's word is lost.

[4] In the 18th century it was supposed, by an incorrect translation of the Hebrew, that the substitute word signified " The Master is smitten."   Dr. Oliver adopted that interpretation.

[5] By " the wisdom of the ancients " is meant the two preceding stages of Masonry represented, as we have seen, by the Apprentices and the Fellow Craft.   In the allegory of Hiram, the knowledge of each of these degrees is unsuccessfully applied to effect the raising.

[6] Acacia.   The Greek word *akakia* means innocence.   Hence in the succeeding paragraph he calls Masons " true Acacians."

[7] "Spirit of Masonry," lect. ix., p. 100.

dogmas, is not peculiar to nor original with Hutchinson. It was the accepted doctrine of almost all his contemporaries, and several of the rituals of the 18th century contain unmistakable traces of it. It was not, indeed, until the revisal of the lectures by Dr. Hemming, in 1813, that all references in them to Christianity were expunged. Even as late as the middle of the 19th century, Dr. Oliver had explicitly declared that if he had not been fully convinced that Freemasonry is a system of Christian ethics—that it contributes its aid to point the way to the Grand Lodge above, through the Cross of Christ—he should never have been found among the number of its advocates.[1]

Notwithstanding that the Grand Lodge of England had authoritatively declared, in the year 1723, that Masonry required a belief only in that religion in which all men agree,[2] the tendency among all our early writers after the revival of 1717 was to Christianize the institution.

The interpretation of the symbols of Freemasonry from a Christian point of view was, therefore, at the period when Hutchinson advanced his theory, neither novel to the Craft nor peculiar to him.

The peculiarity and novelty of his doctrine consisted not in its Christian interpretation of the symbols, but in the view that he has taken of the origin and historical value of the legend of the Third degree.

At least from the time of Anderson and Desaguliers, the legend of Hiram Abif had been accepted by the Craft as an historical statement of an event that had actually occurred. Even the most skeptical writers of the present day receive it as a myth which possibly has been founded upon events that have been distorted in their passage down the stream of tradition.

Now, neither of these views appears to have been entertained by Hutchinson. We look in vain throughout his work for any reference to the legend as connected with Hiram Abif. In his lecture on "The Temple at Jerusalem," in which he gives the details of the labors of Solomon in the construction of that edifice, the name of Hiram does not once occur, except in the extracts that he makes from the Book of Kings and the *Antiquities* of Josephus. Indeed,

---

[1] "Antiquities of Masonry," chap. vi., p. 166, note.
[2] "Book of Constitutions," 1st ed., "Charges of a Freemason," I.

we must infer that he did not recognize Hiram Abif as a Mason, for he expressly says that all the Masons at the Temple were Israelites and believers in the Jewish faith.

In a subsequent lecture, on "The Secrecy of Masons," he, in fact, undervalues Hiram Abif as an architect, and says that he does not doubt that " Hiram's knowledge was in the business of a statuary and painter, and that he made graven images of stone and wood and molten images in metals," thus placing him in a subordinate position, and completely ignoring the rank given to him in all the Masonic rituals, as the equal and colleague of Solomon and the Master Builder of the Temple.[1]

There is nowhere to be found in the work of Hutchinson any reference, however remote, to the circumstances of the death and raising of the "Widow's Son."   He must have been acquainted with the legend, since it was preserved and taught in the lodges that he visited.   But he speaks, in the most general terms, of the third degree as symbolizing the corruption and death of religion, and the moral resurrection of man in the new or Christian doctrine.

If he believed in the truth of his own theory—and we are bound to suppose that he did—then he could not but have looked upon the details of the Master's legend as absolutely false, for the legend and the theory can in no way be reconciled.

If I rightly understand the language of Hutchinson, which, it must be admitted, is sometimes confused and the ideas are not plainly expressed, he denies the existence of the third degree at the Temple.

That edifice was built, according to his theory, within the period of the second stage of the progress of Masonry. Now, that stage, which was inaugurated by Moses, was represented by the Fellow Craft's degree. It was not until the coming of Christ that the Master's degree with its rites and ceremonies came into existence, in the third stage of the progress of Masonry, which was represented by that degree. Indeed, in the following passage he explicitly makes that statement.

" The ceremonies now known to Masons prove that the testimonials and insignia of the Master's order, in the present state of

---

[1] Hutchinson has here ventured on a truth which, however, none of his successors have accepted.   See hereafter the chapter in this work on " The Legend of Hiram Abif," in which I have advanced and endeavored to sustain the same view of the character of this celebrated artist.

Masonry, *were devised within the ages of Christianity ;* and we are confident there are not any records in being, in any nation or in any language, which can show them to be pertinent to any other system or give them greater antiquity." [1]

We can not explain this language with any respect for consistency and for the meaning of the words except by adopting the following explanation of the Hutchinsonian theory. At the building of the Temple, the Masonry then prevailing, which was the second or Fellow Crafts stage, was merely a system of religious ethics in which the doctrines of the Jewish faith, as revealed to Moses, had been superimposed upon the simple creed of the Patriarchs, which had constituted the first or Apprentice's stage of the institution. There was at that time no knowledge. of the legend of Hiram Abif, which was a myth subsequently introduced in the Third or Master's stage of the progress of the Order. It was not until after the advent of Jesus Christ, "within the ages of Christianity," that the death and raising of the Master Builder was devised as a mythical symbol to constitute what Hutchinson calls "the testimonials and insignia of the Master's order."

The myth or legend thus fabricated was to be used as a symbol of the change which took place in the religious system of Masonry when the third stage of its progress was inaugurated by the invention of the Master's degree.

Here again Hutchinson differs from all the writers who preceded or who have followed him. The orthodox doctrine of all those who have given a Christian interpretation to the legend of the Third Degree is that it is the narrative of events which actually occurred at the building of the Temple of Solomon, and that it was afterward, on the advent of Christianity, adopted as a symbol, whereby the death and raising of Hiram Abif were considered as a type of the sufferings and death, the resurrection and ascension, of Christ.

No words of Hutchinson give expression to any such idea. With him the legend of Hiram the Builder is simply an allegory, invented at a much later period than that in which the events it details are supposed to have occurred, for the purpose of symbolizing

---

[1] "Spirit of Masonry," lect. x., p. 1,062. It is "passing strange" that a man of Hutchinson's learning should, in this passage, have appeared to be oblivious of the mythical character of the ancient Mysteries.

the death and burial of the Jewish law with the Masonry which it had corrupted, and the resurrection of this defunct Masonry in a new and perfect form under the Christian dispensation.

Such is the Hutchinsonian theory of the origin and progress of Masonry. It is *sui generis*—peculiar to Hutchinson—and has been advanced or maintained by no other Masonic writer before or since. It may be summarized in a very few words :

1. Masonry was first taught by Adam, after the fall, to his descendants, and continued through the patriarchal age. It consisted of a simple code of ethics, teaching only a belief in the God of Nature. It was the Masonry of the Entered Apprentice.

2. It was enlarged by Moses and confirmed by Solomon, and thus lasted until the era of Christ. To its expanded code of ethics was added a number of symbols derived from the Egyptian priesthood. Its religion consisted in a belief in God as he had been revealed to the Jewish nation. It was the Masonry of the Fellow Craft.

3. The Masonry of this second stage becoming valueless in consequence of the corruption of the Jewish law, it was therefore abolished, and the third stage was established in its place. This third stage was formed by the teachings of Christ, and the religion it inculcates is that which was revealed by Him. It is the Masonry of the Master Mason.

4. Hence the three stages of Masonry present three forms of religion : first, the Patriarchal ; second, the Jewish ; third, the Christian.

Masonry, having thus reached its ultimate stage of progress, has continued in this last form to the present day. And now Hutchinson proceeds to advance his theory as to its introduction and growth in England. He had already accounted for its extension into other quarters of the world in consequence of the dispersion and travels of King Solomon's Masons, after the completion of the Temple. He thinks that during the first stage of Masonry—the Patriarchal— its principles were taught and practiced by the Druids. They received them from the Phœnicians, who visited England for trading purposes in very remote antiquity. The second stage—the Judaic —was with its ceremonials introduced among them by the Masons of Solomon, after the building of the Temple, but at what precise period he can not determine. The third and perfect form, as developed in the third stage, must have been adopted upon the conversion of the Druidical worshippers to Christianity, having been introduced into England, as we should infer, by the Christian missionaries who came from Rome into that country.

While Hutchinson denies that there was ever any connection between the Operative and the Speculative Masons, he admits that among the former there might have been a few of the latter. He accounts for this fact in the following manner :

After Christianity had become the popular religion of England, the ecclesiastics employed themselves in founding religious houses and in building churches. From the duty of assisting in this pious work, no man of whatever rank or profession was exempted. There were also a set of men called " holy werk folk," to whom were assigned certain lands which they held by the tenure of repairing, building, or defending churches and sepulchers, for which labors they were released from all feudal and military services. These men were stone-cutters and builders, and might, he thinks, have been Speculative Masons, and were probably selected from that body. " These men," he says, " come the nearest to a similitude of Solomon's Masons, and the title of Free and Accepted Masons, of any degree of architects we have gained any knowledge of." But he professes his ignorance whether their initiation was attended with peculiar ceremonies or by what laws they were regulated. That they had any connection with the Speculative Order whose origin from Adam he had been tracing, is denied.

Finally, he attributes the moral precepts of the Masonry of the present day to the school of Pythagoras and to the Basilideans, a sect of Christians who flourished in the 2d century. For this opinion, so far as relates to Pythagoras, he is indebted to the celebrated Leland manuscript, of whose genuineness he had not the slightest doubt. These precepts and the Egyptian symbols introduced by Moses with Jewish additions constitute the system of modern Masonry, which has, however, been perfected by a Christian doctrine.

Such is the theory of Hutchinson as to the origin and progress of Speculative Masonry. That it has been accepted as a whole by no other writer, is not surprising, as it not only is not supported by the facts of history, but is actually contradicted by every Masonic document that is extant.

It is, indeed, a mere body of myths, which are not clad with the slightest garment of probability.

And yet there are here and there some glimmerings of truth, such as the appropriation of his real character to Hiram Abif, and the allusions to the "holy werk folk," as showing a connection between Operative and Speculative Masonry, which, though not pushed far enough by Hutchinson, may afford valuable suggestions, if extended, to the searcher after historic truth in Freemasonry.

CHAPTER XXIII

N commendation of the Rev. Dr. Oliver as a learned and prolific writer on Freemasonry, too much can not be said. His name must ever be *clarum et venerabile* among the Craft. To the study of the history and the philosophy of the Institution he brought a store of scholarly acquirements, and a familiarity with ancient and modern literature which had been possessed by no Masonic author who had preceded him. Even Hutchinson, who certainly occupied the central and most elevated point in the circle of Masonic students and investigators who flourished in the 18th century, must yield the palm for erudition to him whose knowledge of books was encyclopedical.

In his numerous works on Freemasonry, of which it is difficult to specify the most important, the most learned, or the most interesting, Dr. Oliver has raised the Institution of Masonry to a point of elevation which it had never before reached, and to which its most ardent admirers had never aspired to promote it.

He loved it for its social tendencies, for he was genial in his inclination and in his habits, and he cherished its principles of brotherly love, for his heart was as expanded as his mind. But he taught that within its chain of union there was a fund of ethics and philosophy, and a beautiful science of symbolism by which its ethics was developed to the initiated, which awakened scholars to the contemplation of the fact never before so completely demonstrated, that Speculative Masonry claimed and was entitled to a prominent place among the systems of human philosophy.

No longer could men say that Freemasonry was merely a club of good fellows. Oliver had proved that it was a school of inquirers after truth. No longer could they charge that its only design was the cultivation of kindly feelings and the enjoyment of good cheer.

He had shown that it was engaged in the communication to its disciples of abstruse doctrines of religion and philosophy in a method by which it surpassed every other human scheme for imparting such knowledge.

But, notwithstanding this eulogium, every word of which is merited by its subject, and not one word of which would I erase, it must be confessed that there were two defects in his character that materially affect the value of his authority as an historian.

One was, that as a clergyman of the Church of England he was controlled by that clerical *esprit du corps* which sought to make every opinion subservient to his peculiar sectarian views. Thus, he gave to every symbol, every myth, and every allegory the interpretation of a theologian rather than of a philosopher.

The other defect, a far more important one, was the indulgence in an excessive credulity, which led him to accept the errors of tradition as the truths of history. In reading one of his narratives, it is often difficult to separate the two elements. He so glosses the sober facts of history with the fanciful coloring of legendary lore, that the reader finds himself involved in an inextricable web of authentic history intermixed with unsupported tradition, where he finds it impossible to discern the true from the fabulous.

The canon of criticism laid by Voltaire, that all historic certainty that does not amount to a mathematical demonstration is merely extreme probability, is far too rigorous. There are many facts that depend only on contemporaneous testimony to which no more precise demonstration is applied, and which yet leave the strong impression of certainty on the mind.

But here, as in all other things, there is a medium—a measure of moderation—and it would have been well if Dr. Oliver had observed it. But not having done so, his theory is founded not simply on the *Legend of the Craft*, of which he takes but little account, but on obscure legends and traditions derived by him, in the course of his multifarious reading, sometimes from rabbinical and sometimes from unknown sources.[1]

---

[1] He divides the legends of Masonry into two classes, neither of which embraces the incredible. He says that " many of them are founded in fact, and capable of unquestionable proof, whilst others are based on Jewish traditions, and consequently invested with probability, while they equally inculcate and enforce the most solemn and important truths."—" Historical Landmarks," vol. i., p. 399.

The theoretical views of Oliver as to the origin and progress of Masonry from a legendary point of view are so scattered in his various works that it is difficult to follow them in a chronological order. This is especially the case with the legends that relate to the periods subsequent to the building of the Temple at Jerusalem. Up to that era, the theory is enunciated in his *Antiquities of Freemasonry*, upon which I shall principally depend in this condensation. It was, it is true, written in the earlier part of his life, and was his first contribution to the literature of Masonry, but he has not in any of his subsequent writings modified the views he there entertained. This work may therefore be considered, as far as it goes, as an authoritative exposition of his theory. His *Historical Landmarks*, the most learned and most interesting of his works, if we except, perhaps, his *History of Initiation*, will furnish many commentaries on what he has advanced in his *Antiquities*, but as it is principally devoted to an inquiry into the origin and interpretation of the symbols and allegories of Masonry, we can not obtain from its pages a connected view of his theory.

Preston had introduced his history of Masonry by the assertion that its foundations might be traced " from the commencement of the world." Dr. Oliver is not content with so remote an origin, but claims, on the authority of Masonic traditions, that the science " existed before the creation of this globe, and was diffused amidst the numerous systems with which the grand empyreum of universal space is furnished." [1]

But as he supposes that the globes constituting the universe were inhabited long before the earth was peopled, and that these inhabitants must have possessed a system of ethics founded on the belief in God, which he says is nothing else but Speculative Masonry, we may regard this opinion as merely tantamount to the expression that truth is eternal.

Passing by this empyreal notion as a mere metaphysical idea, let us begin with Oliver's theory of the mundane origin of the science of Masonry.

While in the Garden of Eden, Adam was taught that science which is now termed Masonry.[2] After his fall, he forfeited the gift of inspiration, but certainly retained a recollection of those degrees

---

[1] " Antiquities," Period I., ch. ii., p. 26. [2] Oliver, " Antiquities," I., ii., 37.

of knowledge which are within the compass of human capacity, and among them that speculative science now known as Freemasonry.[1]

These, in the course of time, he communicated to his children. Of these children, Seth and his descendants preserved and cultivated the principles of Masonry which had been received from Adam, but Cain and his progeny perverted and finally abandoned it. However, before his complete secession, the latter, with some of his descendants, reduced the knowledge he had received from Adam to practice, and built a city which he called Hanoch. The children of Lamech, the sixth in descent from Cain, also retained some faint remains of Masonry, which they exerted for the benefit of mankind.

It is in this way that Dr. Oliver attempts to reconcile the story of the children of Lamech, as detailed in the *Legend of the Craf.,* with his theory, which really ousts Cain and all his descendants from the pale of Masonry. The sons of Lamech were Masons, but their Masonry had been greatly corrupted.

Dr. Oliver makes the usual division of Masonry into Operative and Speculative. The former continued to be used by the Cainites after they had lost all pretensions to the latter, and the first practical application of the art was by them in the building of the city of Hanoch, or, as it is called in Genesis, Enoch.

Thus Masonry was divided, as to its history, into two distinct streams, that of the Operative and that of the Speculative; the former cultivated by the descendants of Cain, the latter by those of Seth. It does not, however, appear that the Operative branch was altogether neglected by the Sethites, but was only made subordinate to their Speculative science, while the latter was entirely neglected by the Cainites, who devoted themselves exclusively to the Operative art. Finally they abandoned it and were lost in the corruptions of their race, which led to their destruction in the flood.

The Speculative stream, however, flowed on uninterruptedly to the time of Noah. Oliver does not hesitate to say that Seth, "associating himself with the most virtuous men of his age, they formed lodges and discussed the great principles of Masonry," and were called by their contemporaries the "Sons of Light."

Seth continued to preside over the Craft until the time of

---

[1] Oliver, "Antiquities," I., ii., 40.

Enoch, when he appointed that patriarch as his successor and Grand Superintendent.[1]

Enoch, as Grand Master, practiced Masonry with such effect that God vouchsafed to reveal to him some peculiar mysteries, among which was the sacred WORD, which continues to this day to form an important portion of Masonic speculation, and for the preservation of which from the impending destruction of the world he constructed a subterranean edifice in which he concealed the sacred treasure. He also erected two pillars, one of brass and one of stone, on which he engraved the elements of the liberal sciences, including Masonry.[2] Enoch then resigned the government of the Craft to Lamech, who afterward surrendered it to Noah, in whose hands it remained until the occurrence of the flood.

Such is Oliver's legendary narrative of the progress of Masonry from the creation to the flood. The Craft were organized into lodges and were governed during that long period by only five Grand Masters—Adam, Seth, Enoch, Lamech, and Noah.

To the Institution existing at that time he gives the appropriate title of "Antediluvian Masonry," and also that of "Primitive Masonry."

Of its character he says that it had but few symbols or ceremonies, and was indeed nothing else but a system of morals or pure religion. Its great object was to preserve and cherish the promise of a Messiah.

On the renewal of the world by the subsidence of the waters of the deluge, it was found that though Enoch's pillar of brass had given way before the torrent of destruction, the pillar of stone had been preserved, and by this means the knowledge of the state of Masonry before the flood was transmitted to posterity.

Of the sons of Noah, all of whom had been taught the pure system of Masonry by their father, Shem and his descendants alone preserved it. Ham and Japhet having dispersed into Africa and Europe, their descendants became idolaters and lost the true principles

---

[1] Anderson gives the direction of the Craft, after Seth, successively to Enoch, Kainan, Mahalaleel, and Jared, whom Enoch succeeded. Const. 2d edit., p. 3.

[2] This legend of the vault of Enoch was not known to the mediæval Masons. It forms, therefore, no part of the ritual of Ancient Craft Masonry. It is an invention of a later period, and is recognized only by the more modern "high degrees." The form of the legend as known to Anderson in 1722 was that he erected pillars on which the science of Masonry was inscribed.

of Masonry, which consisted in the worship of the one true God. The descendants of Japhet not only fell from the worship of God and embraced the adoration of idols, but they corrupted the form of Masonry by the establishment on its basis of a system of secret rites which are known in history as the "Mysteries."

This secession of the children of Japhet from the true system which their ancestor had received from Noah, has been called by Dr. Oliver "Spurious Freemasonry," while that practiced by the descendants of Shem he styles "Pure Freemasonry."

Of these two divisions the Spurious Freemasons were more distinguished for their cultivation of the Operative art, while the Pure Freemasons, although not entirely neglectful of Operative Masonry, particularly devoted themselves to the preservation of the truths of the Speculative science.

Shem communicated the secrets of Pure Freemasonry to Abraham, through whose descendants they were transmitted to Moses, who had, however, been previously initiated into the Spurious Masonry of the Egyptians.

Masonry, which had suffered a decay during the captivity of the Israelites in Egypt, was revived in the wilderness by Moses, who held a General Assembly, and, as the first act of the reorganized Institution, erected the Tabernacle.

From this time Masonry was almost exclusively confined to the Jewish nation, and was propagated through its judges, priests, and kings to the time of Solomon.

When Solomon was about to erect the Temple at Jerusalem, he called to his assistance the artists of Tyre, who were disciples of the Spurious Masonry and were skillful architects, as members of the Dionysiac fraternity of artificers.

By this association of the Tyrian Masons of the spurious order with the Jewish workmen who practiced the pure system, the two classes were united, and King Solomon reorganized the system of Freemasonry as it now exists.

For the subsequent extension of Masonry throughout the world and its establishment in England, Dr. Oliver adopts the legendary histories of both Anderson and Preston, accepting as genuine every mythical narrative and every manuscript. From the Leland manuscript he quotes as if he were citing an authority universally admitted to be authentic. Receiving the narrative of the General Assembly which was called at York by Prince Edwin as an event of whose occurrence there canbe no possible doubt, he claims that the Halliwell poem is a veritable copy of the Constitutions enacted by that Assembly.

On the subject of the religious character of Freemasonry, Dr. Oliver in the main agrees with Hutchinson, that it is a Christian Institution, and that all its myths and symbols have a Christian interpretation. He differs from Hutchinson in this, that instead of limiting the introduction of the Christian element to the time of Christ, he supposes it to have existed in it, from the earliest times. Even the Masonry of the patriarchs he believes to have been based upon the doctrine of a promised Messiah.

But his views will be best expressed in his own language, in a passage contained in the concluding pages of his *Historical Landmarks:* "The conclusion is therefore obvious. If the lectures of Freemasonry refer only to events which preceded the advent of Christ, and if those events consist exclusively of admitted types of the Great Deliverer, who was preordained to become a voluntary sacrifice for the salvation of mankind, it will clearly follow that the Order was originally instituted in accordance with the true principles of the Christian religion ; and in all its consecutive steps bears an unerring testimony to the truth of the facts and of their typical reference to the founder of our faith."

He has said, still more emphatically, in a preceding part of the same work, that " Freemasonry contains scarcely a single ceremony, symbol, or historical narration which does not apply to this glorious consummation of the divine economy of the Creator towards his erring creatures "; by which economy he, of course, means the Christian dispensation and the Christian scheme of redemption.

If in the multifarious essays in which he has treated the subject Dr. Oliver meant to announce the proposition that in the very earliest ages of the world there prevailed certain religious truths of vast importance to the welfare and happiness of mankind, which had been communicated either by direct inspiration or in some other mode, and which have been traditionally transmitted to the present day, which truths principally consisted in an assertion of a belief in God and in a future life, such a proposition will hardly meet with a denial.

But if he also meant to contend that the transmission of these truths to posterity and to the present age was committed to and preserved by an order of men, an association, or a society whose form and features have been retained in the Freemasonry of the present day, it will, I imagine, be admitted that such a proposition is wholly untenable.   And yet this appears to be the theory that was entertained by this learned but too credulous scholar.

CHAPTER XXIV

THE TEMPLE LEGEND

THE Temple Legend is a name that I give to that legend or tradition which traces the origin of Freemasonry as an organized institution to the Temple of Solomon and to the builders, Jewish and Tyrian, who were employed in the construction of that edifice.

This is the legend that is now almost universally accepted by the great mass of the Masonic fraternity. Perhaps nine out of ten of the Freemasons of the present day—that is to say, all those who receive tradition with the undoubting faith that should be given to history only—conscientiously believe that Freemasonry, as we now see it, organized into lodges and degrees, with Grand Masters, Masters, and Wardens, with the same ritual observances, was first devised by Solomon, King of Israel, and assumed its position as a secret society during the period when that monarch was engaged in the construction of the Temple on Mount Moriah.[1]

This theory is not a new one. It was probably at first suggested by the passage in the *Legend of the Craft* which briefly describes the building of the Temple and the confirmation by Solomon of the charges which his father David had given to the Masons.

There can be no doubt from this passage in the Legend that the Temple of Solomon occupied a prominent place in the ideas of the mediæval Masons. How much use they made of it in their esoteric ceremonies we, of course, are unable to learn. It is, however, a

---

[1] In a sermon by the Rev. A. N. Keigwin, at the dedication of the Masonic Temple in Philadelphia (1873), we find the following passage : "Historically, Masonry dates from the building of the Temple of Solomon. No one at the present day disputes this claim." I cite this out of hundreds of similar passages in other writers, to show how universal among such educated Masons is the belief in the Temple theory. It is, in fact, very true that only those scholars who have made the history of the Order an especial study have any doubts upon the subject.

significant coincidence, if nothing more, that there was a somewhat similar legend among the "Compagnons de la Tour," those mystical associations of workmen who sprang up in France about the 12th century, and who are supposed to have been an offshoot of dissatisfied journeymen from the body of oppressive Masters, who at that period constituted the ruling power of the corporate guilds of operative Masons and other crafts.

As the traditions of this society in reference to the Temple of Solomon are calculated to throw much light on the ideas which prevailed among the Masons in respect to the same subject, and as the Temple legends of the "Compagnons" are better known to us than those of the mediæval operative Masons, and finally, as it is not at all unlikely that the ideas of the former were derived from those of the latter, it will not be inexpedient to take a brief view of the Temple legend of the Compagnonage.

The Compagnons de la Tour have three different legends, each of which traces the association back to the Temple of Solomon, through three different founders, which causes the Compagnonage to be divided into three distinct and, unfortunately, hostile associations. These are the Children of Solomon, the Children of Maître Jacques, and the Children of Père Soubise.

The Children of Solomon assert that they were associated into a brotherhood by King Solomon himself at the building of the Temple.

The Children of Maître Jacques and those of Père Soubise declare that both of these workmen were employed at the Temple, and after its completion went together to Gaul, where they taught the arts which they had learned at Jerusalem.[1]

The tradition of Maître Jacques is particularly interesting. He is said to have been the son of a celebrated architect named Jacquain, who was one of the chief Masters of Solomon and a colleague of Hiram Abif. From the age of fifteen he was employed as a stone-cutter. He traveled through Greece, where he acquired a knowledge of architecture and sculpture. He then went to Egypt and thence to Jerusalem, where, being engaged in the construction of the Temple, he fabricated two pillars with such consummate skill that he was at once received as a Master of the Craft.

---

[1] The reader will remember the story in the "Legend of the Craft" of one Namus Grecus, who came from Jerusalem and from the Temple in the time of Charles Martel and propagated Masonry in France.

It is not necessary to pursue the legend of the French Compagnonage any further. Sufficient has been told to show that they traced
their origin to the Temple of Solomon and that the legend referred
to events connected with that edifice.

Now, as these traveling Journeymen (for thus may we translate
their French title) are known to have separated themselves in the
12th century from the corporations of Master Workmen in consequence of the narrow and oppressive policy of these bodies, making
what in modern times would be called a "strike," it is reasonable to
suppose that they carried with them into their new and independent
organization many of the customs, ceremonies, and traditions which
they had learned from the main body or Master's guilds of which
they were an offshoot. Therefore, although we have not been able
to find any legend or tradition of the mediæval operative Masons
which traced their origin to the Temple of Solomon, yet as we find
such a tradition prevailing among an association of workmen who,
as we know, were at one time identified with the Operative Masons
and seceded from them on a question of policy, we have a reasonable right to believe that the legend of the Compagnons de la Tour,
or Traveling Journeymen, which traced their origin to the Temple
of Solomon, was derived by them from the Corporations of Masters
or Guilds of Operative Masons, among whom it was an accepted
tradition.

And therefore we have in this way the foundation for a reasonable belief that the Legend of the Temple origin of Masonry is
older than the era of the Revival in the beginning of the 18th century, and that it had been a recognized doctrine among the operative
Masons of the Middle Ages.

The absence of the Legend in any formal detail from all the old
manuscripts does not prove that there was no such Legend, for
being of an esoteric character, it may, from conscientious motives, or
in obedience to some regulation, never have been committed to writing. This is, however, a mere supposition and can not in any way
interfere with deductions drawn from positive data in reference to
the Legend of the Third Degree. There may have been a Temple
Legend, and yet the details narrated in it may have been very incomplete and not have included the events related in the former
Legend.

The first reference in the old records to the Temple of Solomon as connected with the origin of Freemasonry is to be found in the Cooke MS. and is in the following words:

"What tyme that the children of isrl dwellid in Egypte they lernyd the craft of masonry. And afterward they were driven out of Egypte they come into the lond of bihest (promise) and is now callyd Jerl'm (Jerusalem) and it was ocupied and chsrgys yholde. And the makyng of Salomonis tempull that kyng David began. Kyng David lovyd well masons and he gaf hem rygt nye as thay be nowe. And at the makyng of the temple in Salomonis tyme as hit is seyd in the bibull in the iij boke of Regum in teicio Regum capito quinto (1 Kings, Cap. 5) That Salomon had iiij score thowsand masons at his werke. And the kyngis sone of Tyry was his master mason, And (in) other cronyclos hit is seyd and in olde bokys of masonry that Salomon confirmed the chargys that David his fadir had geve to masons. And Salomon hymself taught hem here (their) maners (customs) but lityll differans fro the maners that now ben usyd. And fro thens this worthy sciens was brought into Fraunce and into many other regions." [1]

The Dowland MS., whose supposed date is some fifty or sixty years later than the Cooke, gives substantially the same Legend, but with the additional circumstances, that David learned the charges that he gave, from Egypt, where they had been made by Euclid; that he added other charges to these; that Solomon sent into various countries for Masons, whom he gathered together; that the name of the King of Tyre was Iram, and that of his son, who was Solomon's chief Master, was Aynon; and finally that he was a Master of Geometry and of carving and graving.

In this brief narrative, the first edition of which dates back as far as the close of the 15th century, we see the germs of the fuller Legend which prevails among the Craft at the present day. That there was an organization of Masons with "Charges and Manners," that is, laws and customs at the building of the Temple of Jerusalem, and that King Solomon was assisted in the work by the King of Tyre and by a skillful artist who had been sent to him by Hiram, are the two most important points in the theory of the Temple origin of Masonry, and both are explicitly stated in these early legends. We next find the Legend repeated, but with more

---

[1] Cooke MS., lines 539–575.

elaborate details, most of which, however, are taken from the Book of Kings as referred to in the *Legend of the Craft* by Anderson, in the first edition of the *Constitutions*, and with a few additional particulars in the second edition of the same work.

Preston, the next important Masonic writer after Anderson, does not indeed relate or refer to the Legend in any part of his *Illustrations of Masonry*, but the theory that Masonry found its origin at the Temple is to be deduced from the historical traditions contained in the third lecture of the Prestonian system, from which Webb derived it, and has perpetuated it among American Masons to the present day.

Hutchinson, who followed Preston, although, as has been seen, he inclined to a remoter origin of the Order, repeatedly refers in his *Spirit of Masonry*, and especially in his Sixth Lecture, to the Temple of Solomon as the place where "the true craftsmen were proved in their work," and where Solomon distinguished them into different ranks, giving to each appropriate signs and secret tokens, and organized them for the first time into an association of builders, the predecessors of the Masons being previous to that time sages who, though acquainted with the principles of geometry and architecture, were engaged solely in philosophical speculations. In this way Hutchinson gave the weight of his influence in favor of the Legend which ascribed the origin of operative and speculative Masonry to Solomon and to his Temple, although his views on this subject differ from those of other writers.

Dr. Oliver, one of the latest and the most prolific of the legendary writers, although in his own theory he seeks to trace the origin of Freemasonry to a much more remote antiquity, yet speaks so much in detail in most of his works, but principally in his *Antiquities* and in his *Historical Landmarks*, of the system which was for the first time organized at the building of the Solomonic Temple, that most readers who do not closely peruse his writings and carefully scan his views are under the impression that he had fully adopted the Legend of the Temple origin, and hence his authority has been lent to the popular belief.

Existing, as may be supposed from the analogy of a similar legend of the Compagnons de la Tour, among the craftsmen of the Middle Ages; transmitted to the Revival era of the beginning of the 18th century, and since then taught in all the rituals and sustained by the best Masonic writers up to a recent period, this **Legend** of the Temple origin of Freemasonry, or, in plainer words, the theory that Freemasonry received at the time of the building of the Temple of Jerusalem that form and organization which it holds at the present day, has been and continues to be a dogma of faith implicitly believed by the masses of the fraternity.

It is well, therefore, that we should now see what precisely is the form and substance of this popular Legend. As received at the present day by the body of the Craft, it may be stated as follows:

When Solomon was about to commence the building of his Temple, his own people not being expert or experienced architects, he applied to his friend Hiram, the monarch of the neighboring kingdom of Tyre, for assistance. Hiram, in complying with his request, sent to him a numerous body of workmen, and at their head a distinguished artist called, as a mark of distinction, Hiram Abif,[1] equivalent to the title, " Hiram his father," who is described as " a cunning man endued with understanding."

King Solomon then proceeded to organize the institution into a form, which has been adopted as the model of that which exists at the present day in every country where Freemasonry exists. The Legend that contains the classification of the workmen at the Temple, which has been adopted in the rituals of modern Masonry, is derived partly from Scripture and partly from tradition. An examination of it will not be inappropriate.

There are two accounts, slightly conflicting, in the Scriptural narrative. In the Second Book of Chronicles, chapter ii., verses 17 and 18, are the following words:

"And Solomon numbered all the strangers that were in the land of Israel, after the number wherewith David his father had numbered them, and there were found an hundred and fifty thousand and three thousand and six hundred.

"And he set three score and ten thousand of them to be bearers of burdens and four score thousand to be hewers in the mountains and three thousand six hundred overseers to set the people at work."

The same numerical details are given in the second verse of the

---

[1] Of Hiram Abif a more detailed account will be given when we come to consider the legend connected with him.

same chapter. Again in the First Book of Kings, chapter v., verses 13 and 14, it is said:

"And King Solomon raised a levy out of all Israel; and the levy was thirty thousand men.

"And he sent them to Lebanon, ten thousand a month by courses; a month they were in Lebanon, and two months at home: and Adoniram was over the levy."

In the *Legend of the Craft* this enumeration was not strictly adhered to. The Cooke MS. says that there were "four score thousand masons at work," out of whom three thousand were chosen as Masters of the work. The Landsdowne MS. says that the number of Masons was twenty-four thousand. But this number must have been a clerical error of the copyist in which he is followed only by the Antiquity MS. All the other manuscripts agree with the Dowland and make the number of Masons eighty thousand, including the three thousand overseers or Masters of the Work.

This statement does not accord with that which is in the Book of Kings nor with that in Chronicles, and yet it is all that the *Legend of the Craft* furnishes.

Dr. Anderson, who was the first author after the Revival who made an enumeration and classification of the workmen at the Temple, abandoned the Legend altogether and made up his account from the Bible. This he published in the first edition of the *Constitutions* and tempered it with some traditional information, whence derived I do not know. But it is on this classification by Anderson that all the rituals that have been in use since his time are framed. Hence he may justly be considered as the author of the Legend of the Workmen at the Temple; for notwithstanding the historical element which it contains, derived from Scripture, there are so many traditional interpolations that it properly assumes a legendary character.

Anderson's account is that there were employed on the building three thousand six hundred Master Masons, to conduct the work according to Solomon's directions; eighty thousand hewers of stone in the mountains who he says were Fellow Craftsmen, and seventy thousand laborers who were not Masons, besides the levy of thirty thousand who worked under the superintendence of Adoniram, making in all one hundred and eighty-three thousand six hundred. For this great number, Anderson says Solomon was "much obliged" to Hiram, King of Tyre, who sent his Masons and carpenters to Jerusalem.

Over this immense number of builders and laborers, Anderson says that King Solomon presided as Grand Master at Jerusalem, King Hiram in the same capacity at Tyre, and Hiram Abif was the Master of Work.

Fifteen years afterward, Anderson, in the second edition of his *Constitutions* somewhat modified these views and added certain other particulars. He promotes Hiram Abif from the position of *Magister Operis* or Master of the Work, to that of Deputy Grand Master in Solomon's absence and to that of Senior Grand Warden in his presence. He also says:

"Solomon partitioned the Fellow Crafts into certain Lodges with a Master and Wardens in each; that they might receive commands in a regular manner, might take care of their tools and jewels, might be paid every week, and be duly fed and clothed, etc., and the Fellow Crafts took care of their succession by educating Entered Apprentices."[1]

Anderson adds in a marginal note that his authority for this statement is "the traditions of old Masons, who talk much of these things."

If such a tradition ever existed, it is now lost, for it can not be found in any of the old manuscripts which are the record of the Masonic traditions. It is admitted that similar usages were practiced by the Operative Masons of the Middle Ages, but we have no historical authority, nor even legendary, outside of Anderson's work, for tracing them to the Temple of Jerusalem.

Out of these materials the ritualists have manufactured a Legend; which exists in all the Masonic rituals and which must have been constructed in London, at a very early period after the Revival, to have secured such an universal acceptance among all the nations who derived their Masonry from the Grand Lodge of England. The Legend of the Temple origin of Masonry, as generally accepted by the Craft at the present day, is that there were one hundred and fifty-three thousand, three hundred workmen employed in the construction of the Temple. Three thousand three hundred of these were overseers, who were among as well as over the Craft, but who at

---

[1] "Constitutions," 2d edit., p. 13.

the completion of the Temple were promoted to the rank of Master Masons. The remaining workmen were divided into eighty thousand Fellow Crafts and seventy thousand Entered Apprentices.

Three Grand Masters presided over the large number of work. men, namely, Solomon, King of Israel; Hiram, King of Tyre, and Hiram Abif. These were the only persons who at the building of the Temple were Master Masons and in possession of the secrets of the Third Degree.

The statement in the ritual is that the workmen were divided into Lodges. The Lodge of Master Masons, for there could be only one of that degree, consisted of three members; the Lodges of Fellow Crafts, of which there must have been sixteen thousand, was composed of five members each; and the Lodges of Entered Apprentices, of which there must have been ten thousand, was composed of seven each.

But as this statement has neither historical authority nor logical possibility to support it, it must be considered, as it undoubtedly was originally intended to be considered, merely as a reference to the symbolic character of those sacred numbers in Masonry—three, five, and seven. In the same spirit of symbolic reference the steps of the winding stairs leading to the middle chamber were divided into a series of three, five, and seven, with the addition in the English ritual of nine and eleven. All of this is, therefore, to be rejected from the class of legends and referred to that of symbols.

Viewing then this Legend or theory of the origin of Masonry at the Temple, tracing it from the almost nude state in which it is presented in the *Legend of the Craft* through the extraneous clothing which was added by Anderson and I suppose by Desaguliers, to the state of tinsel ornamentation in which it appears in the modern ritual, we will come to the following conclusion:

In the *Legend of the Craft* we find only the following statement: That King Solomon was assisted in the building of the Temple by the King of Tyre, who sent him materials for the edifice and a skillful artist, on whose name scarcely any two of them agree, and whom Solomon appointed as his Master of the Work; that Solomon invited Masons from all lands and having collected them together at Jerusalem, organized them into a body by giving them a system of laws and customs for their government. Now, most of these facts are sustained by the historical authority of the Books of Kings and

Chronicles, and those that are not have the support of extreme probability.

That Solomon, King of Israel, built a Temple in Jerusalem is an historical fact that can not be doubted or denied. Richard Carlile, it is true, says, " My historical researches have taught me that that which has been called Solomon's Temple never existed upon earth ; that a nation of people called Israelites never existed upon earth, and that the supposed history of the Israelites and their Temple is nothing more than an allegory."[1]

But the measure of the moral and mental stature of Carlile has long been taken, and even among the most skeptical critics he remains alone in his irrational incredulity.

Doubtless there are Oriental exaggerations in respect to the amount of money expended and the number of workmen employed on the building, which have been overestimated. But the simple, naked fact that King Solomon built a temple remains uncontradicted, and is as historically true and undoubted as that of the construction of any other public edifice in antiquity.

It is equally historical that the King of Tyre gave assistance to Solomon in carrying out his design. However fiercely the skeptics may have attacked certain portions of the Bible, the Books of Kings and Chronicles have been placed upon the footing of other ancient historical records and subjected to the same canons of criticism.

Now we are distinctly told that Hiram, King of Tyre, "sent masons and carpenters to David to build him a house ;"[2] we learn subsequently that the same Hiram (some say his son) was equally friendly with Solomon, and although there is no distinct mention either in Kings or Chronicles that he sent workmen to Jerusalem,[3] except his namesake, the artificer, yet we may infer that he did so, from the friendship of the two kings, from the need of Solomon for expert workmen, and from the fact which we learn from the First Book of Kings, that the stones for the edifice were hewn by " Solomon's builders and Hiram's builders and the Giblim." The authorized version, on what authority I know not, translates this word " Giblim " as " stone-squarers." They were, however, the inhabitants

---

[1] " Manual of Freemasons," Part I., p. 4.   [2] 1 Chronicles, xiv., 1.

[3] We are told in 1 Kings, v., and it is repeated in 2 Chron., ii., that Hiram sent his workmen to Lebanon to cut down trees. The timber they were to carry to Joppa, where Solomon was to receive it, and, presumably, the workmen were to return to the forest.

of the city of Gebal, called by the Greeks, Byblos, which was the principal seat of the worship and the mysteries of Adonis. The inhabitants were celebrated for their skill in stone-carving and in shipbuilding.

Thus we see that there were, according to the Scriptural account, three classes of Masons engaged at the building of the Temple. First there were the workmen of Solomon : these were of the "four score thousand hewers in the mountains"[1] who were taken by Solomon from "the strangers that were in the land of Israel"[2]—men whom Dr. Adam Clarke supposes to have been not pure Israelites, but proselytes to the Jewish religion so far as to renounce idolatry and to keep the precepts of Noah. But we must believe that among these four score thousand strangers were to be enumerated the workmen who came from Tyre, or there will be no place allotted to them in the distribution in the First Book of Kings. The three thousand three hundred who were "over the work," are said to have been chief officers of Solomon and therefore Israelites, and the remaining seventy thousand were mere laborers or bearers of burden—a class for whom Solomon need not have been indebted to the King of Tyre.

Secondly, there were the workmen of Hiram, King of Tyre. These I have already said were probably, and indeed necessarily, included in the number of four score thousand strangers or foreigners. The words in the original are *anoshim gherim*, men who are foreigners, for Gesenius defines the word *gherim*, to be "*sojourners, strangers, foreigners*, men living out of their country."[3]

Thirdly, we have the Giblim, the inhabitants of the city of Gebal in Phœnicia, who came to Jerusalem, invited there by Solomon, to assist in the construction of the Temple, and who must also be reckoned among the four score thousand strangers.

Thus the *Legend of the Craft* is justified in saying that Solomon "sent after Masons into divers countries and of divers landes," and that he had "four score workers of stone and were all named Masons." For these were the foreigners or sojourners, whom he found in Jerusalem, many of whom had probably come there on his invitation, and the Tyrians who had been sent to him by King Hiram, and the Phœnicians, whom he had called out of Gebal on account of their well-known skill in stone-cutting. And all of these

---

[1] 1 Kings, v., 15.   [2] 2 Chron. ii., 17.   [3] Lexicon, *in voce*.

amounted to eighty thousand, the number stated in the Books of Kings and Chronicles, and just the number mentioned in the *Legend of the Craft.*

It will be seen that the *Legend of the Craft* takes no notice of the levy of thirty thousand who worked under Adoniram on Mount Lebanon, nor of the seventy thousand who were employed as bearers of burdens. As the former were merely wood-cutters and the latter common laborers, the *Legend* does not class them among the Masons, any more than it does the three thousand three hundred who were, according to the Biblical account, officers of the court of Solomon, who were appointed merely to overlook the Masons and to see that they worked faithfully ; perhaps also to pay them their wages, or to distribute their food, and to supervise generally their conduct.

In all this, the *Legend of the Craft* differs entirely from the modern rituals, which have included all these classes, and therefore reckon that at the building of the Temple there were one hundred and fifty-three thousand three hundred Masons, instead of eighty thousand. The *Legend* is certainly more in accord with the authority of the Bible than are the rituals.

The *Legend of the Craft* is also justified in saying that Solomon organized these Masons into what might be called a guild, that is, a society or corporation,[1] by giving them " charges and manners " —in other words, a code of laws and regulations. On this question the Bible account is silent, but it amounts to an extreme probability, the nearest approximation to historical evidence, that there must have been some regulations enacted for the government of so large a number of workmen. It is also equally probable that to avoid confusion these workmen must have been divided into sections, or what, in modern parlance, would be called " gangs," engaged in various parts of the building and in different employments. There must have been a higher and more skillful class occupied in directing the works of these several sections ; there must have been others less skillful and yet competent to discharge the duties of stone-cutters and layers, and there must have been another and still inferior class who were only acquiring the rudiments of the profession.

Founded on these evident propositions, Anderson made his

---

[1] The Latin original of the Krause MS. calls it " Societas architedonica "—an architectural society.

division of the workmen at the Temple into the three classes of Master Masons, Fellow Crafts, and Entered Apprentices. But he abandoned the *Legend* in calling the three thousand six hundred officers of King Solomon Master Masons, and making the whole number, exclusive of the seventy thousand laborers and the thirty thousand wood-cutters on Mount Lebanon, eighty-three thousand, and afterward stating that there were one hundred and eighty-three thousand Masons in all—a contradiction of his own previous statement as well as of the *Legend of the Craft* which states the whole number of Masons to have been eighty thousand.

The modern ritual may, however, be considered as having adopted the Temple of Jerusalem as a type of that abstruse symbol of a spiritual temple, which forms, as will be hereafter seen, one of the most important and most interesting symbolic lessons on which the philosophy of Speculative Masonry depends. But viewing it as an historical statement, it is devoid of all claims to credence. The facts stated in the ritual are an outgrowth of those contained in the *Legend of the Craft* which it has greatly altered by unauthorized additions, and it is in entire contradiction to those given in the Books of Kings and Chronicles.

The claim that Freemasonry took its origin at the building of the Temple is without any historical authority. The *Legend of the Craft*, upon which, to be consistent, all Masonic rituals should be founded, assigns its origin equally to two other periods—to that of the building of the Tower of Babel, when Nimrod was Grand Master, and to Egypt under the geometrician Euclid. Why the Temple of Solomon was exclusively selected by the modern Masons as the incunabulum of their Order can be only conjecturally accounted for.

I am not unwilling to believe, for reasons that have been already assigned, that the Operative or Stone Masons of the Middle Ages had some tradition or Legend of the origin of the Institution at the Temple of Solomon. If so, I am inclined to attribute their selection of this in preference to any other stately edifice of antiquity to these reasons.

The mediæval Masons were, as an association of builders, most intimately connected with the ecclesiastics of that age. Their principal home at one time was in the monasteries, they worked under the immediate patronage and supervision of bishops and abbots, and were chiefly engaged in the construction of cathedrals and other religious edifices. Private houses at that early period were mostly built of wood, and the building of them was the business of carpenters. The *treow-wyr-hta*, literally the tree-workman, in modern phrase the carpenter, was one of the most important handicrafts of the early Anglo-Saxons. He was the builder of their ships as well as of their houses, and the trade is frequently spoken of in ancient Saxon documents. He was constantly employed in the construction of vessels for the carrying on of trade, or the erection of dwellings for the residences of the people.

To the stone-masons was exclusively entrusted the nobler vocation of building religious edifices.

Imbued, from their connection with the priests as well as from their peculiar employment, with religious sentiments, they naturally looked for the type of the great cathedrals which they were erecting, not to Pagan temples, however splendid might be their architecture, but rather to that Jewish cathedral which had been consecrated on Mount Moriah to the worship of the true God. Hence the brief notice of that building in the *Legend of the Craft* was either the suggestion of that esoteric Legend of the Temple which has not, from its necessarily oral character, been handed down to us, or if the written Legend was posterior in time to the oral one, then it was a brief record of it.

But I do not believe that this lost Legend of the stone-masons was ever intended to be historical. It was simply a symbol to illustrate the idea that the Temple at Jerusalem was the type of all Christian cathedrals.

This symbolic Legend, which I suppose to have existed among the stone-masons of the Middle Ages, was probably lost before the revival of Masonry in the year 1717. Anderson therefore framed a new Legend out of the *Legend of the Craft*, the Scriptural account, and his own invention.

Upon this Andersonian Legend, simple in the first edition of the *Constitutions*, but considerably expanded in the second, the modern ritualists have framed another Legend, which in many important details differs from Anderson's, from the *Legend of the Craft*, and from the account in the Bible.

This is the Legend now accepted and believed by the great body of the Craft to be historically true. That it has no claim to historical credence is evident from the fact that it is, in its most important details, unauthorized, and in fact contradicted by the Scriptural account, which is the only authentic memorial that we have of the transactions that took place at the building of the Solomonic Temple.

And moreover, the long period that elapsed between the building of the Temple, a thousand years before the Christian era, and the time, not earlier than the 3d century after Christ, during which we have no traces of the existence of such an architectural association connected with Jewish Masons and transmitted from them to the Christian architects, presents an extensive lacuna which must be filled by authentic records, before we can be enabled, as scholars investigating truth, to consent to the theory that the Freemasons of the present day are, by uninterrupted successions, the representatives of the Masons who wrought at King Solomon's Temple.

The Legend of the ritual is, in fact, a symbol—but a very important and a very interesting one, and as such will be fully discussed when the subject of Masonic symbols comes to be treated in a subsequent part of this work.

CHAPTER XXV

LEGEND OF THE DIONYSIAC ARTIFICERS

E now approach a very interesting topic in the legendary history of Masonry. The reader has already seen in the last chapter that the Masons of the kingdom of Tyre were invited to join with the Jewish builders in the construction of the Temple. Who these Tyrian Masons were, what was their character, whence they came, and what was the influence exerted by them on the Jewish workmen with whom they were united in a common labor, are questions which can only be solved by a reference to what may be called the *Legend of the Dionysiac Artificers.*

This Legend was entirely unknown to the old Masons of the Middle Ages. There is no reference to it in any of the manuscripts. The brief allusion to the Dionysiacs of Asia Minor in Robison's anti-Masonic work does not necessarily connect them with the Masons of King Solomon.[1]

The first writer who appears to have started the theory that the Masons sent by King Hiram to the King of Israel were members of the Dionysiac fraternity, is Sir David Brewster, who presented the Legend under the guise of an historic statement in the *History of Freemasonry*, published in the beginning of this century, and the authorship of which, although it was actually written by him, has been falsely attributed to Alexander Lawrie, the bookseller of Edinburgh and at the time the Grand Secretary of the Grand Lodge of Scotland. Brewster may therefore, I think, be fairly considered as the original framer of the Legend.

The origin of the mystical and architectural society which Brew-

---

[1] " Proofs of a Conspiracy," p. 20.

ster closely connects with the Masons of the Temple may be given in almost his own words:[1]

Between 1055 and 1044 years before Christ, or something more than half a century anterior to the building of the Temple, the inhabitants of Attica, complaining of the narrowness of their territory and the unfruitfulness of the soil, went in quest of more extensive and fertile settlements. Being joined by a number of the inhabitants of the surrounding provinces of Greece, they sailed to Asia Minor and drove out the inhabitants of that portion of the western coast from Phocœa in the north to Miletus in the south. To this narrow strip of land they gave the name of Ionia, because the greatest number of the adventurers were natives of that Grecian state. After partly subduing and partly expelling the original inhabitants, they built several towns, of which one of the principal was Teos.

Prior to this emigration the Greeks had made considerable progress in the arts and sciences, which the adventurers carried with them into their new territory, and they introduced into Ionia the Mysteries of Pallas and Dionysus, before they had become corrupted by the licentiousness of the Athenians.

Especially popular, not only in Ionia but throughout Asia Minor, were the Mysteries of Dionysus, the Roman Bacchus. In these, as in all the religious Mysteries of antiquity, there was a funereal legend.

In the Dionysiac Mysteries the legend of initiation recounted or represented the death of the demi-god Dionysus, the search for and discovery of his body, and his subsequent restoration to life.

In the initiations the candidate was made to represent in his own person, the events connected with the slaying of the hero-god. After a variety of preparatory ceremonies, intended to call forth all his fortitude and courage, the aphanism or mystical death of Dionysus—torn to pieces by the Titans—was presented in a dramatic form and followed by the confinement or burial of the candidate, as the representative of Dionysus in the pastos, couch, or coffin, all of which constituted the first part of the ceremony of initiation. Then began the search for the remains of Dionysus, which was continued amid scenes of the greatest confusion and tumult, until at last, the search having been successful, the morning was turned to joy, light suc-

---

[1] Lawrie's "History of Freemasonry," 1st edit., p. 27.

ceeded to darkness, and the candidate was invested with the knowledge of the secret doctrine of the Mysteries—the belief in the existence of one God and a future and immortal state.[1]

Now these Mysteries of Dionysus were very intimately connected with a society of architects. As this association, according to the Legend which we are now considering, had much to do with the organization of Masonry at the Solomonic Temple, it is necessary to take a brief notice of its origin and character.

It is an historical fact that at the time of the building of the Temple at Jerusalem, there existed at Tyre as well as in other parts of Asia Minor an association known as the *Dionysian Architects*, because they joined to the practice of operative architecture the observance of the religious rites of the Dionysiac Mysteries.

It has been already stated that the priests of Dionysus had devoted themselves to the study and the practice of architecture, and about one thousand years before the Christian era, or at the time that King Solomon began the construction of the Temple at Jerusalem, had emigrated from Greece and established themselves as a society or fraternity of builders in Asia Minor, and devoted themselves to the construction of temples and other public edifices.[2]

Hiram, who then reigned over the kingdom of Tyre, and who from his cultivation of the sciences has been styled the Augustus of his age, is said to have patronized these religious builders, and to have employed them in the magnificent works by which he adorned and strengthened his capital.

The internal government and the usages of this association were very similar to those exhibited by the Masonic society in the present day, and which the legendary theory supposes to have prevailed among the builders of the Solomonic Temple.

The fraternity was divided into communities called synœciæ,[3] having houses or dwellings in common, which might well be com-

---

[1] Le meurtre de Bacchus mis à mort et déchiré en pièces par les Titans, et son retour à la vie, ont été le sujet d'explications allégoriques tout-à-fait analogues à celles que l'on à données de l'enlèvement de Proserpine et du meurtre d'Osiris.—Sylvestre de Tracy in Sainte-Croix's "Recherches sur les Mysteres du Paganisme," T. ii., p. 86.

[2] Chandler says "the Dionysiasts were artificers or contractors for the Asiatic theaters, and were incorporated and settled at Teos, under the Kings of Pergamum."—"Travels in Asia Minor," vol. i., ch. xxviii., p. 123. [This was at a later period than the era of the Temple.]

[3] "Antiquitates Asiaticæ Christianam Aeram Antecedentes," p. 139.

pared to the Masonic Lodges of the present day. Their plans of meeting were also called in Greek koina, which signifies communities, and each received a distinctive name, just as our Lodges do. Thus Chishull speaks in his account of the pre-Christian antiquities of Asia of a koinon ton Attaliston, or a "community of the Attalistæ," so called, most probably in honor of King Attalus, who was their patron.[1]

There was an annual festival, like the General Assembly or Grand Lodge of the Masons, which was held with great pomp and ceremony. Chandler says (but he speaks of a later period, when they were settled at Teos) that it was the custom of their synod to hold yearly a General Assembly, at which they sacrificed to the gods and poured out libations to their deceased benefactors. They likewise celebrated games in honor of Bacchus, when the crowns which had been bestowed by any of the communities as rewards of merit were announced by heralds, and the wearers of them were applauded by the other members. These meetings, he adds, were solemnized with great pomp and festivity.[2]

The same traveler mentions a long decree made by one of the communities in honor of its magistrates, which he found inscribed on a slab in a Turkish burying-ground. The thanks of the community with a crown of olives are given as a recompense to these officers for their great liberality and trouble while in office ; and to perpetuate their memory and to excite an emulation of their merit, it is besides enacted that the decrees be engraved, but at their expense, "so desirable," says Chandler, "was the testimony to the individuals and so frugal the usage in bestowing it."[3]

Of course as an architectural association the Dionysiacs used many of the implements employed by Operative Masons, and as a secret brotherhood they had a system of signs and tokens by which any one of the members could make himself known to the others. Professor Robison, who may be accepted on this point as authority, admits that they were "distinguished from the uninitiated or profane inhabitants by the science which they possessed and by many private signs and tokens by which they recognized each other."[4]

---

[1] Rollin's "Universal History" places Attalus in the rank of those princes who loved and patronized letters and the arts.

[2] Chandler, " Travels in Asia Minor," vol. i., ch. xxx., p. 126.

[3] Ibid., vol. i., ch. xxviii., p. 124.   [4] " Proofs of a Conspiracy," p. 20.

Each of the *koina* or separate communities into which they were divided was under the direction of officers corresponding to a Master and Wardens.[1]

The Masonic principle of charity was practiced among them and the opulent members were bound to provide for the wants and necessities of their poorer brethren.

The Legend which connects these architects with the building of the Temple at Jerusalem, assumes that Hiram Abif was a member of this secret association. Although the Scriptural narrative is adverse to this theory, since it states that he was simply a worker in metals and precious stones, yet we may reconcile it with possibility by supposing that such craftsmen were admitted into the association of the Dionysiacs because their decorative art was necessary for the completion and perfection of the temples and public buildings which they constructed. This is, however, merely conjectural.

The Legend, now connecting itself in part with history, proceeds to state that when Solomon was about to build a temple to Jehovah, he made his intention known to his friend and ally, Hiram, King of Tyre, and because he was well aware of the architectural skill of the Tyrian Dionysiacs, he besought that monarch's assistance to enable him to carry his pious design into execution. Hiram complied with his request and sent him the necessary workmen, who by their skill and experience might supply the mechanical deficiencies and ignorance of the Israelites.

With the body of builders he sent this Hiram Abif, who as "a curious and cunning workman," highly recommended by his patron, was entrusted by King Solomon with the superintendence of the construction and placed at the head of both the Tyrian and Jewish craftsmen as the chief builder and principal conductor of the work.

To this distinguished artist, on account of the large influence which his position gave him and the exalted personal virtues which are traditionally supposed to have characterized him, is to be attributed, according to the Legend, the intimate union of two peoples so dissimilar in manners and so antagonized in religion as the Jews and the Tyrians, which resulted in the organization of the Institution of Freemasonry.

Supposing Hiram Abif, as the Legend does, to have been con-

---

[1] Brewster in Lawrie's " History," p. 29.

nected with the Dionysiac fraternity, we may also suppose that he could not have been a very humble or inconspicuous member, if we may judge of his rank in the society, from the amount of talent which he is said to have possessed, and from the elevated position that he held in the affections and at the court of the King of Tyre.

He must therefore have been very familiar with all the ceremonial usages of the Dionysiac artificers and must have enjoyed a long experience of the advantages derived from the government and discipline which they practiced in the erection of the many sacred edifices which they had constructed.   A portion of these ceremonial usages and of this discipline he would naturally be inclined to introduce among the workmen at Jerusalem.   He therefore united them in a society, similar in many respects to that of the Dionysiac artificers.   He inculcated lessons of charity and brotherly love; he established a ceremony of initiation to test experimentally the worth and fortitude of the candidate; adopted secret methods of recognition; and impressed the obligations of duty and the principles of morality by means of symbols and allegories.

Just at this point a difficulty must have arisen in reconciling the pagan symbolic instruction of the Tyrians with the religious notions of the Jews, which, however, the Legend ingeniously overcomes.

The most prominent symbol of Speculative Masonry, that, indeed, on which the whole of the ethical instructions is founded, is contained in the lesson of resurrection to a future life as developed in the allegorical Legend of the Master's Degree.

In the Pagan Mysteries, of which the Dionysia were a part, this doctrine was also illustrated by an allegorical legend.   In the Mysteries of Dionysus which were practiced by the Tyrian architects the legend related to the death and subsequent resuscitation of Bacchus or Dionysus.

But it would have been utterly impossible to have introduced such a legend as the basis of any instructions to be communicated to Jewish initiates.   Any allusion to the mythological fables of their Gentile neighbors would have been equally offensive to the taste and repugnant to the religious prejudices of a nation educated from generation to generation in the worship of a Divine Being, who, they had been taught, was jealous of his prerogatives, and who had made himself known to their ancestors as the JEHOVAH, the only God of time present, past, and future.

The difficulty of obtaining a legend on which the dogma of the Third Degree might be founded was obviated by substituting Hiram Abif, after his death (at which time only the system could have been perfected), in the place of Dionysus. The lesson taught in the Mysteries practiced by the Dionysiac artificers was thus translated into the Masonic initiation, the form of the symbolism remaining the same, but the circumstances of the legend necessarily varying.

By this union of the Dionysiacs with the Jewish workmen and the introduction of their mystical organization, the Masonic Order assumed at the building of the Temple that purely speculative form connected with the operative which it has ever since retained.

From its Jewish element it derived its religious character as a pure theism.

From its Tyrian element it borrowed its peculiar mystical character and its system of symbolism, which so much assimilated it to the ancient Pagan Mysteries, that a Legend has been framed (to be hereafter considered) which traces its origin directly to those secret associations of antiquity.

Upon the completion of the Temple, the workmen, invested with all the secrets which had been promised in their initiation, and thus becoming Master Masons, dispersed, that they might be enabled to extend their knowledge and to renew their labors in other lands.

Such is the Legend which seeks to attribute the present form of Freemasonry to the connection of the Dionysiac artisans of Tyre with the Jewish workmen at the building of the Temple. So much of the Legend as relates to the existence of a building sodality at Tyre (leaving out the question whether they were or were not Dionysiacs), some of whose members went to Jerusalem to assist in the construction of the Solomonic Temple, may, I think, be accepted as indisputably historic. What were the real influences exerted by them on the Jewish people, is a question whose answer finds no place in the realm of history, but must be relegated to the doubtful domain of conjecture. Brewster has described the Dionysiacs as they existed in about the 3d century before Christ, and after their incorporation by King Attalus, as if they maintained the same condition in the reign of Hiram of Tyre seven hundred years before. For this statement there is no warrant in any historical record. The supposition that the Dionysiacs of Tyre and those of Teos were identical in organization, is simply a theory based on a mere assump-

tion.   It is, however, certain that they who adopt the legendary theory that Freemasonry was first organized at the Temple of Solomon,
will find much to sustain their theory in the Legend of the Dionysiac Artificers.

It is equally certain that those who deny the Temple theory will
have to reject the Dionysiac, for the two are too closely connected
to be arbitrarily dissevered.

But laying the subject of Freemasonry altogether aside, and considering the connection of the Tyrians and the Jews at the Temple
as a mere historical question, it would present a very interesting
study of history to determine what were the results of that connection, if there were any way of solving it except by mere conjecture.

The subsequent history of the association of Dionysiac Architects forms no part of the Legend which has just been recited ; but
it may be interesting to trace their progress.   About seven hundred
years after the building of the Temple at Jerusalem, they are said
to have been incorporated by the King of Pergamum, an ancient
province of Mysia, as a society exclusively engaged in the erection
of public buildings such as theaters and temples.   They settled at
Teos, an Ionian city, on the coast of Asia Minor, where, notwithstanding its intestine troubles, they remained for several centuries.
Among the works accomplished by them were a magnificent theater
and a splendid temple of Dionysus, some ruins of which still remain.

But proving turbulent and seditious they were at length expelled
from Teos and removed to the city of Ephesus.   Thence they were
transferred by King Attalus to the town of Myonessus.   The Teians
having sent an embassy to Rome to request that the Myonessians
should not be permitted to fortify their city, the Dionysiacs removed
to Lebedos, about fifteen miles from Teos, where they were joyfully
welcomed.

In the 5th century of the Christian era the Emperor Theodosius
abolished all mystical associations, but the Dionysiacs are said to
have continued their existence until the time of the Crusades, when
they passed over into Europe and were merged in the association of
builders known as the *Traveling Freemasons* of the Middle Ages.
This latter part of the narrative is, I think, merely legendary or traditional, and will find no support in authentic history.   It is, however, an historical study to be examined hereafter.

CHAPTER XXVI

FREEMASONRY AND THE ANCIENT MYSTERIES

HE theory which ascribes the origin of Freemasonry as a secret society to the Pagan Mysteries of the ancient world, and which derives the most important part of its ritual and the legend of its Third Degree from the initiation practiced in these religious organizations, necessarily connects itself with the Legend of the Temple origin of the Institution, because we can only link the initiation in the Mysteries with that of Freemasonry by supposing that the one was in some way engrafted on the other, at the time of the building of the Temple and the union of the Jewish and Tyrian workmen.

But before we can properly appreciate the theory which associates Freemasonry with the Pagan Mysteries, we must make ourselves acquainted with the nature and the design as well as with something of the history of those mystical societies.

Among all the nations of antiquity in which refinement and culture had given an elevated tone to the religious sentiment, there existed two systems of worship, a public and a private one. "Each of the pagan Gods," says Warburton, "had (besides the public and open) a secret worship paid unto him, to which none were admitted but those who had been selected by preparatory ceremonies, called INITIATION. This secret worship was called the MYSTERIES."[1]

The public worship was founded on the superstitious polytheism whose numerous gods and goddesses were debased in character and vicious in conduct. Incentive to virtue could not be derived from their example, which furnished rather excuses for vice. In the *Eunuchus* of Terenie, when Chærea is meditating the seduction of the virgin Pamphila, he refers to the similar act of Jupiter,

---

[1] "Divine Legation of Moses," B. I., sect. iv., p. 193.

who in a shower of gold had corrupted Danæ, and he exclaims, "If a god, who by his thunders shakes the whole universe, could commit this crime, shall not I, a mere mortal, do so also?"[1] Plautus, Euripides, and other Greek and Roman dramatists and poets repeatedly used the same argument in defense of the views of their heroes, so that it became a settled principle of the ancient religion. The vicious example of the gods thus became an insuperable obstacle to a life of purity and holiness.[2]

The assurance of a future life of compensation constituted no part of the popular theology. The poets, it is true, indulged in romantic descriptions of an Elysium and a Tartarus, but their views were uncertain and unsatisfactory, as to any specific doctrine of immortality, and were embodied in the saying of Ovid[3] that of the four elements which constituted the human organization, "the earth covers the flesh; the shade flits around the tomb; the spirit seeks the stars."

Thus did the poet express the prevalent idea that the composite man returned after death to the various primordial elements of which he had been originally composed. In such a dim and shadowy hypothesis there was no incentive for life, no consolation in death. And hence Alger, to whom the world has been indebted for a most exhaustive treatise on the popular beliefs of all nations, ancient and modern, on the subject of the future life, has after a full and critical examination of the question, come to the following conclusion:

"To the ancient Greek in general, death was a sad doom. When he lost a friend, he sighed a melancholy farewell after him to the faded shore of ghosts. Summoned himself, he departed with a lingering look at the sun and a tearful adieu to the bright day and the green earth. To the Roman death was a grim reality. To meet it himself he girded up his loins with artificial firmness. But at its ravages among his friends, he wailed in anguished abandonment. To his dying vision there was indeed a future, but shapes of distrust and shadow stood upon its disconsolate borders; and

---

[1] At quem Deum, qui templa caeli summa sonitu concutit;
Ego homuncio hoc non facerem?
—Act iii., sc. 5.

[2] Warburton, "Divine Legation," B. II., sect. iv.

[3] Terra tegit carnem; tumulum circumvolat umbra; orcus habet manes; spiritus astra petit.

when the prospect had no horror, he still shrank from the poppied gloom." [1]

Yet as each nation advanced in refinement and intellectual culture the priests, the poets, and the philosophers [2] aspired to a higher thought and cherished the longing for and inculcated the consoling doctrine of an immortality, not to be spent in shadowy and inert forms of existence, but in perpetual enjoyment, as a compensation for the ills of life.

The necessary result of the growth of such pure and elevated notions must have been a contempt and condemnation of the absurdities of polytheism. But as this was the popular religion it was readily perceived that any open attempt to overthrow it and to advance, publicly, opinions so antagonistic to it would be highly impolitic and dangerous. Whenever any religion, whether true or false, becomes the religion of a people, whoever opposes it, or ridicules it, or seeks to subvert it, is sure to be denounced by popular fanaticism and to be punished by popular intolerance.

Socrates was doomed to drink the poisoned bowl on the charge that he taught the Athenian youth not to worship the gods who are worshipped by the state, but new and unknown deities. Jesus was suspended from the cross because he inculcated doctrines which, however pure, were novel and obnoxious to the old religion of his Jewish countrymen.

The new religious truths among the Pagan peoples were therefore concealed from common inspection and taught only in secret societies, admission to which was obtained only through the ordeal of a painful initiation, and the doctrines were further concealed under the veil of symbols whose true meaning the initiated only could understand. "The truth," says Clemens of Alexandria, "was taught involved in enigmas, symbols, allegories, metaphors, and tropes and figures." [3]

The secret associations in which the principles of a new and

---

[1] "Critical History of the Doctrine of a Future Life," p. 196.

[2] Many of the philosophers were, however, skeptics. The Stoics, for instance, and they were the leading sect, denied the survival of the soul after the death of the body; or, if any of them conceded its survival, they attributed to it only a temporary duration before it is dissolved and absorbed into the universe. Seneca ("Troades," I., 397) says "there is nothing after death, and death itself is nothing." *Post mortem nihil, est ipsaque mors nihil.*

[3] "Stromat.," lib. v., p. 658.

Time

Youth, Manhood, and Old Age

purer theology were taught have received in history the name of the MYSTERIES.

Each country had its own Mysteries peculiar to itself. In Egypt were those of Osiris and Isis; in Samothrace those of the Cabiri; in Greece they celebrated at Eleusis, near Athens, the Mysteries of Demeter; in Syria of Adonis; in Phœnicia of Dionysus; and in Persia those of Mithras, which were the last to perish after the advent of Christianity and the overthrow of polytheism.

These Mysteries, although they differed in name and in some of the details of initiation, were essentially alike in general form and design. "Their end as well as nature," says Warburton, "was the same in all: to teach the doctrine of a future state."[1] Alger says: "The implications of the indirect evidence, the leanings and guidings of all the incidental clews now left us as to the real aim and purport of the Mysteries, combine to assure us that their chief teaching was a doctrine of a future life in which there should be rewards and punishments."[2]

Thomas Taylor, the Platonist, than whom no better modern authority on this subject could be cited, says that "the initiated were instructed in the doctrine of a state of future rewards and punishments,"[3] and that the greater Mysteries "obscurely intimated, by mystic and splendid visions, the felicity of the soul both here and hereafter, when purified from the defilements of a material nature and constantly elevated to the realities of intellectual vision."[4]

All the ancient writers who were contemporary with these associations, and must have been familiar with their character, concur in the opinion that their design was to teach the doctrine of a future life of compensation.

Pindar says, "Happy the man who descends beneath the hollow earth having beheld these Mysteries. He knows the end, he knows the divine origin of life."

Sophocles says that "they are thrice happy who descend to the shades below, after having beheld these rites; for they alone have life in Hades, while all others suffer there every kind of evil."

---

[1] "Divine Legation," B. I., sect. iv., p. 194.
[2] "Crit. Hist. of the Doctrine of a Future Life," p. 454.
[3] "Dissertation on the Eleusinian and Bacchic Mysteries" *apud Pamphleteer*, vol. viii., p. 40.
[4] Ibid., p. 53.

And lastly, Isocrates declares that "those who have been initi-ated in the Mysteries of Ceres entertain better hopes both as to the end of life and the whole of futurity."

It is then evident from all authorities that the great end and design of the initiation into these Mysteries was to teach the aspir-ant the doctrine of a future life—not that aimless, uncertain, and shadowy one portrayed by the poets and doubtfully consented to by the people, but that pure and rational state of immortal existence in which the soul is purified from the dross of the body and elevated to eternal life. It was, in short, much the same in its spirit as the Christian and Masonic doctrine of the resurrection.

But this lesson was communicated in the Mysteries in a peculiar form, which has in fact given rise to the theory we are now consid-ering that they were the antetype and original source of Speculative Masonry. They were all dramatic in their ceremonies; each one exhibited in a series of scenic representations the adventures of some god or hero ; the attacks upon him by his enemies; his death at their hands; his descent into Hades or the grave, and his final resurrection to renewed life as a mortal, or his apotheosis as a god.

The only important difference between these various Mysteries was, that there was to each one a different and peculiar god or hero, whose death and resurrection or apotheosis constituted the subject of the drama, and gave to its scenes the changes which were depend-ent on the adventures of him who was its main subject. Thus, in Samothrace, where the Mysteries of the Cabiri were celebrated, it was Atys, the lover of Cybele, who was slain and restored; in Egypt it was Osiris whose death and resurrection were represented ; in Greece it was Dionysus, and in Persia Mithras.

But in all of these the material points of the plot and the relig-ious design of the sacred drama were identical. The dramatic form and the scenic representation of the allegory were everywhere pre-served.

This dramatic form of the initiatory rites in the Mysteries—this acted allegory in which the doctrine of the resurrection was shad-owed forth by the visible representation of some fictitious event—was, as the learned Dr. Dollinger[1] has justly observed, "eminently calculated to take a powerful hold on the imagination and the heart,

---

[1] " Jew and Gentile," I., p. 136, Darnell's Translation.

and to excite in the spectators alternately conflicting sentiments of terror and calmness, of sorrow and fear and hope."

As the Mysteries were a secret society, whose members were separated from the rest of the people by a ceremony of initiation, there resulted from this form of organization, as a necessary means of defense and of isolation, a solemn obligation of secrecy, with severe penalties for its violation, and certain modes of recognition known only to those who had been instructed in them.

There was what might be called a progressive order of degrees, for the neophyte was not at once upon his initiation invested with a knowledge of the deepest arcana of the religious system.

Thus the Mysteries were divided into two classes called the Lesser and the Greater Mysteries, and in addition there was a preliminary ceremony, which was only preparatory to the Mysteries proper. So that there was in the process of reception a system of three steps, which those who are fond of tracing analogies between the ancient and the modern initiations are prone to call degrees.

A brief review of these three steps of progress in the Mysteries will give the reader a very definite idea of the nature of this ancient system in which so many writers have thought that they had found the incunabulum of modern Freemasonry, and will enable him to appreciate at their just value the analogies which these writers have found, as they suppose, between the two systems. The first step was called the *Lustration*, or purification by water. When the neophyte was ready to be received into any of the ancient Mysteries, he was carried into the temple or other place appropriated to the ceremony of initiation, and there underwent a thorough cleansing of the body by water. This was the preparation for reception into the Lesser Mysteries and was symbolic of that purification of the heart that was absolutely necessary to prepare the aspirant for admission to a knowledge of and participation in the sacred lessons which were to be subsequently communicated to him. It has been sought to find in this preparatory ceremony an analogy to the first degree of Masonry. Such an analogy certainly exists, as will hereafter be shown, but the theory that the Apprentice's degree was derived from and suggested by the ceremony of Lustration in the Mysteries is wholly untenable, because this ceremony was not peculiar to the Mysteries.

An ablution, lustration, or cleansing by water, as a religious rite was practiced among all the ancient nations. More especially was it observed among the Hebrews, Greeks, and Romans. With the Hebrews the lustration was a preliminary ceremony to every act of expiation or sin-offering. Hence the Jewish prophets continually refer to the ablution of the body with water as a symbol of the purification of the heart. Among the Greeks lustration was always connected with their sacrifices. It consisted in the sprinkling of water by means of an olive or a laurel branch. Among the Romans, the ceremony was more common than among the Greeks. It was used not only to expiate crime, but also to secure the blessing of the Gods. Thus, fields were lustrated before the corn was put into the ground; colonies when they were first established, and armies before they proceeded to battle. At the end of every fifth year, the whole people were thus purified by a general lustration. Everywhere the rite was connected with the performance of sacrifice and with the idea of a moral purification.

The next step in the ceremonies of the ancient Mysteries was called the *Initiation*. It was here that the dramatic allegory was performed and the myth or fictitious history on which the peculiar Mystery was founded was developed. The neophyte personated the supposed events of the life, the sufferings, and the death of the god or hero to whom the Mystery was dedicated, or he had them brought in vivid representation before him. These ceremonies constituted a symbolic instruction in the *initia*—the beginnings—of the religious system which it was the object of the Mysteries to teach.

The ceremonies of initiation were performed partly in the Lesser, but more especially and more fully in the Greater Mysteries, of which they were the first part, and where only the allegory of death was enacted. The Lesser Mysteries, which were introductory to the Greater, have been supposed by the theorists who maintain the connection between the Mysteries and Freemasonry to be analogous to the Fellow Craft's degree of the latter Institution.

There may be some ground for this comparison in a rather inexact way, for although the Lesser Mysteries were to some extent public, yet as they were, as Clemens of Alexandria[1] says, a certain groundwork of instruction and preparation for the things that were to follow, they might perhaps be considered as analogous to the Fellow Craft's degree.

---

[1] " Stromat.," v., p. 424.

The third and last of the progressive steps or grades in the Mysteries was *Perfection*. It was the ultimate object of the system. It was also called the autopsy, from a Greek word which signifies *seeing with one's own eyes*. It was the complete and finished communication to the neophyte of the great secret of the Mysteries; the secret for the preservation of which the system of initiation had been invented, and which, during the whole course of that initiation, had been symbolically shadowed forth.

The communication of this secret, which was in fact the explanation of the secret doctrine, for the inculcation of which the Mysteries in every country had been instituted, was made in the most sacred and private place of the temple or place of initiation.

As the *autopsy* or *Perfection* of the Mysteries concluded the whole system, the maintainers of the doctrine that Freemasonry finds its origin in the Mysteries have compared this last step in the ancient initiation to the Master's degree. But the analogy between the two as a consummation of the secret doctrine is less patent in the third degree, as it now exists, than it was before the disseverance from it of the Royal Arch, accepting, however, the Master's degree as it was constituted in the earlier part of the 18th century, the analogies between that and the last stage of the Mysteries are certainly very interesting, although not sufficient to prove the origin of the modern from the ancient systems. But of this more hereafter.

This view of the organization of the Pagan Mysteries would not be complete without some reference to the dramatized allegory which constituted so important a part of the ceremony of initiation, and in connection with which their relation to Freemasonry has been most earnestly urged.

It has been already said that the Mysteries were originally invented for the purpose of teaching two great religious truths, which were unknown to, or at least not recognized, in the popular faith. These were the unity of God and the immortality of the soul in a future life. The former, although illustrated at every point by expressed symbols, such, for instance, as the all-seeing eye, the eye of the universe, and the image of the Deity, was not allegorized, but taught as an abstract doctrine at the time of the autopsy or the close of the grade of *Perfection*. The other truth, the dogma of a future life, and of a resurrection from death to immortality, was communicated by an allegory which was dramatized in much the same way in each of the Mysteries, although, of course, in each nation the person and the events which made up the allegory were different. The interpretation was, however, always the same.

As Egypt was the first country of antiquity to receive the germs of civilization, it is there that the first Mysteries are supposed to have been invented.[1] And although the Eleusinian Mysteries, which were introduced into Greece long after the invention of the Osiriac in Egypt, were more popular among the ancients, yet the Egyptian initiation exhibits more purely and more expressively the symbolic idea which was to be developed in the interpretation of its allegory. I shall therefore select the Osiriac, which was the most important of the Egyptian Mysteries, as the exemplar from which an idea may be obtained of the character of all the other Mysteries of paganism.

All the writers of antiquity, such as Plutarch, Diodorus Siculus, and Herodotus, state that the Egyptian Mysteries of Osiris, Isis, and Horus were the model of all the other systems of initiation which were subsequently established among the different peoples of the Old World. Indeed, the ancients held that the Demeter of the Greeks was identical with the Isis of the Egyptians, and Dionysus with Osiris. Their adventures were certainly very similar.

The place of Osiris in Egyptian history is unknown to us. The fragments of Sanchoniathon speak of Isiris, the brother of Chna or Canaan ; in the lists of Manetho, he is made the fifth king under the dynasty of the demi-gods, being conjoined with Isis ; but as the four preceding kings are named as Hephœstus, Helios, Agathodomon and Kronos, the whole is evidently a mere mythological fable, and we have as far to seek as ever. Herodotus is not more satisfactory, for he says that Osiris and Isis were two great deities of the Egyptians. Banier, however, in his *Mythology* thinks that he was the same as Mizraim, the son of Cham, and grandson of Noah. Bishop Cumberland concurs in this and adds that Cham was the first king of Egypt, that Osiris was a title appropriated by him, signifying Prince, and that Isis was simply Ishah, his wife. Lastly, Diodorus Siculus says that he was Menes, the first King of Egypt. Some later writers have sought to identify Osiris and Isis with the

---

[1] The first and original Mysteries of which we have any account were those of Isis and Osiris in Egypt, from whence they were derived by the Greeks.—Warburton, " Divine Legation," I., p. 194. Diodorus says the same thing in the first book of his " History," I., xxxvii.

Iswara and Isi of India. There is certainly a great deal of etymological plausibility in this last conjecture.

The ubiquitous character of Osiris as a personality among the ancients is best shown in an epigram of Ausonius, wherein it is said that in Greece, at Eleusis, he was called Bacchus; the Egyptians thought that he was Osiris, the Mysians of Asia Minor named him Phanœus or Apollo; the Indians supposed that he was Dionysus; the sacred rites of the Romans called him Liber; and the Arabians, Adonis.[1]

But the only thing that is of any interest to us in this connection is that Osiris was the hero of the earliest of the Mysteries, and that his death and apotheosis—his change from a mortal king to an immortal God—symbolized the doctrine of a future life.

His historical character was that of a mild and beneficent sovereign, who had introduced the arts of civilization among his subjects, and had then traveled for three years for the purpose of extending them into other nations, leaving the government of his kingdom, during his absence, to his wife Isis. According to the legend, his brother Typhon had been a rival claimant for the throne, and his defeat had engendered a feeling of ill-will. During the absence of Osiris, he, therefore, formed a secret conspiracy with some of his adherents to usurp the throne.

On the return of Osiris from his travels he was invited by Typhon to a banquet, ostensibly given in his honor, at which all the conspirators were present. During the feast Typhon produced a chest, inlaid with gold, and promised to present it to that person of the company, whose body, upon trial, would be found most exactly to fit it. Osiris tried the experiment, but as soon as he had laid himself in the chest, Typhon closed and nailed down the lid.

The chest was then thrown into the river Nile, whence it floated into the sea, and, after being for some time tossed upon the waves, it was finally cast ashore at the town of Byblos, in Phœnicia, and left at the foot of a Tamarisk tree. Isis, the wife of Osiris, over-

---

[1] Ogygia me Bacchum vacat;
Osisin Egyptus putat;
Mysi Phanacem nominant;
Dionuson Indi existimant;
Romana sacra Liberum;
Arabica gens Adoneum.
      —Ausonius, Ep. 30.

whelmed with grief for the loss of her husband, commenced a search for the body, being accompanied by her son, Anubis, and his nurse, Nepthe.

After many adventures Isis arrived on the shores of Phœnicia and in the neighborhood of Byblos, where she at length discovered the body at the foot of the Tamarisk tree. She returned with it to Egypt. It was received by the people with great demonstrations of joy, and it was proclaimed that Osiris had risen from the dead and had become a god.

The sufferings of Osiris, his death, his resurrection, and his subsequent office as judge of the dead in a future state, constituted the fundamental principles of the Egyptian religion. They taught the secret doctrine of a future life, and initiation into the mysteries of Osiris was initiation into the rites of the religion of Egypt. These rites were conducted by the priests, and into them many sages from other countries, especially from Greece, such as Herodotus, Plutarch, and Pythagoras, were initiated.

In this way it is supposed that the principles and general form of the Mysteries were conveyed into other countries, although they everywhere varied in the details. The most important of the Mysteries besides the Egyptian were those of Mithras in Persia, of Atys or of the Cabiri in Thrace, of Adonis in Syria, and of Dionysus in Greece. They extended even beyond the then more civilized parts of the world into the northern regions of Europe, where were practiced the Scandinavian rites of the Norsemen and the Druidical Mysteries of Gaul and Britain, though these were probably derived more directly from a primitive Aryan source.

But wherever they existed we find in them a remarkable unity of design and a similarity of ceremonies from which we are compelled to deduce a common origin, while the purity of the doctrines which they taught evidently show that this common origin was not to be sought in the popular theology.

In all of the Mysteries the ceremonies of initiation were of a funereal character. They allegorized in a dramatic form the sufferings, the death, and the resurrection of some god or hero. There was a death, most generally by violence,[1] to symbolize, as certain

---

[1] Thus Clemens of Alexandria describes the legend or allegory of the Cabiri Mysteries as the sacred mystery of a brother slain by his brethren, " frater trucidatus a fratribus."

interpreters of the Mysteries have supposed, the strife of certain antagonistic powers in nature, such as life and death, virtue and vice, light and darkness, or summer and winter.

The person thus slain was represented in the allegorical drama by the candidate. After the death followed the disappearance of the body, called by the Greeks the *aphanism*, and the consequent search for it. This search for the body, in which all the initiates joined, constituted what Faber calls "the doleful part," and was succeeded by its discovery, which was known as the *heuresis*.[1] This was accompanied by the greatest demonstrations of joy. The candidate was afterward instructed in the *apporheta*, or secret dogmas of the Mysteries.

In all of the Pagan Mysteries this dramatic form of an allegory was preserved, and we may readily see in the groans and lamentations on the death of the god or hero and the disappearance of the body a symbol of the death of man, and in the subsequent rejoicings at his discovery and restoration, a symbol of the restoration of the spirit to eternal life.

In view of the purity of the lessons taught in the Mysteries and their inculcation of the elevated dogmas of the unity of God and the immortality of the soul, it is not surprising to read the encomiums passed upon them by the philosophers of antiquity.

The reader, if he has carefully considered the allegorical drama which was represented in the ancient Mysteries, and compared it with the drama which constitutes the principal portion of the initiation in Freemasonry, will be at no loss to account for the reasons which have led so many writers to attribute the origin of the Masonic system to these mystical associations of antiquity.

It has been a favorite theory with several German, French, and British scholars to trace the origin of Freemasonry to the Mysteries of Paganism, while others, repudiating the idea that the modern association should have sprung from them, still find analogies so remarkable between the two systems as to lead them to suppose that the Mysteries were an offshoot from the pure Freemasonry of the Patriarchs.

In my opinion there is not the slightest foundation in historical

---

[1] "Concerning Adonis, whom some call Osiris, there are two things remarkable: *aphanismos*, the death or loss of Adonis; and *heuresis*, the finding of him again."—Godevyn in "Moses and Aaron," lib. iv., c. 2.

evidence to support either theory, although I admit the existence of many analogies between the two systems, which can, however, be easily explained without admitting any connection in the way of origin and descent between them.

Of the theory that the Mysteries were an offshoot or imitation of the pure patriarchal Freemasonry, Hutchinson and Oliver are the most distinguished supporters.

While Hutchinson strongly contends for the direct derivation of Freemasonry from Adam, through the line of the patriarchs to Moses and Solomon, he does not deny that it borrowed much from the initiations and symbols of the Pagans.

Thus he unhesitatingly says, that "there is no doubt that our ceremonies and Mysteries were derived from the rites, ceremonies, and institutions of the ancients, and some of them from the re-motest ages."[1]

But lest the purity of the genuine patriarchal Masonry should be polluted by borrowing its ceremonies from such an impure source, he subsequently describes, in that indefinite manner which was the peculiarity of his style, the separation of a purer class from the debasement of the popular religion, wherein he evidently alludes to the Mysteries. Thus he says :

"In the corruption and ignorance of after ages, those hallowed places[2] were polluted with idolatry; the unenlightened mind mis-took the type for the original, and could not discern the light from darkness; the sacred groves and hills became the objects of enthu-siastic bigotry and superstition ; the devotees bowed down to the oaken log and the graven image as being divine. Some preserved themselves from the corruptions of the times, and we find those sages and select men to whom were committed, and who retained, the light of understanding and truth, unpolluted with the sins of the world, under the denomination of Magi among the Persians ; wise men, soothsayers, and astrologers among the Chaldeans ; philoso-phers among the Greeks and Romans ; Brahmins among the Ind-ians ; Druids and bards among the Britons ; and with the people of God, Solomon shone forth in the fullness of human wisdom."[3]

Dr. Oliver expresses almost the same views, but more explicitly.

---

[1] "Spirit of Masonry," lect. ii., p. 15.   [2] "The highest hills and lowest valleys."
[3] "Spirit of Masonry," lect. iv., p. 59.

He was, I think, the first to advance the theory that two systems of Masonry had come down the course of time, both derived from a common source, which he called the Pure and the Spurious Freemasonry of antiquity—the former descending without interruption from the Patriarchs, and especially from Noah, and which system was the progenitor of that which is now practiced, and the latter, being a schism, as it were, from the former, and impure and corrupted in its principles, and preserved in the Pagan Mysteries. He admits, however, that there were certain analogies between the two in their symbols and allegories. His own language on this subject, which is as follows, leaves no doubt of the nature of his views. In a note to his *History of Initiation*, an elaborate and learned work on certain of these Mysteries, he says:

"I have denominated the surreptitious initiations *earth-born*, in contra-distinction to the purity of Freemasonry, which was certainly derived from above; and to those who contend that Masonry is nothing more than a miserable relic of the idolatrous Mysteries (vide *Fab. Pag. Idol.*, vol. iii., p. 190), I would reply, in the words of an inspired apostle, 'Doth a fountain send forth at the same place sweet water and bitter? Can the fig tree bear olive berries or a vine figs? So can no fountain both yield salt water and fresh. The wisdom that is from above is first pure, then peaceable, full of mercy and good fruits' (James iii. 11, 12, 17). I wish to be distinct and intelligible on this point, as some misapprehensions are afloat respecting the immediate object of my former volume of Signs and Symbols; and I have been told that the arguments there used afford an indirect sanction to the opinion that Masonry is derived from the Mysteries. In answer to this charge, if it requires one, I only need reply to the general tenor of that volume, and to declare explicitly my firm opinion, founded on intense study and abstruse research, that the science which we now denominate Speculative Masonry, was coeval, at least, with the creation of our globe, and the far-famed Mysteries of idolatry were a subsequent institution founded on similar principles, with the design of conveying unity and permanence to the false worship, which it otherwise could never have acquired."[1]

I do not know of any other prominent Masonic writer who en-

---

[1] "History of Initiation," lect. i., p. 13, notes.

tertains the theory of the common origin but diverse descent of the Mysteries and Freemasonry, although there are many who, subscribing with implicit faith to the teachings of Dr. Oliver as a Masonic historian, necessarily give their assent to his opinion on this subject.

There is another class of Masonic scholars who have advanced the theory that the Speculative Freemasonry of the present day is derived directly from and is a legitimate successor of the Mysteries of antiquity. They found this theory on the very many and striking analogies that are to be found in the organization, the design, and the symbols of the two systems, and which they claim can only be explained on the theory that the one is an offshoot from the other.

The Abbé Robin was, perhaps, the first writer who advanced this idea in a distinct form. In a work on the Ancient and Modern Initiations,[1] published in 1780, he traces the origin of the ancient systems of initiation to that early period when wicked men, urged by the terror of guilt, sought among the virtuous for intercessors with the Deity. The latter, he says, retired into solitary places to avoid the contagion of the growing corruption, and devoted themselves to a life of contemplation and to the cultivation of the arts and sciences. In order to associate with them in their labors and functions only such as had sufficient merit and capacity, they appointed strict courses of trial and examination. This, he thinks, must have been the source of the initiations which distinguished the celebrated Mysteries of antiquity. The Magi of Chaldea, the Brahmins and Gymnosophists of India, the Priests of Egypt, and the Druids of Gaul and Britain thus lived in sequestered places and obtained great reputation by their discoveries in astronomy, chemistry, and mechanics, by the purity of their morals, and by their knowledge of the science of legislation.

It was in these schools, says the abbé, that the first sages and legislators of antiquity were formed, where the doctrines taught were the unity of God and the immortality of the soul, and it was from these Mysteries that the exuberant fancy of the Greeks drew much of their mythology. From these ancient initiations he deduces the orders of Chivalry which sprang into existence in the Middle Ages,

---

[1] " Recherches sur les Initiations Anciennes et Modernes."

and certain branches of these, he thinks, produced the institution of Freemasonry.

The theory of the Abbé Robin therefore traces the institution of Masonry to the ancient Mysteries, but in an indirect way, through the orders of Chivalry. He might therefore more correctly be classed among those who maintain the doctrine of the Templar origin of Freemasonry.

But it is Alexander Lenoir, the French archæologist, who has attempted in the most explicit and comprehensive manner to establish the doctrine of the direct descent of Freemasonry from the ancient Mysteries, and especially from the Egyptian. In the year 1814 he published an elaborate work on this subject.[1] In this he begins by affirming that we cannot expect to find in the Egyptian and Greek initiations those modes of recognition which are used by the Freemasons of the present day, because these methods, which are only conventional and had been orally communicated under the obligation of secrecy, can not be known to us, for they could not have been transmitted through the lapse of ages. Omitting, therefore, all reference to these as matters of no real importance, he confines himself to a comparison of the Masonic with the ancient rites of initiation. In this view he comes to the conclusion that Freemasonry in all the points that it essentially comprehends is in direct relation with the Mysteries of the ancient world, and that hence, abstracting certain particular usages practiced by the modern Freemasons, it is evident that Freemasonry in no respect differs from the ancient initiations of the Egyptians and the Greeks.

This theory has been embraced by nearly all the French Masonic writers except Rebold, who traces Masonry to the Roman Colleges of Artificers.

Unfortunately for the general acceptance of this theory, M. Lenoir has in the first place drawn his comparisons from the system of ceremonies of initiation which are practiced in the lodges of France, and especially from the "proofs and trials" of the Entered Apprentice's degree. But the tedious ceremonies and painful trials of the candidate as they are practiced in the French Rite constitute no part of the original English Masonry whence the French Masonry derives its existence, and were adopted as a pure innovation

---

[1] "La Franche–Maçonnerie rendue à sa veritable origine," etc. Par M. Alexander Lenoir. Paris, 1814.

long after the establishment of the Order in France by the Grand Lodge of England.

And again, the Egyptian initiations, with which they have been compared by Lenoir, were not those which were actually practiced by the priests of Egypt, or at least we have no authentic proof of that fact, but were most probably suggested by the imaginative details given by the Abbé Terrasson in his romance entitled *Sethas*, in which he pretends to portray the initiation of an Egyptian prince.

The truth is that Lenoir and those writers who have followed him and adopted his theory have not instituted a comparison between the original ceremonies of Masonic initiation and those of the ancient Mysteries, but merely a comparison between a recent system of ceremonies, certainly not earlier than the middle of the last century, and a fictitious system indebted for its birth to the inventive genius of a French abbé, and first promulgated in a work published by him in the year 1731.

As well might Mr. Turner or any other writer on Anglo-Saxon history have cited, as authentic materials for his description of the customs of the Anglo-Saxon, the romantic incidents given by Sir Walter Scott in his novel of *Ivanhoe*.

Hence all the references of the *voyages* of an Entered Apprentice in a French Lodge to the similar voyages of an Aspirant in the Mysteries of Osiris or Isis become nothing more than "the baseless fabric of a vision," which must fade and dissolve like an "insubstantial pageant" when submitted to the crucial test of authentic historical investigation.[1]

The Rev. Mr. King, the author of a very interesting treatise on the Gnostics,[2] has advanced a theory much more plausible than either of those to which I have adverted. He maintains that some of the Pagan Mysteries, especially those of Mithras, which had been instituted in Persia, extended beyond the period of the advent of Christianity, and that their doctrines and usages were adopted by the secret societies which existed at an early period in Europe and

---

[1] "Many of the explanations given as to the ceremonies used in Egyptian initiations are modern inventions, abounding in absurdities and purely imaginary."—Tho. Pryer, "On the study of Masonic Antiquities," in *Freemasons' Quarterly Review*, 1847, p. 262. Wilkinson was of the same opinion. See "Manners and Customs of the Ancient Egyptians," vol. i.

[2] "The Gnostics and their Remains, Ancient and Mediæval." By C. W. King, M.A., London, 1865, p. 47 *et seq.*

which finally assumed the form of Freemasonry. I have said that this theory is a plausible one. It is so because its salient points are sustained by historical evidence.

It is, for instance, a fact that some of the Mysteries of Paganism were practiced in Europe long after the commencement of the Christian era. They afforded a constant topic of denunciation to the fathers of the church, who feared and attacked what they supposed to be their idolatrous tendencies. It was not until the middle of the 5th century that they were proscribed by an edict of the Emperor Theodosius. But an edict of proscription is not necessarily nor always followed by an immediate abolition of the thing proscribed.

The public celebration of the Mysteries must, of course, have ceased at once when such celebration had been declared unlawful. But a private and secret observance of them may have continued, and probably did continue, for an indefinite time, perhaps even to as late a period as the end of the 5th or the beginning of the 6th century.

Mosheim tells us that in the 4th century, notwithstanding the zeal and severity of the Christian emperors, there still remained in several places, and especially in the remoter provinces, temples and religious rites consecrated to the Pagan deities; that rites instituted in honor of them were, in the 5th century, celebrated with the utmost freedom and impunity in the western empire; and that even in the 6th century remains of the Pagan worship were to be found among the learned and the officers of state.[1]

During all this time it is known that secret associations, such as the Roman Colleges of Artificers, existed in Europe, and that from them ultimately sprang up the organizations of Builders, which, with Como in Lombardy as their center, spread over Europe in the Middle Ages, and whose members, under the recognized name of *Traveling Freemasons*, were the founders of Gothic architecture.

There is no forced or unnatural succession from them to the Guilds of Operative Masons, who undoubtedly gave rise, about the end of the 17th or the beginning of the 18th century, to the Speculative Order or the Free and Accepted Masons, which is the organization that exists at the present day.

---

[1] Mosheim, "Ecclesiast. History," Maelaine's Translation, vol. i., pp. 251, 332, 401.

There is, therefore, nothing absolutely untenable in the theory that the Mithraic Mysteries which prevailed in Europe until the 5th or perhaps the 6th century may have impressed some influence on the ritual, form, and character of the association of early Builders, and that this influence may have extended to the Traveling Free-masons, the Operative Guilds, and finally to the Free and Accepted Masons, since it can not be proved that there was not an uninter-rupted chain of succession between these various organizations.

The theory of Mr. King can not, therefore, be summarily re-jected. It may not be altogether true, but it has so many elements of truth about it that it claims our serious consideration.

But, after all, we may find a sufficient explanation of the analogy which undoubtedly exists between the rites of the ancient Mysteries and those of the modern Freemasons in the natural tendency of the human mind to develop its ideas in the same way when these ideas are suggested by the same or similar circumstances. The fact that both institutions have taught the same lessons by the same method of instruction may be attributed not to a direct and uninterrupted succession of organizations, each one a link of a long chain leading consequentially to another, but rather to a natural and usual coin-cidence of human thought.

The believers in the lineal and direct descent of Freemasonry from the ancient Mysteries have of course discovered, or thought that they had discovered, the most striking and wonderful analogies between the internal organizations of the two institutions. Hence the most credulous of these theorists have not hesitated to compare the *Hierophant*, or the Explainer of the sacred rites in the Mys-teries, with the *Worshipful Master* in a Masonic Lodge, nor to style the *Dadouchos*, or Torch-Bearer, and the *Hieroceryx*, or Herald of the Mysteries, *Wardens*, nor to assign to the *Epibomos*, or Altar-Server, the title and duties of a *Deacon*.

That there are analogies, and that many of them are very curi-ous, can not be denied, but I shall attempt, before leaving this sub-ject, to explain the reason of their existence in a more rational way than by tracing the modern as a succession from the ancient system.

The analogies existing between the ancient Mysteries and Free-masonry, upon which the theory of the descent of the one from the other has been based, consist in the facts that both were secret so-cieties, that both taught the same doctrine of a future life, and that both made use of symbols and allegories and a dramatic form of instruction. But these analogies do not necessarily support the doctrine of descent, but may be otherwise satisfactorily explained.

Whether the belief in a personal immortality was communicated to the first man by a divine revelation, and subsequently lost as the intellectual state of future generations declined into a degraded state of religious conceptions; or whether the prehistoric man, created but little superior to the wild beast with whom he daily contended for dominion with insufficient weapons, was at first without any conception of his future, until it had by chance dawned upon some more elevated intellect and by him been communicated to his fellows as a consoling doctrine, afterward to be lost, and then in the course of time to be again recovered, but not to be universally accepted by grosser minds, are questions into which we need not enter here.

It is sufficient to know that there has been no period in the world's history, however dark, in which some rays of this doctrine have not been thrown upon the general gloom. The belief in a future life and an immortal destiny has always been so inseparably connected with elevated notions of God that the deep and reverent thinkers in all ages have necessarily subscribed to its truth. It has inspired the verses of poets and tempered and directed the discussions of philosophers.

As both the Mysteries of the ancients and the Freemasonry of the moderns were religious institutions, the conceptions of the true nature of God which they taught to their disciples must of course have involved the ideas of a future life, for the one doctrine is a necessary consequence of the other. To seek, therefore, in this analogy the proof of a descent of the modern from the ancient institution is to advance an utterly fallacious argument.

As to the secret character of the two institutions, the argument is equally untenable. Under the benighted rule of Pagan idolatry the doctrine of a future life was not the popular belief. Yet there were also some who aspired to a higher thought—philosophers like Socrates and Plato, who nourished with earnest longing the hope of immortality. Now, it was by such men that the Mysteries were originally organized, and it was for instruction in such a doctrine that they were instituted. But opposed as this doctrine was to the general current of popular thought, it became, necessarily and defensively, esoteric and exclusive. And hence we derive the reason for the secret character of the Mysteries. "They were kept secret," says Warburton, "from a necessity of teaching the initiated some things improper to be communicated to all."[1] The learned bishop assigns another reason, which he sustains with the authority of ancient writers, for this secrecy. "Nothing," he says, "excites our curiosity like that which retires from our observation, and seems to forbid our search."[2]

Synesius, who lived in the 4th century, before the Mysteries were wholly abolished, says that they owed the veneration in which they were held to a popular ignorance of their nature.[3]

And Clemens of Alexandria, referring to the secrecy of the Mysteries, accounts for it, among other reasons, because the truth seen through a veil appears greater and more venerable.[4]

Freemasonry also teaches the doctrine of a future life. But al. though there was no necessity, as in the Pagan Mysteries, to conceal this doctrine from the populace; yet there is, for the reasons that have just been assigned, a proneness in the human heart, which has always existed, to clothe the most sacred subjects with the veil of mystery. It was this spirit that caused Jesus to speak to the Jewish multitudes in parables whose meaning his disciples, like initiates, were to comprehend, but which would be unintelligible to the people, so that "seeing they might not see, and hearing they might not understand."

The Mysteries and Freemasonry were both secret societies, not necessarily because the one was the legitimate successor of the other, but because both were human institutions and because both partook of the same human tendency to conceal what was sacred from the unhallowed eyes and ears of the profane. In this way may be explained the analogy between the two institutions which arises from their secret character and their esoteric method of instruction.

The symbolic form of imparting the doctrines is another analogy which may be readily explained. For when once the esoteric or secret system was determined on, or involuntarily adopted by the force of those tendencies to which I have referred, it was but natural that the secret instruction should be communicated by a method of symbolism, because in all ages symbols have been the cipher by which

---

[1] "Div. Legat.," I., p. 201. [2] Ibid., I., p. 200. [3] "De Providentia." [4] "Stromat.," v., 419.

secret associations of every character have restricted the knowledge which they imparted to their initiates only.

Again, in the Mysteries, the essential doctrine of a resurrection from death to eternal life was always taught in a dramatic form. There was a drama in which the aspirant or candidate for initiation represented, or there was visibly pictured to him, the death by violence and then the resuscitation or apotheosis—the resurrection to life and immortality of some god or hero, in whose honor the peculiar mystery was founded. Hence in all the Mysteries there were the *thanatos*, the death or slaying of the victim; the *aphanism*, the concealment or burial of the body by the slayers; and the *heuresis*, the finding of the body by the initiates. This drama, from the character of the plot, began with mourning and ended with joy.

The traditional " *heureka*," sometimes attributed to Pythagoras when he discovered the forty-seventh problem, and sometimes to Archimedes when he accidentally learned the principle of specific gravity, was nightly repeated to the initiates when, at the termination of the drama of the Mysteries, they had found the hidden body of the Master.

Now, the recognized fact that this mode of inculcating a religious or a philosophical idea by a dramatic representation was constantly practiced in the ancient world, for the purpose of more permanently impressing the conception, would naturally lead to its adoption by all associations where the same lesson was to be taught as that which was the subject of the Mysteries. The tendency to dramatize an allegory is universal, because the method of dramatization is the most expedient and has been proved to be the most successful. The drama of the third or Master's degree of Freemasonry is, as respects the subject and the development of the plot and the conduct of the scenes, the same as the drama of the ancient Mysteries. There is the same *thanatos*, or death; the same *aphanism*, or concealment of the body, and the same *heuresis*, or discovery of it. The drama of the Master's degree begins in sorrow and ends in joy. Everything is so similar that we at once recognize an analogy between Freemasonry and the ancient Mysteries; but it has already been explained that this analogy is the result of natural causes, and by no means infers a descent of the modern from the ancient institution.

Another analogy between the Mysteries and Freemasonry is

the division of both into steps, classes, or degrees—call them what you may—which is to be found in both. The arrangement of the Masonic system into three degrees certainly bears a resemblance to the distribution of the Mysteries into the three steps of Preparation, Initiation, and Perfection which have been heretofore described.

But this analogy, remarkable as it may at first view appear, is really an accidental one, which in no way shows an historical connection between the two institutions.

In every system of instruction, whether open or secret, there must be a gradual and not an immediate attainment of that which is intended to be imparted. The ancient adage that "no one suddenly becomes wicked" might with equal truth be read that "no one suddenly becomes learned." There must be a series of gradual approaches to the ultimate point in every pursuit of knowledge, like the advancing parallels of a besieging army in its efforts to attain possession of a beleaguered city. Hence the ladder, with its various steps, has from the earliest times been accepted as a symbol of moral or intellectual progress from an inferior to a superior sphere.

In this progress from the simplest to the most profound arena of initiation—from the inception to the full accomplishment of the instruction whereby the mind was to be gradually purged of many errors, by preparatory steps, before it could bear the full blaze of truth—both the Mysteries and Freemasonry have obeyed a common law of intellectual growth, independently of any connection of the one with the other institution.

The fact that there existed in both institutions secret modes of recognition presents another analogy. It is known that in the Mysteries, as in Freemasonry, there was a solemn obligation of secrecy, with penalties for its violation, which referred to certain methods of recognition known only to the initiates. But this may safely be attributed to the fact that such peculiarities are and always will be the necessary adjuncts of any secret organization, whether religious, social, or political. In every secret society isolated from the rest of mankind, we must find, as a natural outgrowth of its secrecy and as a necessary means of defense and isolation, an obligation of secrecy and methods of recognition. On such analogies it is, therefore, scarcely worth while to dilate.

Thus, then, I have traced the analogies between the ancient

Mysteries and modern Freemasonry in the following points of re-semblance.

1. The *Preparation*, which in the Mysteries was called the *Lustration*. It was the first step in the Mysteries, and is the Entered Apprentice's degree in Freemasonry. In both systems the candidate was purified for the reception of truth by washing. In one it was a physical ablution; in the other a moral cleansing; but in both the symbolic idea was the same.

2. The *Initiation*, which in the ancient system was partly in the Lesser Mysteries, but more especially in the Greater. In Masonry it is partly in the Fellow Craft's, but more especially in the Master's degree.

3. The *Perfection*, which in the Mysteries was the communication to the aspirant of the true dogma—the great secret symbolized by the *Initiation*. In Freemasonry it is the same. The dogma communicated in both is, in fact, identical. This *Perfection* came in the Mysteries at the end of the Greater Mysteries. In Masonry it is communicated at the close of the Master's degree. In the Mysteries the communication was made in the *saceeum* or holiest place. In Masonry it is made in the Master's Lodge, which is said to represent the holy of holies of the Temple.

4. The secret character of both institutions.

5. The use of symbols.

6. The dramatic form of the initiation.

7. The division of both systems into degrees or steps.

8. And the adoption by both of secret methods of recognition.

These analogies, it must be admitted, are very striking, and, if considered merely as coincidences, must be acknowledged to be very singular.

It is not, therefore, surprising that scholars have found it difficult to resolve the following problem:

Is modern Freemasonry a lineal and uninterrupted successor of the ancient Mysteries, the succession being transmitted through the Mithraic initiations which existed in the 5th and 6th centuries; or is the fact of the analogies between the two systems to be attributed to the coincidence of a natural process of human thought, common to all minds and showing its development in symbolic forms?

For myself, I can only arrive at what I think is a logical con clusion; that if both the Mysteries and Freemasonry have taught the same lessons by the same method of instruction, this has arisen not from a succession of organizations, each one a link of a long chain of historical sequences leading directly to another, until Hiram is simply substituted for Osiris, but rather from those usual and natural coincidences of human thought which are to be found in every age and among all peoples.

It is, however, hardly to be denied that the founders of the Speculative system of Masonry, in forming their ritual, especially of the third degree, derived many suggestions as to the form and character of their funereal legend from the rites of the ancient initiations.

But how long after Freemasonry had an organized existence this funereal legend was devised, is a question that must hereafter be entitled to mature consideration.

CHAPTER XXVII

DRUIDISM AND FREEMASONRY

R. PRESTON, in commencing his history of Masonry in England, asserts that there are convincing proofs that the science of Masonry was not unknown to the early Britons even before the time of the invasion of the Romans. Hence he suggests the probability that the Druids retained among them many usages similar to those of Masons; but he candidly admits that this is a mere conjecture.[1]

Hutchinson thinks it probable that many of the rites and institutions of the Druids were retained in forming the ceremonies of the Masonic society.[2]

Paine, who knew, by the way, as little of Masonry as he did of the religion of the Druids, dogmatically asserts that " Masonry is the remains of the religion of the ancient Druids, who, like the Magi of Persia and the priests of Heliopolis in Egypt, were priests of the sun."[3]

The learned Faber, a much more competent authority than Paine, expresses the opinion that the Druidical Bards "are probably the real founders of English Freemasonry."[4]

Godfrey Higgins, whose inventive genius, fertile imagination, and excessive credulity render his great work, the *Anacalypsis*, altogether unreliable, says that he has "no doubt that the Masons were Druids, Culidei, or Chaldei, and Casideans."[5]

Dr. Oliver, it is true, denies that the Masons of the present day were derived from the Druids. He thinks that the latter were a branch of what he calls the Spurious Freemasonry, which was a secession from the Pure Freemasonry of the Patriarchs. But he finds many analogies in the rites and symbols of the two institu-

---

[1] " Illustrations of Masonry," B. IV., sec. i., p. 121, Oliver's ed.
[2] " Spirit of Masonry," lect. iii., p. 41. [3] " Essay on Freemasonry," p. 6.
[4] " Pagan Idolatry." [5] "Anacalypsis," vol. i., p. 718.

tions which indicate their common origin from a primitive system, namely, the ancient Mysteries of the Pagans.

The theory of those who find a connection either in analogy or by succession between the Druids and the Freemasons accounts for this connection by supposing that the Druids derived their system either from Pythagoras or from the ancient Mysteries through the Phœnicians, who visited Britain at an early period for commercial purposes.

But before we can profitably discuss the relations of Druidism to Freemasonry, or be prepared to determine whether there were any relations whatever between the two, it will be necessary to give a brief sketch of the history and character of the former. This is a topic which, irrespective of any Masonic reference, is not devoid of interest.

Of all the institutions of antiquity, there is none with which we are less acquainted than that of the Druidism of Britain and Gaul. The investigations of recent archæologists have tended to cast much doubt on the speculations of the antiquaries of the 17th and 18th centuries. Stukely, for instance, one of the most learned of those who have sought to establish out of the stone monuments of England a connected history of Druidism, has been said by Ferguson, in his work on *Rude Stone Monuments*, to have been indebted more to a prolific imagination than to authentic facts for the theory which he has sought to establish.

The skepticism of Ferguson is, however, not less objectionable in a critical inquiry than the credulity of Stukely. There is evidently a middle way between them.

Ferguson can not deny the existence of Druids in Gaul and Britain, since the fact is stated by Cæsar. He supposes that there were two distinct races in the island; the original inhabitants, who were of Turanian origin, and, being more uncivilized, were driven by the other race, who were Celts, into the fastnesses of the Welsh hills long before the Roman invasion. Among the former he thinks that the religion of Druidism, consisting of tree and serpent worship, may have been practiced. And he accounts for the error of the classical writers in describing the priests of the latter race as Druids by attributing it to the confounding of the two races by the "uncritical Romans."[1]

---

[1] "Tree and Serpent Worship," p. 29.

Very recently a bold and very skeptical theory has been advanced by Dr. Ignaz Goldziher, in his work on *Mythology Among the Hebrews*,[1] which aims at a total annihilation of Druidism as a system of secret initiation among the ancient Britons (whose Druidism was only a national religion), and attributes its invention to the modern Welsh, who created it for the purpose of elevating and strengthening their own nationality in their rivalry with the English.   He says:

" The Cymri of Wales, becoming alive to the opposition in nationality between themselves and the English, felt the need of finding a justification of this opposition in the oldest prehistoric times. It was then first suggested to them that they were descendants of the ancient, renowned Celtic nation ; and to keep alive this Celtic national pride they introduced an institution of New Druids, a sort of secret society like the Freemasons.   The New Druids, like the old ones, taught a sort of national religion, which, however, the people having long become Christian and preserved no independent national traditions, they had mostly to invent themselves.   Thus arose the so-called Celtic mythology of the god Hu and the goddess Ceridolu (Ceridwen), etc.—mere poetical fictions which never lived in popular belief."

The questions involved in this difference of opinion are as yet not critically decided, and I shall therefore content myself with giving the views of the history and religion of the Druids as they have been generally received and believed, without confusing the subject with the contending speculations which have been fostered by the credulity or the imagination of one side and impugned by the skepticism of the other.

The Druids, which word signifies magicians,[2] were the priests of the religion of the ancient Britons, among whom they exercised almost unlimited influence and authority.   They presided over and directed the education of the youths ; they decided without appeal all judicial controversies; they were exempted from all taxes and legal impositions ; and whoever refused to submit to their decisions on any question was subjected to excommunication, by which he was forbidden access to the altars or the performance of religious

---

[1] Ably translated from the German by Mr. Russell Martineau, of the British Museum, with valuable additions.   For the passage quoted, see p. 252.

[2] In Anglo-Saxon *dry* is a magician ; and *drycroft*, magic.

rites, and was debarred from all intercourse with his relatives, his friends, or his countrymen. Hence no superstition was ever more terrible than that of the priest-ridden Britons.

The Druids were under the chief authority of an Archdruid, which office was for life, but originally elective. They were divided into three orders, the highest being the *Druids*, below which were the *Prophets* and the *Vates* or *Bards*. They held an annual assembly, at which litigated questions were decided and new laws were made or old ones abrogated. They held also four quarterly meetings, on the days of the equinoxes and the solstices.

They permitted none of their doctrines or ceremonies to be committed to common writing, but used a cipher for their concealment. This, Cæsar says, consisted of the letters of the Greek alphabet; a statement by no means probable, since it would infer a knowledge by them of the Greek language, of which we have no evidence.

The opinion of Toland is more plausible—that the characters used were those of the Irish *Ogum* alphabet. Sir James Ware, who wrote in Latin, about the middle of the 17th century, a work on the *Antiquities of Ireland*, says that "the ancient Irish, besides the vulgar characters, used also various occult or artificial forms of writing, called *Ogum*, in which they wrote their secrets;" and he adds that he himself was in possession of an ancient book or parchment filled with these characters.[1]

Their places of worship were, according to the contemporaneous authority of Cæsar and Tacitus, in sacred groves. Stukely and other antiquaries of his school suppose that the megalithic monuments found in Britain, such as at Stonehenge and Avebury, were Druidical temples, but Ferguson denies this, and asserts that "there is no passage in any classical author which connects the Druids either directly or indirectly with any stone temples or stones of any sort."[2] The question remains unadjudicated, but the position taken by Ferguson seems to be supported by better archæological evidence.

Their worship, like that of the ancient Mysteries, was accompanied by a secret initiation. Their doctrines were communicated only to the initiated, who were strictly forbidden to expose them to the profane.

What were the precise forms of this initiation it is impossible to

---

[1] "Antiq. Hibern.," cap. 2. [2] "Rude Stone Monuments," p. 20.

say. The Druids themselves, wedded to their oral system of instruction, have left no records. But Dr. Oliver, depending on inferences that he has drawn from the Welsh triads, from the poem of the ancient bard Taleisin, and some other Cambrian authorities, aided by the inventive genius of his own imagination, has afforded us a very minute, if not altogether accurate, detail of these initiatory ceremonies. The account is entirely too long for reproduction, but a condensed view of it will not be uninteresting.[1]

Previous to admission to the first degree, or that of the *Vates*, the candidate was submitted to a careful preparation, which in especial cases extended to the long period of twenty years.

The ceremony of initiation began by placing the candidate in the *pastos*, chest or coffin, in which he remained enclosed for three days, to represent death, and was liberated or restored to life on the third day.[2]

The sanctuary being now prepared for the business of initiation, the Druids are duly arranged, being appropriately clothed and crowned with ivy. The candidate, representing a blind man, is then introduced while a hymn to the Sun is being chanted. He is placed under the care of an officer whose duty it is to receive him in the land of rest, and he is directed to kindle the fire under the cauldron of Ceridwen, the Druidical goddess. A pageant is then formed, and the candidate makes a circumambulation of nine times around the sanctuary, in circles from east to west by the south. The procession is first slow and amid a death-like silence; at length the pace is increased into a rapid and furious motion, accompanied with the tumultuous clang of musical instruments and the screams of harsh and dissonant voices reciting in verse the praises of those heroes who were brave in war, courteous in peace, and patrons of religion.[3]

This sacred ceremony was followed by the administration of an oath of secrecy, violation of which could be expiated only by death.

Then succeeded a series of ceremonies in which, by means of masks, the candidate was made to assume the character of various animals, such as the dog, the deer, the mare, the cock, etc.[4]

This, according to Oliver, concluded the first part of the cere-

---

[1] " History of Initiation," lect. viii., p. 199 *et seq.*

[2] Ibid., p. 201. That this ceremony represented a death and resurrection is altogether conjectural.   [3] Ibid., p. 204.   [4] Ibid., p. 205.

mony of initiation. The second part began with striking the candidate a violent blow on the head with an oar, and a pitchy darkness immediately ensued, which was soon changed into a blaze of light which illuminated the whole area of the shrine.

This sudden transition from darkness to light was intended to shadow forth the same transition which Noah experienced on emerging from the gloom of the ark to the brightness of the renovated world.[1]

Thus it is contended that the Druids were Arkite worshippers—a concession by Oliver to the theories of Faber and Bryant.

The light was then withdrawn and the candidate was again involved in chaotic darkness The most dismal howlings, shrieks, and lamentations salute his astonished ear. Thus the figurative death of Noah, typified by his confinement in the ark, was commemorated with every external mark of sorrow. Alarmed at the discordant noises, the candidate naturally sought to escape, but this was rendered impossible, for wherever he turned he was opposed by dogs who pursued him. At length the gigantic goddess Ceridwen seized him and bore him by main force to the mythological sea which represented the flood of waters over which Noah floated.

Here he is supposed to have remained for a year in the character of Arawn, or Noah.[2] The same appalling sounds continued, until at length, having emerged from the stream, the darkness was removed and the candidate found himself surrounded by the most brilliant coruscations of light. This change produced in the attendants corresponding emotions, which were expressed by shouts and loud pæans that testified their rejoicings at the resuscitation of their god.[3]

The aspirant was then presented to the Archdruid, who explained to him the design of the mysteries and imparted some portion of the secret knowledge of Druidism, and recommended to him the practice of fortitude, which was considered as one of the leading traits of perfection.

With the performance of these painful ceremonies, the first degree of initiation into the Druidical Mysteries was concluded.

In the second degree, where the trials appear, from Oliver's

---

[1] " History of Initiation," p. 208.

[2] This detention of a year in the waters of the deluge was, I presume, like the fourteen days of interment in the Master Mason's degree, which period passes in the space of a few minutes—only a symbolic idea.   [3] " History of Initiation," p. 211.

description, to have been of a less severe character, the candidate underwent lustration, or a typical ablution, which was followed by his enlightenment. He was now instructed in the morality of the order; taught that souls are immortal and must live in a future state; solemnly enjoined to the performance of divine worship and the practice of virtue; and was invested with some of the badges of Druidism. Among these was the crystal, the unequivocal test of his initiation. This crystal, or talisman against danger, was manufactured exclusively by the Druids, and its color varied in the three degrees. In the first it was green, in the second blue, and in the third white. The one presented to the aspirant was a combination of these colors.[1]

Beyond the second degree very few advanced. The third was conferred only on persons of rank and consequence, and in it the aspirant passed through still more arduous ceremonies of purification.

The candidate was committed to secluded solitude for a period of nine months, which time was devoted to reflection and to the study of the sciences, so that he might be prepared more fully to understand the sacred truths in which he was about to be instructed. He was again submitted to a symbolic death and regeneration, by ceremonies different from those of the first degree. He was then supposed to represent a new-born infant, and, being placed in a coracle or boat, was committed to the mercy of the waters. The candidate, says Oliver, was actually set adrift in the open sea, and was obliged to depend on his own address and presence of mind to reach the opposite shore in safety.[2]

This was done at night, and this nocturnal expedition, which sometimes cost the candidate his life, was the closing act of his initiation. Should he refuse to undertake it, he was contemptuously rejected and pronounced unworthy of a participation in the honors to which he aspired and for which he was forever afterward ineligible. But if he courageously entered on the voyage and landed safely, he was triumphantly received by the Archdruid and his companions. He was recognized as a Druid, and became eligible for any ecclesiastical, civil, or military dignity. "The whole circle of human science was open to his investigation; the knowledge of divine things was communicated without reserve; he was now en-

---

[1] "History of Initiation," p. 212. [2] Ibid., p. 216.

abled to perform the mysterious rites of worship, and had his under-standing enriched with an elaborate system of morality."[1]

But little is known of the religion of the Druids, on which these ceremonies are supposed to be founded, and concerning that little the opinions of the learned greatly differ. "Among those institutions," says Toland, "which are thought to be irrecoverably lost, one is that of the Druids; of which the learned have hitherto known nothing but by some fragments concerning them out of the Greek and Roman authors."[2] Hence the views relating to their true worship have been almost as various as the writers who have discussed them.

Cæsar, who derived his knowledge of the Druids, imperfect as it was, from the contemporary priests of Gaul, says that they worshipped as their chief god Mercury, whom they considered as the inventor of all the arts, and after him Apollo, Mars, Jupiter, and Minerva.[3] But the Romans had a habit of applying to all the gods or idols of foreign nations the names and qualities of the deities of their own mythology. Hence his statement will scarcely amount to more than that the Druids worshipped a variety of gods.

Yet Davies, who, notwithstanding his national prejudices and prepossessions, is, from his learning, an authority not to be contemned, concurs in the view of Cæsar so far as to say that "it is an historical fact, that the mythology and the rites of the Druids were the same, in substance, with those of the Greeks and Romans and of other nations which came under their observation."[4]

Dionysius the Geographer, another writer of the Augustan age, says that the rites of Bacchus were celebrated in Britain,[5] and Strabo, on the authority of Artemidorus, who wrote a century before Christ, asserts that in an island close to Britain (probably the isle of Mona, where the Druids held their principal seat) Ceres and Proserpine were venerated with rites similar to those of Samothracia.[6]

Bryant, who traced all the ancient religions, principally on the basis of etymology, to traditions of the deluge and the worship of

---

[1] Oliver, "History of Initiation," p. 217.
[2] "History of the Druids," in miscellaneous works, vol. i., p. 6.
[3] "De Bello Gallico." [4] "Mythology and Rites of the British Druids," p. 89.
[5] "Perieget," v., 565. [6] Letter IV.

the patriarch Noah, conceived, of course, that Druidism was but a part of this universal cult.[1]

Faber, who followed in the footsteps of his learned predecessor, adopted the same hypothesis, and held the doctrine that the Druids were addicted to what he denominated Arkite worship, or the worship of Noah, and that all their religious rites referred to the deluge, death and immortality being typified by the confinement of the patriarch in the ark and his subsequent emergence from it into a new and renovated world, the symbol of the future life.[2]

It will be evident from the description already given of the Druidical initiations as portrayed by Dr. Oliver, that he concurred to a great extent in the views of Bryant and Faber.

Stukely, one of the most learned of English antiquarians, believed that the Druids were addicted to tree and serpent worship, and he adduces as evidence of the truth of this theory the megalithic monuments of Stonehenge and Avebury, in the arrangement of whose stones he thought that he had traced a serpentine form.

On the contrary, Mr. Ferguson[3] scoffs, in language not always temperate, at the views of Stukely, and not only denies the serpentine form of the stone remains in England, as described by that antiquary, but repudiates the hypothesis that the Druids ever erected or had any connection with stone temples or monuments in any part of the world. But as Ferguson adduces nothing but negative arguments in proof of his assertion, and as he even casts some doubt upon the existence of Druids at all in Britain, his views are by no means satisfactory. He has sought to demolish a palace, but he has not attempted to build even a hovel in its place. Repudiating all other theories, he has offered none of his own.

If the Druids did not erect the stone monuments of Britain, who did? Until the contrary is conclusively proved, we have but little hesitation in attributing them to the Druids. But we need not enter into this discussion, which pertains more properly to the province of archæology than of Freemasonry.

Some writers have held that the Druids were Sun-worshippers, and that the adoration of the solar orb constituted the national religion of the ancient Britons. Hence these theorists are inclined to

---

[1] "Analysis of Ancient Mythology." Drummond says of him : "Mr. Bryant was a man possessed of much learning and talent, but his etymologies are generally untenable." —"Origines," vol. iii., p. 191.   [2] "Pagan Idolatry."   [3] "Old Stone Monuments."

believe that Stonehenge and Avebury were really observatories, where the worshippers of the Sun might behold his rising, his diurnal course, and his setting.

Mr. Davies, in his *Celtic Researches* and in his *Mythology and Rites of the British Druids*, maintains that there was among them a mutilated tradition of the Noachic deluge,[1] as there was among all heathen nations. The legend was similar to that of the flood of Deucalion, and was derived from Samothrace and the East, having been brought by a colony from one nation to another and preserved without interruption.[2]

Hu, the supreme god of the Druids, he therefore supposes to have been identical with Noah, and he bestows upon him the various attributes that were distributed among the different gods of the more prolific mythology of the Greeks and Romans, all of which, with Bryant and Faber, he considers were allusive to Sun-worship and to the catastrophe of the deluge.

He therefore asserts that the Helio-Arkite god of the Britons, the great *Hu*, was a Pantheon (a collection of deities), who under his several titles and attributes comprehended the group of superior gods whom the Greeks and other refined nations separated and arranged in distinct personages.[3]

In propounding his theory that the Druids were of Eastern origin, and that they had brought from that source their religion and their rites, Mr. Davies has been sustained by the opinions of more recent scholars, though they have traced the birthplace to a more distant region than the island of Samothracia.

It is now very generally believed that the Druids were Buddhists, and that they came into Britain with the great tide of emigration from Asia which brought the Aryan race westward into Europe.

If this be true, the religion of India must have greatly degenerated in the course of its migration. It is admitted that the Druids cultivated the art of magic and in their rites were accustomed to sacrifice human victims, both of which practices were repugnant to the philosophic spirit of Buddhism.

The fact is that, notwithstanding the authority of the Welsh Bards and the scanty passages in Cæsar, Tacitus, and a few other

---

[1] " British Druids," p. 95.   [2] Ibid., p. 99.   [3] Ibid., p. 126.

Roman writers, we are entirely at sea in reference to everything connected with the religious system of Druidism. Almost all on this mysterious subject is guesswork and conjecture—extravagant theories, the only foundation of which is in the imaginations of their framers and bold assertions for the truth of which no competent authority can be given.

Much of the confusion of ideas in respect to the customs and manners of the ancient Britons has arisen from the ignorance of the old writers in supposing that the inhabitants of Britain, at the time of the Roman invasion and long before, were a homogeneous race. The truth is that the island was inhabited by two very distinct races. Those on the coast, derived from the opposite shores of Gaul, Germany, and Scandinavia, were a people who had made some progress in civilization. The interior of the island was populated by the original natives, who were a very uncivilized and even barbarous race, and it was among these that the Druidical religion prevailed and its mystical and inhuman rites were practiced.

Mr. Ferguson, in his elaborate work on *Tree and Serpent Worship*, sustains this view. He says:

"From whatever point of view the subject is looked at, it seems almost impossible to avoid the conclusion that there were two races in England—an older and less civilized people, who in the time of the Romans had already been driven by the Celts into the fastnesses of the Welsh hills, and who may have been serpent-worshippers and sacrificers of human victims, and that the ecumenical Romans confounded the two." [1]

He is, however, in error in supposing that the Romans were ignorant of this fact, for Cæsar distinctly alludes to it. He says in his *Gallic War* that "the interior part of Britain was inhabited by those who were natives of the island," thus clearly distinguishing the inhabitants of the interior from those who dwelt on the coast and who, he states, "had passed over from Belgium."

In another place he speaks of them as a rude and barbarous race, who in one of their embassies to him describe themselves as a savage and unpolished people wholly unacquainted with Roman customs.

In speaking of the ancient Gauls, M. Thierry, in his history of

---

[1] " Tree and Serpent Worship," p. 29.

that people, makes the following remarks, every one of which may be equally attributed to the ancient Britons. He says:

"When we attentively examine the character of the facts concerning the religious belief of the Gauls, we are enabled to recognize two systems of ideas, two bodies of symbols and superstitions altogether distinct—in a word, two religions. One of these is altogether sensible, derived from the adoration of the phenomena of nature ; and by its forms and by its literal development it reminds us of the polytheism of the Greeks. The other is founded upon a material pantheism, mysterious, metaphysical, and sacerdotal, and presents the most astonishing conformity with the religions of the East. This last has received the name of Druidism, from the Druids who were its founders and priests." [1]

To the former religion M. Thierry gives the name of Gaulish polytheism. A similar distinction must have existed in Britain, though our own writers do not seem generally to have carefully observed it. In no other way can we attempt, with any prospect of success, to reconcile the contending traditions in relation to the religion of the ancient Britons. The Roman writers have attributed a polytheistic form of religion to the people of the coast, derived apparently from Greece, the gods having only assumed different names. But this religion was very far removed in its character from the bloody and mysterious rites of the Druids, who seem to have brought the forms and objects, but not the spirit of their sanguinary and mysterious worship from the far East.

The Masonic writers who have sought to trace some connection between Druidism and Freemasonry have unfortunately too much yielded their judgment to their imagination. Having adopted a theory, they have, in their investigations, substituted speculation for demonstration and assumptions for facts. By a sort of Procrustean process of reasoning, they have fitted all sorts of legends and traditions to the length required for their preconceived system.

Preston had said that "the Druids retained among them many usages similar to those of the Masons," and hence he conjectured that there might be an affinity between the rites of the two institutions, leaving his readers, however, to determine the question for themselves.

Godfrey Higgins—of all writers not claiming to write fiction,

---

[1] " Histoire des Gaulois," tom. ii., p. 73.

the most imaginative and the most conjectural—goes a step further and asserts that he has "no doubt that the Masons were Druids," and that they may be "traced downward to Scotland and York." Of this he thinks "the presumption is very strong."[1]

Hutchinson thinks it probable that some of the rites and institutions of the Druids might be retained in forming the ceremonies of the Masonic society.[2]

The theory of Dr. Oliver connected Druidism and Freemasonry in the following way. The reader must be aware, from what has already been said, that the Doctor held that there were two currents of Masonry that came contemporaneously down the stream of time. These were the Pure Freemasonry of the Patriarchs, that passed through the Jewish people to King Solomon and thence onward to the present day, and a schism from this pure system, fabricated by the Pagan nations and developed in the ancient Mysteries, which impure system he called the Spurious Freemasonry of antiquity. From this latter system he supposes Druidism to have been derived.

Therefore, in support of this opinion, he collates in several of his works, but especially in his *History of Initiation*, the rites and ceremonies of the Druids with those of the Eleusinian, Dionysian, and other mysteries of the Pagan nations, and attempts to show that the design of the initiation was identical in all of them and the forms very similar.

But, true to his theory that the Spurious Freemasonry was an impure secession or offshoot from the Pure or Patriarchal system, he denies that modern Freemasonry has derived anything from Druidism, but admits that similarity in the design and form of initiation in both which would naturally arise from the origin of both from a common system in remote antiquity.

We have therefore to consider two theories in reference to the connection of Druidism and Masonry.

The first is that Freemasonry has derived its system from that of the British Druids. The second is that, while any such descent or succession of the one system from the other is disclaimed, yet that there is a very great similarity in the character of both which points to some common origin.

I shall venture, before concluding this essay, to advance a third

---

[1] "Anacalypsis," vol. i., p. 769.   [2] "Spirit of Masonry," lect. iii., p. 41.

theory, which I think is far more reconcilable than either of the others with the true facts of history.

The second of these theories may be dismissed with the remark that it depends for its support on the truth of the theory that there was any kind of historical connection between the Mysteries of the Pagans and Freemasonry. But I think it has been conclusively proved that any similarity of form or design in these institutions is to be attributed not to any dependence or succession, but simply to the influences of that law of human thought which makes men always pursue the same ends by the same methods.

Dr. Oliver has gone so far in the attempt to sustain his theory of two systems of Masonry existing at the same time as to assert that at the time of the Roman invasion, and after the establishment of Christianity in the island, the True and the Spurious Freemasonry—that is, the Masonic system as now practiced and the impure Masonry of Druidism—" flourished at the same period and were considered as distinct institutions in Britain."[1]

Of the truth of this statement, there is not a scintilla of historical testimony. Even if we were to accept the doctrine of Anderson, that all great architects in past times were Freemasons, we could hardly dignify the rude carpenters of the early Britons and Anglo-Saxons with the title of Masonry.

The first of the theories to which I have alluded, which derives Freemasonry, or at least its rites and ceremonies, from Druidism, will require a more extended review.

In the first place, we must investigate the methods by which it is supposed that the Greeks and Pythagoras communicated a knowledge of their mysteries to the Druids in their secluded homes in uncivilized Britain.

It is supposed that the principal seats of the British Druids were in Cornwall, in the islands adjacent to its coast, in Wales, and in the island of Mona; that is to say, on the southwestern shores of the island.

It is evident that in these localities they were accessible to any of the navigators from Europe or Asia who should have penetrated to that remote distance for the purpose of commerce. Now, just such

---

[1] "On Freemasonry, Evidences, Doctrines, and Traditions," No. 1, in *Freemasons' Quarterly Review*, 1840, p. 15.

a class of navigators was found in the Phœnicians, an adventurous people who were distinguished for their spirit of maritime enterprise.

The testimony of the Greek and Roman writers is, that in their distant voyages in search of traffic the Phœnicians had penetrated to the southwestern shores of Britain, and that they loaded their vessels with tin, which was found in great abundance in Cornwall and the Scilly islands on its coast.

The theorists who suppose that the religious rites practiced by the Phœnicians at home were introduced by them into Britain are required, in proof of their theory, to show that the Phœnicians were missionaries as well as merchants ; that they remained long enough in Britain, at each voyage, to implant their own religious rites in the island; that these merchant-sailors, whose paramount object was evidently the collection of a valuable and profitable cargo, would divert any portion of the time appropriated to this object to the propagation among the barbarians, whom they encountered in the way of business, of the dogmas of their own mystical religion ; that if they were so disposed, the Britons were inclined during these necessarily brief visitations to exchange their ancient religion, whatever it was, for the worship attempted to be introduced by the newcomers ; and, finally, that the fierce and sanguinary superstition of the Druids, with its human sacrifices, bore any resemblance to or could have possibly been derived from the purer and more benign religion of the Phœnicians.

For not one of these points is there a single testimony of history, and over every one of them there is cast an air of the greatest improbability. History tells us only that the Phœnician merchants visited Britain for the purpose of obtaining tin. On this the Masonic theorists have erected a fanciful edifice of missionary enterprises successfully ending in the implanting of a new religion.

Experience shows us how little in this way was ever accomplished or even attempted by the modern navigators who visited the islands of the Pacific and other unknown countries for the purposes of discovery. Nor can we be ignorant of how little progress in the change of the religion of any people has ever been effected by the efforts of professed missionaries who have lived and labored for years among the people whom they sought to convert. They have made, it is true, especial converts, but in only a very few exceptional instances have they succeeded in eradicating the old faith of a nation or a tribe and in establishing their own in its place. It is not to be presumed that the ancient Phœnician merchants could, with less means and less desires, have been more successful than our modern missionaries.

For these reasons, I hold that the proposition that Druidism was introduced from Greece and Asia into Britain by the Phœnicians is one that is wholly untenable on any principle of historic evidence or of probable conjecture.

It has also been asserted that Pythagoras visited Britain and instructed the inhabitants especially in the doctrine of metempsychosis, or the transmigration of souls.

There is, however, not the slightest historical evidence that the sage of Samos ever penetrated in his travels as far as Britain. Nor is it certain that the dogma of the transmigration as taught by him is of the same character as that which was believed by the Druids. Besides, it is contrary to all that we know of the course pursued by Pythagoras in his visits to foreign countries. He went to learn the customs of the people and to acquire a knowledge of whatever science they might possess. Had he visited Britain, which, however, he never did, it would have been to receive and not to impart instruction.

As to the further explanation offered by these theorists, of a connection between Druidism and Masonry, that the former acquired a knowledge of the Eleusinian and other rites in consequence of their communication with the Greeks, during the celebrated invasion of the Celts, which extended to Delphos, and during the intercourse of the Gauls with the Grecian colony of Marseilles, it is sufficient to say that neither of these events occurred until after the system of Druidism must have been well established among the people of Britain and of Gaul.

But the great argument against any connection of Druidism and Freemasonry is not only the dissimilarity of the two systems, but their total repugnance to each other. The sanguinary superstition of the Druids was developed in their sacrifice of human victims as a mode of appeasing their offended deities, and their doctrine of a future life was entirely irreconcilable with the pure belief in immortality which is taught in Freemasonry and developed in its symbols.

The third theory to which I have referred, and which I advanced in the place of the two others which I have rejected, traces Druidism neither to the Phœnicians, nor to Pythagoras, nor to the Greeks. It is that the ancient inhabitants of Britain were a part of the Celtic division of that great Cimmerian race who, springing from their Aryan origin in the Caucasian mountains, first settled for a time in the region of Asia which lies around the Euxine Sea, and then passed over into the north and west of Europe. One detachment of them entered Gaul, and another, crossing the German Ocean, made their home in Britain.

It is not at all improbable that these nomadic tribes carried with them some memories of the religious faith which they had learned from the original stock whence they sprung. But there is no fact more patent in ethnology than that of the tendency of all nomadic races springing from an agricultural one to degenerate in civilization.

It has been said that the Druids were Buddhists. This might be so, for Brahmanism and its schism, Buddhism, were the religions of the early Aryan stock whence the Druids descended. But it is very evident that in the course of their migrations the faith of their fathers must have become greatly corrupted. Between Buddhism and Druidism the only connecting link is the dogma of the transmigration of souls. Between the rites of the two sects there is no similarity.

I suppose, therefore, that the system of Druidism was the pure invention of the Britons, just as the Mysteries of Osiris were the fabrication of some Egyptian priest or body of priests. What assistance the Britons had in the formation of their mystical system must have been derived from dim recollections of the dogmas of their fatherland, which, however, from the very dimness of those recollections, must have been greatly perverted. I do not find any authentic proof or any reasonable probability that they had obtained any suggestions in the fabrication or the improvement of their system of religious rites from the Phœnicians, from the Greeks, or from Pythagoras.

If, for the sake of argument, we accept for a time the theory that Freemasonry and the Mysteries originated from a common source, whence is derived a connection between the two, we can not fail to see, on an examination of the doctrines and ceremonies of the Druids, that they bore no relation to those of the Mysteries of Egypt or of Greece. Hence the link is withdrawn which would connect Druidism with Freemasonry through the initiations of the East.

But the fact is that there is not in Druidism the slightest resemblance to Freemasonry, except in the unimportant circumstance that both have mystical ceremonies. The voyages of the candidate in Druidism, after a period of long solitude and confinement, his pursuit by the angry goddess Ceridwen and her accompanying dogs, his dangerous passage in a coracle or small boat over the rough waters, and his final landing and reception by the Archdruid, may have referred, as Dr. Oliver thought, to the transmigration of the soul through different bodies, but just as probably symbolized the sufferings and vicissitudes of human life in the progress to intellectual and moral perfection. But they bear not the slightest analogy to the mystical death in Freemasonry, which is the symbol of a resurrection to a future and immortal life.

Hence the bold assertion of Payne, in his frivolous *Essay on the Origin of Freemasonry*, that "it is derived from and is the remains of the religion of the ancient Druids," simply shows that he was a mere sciolist in the subject of what he presumptuously sought to treat. Equally untenable is the proposition of the more learned Faber, when he says that "the Druids are probably the real founders of English Freemasonry."

The conclusion to which I think we must arrive, from what we learn of the two institutions from historical knowledge of one and personal experience of the other, is that Freemasonry has no more relation or reference or similitude to Druidism than the pure system of Christianity has to the barbarous Fetichism of the tribes of Africa.

CHAPTER XXVIII

N all the legendary history of Freemasonry there is nothing more interesting or more romantic than the stories which connect its origin with the Crusades; nothing in which the judgment and reasoning powers have been more completely surrendered to the imagination of the inventors of the various theories on this subject or to the credulity of the believers.

Before proceeding to discuss the numerous phases which have been given by different writers to the theory which traces the origin of Freemasonry to the Crusades, to the chivalric orders of the Middle Ages, and especially to the Knights Templars, it will be proper to take a very brief view of those contests between the Christians and the Saracens which, under the name of the Crusades, cost Europe so vast an amount of blood and treasure in the unsuccessful attempt to secure and maintain possession of the Holy Land. This view, or rather synopsis, need not be more than a brief one, for the topic has been frequently and copiously treated by numerous historians, from Joinville to Michaux and Mills, and must therefore be familiar to most readers.

About twenty years after the Moslems had conquered Jerusalem, a recluse of Picardy in France had paid a pious visit to the city. Indignant at the oppressions to which the Christians were subjected in their pious pilgrimages to the sepulcher of their Lord, and moved by the complaints of the aged patriarch, Peter the Hermit—for such is the name that he bears in history—resolved on his return to Europe to attempt to rouse the religious sentiment and the military spirit of the sovereigns, the nobles, and the populace of the West. Having first obtained the sanction of the Roman pontiff, Peter the Hermit traveled through Italy and France, and by fervent addresses in every place that he visited urged his auditors to the sacred duty of rescuing Palestine from the hands of infidels. The superstitious feelings of a priest-governed people and the military spirit of knights accustomed to adventure were readily awakened by the eloquence of a fanatical preacher. In every city and village, in the churches and on the highways, his voice proclaimed the wrongs and the sufferings of pious pilgrims, and his reproaches awoke the remorse of his hearers for their past supineness and indifference to the cause of their brethren, and stimulated their eagerness to rescue the sacred shrines from the pollution of their Saracen possessors.

The spirit of enthusiasm which pervaded all classes of the people—nobles and priests, princes and peasants—presented a wonderful scene, which the history of the world had never before and has never since recorded. With one voice war was declared by the nations of western Europe against the sacrilegious Moslems. Tradesmen and mechanics abandoned the pursuits by which they were accustomed to gain their livelihood, to take up arms in a holy cause; peasants and husbandmen left their fields, their flocks, and their herds; and barons alienated or mortgaged their estates to find the means of joining the expedition.

The numerous conflicts that followed for the space of two hundred years were called the Crusades, or, in French, *Croisades*, from the blood-red cross worn by the warriors on the breast or shoulder, first bestowed at the council of Clermont, by Pope Urban, on the Bishop of Puy, and ever afterward worn by every Crusader as a badge of his profession.

The first detachment of the great army destined for a holy war issued, in the year 1096, from the western frontiers. It consisted of nearly three hundred thousand men, composed for the most part of the lowest orders of society, and was headed by Peter the Hermit. It was, however, a huge, undisciplined mob rather than an army, whose leader was entirely without military capacity to govern it or to restrain its turbulence.

The march, or rather the progress, of this immense rabble toward Asia Minor was marked at every step by crime. They destroyed the towns and plundered the inhabitants of every province through which they roamed in undisciplined confusion. The outraged inhabitants opposed their passage with arms. In many conflicts in Hungary and in Bulgaria they were slaughtered by thousands. Peter the Hermit escaped to the mountains, and of his deluded and debased followers but few reached Constantinople, and still fewer the shores of Asia Minor. They were speedily destroyed by the forces of the Sultan. The war of the Crusades had not fairly begun before three hundred thousand lives were lost in the advance guard of the army.

The first Crusade was undertaken in the same year, and speedily followed the advanced body whose disastrous fate has just been recorded. This body was composed of many of the most distinguished barons and knights, who were accompanied by their feudal retainers.

At the head of this more disciplined army, consisting of a hundred thousand knights and horsemen and five times that number of foot-soldiers, was the renowned Godfrey of Bouillon, a nobleman distinguished for his piety, his valor, and his military skill.

This army, although unwieldy from its vast numbers and scarcely manageable from the diverse elements of different nations of which it was composed, was, notwithstanding many reverses, more fortunate and more successful than the rabble under Peter the Hermit which had preceded it. It reached Palestine in safety, though not without a large diminution of knights and soldiers. At length Jerusalem, after a siege of five weeks, was conquered by the Christian warriors, in the year 1099, and Godfrey was declared the first Christian King of Jerusalem. In a pardonable excess of humility he refused to accept a crown of gems in the place where his Lord and Master had worn a crown of thorns, and contented himself with the titles of Duke and Defender of the Holy Sepulcher.

In the course of the next twenty-five years Palestine had become the home, or at least the dwelling-place, of much of the chivalry of Europe. The Latin kingdom of Jerusalem had extended eastward from the shores of the Mediterranean Sea to the deserts of Arabia, and southward from the city of Beritus (now Beirut), in Syria, to the frontiers of Egypt, besides the country of Tripoli, which stretched north of Beritus to the borders of the principality of Antioch.

The second Crusade, instigated by the preaching of the monk St. Bernard, and promoted by Louis VII. of France, was undertaken in the year 1147. The number of knights, soldiers, priests, women, and camp-followers who were engaged in this second Crusade has been estimated as approaching a million. At its head were the

Emperor Conrad III. of Germany and King Louis VII. of France. This effort to relieve and to strengthen the decaying Christian power in Palestine was not a successful one. After a futile and inglorious attempt to take the city of Damascus, whose near vicinity to Jerusalem was considered dangerous to the Latin kingdom, Louis returned home with the small remnant of his army, in 1149, and was followed in the succeeding year by the Emperor Conrad. Thus ended abortively the second Crusade, and the Christian cause in Palestine was left to be defended by the feeble forces but invincible courage of the Christian inhabitants.

The next thirty-five or forty years is a sad and continuous record of the reverses of the Christians. They had to contend with a new and powerful adversary in the person of the renowned Saracen, Sallah-ud-deen, better known as Saladin, who, after sixteen years of warfare with the Christian knights, in which he was sometimes defeated but oftener a victor, succeeded in taking Jerusalem, on the 2d of October, in the year 1187.

Thus, after a possession by the Christians of eighty-eight years, the city of Jerusalem and the holy shrine which it contained fell again into the power of the Moslems.

When the tidings of its fall reached Europe, the greatest sorrow and consternation prevailed. It was at once determined to make a vigorous effort for its rescue from its infidel conquerors. The enthusiasm of the people for its recovery was scarcely less than that which had preceded the first and second Crusades under the eloquent appeals of Peter the Hermit and St. Bernard. The principal sovereigns of Europe, Spain alone excepted, which was engaged in its own struggles for the extirpation of the Moors, resolved to lead the armies of their respective nations to the reconquest of Jerusalem. Thus was inaugurated the third Crusade.

In the year 1188, innumerable forces from England, France, Italy, and other countries rushed with impetuous ardor to Palestine. In the year 1189 one hundred thousand Crusaders, under Guy de Lusignan, sat down before the city of Acre. The siege lasted for two years, with a vast consumption of lives on both sides. At length the city capitulated and the Mussulmans surrendered to the victorious arms of Richard the Lionhearted, King of England.

This third Crusade is remarkable for the number of European sovereigns who were personally engaged in it. Richard of England,

Philip Augustus of France, Frederick Barbarossa of Germany, and the Dukes of Suabia and of Burgundy, had all left their dominions to be governed by regents in their absence and had joined in the pious struggle to redeem the Holy Land from Mohammedan rule.

But, notwithstanding many victories over Saladin in hard-fought fields, and the conquest of many important places, such as Acre, Ascalon, Jaffa, and Cæsarea, the Crusaders failed in their great design of recovering Jerusalem, which still remained in the possession of Saladin, who, however, having made a truce with King Richard, granted, as one of the terms, free and undisturbed access to all pilgrims who should visit the holy city.

Thus terminated the third Crusade. It can scarcely be called an absolute failure, notwithstanding that Jerusalem still remained in the hands of the infidels, but the total ruin with which, at its commencement, the Latin kingdom had been threatened was averted; the conquering progress of the Mussulmans had been seriously checked; the hitherto victorious Saladin had been compelled to make a truce; the greater part of the seacoast of Palestine, with all its fortresses and the cities of Acre, Jaffa, Antioch, and Tyre, remained in the possession of the Christians.

Saladin had survived the truce which he had made with Richard but a few months, and on his death his dominions were divided between three of his sons and his brother Saphadin. The last of these, to whom most of the veterans who had fought under Saladin adhered, secured for himself a sovereignty in Syria.

The death of their renowned and powerful foe had encouraged the Christians of Palestine to make renewed efforts to recover Jerusalem as soon as the truce had expired. To aid in this design, a new Crusade was invoked in Europe. The appeal, heard with apathy in England and France, met with more favor in Germany. Three large armaments of German chivalry arrived at Acre in 1195. The campaign lasted, however, less than two years, and the troops, having effected no decisive results, were recalled to Germany in consequence of the death of the Emperor Henry VI. This, which has been dignified by some writers with the name of a fourth Crusade, has, however, more generally been considered as a mere episode in the history of the Holy Wars.

The fourth Crusade proper began in the year 1203, when a large armament of knights and men-at-arms of France, Germany, Italy, and Flanders sailed for Constantinople in transports furnished by the Venetians and commanded by the blind Doge Dandolo. The throne of the Byzantine Empire had been usurped by the elder Alexius, who had imprisoned his brother, the legitimate monarch, after having caused his eyes to be put out. The first object of the Crusaders was to dethrone the usurper and to restore the government to Isaac and his son, the younger Alexius, who had instigated the enterprise and accompanied the expedition.

The siege and the conquest of Constantinople is told in the graphic language of Gibbon; but it is so wholly unconnected with the subject of our present inquiry as not to claim further attention. It is sufficient to say that by it the Crusaders were entirely diverted from the great object for which they had left Europe. None ever reached or sought to reach the land of Palestine, and the fourth Crusade terminated without a blow having been struck for the recovery of Jerusalem and the deliverance of the Holy Sepulcher from the pollution of its Paynim possessors.

The fifth Crusade commenced in the year 1217. In this war the Crusaders attacked Egypt, believing that that country was the key to Palestine. At first they were successful, and besieged and captured the city of Damietta. But, influenced and directed by the cupidity and ignorance of the papal legate, they refused the offer of the Saracens, that if the Christians would evacuate Egypt they would cede Jerusalem to them, they continued the campaign with most disastrous results, and, finally abandoning the contest, the Crusaders returned to Europe in 1229, never having even seen the shores of the Holy Land.

A sixth Crusade was undertaken by the French in 1238. They were subsequently joined by Richard, Earl of Cornwall, the nephew of Richard the Lionhearted. The military capacity and prowess of this able leader led to successful results, and in 1240 to the restoration of Jerusalem to the Christians. The Crusade ended with the return of the Earl of Cornwall to England in 1240.

The fortifications of Jerusalem were rebuilt by the Knights Templars, but the necessary measures for defense had scarcely been completed when the Christian kingdom was attacked by a new enemy. The descendants of those barbaric tribes of Tartars who, under the name of Huns, had centuries before overwhelmed the Roman Empire, now commenced their ravages in Asia Minor.

Twenty thousand Turcoman horsemen, under Barbacan, their chief, assisted by Egyptian priests, were enabled in 1242 to wrest Jerusalem from the Christians, who never again recovered it. The war continued with scarcely varying disasters to the Christians. Palestine was overrun by the barbarous hordes of Turcomans. The Moslems of Damascus, Aleppo, and Ems, forgetful of their ancient hatred and religious conflicts, united with the Knights Templars to oppose a common enemy.

But the effort to stay the progress of the Turcoman invasion was vain. Every city of the Latin kingdom, such as Tiberias, Ascalon, Jaffa, and others, were conquered. Acre alone remained to the Christian chivalry, and the Holy Sepulcher was again in the possession of the infidels.

A seventh Crusade was commenced in 1245, to recover what had been lost. It was undertaken by the chivalry of England and France. Louis IX. commanded the French portion of the forces in person, and William Longsword, who had distinguished himself in the fifth Crusade, with many other English knights and nobles, vowed that they would serve under his banner.

Egypt was again made the objective point of the expedition, and after an unnecessary and imprudent delay of eight months at Cyprus, Louis sailed, in 1248, for Egypt, with a force of fifty thousand men. The history of this Crusade is but a narrative of the defeats of the Christians, by the arms of their enemies, by famine, and by pestilence. At Mansora, in 1250, the Crusaders were totally routed; thirty thousand Christians were slain, among them the flower of the French and English chivalry, and King Louis himself was taken prisoner. He was only ransomed by the surrender of Damietta to the Turks, the conquest of which city had been almost the only successful trophy of the Christian arms. The king proceeded to Acre, almost the only possession of the Christians in Syria, and soon afterward returned to France, thus ending the seventh and penultimate Crusade, in the year 1254.

For fourteen years Syria and Palestine were left to the inadequate protection that could be afforded by the Knights Templars and Hospitallers, two Orders who even in the face of their common foe could not restrain their own bitter rivalry and dissensions. These feelings culminated at length in a sanguinary battle between them, in which the Templars were almost completely destroyed.

The Latin kingdom of Palestine being thus enfeebled by the intestine broils of its defenders, city after city was surrendered to the Moslems, until Acre alone remained in the hands of the Christians. In 1268 the heaviest blow was inflicted by the fall of Antioch, the proud capital of Syria. Forty thousand Christians were slain at the time of its surrender and one hundred thousand were sold into slavery.

The fall of the Christian state of Antioch was a catastrophe that once more aroused the military ardor and the pious spirit of Europe, and a new Crusade was inaugurated—the eighth and last—for the recovery of the Holy Land, the restoration of the Latin kingdom, and the extirpation of the infidels from the sacred territory.

This Crusade was conducted entirely by Prince Edward, afterward Edward I. of England. It is true that Louis IX. of France, undeterred by the disasters which had previously befallen him, had with undiminished ardor sought to renew his efforts for the recovery of the Holy Sepulcher, and sailed from France for that purpose in 1270. But he had stopped short at Tunis, the king and people of which he had hoped to convert to Christianity. But, although no decisive battles took place between the Moors and the Christians, the army of the latter was soon destroyed by the heat of the climate, by fatigue, by famine and pestilence, and the king himself died but little more than a month after his arrival on the shore of ancient Carthage. Prince Edward had joined the French army at Tunis with a slender body of knights, but, after the death of the French monarch and the abandonment of the enterprise, he had sailed for Syria with an army of only one thousand knights and men-at-arms, and landed at Acre in 1270. But the knights of the chivalry of Palestine gathered eagerly around his standard and increased his force to seven thousand. With this insignificant body of soldiery, weak in numbers but strong in courage and in the capacity of their leader, Edward attacked the immense horde of Moslems who had been besieging Acre, caused them to retire, and, following them to Nazareth, captured that city, after a battle in which the infidels were defeated with great slaughter.

But the reduction of Nazareth closed the military career of Edward in Palestine. After narrowly escaping death from a poisoned wound inflicted by a Moslem assassin, he returned to England, in 1271, having first effected a truce of ten years with the Sultan of Egypt.

The defense of Palestine, or rather of Acre, the only point occupied by the Christians, as the titular capital of the Latin kingdom, was left to the knights of the three Orders of Chivalry, the Templars, the Hospitallers, and the Teutonic knights. By them the truce was repeatedly violated and peaceable Moslem traders often plundered. Redress for these aggressions having been demanded in vain, the Sultan at length determined to extirpate the "faithless Franks," and marched against Acre with an army of two hundred thousand men.

After a siege of little more than a month, in which prodigies of valor were performed by the knights of the three military orders, Acre was taken, in 1271, by assault, at the cost of sixty thousand Christian lives. The inhabitants who did not submit to the Moslem yoke escaped to Cyprus with the remains of the Templars, the Hospitallers, and the Teutonic knights who had survived the slaughter.

Thus, after a sanguinary contest of two hundred years, the possession of the Holy Land was abandoned forever to the enemies of the Cross.

Thus ends the history of the Crusades. For fifty years afterward the popes endeavored to instigate new efforts for the recovery of the holy places, but their appeals met with no response. The fanatical enthusiasm which had inspired the kings, the nobles, and the knights of Europe for two centuries had been dissolved, and the thirst for glory and the love of arms were thenceforth to be directed in different channels.

It is not my intention to inquire into the influence exerted by the Crusades on the state of religion, of education, of commerce, or of society in Europe. The theme is an interesting one, but it is foreign to the subject of our discussion, which is the possible connection that may have existed between them and the origin of Freemasonry. But, in so far as they may have favored the growth of municipal freedom and the perpetuation of the system of chivalry, it may be necessary in a future part of this discussion that these points should demand some attention.

In the present point of view, the most important subject to attract our attention is the organization during the Crusades of three military Orders of Knighthood, the Knights Hospitallers, the Knights Templars, and the Teutonic Knights. It is through these, but principally through the second, that the attempt is made to find the origin of the Masonic institution in the time of the Crusaders.

Whatever may have been the origin of the institution of chivalry, whether from the equestrian order of the Romans, from the Scandinavians, the Arabians, the Persians, or, what is far more probable, from the peculiar influences of the feudal system, it is certain that that form of knighthood which was embodied in the organization of religious and military orders took its rise in Palestine during the wars of the Crusades, and that before that era no such organizations of knighthood were known in Europe.

The Knights Hospitallers of St. John, now better known as the Knights of Malta, was the first of the military and religious Orders that was established in Palestine. Its origin must be traced to the Hospitallers of Jerusalem, a purely charitable institution established by certain merchants of Amalfi, in the kingdom of Naples, who, trading in the East, built hospitals in Jerusalem for the entertainment and relief of poor and sick pilgrims, about the middle of the 11th century. After the first Crusade had begun, many knights, laying aside their arms, united with the Hospitallers in the pious task of attending the sick. At length Gerard, the Rector of the Hospital, induced his brethren to assume the vows of poverty, obedience, and chastity, and to adopt a peculiar costume consisting of a black robe bearing a white cross of eight points on the left breast. This was in the year 1099. The knights, however, continued their peaceful vocation of attending the sick until 1118, when Gerard, having died, was succeeded by Raymond de Puy as Rector. The military spirit of Raymond was averse to the monastic seclusion which had been fostered by his predecessor. He therefore proposed a change in the character of the society, by which it should become a military order devoted to the protection of Palestine from the attacks of the infidels. The members gladly acceded to this proposition, and, taking new vows at the hands of the Patriarch of Jerusalem, the military Order of Knights of St. John of Jerusalem was established, in the year 1118. The Order continued to reside in Palestine during its occupation by the Christians of the Latin kingdom, taking an active part in all the wars of the eight Crusades.

When the city of Acre fell beneath the victorious army of the Sultan of Egypt, the Hospitallers, with the knights of the other two

Orders, who had escaped the slaughter which attended the siege and followed on the surrender, fled to Cyprus. Thence they repaired to the island of Rhodes, where they remained for two hundred years under the title of the Knights of Rhodes, and afterward permanently established themselves at Malta, where, with a change of name to that of the Knights of Malta, they remained until the island was taken possession of by Napoleon, in the year 1798. This was virtually the end of the career of these valiant knights, although to this day the Order retains some remnant of its existence in Italy.

The Order of Knights Templars was established in the year 1118 by Hugh de Payens, Godfrey de St. Aldemar, and seven other knights whose names history has not preserved. Uniting the characters of the monk and the soldier, they took the vows of poverty, chastity, and obedience in the presence of the Patriarch of Jerusalem ; Baldwin, the King of Jerusalem, assigned them as a residence a part of his palace, which stood near the site of the former Temple, and as a place for an armory the street between the palace and the Temple, from which circumstance they derived their name of Templars. The Templars took a most active part in the defense of Palestine during the two centuries of the Crusades. They had also established houses called Preceptories in every country of Europe, where many of the knights resided. But the head of the Order was always in Palestine. At the close of the contests for the conquest of the Holy Land, when Acre fell and the Latin kingdom was dissolved, the Templars made their escape to Europe and were distributed among their various Preceptories.

But their wealth had excited the cupidity and their power the rivalry of Philip the Fair, King of France, who, with the assistance of a corrupt and weak Pope, Clement V., resolved to extirpate the Order. Charges of religious heresy and of moral licentiousness were preferred against them ; proofs were not wanting when proofs were required by a King and a Pontiff ; and on the 11th of March, 1314, De Molay, the Grand Master, with the three principal dignitaries of the Order, were publicly burnt at the stake, fifty-four knights having suffered the same fate three years before.

The Order was suppressed in every country of Europe. Its vast possessions were partly appropriated by the different sovereigns to their own use and partly bestowed upon the Knights of Malta, between whom and the Templars there had always existed a rivalry, and who were not unwilling to share the spoils of their ancient adversaries. In Portugal alone they were permitted to continue their existence, under the name of the Knights of Christ.

The Teutonic Knights, the last of the three Orders, was exclusively German in its organization. Their humble origin is thus related: During the Crusades, a wealthy gentleman of Germany, who resided at Jerusalem, built a hospital for the relief and support of his countrymen who were pilgrims. This charity was extended by other Germans coming from Lubeck and Bremen, and finally, during the third Crusade, a sumptuous hospital was erected at Acre, and an Order was formed under the name of Teutonic Knights, or Brethren of the Hospital of our Lady, of the Germans of Jerusalem. The rule adopted by the knights closely resembled that of the Hospitallers or Templars, with the exception that none but Germans could be admitted into the Order.

Like the knights of the other two Orders, they remained in Palestine until the fall of Acre, when they returned to Europe. For many years they were engaged in a crusade for the conversion of the Pagans of Prussia and Poland, and afterward in territorial struggle with the Kings of Poland, who had invaded their domains. After centuries of contests with various powers, the Order was at length abolished by Emperor Napoleon, in 1809, although it still has a titular existence in Austria.

In an inquiry into any pretended connection of the Crusaders with Freemasonry, we may dismiss the two Orders of the Knights of Malta and the Teutonic Knights with the single remark that in their organization they bore not the slightest resemblance to that of Freemasonry. They had no arcana in their system, no secret form of initiation or admission, and no methods of recognition. And besides this want of similarity, which must at once preclude any idea of a connection between the Masonic and these Chivalric Orders, we fail to find in history any record of such a connection or the faintest allusion to it.

If Freemasonry owed its origin to the Crusades, as has been asserted by some writers, or if any influence was exerted upon it by the Knights who returned to Europe after or during these wars, and found Freemasonry already existing as an organization, we must look for such connection or such influence to the Templars only.

The probabilities of such a connection have been based upon the following historic grounds. The Knights Templars were a secret society, differing in this respect from the other two Orders. They had a secret doctrine and a secret ceremony of initiation into their ranks. This secret character of their ceremonies was made the subject of one of the charges preferred against them by the pope. The words of this charge are that "when they held their chapters, they shut all the doors of the house or church in which they met so closely that no one could approach near enough to see or hear what they were doing or saying." It is further said, in the next charge, that when they held their secret chapter "they placed a watchman on the roof of the house or church in which they met, to foresee the approach of any one."

Again, it is supposed that the Templars had held frequent and intimate communication with some of the secret societies which, during the Crusades, existed in the East, and that from them they derived certain doctrines which they incorporated into their own Order and introduced into Europe on their return, making them the basis of a system which resulted, if not in the creation of the entire Masonic institution, at least in the invention of the high degrees.

While it may not be possible to sustain this theory of the intercommunion of the Templars and the secret societies of the East by any authentic historical proof, it derives some feature of possibility, and perhaps even of probability, from the admitted character of the Templar Knights during the latter days of their residence in Palestine. They have not been supposed to have observed with strictness their vows of chastity and poverty. That they had lost that humility which made them at first call themselves "poor fellow-soldiers of Christ" and adopt as a seal two knights riding on one horse, is evident from the well-known anecdote of Richard I. of England, who, being advised by a zealous preacher to get rid of his three favorite daughters, pride, avarice, and voluptuousness, replied: "You counsel well. I hereby dispose of the first to the Templars, the second to the Benedictines, and the third to my bishops." In fact, the Templars were accused by their contemporaries of laxity in morals and of infidelity in religion. The Bois du Guilbert drawn by the graphic pen of Walter Scott, although a fiction, had many a counterpart in history. There was, in short, nothing in the austerity of manners or intolerance of faith which would have prevented the Templars of the Crusades from holding frequent communications with the infidel secret Societies around them. The Druses, indeed, are said by some modern writers to have Templar blood in them, from the illegal intercourse of their female ancestors with the Knights.

Of these secret Societies three at least demand a brief attention, from the supposed connection of the Templars with them. These are the Essenes, the Druids, and the Assassins.

The Essenes were a Jewish sect which at the time of the Crusades were dwelling principally on the shores of the Dead Sea. Of the three schools of religion which were cultivated by the Jews in the time of our Saviour, the Pharisees and the Sadducees were alone condemned for their vices and their hypocrisy, while neither He nor any of the writers of the New Testament have referred in words either of condemnation or of censure to the Essenes. This complete silence concerning them has been interpreted in their favor, as indicating that they had not by their doctrines or their conduct incurred the displeasure of our Lord or of his disciples. Some have even supposed that St. John the Baptist, as well as some of the Evangelists and Apostles, were members of the sect—an opinion that is at least not absurd; but we reject as altogether untenable the hypothesis of De Quincey, that they were Christians.

Their ceremonies and their tenets are involved in great obscurity, notwithstanding the laborious researches of the learned Ginsburg. From him and from Josephus, who is the first of the ancient writers who has mentioned them, as well as from Philo and some other authorities, we get possession of the following facts.

The forms and ceremonies of the Essenes were, like those of the Freemasons, eminently symbolical. They were all celibates, and hence it became necessary to recruit their ranks, which death and other causes decimated from time to time, by the admission of new converts. Hence they had adopted a system of initiation which was divided into three degrees. The first stage was preceded by a preparatory novitiate which extended to three years. At the end of the first degree, the trials of which continued for twelve months, he was presented with a spade, an apron, and a white robe, the last being a symbol of purity. In the second degree or stage he was called an *approacher*, which lasted for two years, during which time he was permitted to join in some of the ceremonies of the sect, but not admitted to be present at the common. He was then

accepted as an *associate*.   If his conduct was approved, he was
finally advanced to the third degree and received into full membership as a *companion* or *disciple*.

Brewster, in the work attributed to Lawrie, seeks to find a
common origin for the Freemasons and the Essenes, and sup-
ports his opinion by the following facts, which, if they do not sustain the truth of his hypothesis, are certainly confirmed by other
authorities.   He says: " When a candidate was proposed for admission, the strictest scrutiny was made into his character.   If
his life had hitherto been exemplary, and if he appeared capable
of curbing his passions and regulating his conduct according to
the virtuous though austere maxims of the Order, he was presented
at the expiration of his novitiate with a white garment as an
emblem of the regularity of his conduct and the purity of his
heart.   A solemn oath was then administered to him, that he would
never divulge the mysteries of the Order, that he would make no
innovations on the doctrines of the society, and that he would
continue in that honorable course of piety and virtue which he had
begun to pursue.   Like Freemasons, they instructed the young
members in the knowledge which they derived from their ancestors.   They admitted no women into their Order.   They had
particular signs for recognizing each other, which have a strong
resemblance to those of Freemasons.   They had colleges or
places of retirement, where they resorted to practice their rites and
settle the affairs of the society ; and after the performance of
these duties they assembled in a large hall, where an entertainment
was provided for them by the president or master of the college,
who allotted a certain quantity of provisions to every individual.
They abolished all distinctions of rank, and if preference was ever
given, it was given to piety, liberality, and virtue.   Treasurers
were appointed in every town to supply the wants of indigent
strangers." [1]

Josephus gives the Essenian oath more *in extenso*.   He tells
us that before being admitted to the common meal, that is, before
advancement to full membership, the candidate takes an oath " that
he will exercise piety toward God and observe justice toward men ;
that he will injure no one either of his own accord or by the com-

---

[1] Lawrie, " History of Freemasonry," ed. 1804, p. 34.

mand of others; that he will hate the wicked and aid the good; that he will be faithful to all men, especially to those in authority; that if ever placed in authority he will not abuse his power nor seek to surpass those under him in the costliness of his garments or decorations; that he will be a lover of truth and a reprover of falsehood; that he will keep his hands clear from theft and his soul from unlawful gains; that he will conceal nothing from the members of his own sect, nor reveal their doctrines to others, even at the hazard of his life; nor will he communicate those doctrines to any one otherwise than as he has himself received them; and, finally, that he will preserve inviolate the books of the sect and the names of the angels."

This last expression is supposed to refer to the secrets connected with the Tetragrammaton or Four-lettered Name and the other names of God and the angelical hierarchy which are comprised in the mysterious theosophy taught by the Cabalists and accepted, it is said, by the Essenes. The mystery of the name of God was then, as it is now, a prominent feature in all Oriental philosophy and religion.

I am inclined to the opinion of Brunet, who says that the Essenes were less a sect of religion than a kind of religious order or association of zealous and pious men whom the desire of attaining an exalted state of perfection had united together.[1] But whether they were one or the other, any hypothesis which seeks to connect them with Freemasonry through the Knights Templars is absolutely untenable.

At the time of the Crusades, and indeed long before, the Essenes had ceased to hold a place in history. What little remained of them was to be found in settlements about the northwestern shore of the Dead Sea. They had decreased almost to a fraction in numbers, and had greatly corrupted their doctrines and their manners, ceasing, for instance, to be celibate and adopting the custom of marriage, while they had accepted much of the philosophy of Plato, of Pythagoras, and of the school of Alexandria.

They still retained, however, their Judaic faith and much of their primitive austerity, and it is therefore improbable that there could have been any congenial intercommunion between them and the

[1] Brunet, " Paralèle des Religions," P. VI., sec. xliv.

Templars. Their poverty and insignificance would have supplied no attraction to the Knights, and their austerity of manners and Judaism would have repelled them.

As to the similarity of Essenism and Freemasonry in the establishment by each of a brotherhood distinguished by love, charity, and a secret initiation, we can draw no conclusion from these coincidences that there was a connection of the two associations, since the same coincidences will be found in all fraternities ancient and modern. They arise from no spirit of imitation or fact of descent, but are the natural outgrowth of the social condition of man, which is ever developing itself in such mystical and fraternal associations.

But this subject will be treated more at length when, in a subsequent chapter of this work, I come to treat of the theory which deduces Freemasonry from Essenism by a direct descent, without the invocation of a Christian chivalric medium. It has, however, become inevitable, in considering the Secret Societies of the East at the period of the Crusades, to anticipate to some extent what will have to be hereafter said.

The Druses were another mystical religion with which the Templars are said to have come in contact and from whom they are said to have derived certain dogmas and usages which were transmitted to Europe and incorporated into the system of Freemasonry.

Of the communication of the Templars with the Druses there is some evidence, both traditional and historic, but what influence that communication had upon either Templarism or Masonry is a problem that admits only of a conjectural solution. The one proposed by King, in his work on the Gnostics, will hereafter be referred to.

The Druses are a mystical sect who have always inhabited the southern side of Mount Lebanon and the western side of Anti-Lebanon, extending from Beirut in the north to Sur in the south, and from the shores of the Mediterranean to the city of Damascus. They trace their origin to Hakim, who was Sultan of Egypt in 926, but derive their name from Mohammed Ben Israel Datasi, under whose leadership they fled from Egypt in the 10th century and settled in Syria, in that part around Lebanon which they still inhabit.

Their religion appears to be a mixture of Judaism, Christianity, and Mohammedanism, although what it precisely is it is impossible to tell, since they keep their dogmas a secret, which is imparted only to those of their tribe who have passed through a form of initiation.

Of this initiation, Churchill says that there is a probation of twelve months before the candidate can be admitted to full membership. In the second year, the novitiate having been complete, the Druse is permitted to assume the white turban as a badge of his profession, and is permitted to participate in all the mysteries of his religion.

These mysteries refer altogether to dogma, for their religion is without ceremonies of any kind, and even without prayer.

Their doctrines have been summarized as follows: There is one God, unknown and unknowable, without personal form and of whom we can only predicate an existence. Nine times he has appeared on earth in the form of man. These were not incarnations, for God did not assume flesh, but merely put on flesh as a man puts on a garment. There are five invisible intelligences, called Ministers of Religion, and who have been impersonated by five Druse teachers, of whom the first is *Universal Intelligence*, personated by Hamsa, whose creation was the immediate work of God. The second is the *Universal Soul*, personated by Ismael, and is the female principal as to the first, as the Universal Intelligence is the male. From these two proceed the *Word*, which is personated by Mohammed Wahab. The fourth is the *Right Wing*, or the *Proceeding*, produced from the Word and the Universal Soul and personated by Selama. The fifth is the *Left Wing*, or the *Following*, produced in the same way from the Proceeding and personated by Moctana Behædeen. These form the religious hierarchy of Drusism as the ten sephiroth make the mystical tree of the Cabalists, from which it is probable that the Druses borrowed the idea. But they are taken, as Dr. Jessup says, "in some mysterious and incomprehensible sense which no Druse, man or woman, ever understood or can understand." [1] Yet their sacred books assert that none can possess the knowledge of Drusism except he knows all these Ministers of Religion.

They have also seven precepts or commandments, obedience to

---

which is enjoined but very seldom observed by the modern Druses, and never in their intercourse with unbelievers.

1. To speak the truth.
2. To render each other mutual assistance.
3. To renounce all error.
4. To separate from the ignorant and wicked.
5. To always assert the eternal unity of God.
6. To be submissive under trials and sufferings.
7. To be content in any condition, whether of joy or sorrow.

Of their outward forms and ceremonies we have no reliable information, for their worship is a secret one.   In their sacred edifices, which are embowered among high trees or placed on the mountain summit, there are no ornaments.   They have no prescribed rites and do not offer prayer, but in their worship sing hymns and read the sacred books.   Churchill gives evidence of the profound secrecy in which the Druses envelop their religion. " Two objects," he says, " engrossed my attention—the religion of the Druses and the past history of the races which now occupy the mountain range of Lebanon.   In vain I tried to make the terms of extreme friendship and intimacy which existed between myself and the Druses available for the purpose of informing myself on the first of these points.   Sheiks, akkals, and peasants alike baffled my inquiries, either by jocose evasion or by direct negation." [1]

Finally, as if to complete their resemblance to a secret society, we are told that to enable one Druse to recognize another a system of signs and passwords is adopted, without an interchange of which no communication in respect to their mysteries is imparted.

The Rev. Mr. King, in his work on the Gnostics, thinks that "the Druses of Mount Lebanon, though claiming for their founder the Egyptian caliph Hakim, are in all probability the remains of the numerous Gnostic sects noticed by Procopius as flourishing there most extensively in his own times," [2] which was in the 6th century. And he adds that "the popular belief among their neighbors is that they, the Druses, adore an idol in the form of a calf, and hold in their secret meetings orgies similar to those laid to the charge of the Ophites in Roman times, of the Templars in mediæval, and of the

---

[1] " On the Druses and Maronites under Turkish Rule."
[2] King's " Gnostics," p. 183.

continental Freemasons in modern times."[1]   This statement I have
found confirmed by other writers.   But Mr. King thinks it an interesting and significant point that " the Druses hold the residence
of their Supreme head to be in Scotland;" a tradition which, he
says, has been "evidently handed down from the times when the
Templars were all-powerful in their neighborhood."   This would
prove, admitting the statement to be true, rather that the Druses
borrowed from the Templars than that the Templars borrowed from
the Druses; though it would even then be very difficult to understand why the Templars should have traced their head to Scotland,
since the legend of Scottish Templarism is of more recent growth.

We may, however, judge of the weight to be attached to Mr.
King's arguments from the fact that he deems it to be a "singular
coincidence" that our Freemasons are often spoken of by German
writers as the "Scottish Brethren."   Not being a Mason, he was
ignorant of the meaning of the term, which refers to a particular
rite of Masonry, and not to any theory of its origin, and is therefore
no coincidence at all.   The hypothesis of the supposed connection
of the sect of Gnostics with Freemasonry will be the subject of
future consideration.

But there was another secret society, of greater importance than
the Druses, which flourished with vigor in Syria at the time of the
Crusaders, and whose connection with the Templars, as historically
proved, may have had some influence over that Order in moulding,
or at least in suggesting, some of its esoteric dogmas and ceremonies.   This was the sect of the Assassins.

The Ishmaeleeh, or, as they are more commonly called, the Assassins, from their supposed use of the herb *hashish* to produce a temporary frenzy, was during the Crusades one of the most powerful
tribes of Syria, although their population is now little more than a
thousand.   The sect was founded about the end of the 11th century, in Persia, by Hassan Sahab.   From Persia, where they are
supposed to have imbibed many of the doctrines of the philosophical
sect of the Sofis, they emigrated to Asia Minor and settled in Syria,
to the south of Mount Lebanon.   Their chief was called Sheikh-
el-Jeber, literally translated "the Old Man of the Mountain," a
name familiar to the readers of the Voyages of Sindbad.   Higgins,

---

[1] King's " Gnostics," p. 183.

who, when he had a theory to sustain, became insane upon the subject of etymology, translates it as "the sage of the Kabbala or Traditions," but the plain Arabic words admit of no such interpretation.

The credulity and the ignorance of the Middle Ages had assigned to the sect of the Assassins the character of habitual murderers, an historical error that has been perpetuated in our language by the meaning given to the word assassin. This calumny has been exploded by the researches of modern scholars, who now class them as a philosophical sect whose doctrines and instructions were secret. Of the Sofis, from whom the Ishmaeleeh or Assassins derived their doctrine, it will be necessary soon to speak.

Von Hammer, who wrote a history of the Assassins,[1] has sought to trace a close connection between them and the Templars. He has shown himself rather as a prejudiced opponent than as an impartial critic, but the sophistry of his conclusions does not affect the accuracy of his historical statements. Subsequent writers have therefore, in their accounts of this sect, borrowed largely from the pages of Von Hammer.

The Assassins were a secret society having a religion and religious instructions which they imparted only to those of their tribe who had gone through a prescribed form of initiation. According to Von Hammer, that system of initiation was divided into three degrees. They administered oaths of secrecy and of passive obedience and had modes of mutual recognition, thus resembling in many respects other secret societies which have at all times existed. He says that they were governed by a Grand Master and had regulations and a religious code, in all of which he supposes that he has found a close resemblance to the Templars. Their religious views he states to have been as follows :

"Externally they practice the duties of Islamism, although they internally renounce them ; they believe in the divinity of Ali, in uncreated light as the principle of all created things, and in the Sheikh Ras-ed-dia, the Grand Prior of the Order in Syria, and contemporary with the Grand Master Hassan II., as the last representative of the Deity on earth."[2]

The Rev. Mr. Lyde, who traveled among the remains of the

---

[1] " Die Geschicte der Assassnen aus Morgenländ-ischen Quellen," Tubingen, 1818.
[2] " Geschicte der Assassnen," Wood's Translation, p. 221.

sect in 1852, says that they professed to believe in all the prophets, but had a chief respect for Mohammed and his son-in-law Ali, and he speaks of their secret prayers and rites as being too disgusting to be mentioned.[1]

During the Crusades, the Templars entered at various times into amicable arrangements and treaty stipulations with the Assassins, in whose territory several of the fortresses of the Knights were built, and we may therefore readily believe that at those periods, when war was not raging, there might have been a mutual interchange of courtesies, of visits and of conferences.

Now, the Assassins were by no means incapable of communicating some elements of knowledge to their knightly neighbors. The chivalry of that age were not distinguished for learning and knew little more than their profession of arms, while the Syrian infidels had brought from Persia a large portion of the intellectual culture of the Sofis. Von Hammer, whose testimony is given in the face of his adverse prejudices, admits that they produced many treatises on mathematics and law, and he confesses that Hassan, the founder of the sect, possessed a profound knowledge of philosophy, and of the mathematical and metaphysical sciences. We can not therefore deny the probability that in the frequent communications with this intellectual as well as warlike tribe the Templars may have derived some of those doctrines and secret observances which characterized the Order on its return from Palestine, and which, distorted and misinterpreted by their enemies, formed the basis of those charges which led to the persecution and the eventual extinction of Knight Templarism.

Godfrey Higgins, whose speculations are seldom controlled by a discreet judgment, finds a close connection between the Freemasons and the Assassins, through the Templars. "It is very certain," he says, "that the Ishmalians or Society of Assassins is a Mohammedan sect; that it was at once both a military and religious association, like the Templars and Teutonic Knights; and that, like the Jesuits, it had its members scattered over extensive countries. It was a link that connected ancient and modern Freemasonry."[2] And he subsequently asserts that "the Templars were nothing but one branch of

---

[1] "The Ansyreeh and Ishmaeleeh: a visit to the secret societies of Northern Syria," by Rev. Samuel Lyde, B.A., London, 1853, p. 238.
[2] "Anacalypsis," I., 700.

Masons."[1] And so he goes on speculating, that Templarism and Ishmaelism were identical, and Freemasonry sprung from them both, or rather from the latter through the former. But as Higgins has advanced several other theories of the origin of Masonry, we may let the present one pass.

We may be prepared, however, to admit that the Templars possibly modified their secret doctrines under the influence of their friendly conferences with the Assassins, without recognizing the further fact that the Templars exercised a similar influence over the Freemasons.

I have said that the Assassins are supposed to have derived their doctrines from the sect of the Sofis in Persia. Indeed, the Sofis appear to have been the common origin of all the secret societies of Syria, which will account for their general resemblance to each other. In any inquiry, therefore, into the probable or possible connection of Templarism with these societies, Sofism, or the doctrine of the Sofis, will form an interesting element.

The sect of the Sofis originated in Persia, and was extended over other countries of the East. The name is generally supposed to be derived from the Greek *Sophia*, wisdom, and they bore also the name of *philosauph*, which will easily suggest the word *philosopher*. Dr. Herbelot, however, derived the name from the Persian *sauf* or *sof*, wool, because, as he said, the ancient Sofis dressed in woolen garments. The former derivation is, however, the most plausible.

Sir John Malcolm, who has given a very good account of them in his *History of Persia*, says that among them may be counted some of the wisest men of Persia and the East. The Mohammedan Sofis, he says, have endeavored to connect their mystic faith with the doctrine of the prophet in a manner that will be better shown from Von Hammer. That the Gnostic heresy was greatly infused in the system of Sofism is very evident, and at the same time there appears to have been some connection in ideas with the school of Pythagoras. The object of all investigation is the attainment of truth, and the labors of the initiate are symbolically directed to its discovery.

In Sofism there is a system of initiation, which is divided into

---

[1] " Anacalypsis," I., 712.

four degrees. In the first or preparatory degree, the novice is required to observe the rites of the popular religion in its ordinary meaning. In the second degree, called the *Pale of Sofism*, he exchanges these exoteric rites for a spiritual and secret worship. The third degree is called *Wisdom*, and in this the initiate is supposed to be invested with supernatural knowledge and to have become equal with the angels. The fourth and last degree is called *Truth*, which the candidate is now supposed to have attained, and to have become united with the Deity.

Sir William Jones has given a summary of their doctrines, so far as they have been made known, as follows:

Nothing exists absolutely but God; the human soul is but an emanation from His essence, and, though temporarily separated from its divine source, will eventually be united with it. From this union the highest happiness will result, and therefore that the chief good of man in this world consists in as perfect a union with the Eternal Spirit as the incumbrances of flesh will permit.

Von Hammer's history of the rise, the progress, and the character of Sofism is more minute, more accurate, and therefore more interesting than that of any other writer. In accepting it for the reader, I shall not hesitate to use and to condense the language of Sloane, the author of the *New Curiosities of Literature*.

The German historian of the Assassins says that a certain *House of Wisdom* was formed in Cairo at the end of the 10th century by the Sultan, which had thus arisen. Under Maimun, the seventh Abasside Caliph, a certain Abdallah established a secret society, and divided his doctrines into seven degrees, after the system of Pythagoras and the Ionian schools. The last degree inculcated the vanity of all religion and the indifference of actions, which are visited by neither future recompense or punishment. He sent missionaries abroad to enlist disciples and to initiate them in the different degrees, according to their aptitude.

In a short time Karmath, one of his followers, improved this system. He taught that the Koran was to be interpreted allegorically, and, by adopting a system of symbolism, made arbitrary explanations of all the precepts of that book. Prayer, for instance, meant only obedience to a mysterious Imam, whom the Ishmaeleeh said that they were engaged in seeking, and the injunction of almsgiving was explained as the duty of paying him tithes. Fasting was only silence in respect to the secrets of the sect.

The more violent followers of Karmath sought to subvert the throne and the religion of Persia, and with this intent made war upon the Caliphs, but were conquered and exterminated.

The more prudent portion, under the general name of Ishmaelites, continued to work in secret, and finally succeeded in placing one of their sect upon the throne. In process of time they erected a large building, which they called the House of Wisdom, and furnished it with professors, attendants, and books, and mathematical instruments. Men and women were admitted to the enjoyment of these treasures, and scientific and philosophical disputations were held. It was a public institution, but the secret Order of the Sofis, under whose patronage it was maintained, had their mysteries, which could only be attained by an initiation extending through nine degrees. While Sofism has by most writers been believed to be a religio-philosophical sect, Von Hammer thinks that it was political, and that its principal object was to overthrow the House of Abbas in favor of the Fatimites, which could only be effected by undermining the national religion.

The government at length interfered, and the operations of the society were suspended. But in about a year it resumed its functions and established a new House of Wisdom. Extending its influences abroad, many of the disciples of Sofism passed over into Syria about the close of the 10th century, and there established those secret societies which in the course of the Crusades came into contact, sometimes on the field of battle and sometimes in friendly conferences during temporary truces with the Crusaders, but especially with the Knights Templars.

The principal of these societies were the Ishmaeleeh or Assassins and the Druses, both of whom have been described.

There were other societies in Syria, resembling these in doctrine and ceremonies, who for some especial reasons not now known had seceded from the main body, which appears to have been the Assassins.

Such were the Ansyreeh, who were the followers of that Karmath of whom I have just spoken, who had seceded at an early period from the Sofis in Persia and had established his sect in Syria, on the coast, in the plain of Laodicea, now Ladikeeh.

From them arose another sect, called the Nusairyeh, from the name of their founder, Nusair. They settled to the north of Mount Lebanon, along the low range of mountains extending from Antioch to Tripoli and from the Mediterranean to Hums, where their descendants, numbering about two hundred thousand souls, still remain.

It is from their frequent communications with these various secret societies, but especially with the Assassins, that Von Hammer and Higgins, following Ramsay, have supposed that the Templars derived their secret doctrines and, carrying them to Europe, communicated them to the Freemasons. Rather, I should say, that Von Hammer and Higgins believed these Syrian societies to be Masonic, and that they taught the principles of the institution to the Templars, who were thus the founders of Freemasonry in Europe.

Of such a theory there is not the slightest scintilla of historic evidence. When we come to examine the authentic history of the origin of Freemasonry, it will be seen how such an hypothesis is entirely without support.

But that the Templars did have frequent communication with those secret societies, that they acquired a knowledge of their doctrines, and were considerably influenced in the lives of many of their members, and perhaps in secret modifications of their Order, is an hypothesis that can not be altogether denied or doubted, since there are abundant evidences in history of such communications, and since we must admit the plausibility of the theory that the Knights were to some extent impressed with the profound doctrines of Sofism as practiced by these sects.

Admitting, then, that the Templars derived some philosophical ideas more liberal than their own from these Syrian secret philosophers who were more learned than themselves, the next question will be as to what influences the Templars exerted upon the people of Europe on their return, and in what direction and to what ends this influence was exerted; and to this we must now direct our attention.

But, before entering upon this subject, we may as well notice one significant fact. Of the three Orders of Knighthood who displayed their prowess in Palestine and Syria during the two centuries of the Crusades, the Hospitallers, the Teutonic Knights, and the Templars, it is admitted that the Templars were more intimately acquainted with the Ishmaeleeh or Assassins than either of the others. It is also known that while the admission to membership in the Hospitaller and Teutonic Orders was open and public, the Templars alone had a secret initiation, and held their meetings in houses guarded from profane intrusion.

Now, at what time the Templars adopted this secret formula of initiation is not known. The rule provided for their government by St. Bernard at the period of their organization makes no allusion to it, and it is probable that there was no such secret initiation practiced for many years after their establishment as an order.

Now, this question naturally suggests itself : Did the Templars borrow the idea and in part the form of their initiation from the Assassins, among whom such a system existed, or, having obtained it from some other source, was it subjected at a later period of their career, but long before they left Palestine, to certain modifications derived from their intercourse with the secret societies of Syria ? This is a question that can not be historically solved. We must rest for any answer on mere conjecture. And yet the facts of the Templars being of the three Orders the only secret one, and of their intercourse with the Assassins, who were also a secret order, are very significant. Some light may be thrown upon this subject by a consideration of the charges, mainly false but with certain elements of truth, which were urged against the Order at the time of its suppression.

Let us now proceed to an investigation of the theory that makes the Templars the founders of the Order of Freemasonry, after the return of the Knights to Europe. Rejecting this theory as wholly untenable, it will, however, be necessary to inquire what were the real influences exerted upon Europe by the Knights.

It must be remembered that if any influence at all was exercised upon the people of Europe, the greater portion must be attributed to the Templars. Of the three Orders, the Hospitallers, when they left Palestine, repaired directly to the island of Rhodes, where they remained for two hundred years, and then, removing to Malta, continued in that island until the decadence of their Order at the close of the last century. The Teutonic Knights betook themselves to the uncivilized parts of Germany, and renewed their warlike vocation by crusades against the heathens of that country. The Templars alone distributed themselves in the different kingdoms and cities of the continent, and became familiar with the people who lived around their preceptories. They alone came in contact with the inhabitants, and they alone could have exercised any influence upon the popular mind or taste.

It has been a generally received opinion of the most able architects that the Templars exerted a healthy influence upon the architecture of the Middle Ages. Thus Sir Christopher Wren says that " the Holy Wars gave the Christians who had been there an idea of the Saracens' works, which were afterward imitated by them in their churches, and they refined upon it every day as they proceeded in building." [1]

But the most positive opinion of the influence of the Crusaders upon the architecture of Europe was given in 1836 by Mr. Westmacott, a distinguished artist of England. In the course of a series of lectures before the Royal Academy, he thus spoke of the causes of the revival of the arts.

There were, he said, two principal causes which tended materially to assist the restoration of literature and the arts in England and in other countries of Europe. These were the Crusades and the extension or the establishment of the Freemason's institution in the north and west of Europe. The adventurers who returned from the Holy Land brought back some ideas of various improvements, particularly in architecture, and along with these a strong desire to erect castellated, ecclesiastical, and palatial edifices, to display the taste that they had acquired ; and in less than a century from the first Crusade above six hundred buildings of the above description had been erected in southern and western Europe. This taste, he thinks, was spread into almost all countries by the establishment of the Fraternity of Freemasons, who, it appears, had, under some peculiar form of Brotherhood, existed for an immemorial period in Syria and other parts of the East, whence some bands of them migrated to Europe, and after a time a great efflux of these men, Italian, German, French, Spanish, etc., had spread themselves in communities through all civilized Europe ; and in all countries where they settled we find the same style of architecture from that period, but differing in some points of treatment as suited the climate.

The latter part of this statement requires confirmation. I do not

---

[1] Wren's " Parentalia."

think that there is any historical evidence of the ingress into Europe
of bands of the Syrian secret fraternities during or after the
Crusades, nor is there any probability that such an ingress could
have occurred.

But the historical testimonies are very strong that the literature
and arts of Europe, and especially its architecture, were materially
advanced by the influence of the returning Crusaders, whose own
knowledge had been enlarged and their taste cultivated by their
contact with the nations of the East.

This topic appertains, however, to the historical rather than to
the legendary study of Masonry, and will at a future time in the
course of this work command our attention.   At present we must
restrict ourselves to the consideration of the theory that traditionally connects the Crusaders, and especially the Knights Templars,
with the establishment of the Masonic institution, through their intercourse with the secret societies of Syria.

The inventor of the theory that Freemasonry was instituted in
the Holy Land by the Crusaders, and by them on their return introduced into Europe, was the Chevalier Michael Ramsay, to whom
Masonry is indebted (whatever may be the value of the debt) for
the system of high degrees and the manufacture of Rites.

In the year 1740 Ramsay was the Grand Orator, and delivered
a discourse before the Grand Lodge of France, in which he thus
traces the origin of Freemasonry.

Rejecting as fabulous all hypotheses which trace the foundation
of the Order to the Patriarchs, to Enoch, Noah, or Solomon, he
finds its origin in the time of the Crusades.

" In the time," he says, " of the Holy Wars in Palestine, many
princes, nobles, and citizens associated themselves together and entered into vows to re-establish Christian temples in the Holy Land,
and engaged themselves by an oath to employ their talents and their
fortunes in restoring architecture to its primitive condition.   They
adopted signs and symbolic words, derived from religion, by which
they might distinguish themselves from the infidels and recognize
each other in the midst of the Saracens.   They communicated these
words only to those who had previously sworn a solemn oath, often
taken at the altar, that they would not reveal them.   Some time
after, this Order was united with that of the Knights of St. John of
Jerusalem, for which reason in all countries our Lodges are called

Lodges of St. John. This union of the two Orders was made in imitation of the conduct of the Israelites at the building of the second Temple, when they held the trowel in one hand and the sword in the other.

" Our Order must not, therefore, be regarded as a renewal of the Bacchanalian orgies and as a source of senseless dissipation, of unbridled libertinism and of scandalous intemperance, but as a moral Order instituted by our ancestors in the Holy Land to recall the recollection of the most sublime truths in the midst of the innocent pleasures of society.

"The kings, princes, and nobles, when they returned from Palestine into their native dominions, established Lodges. At the time of the last Crusade several Lodges had already been erected in Germany, Italy, Spain, France, and from the last in Scotland, in consequence of the intimate relations which existed between those two countries.

"James Lord Steward of Scotland was the Grand Master of a Lodge established at Kilwinning in the west of Scotland, in the year 1236, a short time after the death of Alexander III., King of Scotland, and a year before John Baliol ascended the throne. This Scottish Lord received the Earls of Gloucester and Ulster, English and Irish noblemen, as Masons into his Lodge.

" By degrees our Lodges, our festivals, and solemnities were neglected in most of the countries in which they had been established. Hence the silence of the historians of all nations, except Great Britain, on the subject of our Order. It was preserved, however, in all its splendor by the Scotch, to whom for several centuries the kings of France had intrusted the guardianship of their person.[1]

" After the lamentable reverses of the Crusades, the destruction of the Christian armies, and the triumph of Bendocdar, the Sultan of Egypt, in 1263, during the eighth and ninth Crusades, the great Prince Edward, son of Henry III., King of England, seeing that there would be no security for the brethren in the Holy Land when the Christians should have retired, led them away, and thus a colony of the Fraternity was established in England. As this prince was

---

[1] Ramsay here refers to the company of musketeers, composed entirely of Scotchmen of noble birth, which constituted the body-guard of the kings of France. The reader of the Waverley Novels will remember that the renowned Balafrè, in the story of " Quentin Durward," was a member of this company.

endowed with all the qualities of mind and heart which constitute the hero, he loved the fine arts and declared himself the protector of our Order.   He granted it several privileges and franchises, and ever since the members of the confraternity have assumed the name of *Freemasons*.   From this time Great Britain became the seat of our sciences, the conservatrix of our laws, and the depository of our secrets.   The religious dissensions which so fatally pervaded and rent all Europe during the 16th century caused our Order to degenerate from the grandeur and nobility of its origin.   Several of our rites and usages, which were opposed to the prejudices of the times, were changed, disguised, or retrenched.   Thus it is that several of our brethren have, like the ancient Jews, forgotten the spirit of our laws and preserved only the letter and the outer covering.   But from the British islands the ancient science is now beginning to pass into France."

Such was the theory of Ramsay, the principal points of which he had already incorporated into the Rite of six degrees which bears his name.   This Rite might be called the mother of all the Rites which followed it and which in a few years covered the continent with a web of high degrees and of Masonic systems, all based on the hypothesis that Freemasonry was invented during the Crusades, and the great dogma of which, boldly pronounced by the Baron Von Hund, in his Rite of Strict Observance, was that every Freemason was a Templar.

It will be seen that Ramsay repudiates all the legends which ascribe Masonry to the Patriarchs or to the ancient Mysteries, and that he rejects all connection with an Operative association, looking to chivalry alone for the legitimate source of the Fraternity.

Adopting the method of writing Masonic history which had been previously pursued by Anderson, and which was unfortunately followed by other writers of the 18th century, and which has not been altogether abandoned at the present day, Ramsay makes his statements with boldness, draws without stint upon his imagination, presents assumptions in the place of facts, and cites no authority for anything that he advances.

As Mossdorf says, since he cites no authority we are not bound to believe him on his simple word.

Ramsay's influence, however, as a man of ability, had its weight, and the theory of the origin of Freemasonry among the Crusaders continued to be taught in some one form or another by subsequent writers, and it was infused by the system-makers into most of the Rites that were afterward established. Indeed, it may be said that of all the Rites now existing, the English and American are the only ones in which some feature of this Templar theory may not be found.

The theory of Hutchinson varied somewhat from that of Ramsay, inasmuch as while recognizing the influence of the Crusades upon Masonry he is inclined to suppose that it was carried there by the Crusaders rather than that it was brought thence by them to Europe.

After alluding to the organization of the Crusades by Peter the Hermit, and to the outpouring from Europe into Palestine of tens of thousands of saints, devotees, and enthusiasts to waste their blood and treasure in a barren and unprofitable adventure, he proceeds to say that "it was deemed necessary that those who took up the sign of the Cross in this enterprise should form themselves into such societies as might secure them from spies and treacheries, and that each might know his companion and fellow-laborer by dark as well as by day. As it was with Jephtha's army at the passes of the Jordan, so also was it requisite in these expeditions that certain signs, signals, watchwords, or passwords should be known amongst them; for the armies consisted of various nations and various languages."

"No project or device," he thinks, "could answer the purpose of the Crusaders better than those of Masonry. The maxims and ceremonials attending the Master's Order had been previously established and were materially necessary on that expedition; for as the Mohammedans were also worshippers of the Deity, and as the enterprisers were seeking a country where the Masons were in the time of Solomon called into an association, and where some remains would certainly be found of the mysteries and wisdom of the ancients and of our predecessors, such degrees of Masonry as extended only to their being servants of the God of Nature would not have distinguished them from those they had to encounter, had they not assumed the symbols of the Christian faith."

The hypothesis of Hutchinson is, then, that while there was some Masonry in Palestine before the advent of the Crusaders, it was only that earlier stage which he had already described as appertaining to the Apprentice's degree, and which was what both he and

Oliver have called " Patriarchal Masonry." The higher stage represented by the Master's degree was of course unknown to the Saracens, as it was of Christian origin, and the possession of this degree
only could form any distinctive mark between the Crusaders and
their Moslem foes. This degree, therefore, he thinks, was introduced into Palestine as a war-measure to supply the Christians with
signs and words which would be to them a means of protection.
The full force of the language bears only this interpretation, that
Freemasonry was used by the Crusaders not for purposes of peace,
but for those of war, a sentiment so abhorrent to the true spirit of
the institution that nothing but a blind adhesion to a preconceived
theory could have led so good a Mason as Hutchinson to adopt
or to advance such an opinion.

Differing still more from Ramsay, who had attributed the origin
of Masonry to the Knights and nobles of the Crusades, Hutchinson
assigns the task of introducing it into Palestine to the religious and
not the military element of these expeditions.

" All the learning of Europe in those times," he continues, " was
possessed by the religious; they had acquired the wisdom of the
ancients, and the original knowledge which was in the beginning
and now is the *truth;* many of them had been initiated into the
mysteries of Masonry, they were the projectors of the Crusades,
and, as Solomon in the building of the Temple introduced orders
and regulations for the conduct of the work, which his wisdom had
been enriched with from the sages of antiquity, so that no confusion
should happen during its progress, and so that the rank and office
of each fellow-laborer might be distinguished and ascertained beyond the possibility of doubt; in like manner the priests projecting
the Crusades, being possessed of the mysteries of Masonry, the
knowledge of the ancients, and of the universal language which survived the confusion of Shinar, revived the orders and regulations of
Solomon, and initiated the legions therein who followed them to
the Holy Land—hence that secrecy which attended the Crusades."

Mr. Hutchinson concludes this collection of assumptions, cumulated one upon another, without the slightest attempt to verify historically a single statement, by asserting that "among other evidences which authorize us in the conjecture that Masons went to
the Holy Wars, is the doctrine of that Order of Masons called the
Higher Order," that is to say, the higher degrees, which he says

that he was induced to believe was of Scottish origin.   He obtained this idea probably from the theory of Ramsay.   But be that as it may, he thinks " it conclusively proved that the Masons were Crusaders ;" a conclusion that it would be difficult to infer from any known rules of logic.   The fact (if it be admitted) that these higher degrees were invented in Scotland by no means proves that the Masons who possessed them went to the Crusades.   It is impossible, indeed, to find any natural connection or sequence between the two circumstances.

But the legend which refers to the establishment in Scotland of a system of Masonry at the time of the suppression of the Order and the martyrdom of de Molay, belongs to another portion of the legendary history of Freemasonry and will be treated in a distinct chapter.

Von Hammer shows to what shifts for arguments those are reduced who pretend that the institution of Freemasonry was derived at the Crusades, by the Knights Templars, from the secret societies of the East.   He says, as a proof of the truth of this hypothesis, which indeed he makes as a charge against the Templars, that their secret maxims, particularly in so far as relates to the renunciation of positive religion and the extension of their power by the acquisition of castles and strong places, seem to have been the same as those of the Order of Assassins.   The similarity also of the white dress and red fillet of the Assassins with the white mantle and red cross of the Templars he thinks is certainly remarkable.   Hence he assumes that as the Assassins were a branch of the Ishmaeleeh, whom he calls the " Illuminati of the East," and as the former were a secret society of revolutionary principles, which is a characteristic that he gratuitously bestows upon the Freemasons, he takes it for granted that the Assassins supplied the Templars with those ideas of organization and doctrine out of which they created the system of Freemasonry that they afterward introduced into Europe.

A series of arguments like this is scarcely worthy of a serious refutation.   The statement that the Templars ever renounced the precepts of positive religion, either at that early period of their career or at any subsequent time, is a mere assumption, based on the charges made by the malevolence of a wicked King and a still more wicked Pope.   The construction of fortresses and castles for their protection, by both the Templars and the Assassins, arose from the

military instinct which teaches all armies to provide the means of
defense when in the presence of an enemy.   And lastly, the argument drawn from the similarity of the costumes of both Orders is
so puerile as to require no other answer than that as the mantle and
cross of the Templars were bestowed upon them, the former by Pope
Honorius and the latter by Pope Eugenius, therefore they could not
have been indebted to the Assassins for either.   The best refutation
of the slanders of Von Hammer is the fact that to sustain his views
he was obliged to depend on such poverty of argument.

Recognizing as historically true the fact that the Templars, or
rather, perhaps, the architects and builders, who accompanied them
and were engaged in the construction of their fortresses and castles
in the Holy Land, the remains of some of which still exist, brought
with them to Europe some new views of Saracenic architecture
which they communicated to the guilds of Freemasons already established in Europe, we may dismiss the further consideration of
that subject as having nothing to do with the question of how
much Freemasonry as a secret society was indebted for its origin to
Templarism.

On the subject of the direct connection of the Templars with
Freemasonry at the time of the Crusades, there are only two propositions that have been maintained.   One is that the Templars carried
Freemasonry with them to Palestine and there made use of it for
their protection from their enemies, the Saracens.

Of this theory there is not the slightest evidence.   No contemporary historian of the Crusades makes any mention of such a fact.
Before we can begin to even discuss it as something worthy of discussion, we must find the proof, which we can not, that in the 11th
and 12th centuries Freemasonry was anything more than an Operative institution, to which it was not likely that any Crusaders of influence, such as the nobles and knights, were attached as members.
As a mere conjecture it wants every element of probability.   Hutchinson, the most prominent writer who maintains the theory, has
evidently confounded the Crusaders of the 11th and 12th centuries,
who fought in Palestine, with the Templars, who are said to have
fled to Scotland in the 14th century and to have there invented certain high degrees.   This manifest confusion of dates gives a feature
of absurdity to the argument of Hutchinson.

Another form has been given to this theory by a writer in the

London Freemasons' Magazine,[1] which has the air of greater plausibility at least. The theory that he has advanced will be best given in his own language: "The traveling bodies of Freemasons (who existed in Europe at the time of the Crusades) consisted of brethren well skilled in every branch of knowledge; among their ranks were many learned ecclesiastics, whose names survive to the present day in the magnificent edifices which they assisted to erect. The Knights of the Temple, themselves a body of military monks partaking both of the character of soldiers and priests, preserved in their Order a rank exclusively clerical, the individuals belonging to which took no part in warfare, who were skilled in letters, and devoted themselves to the civil and religious affairs of the Order; they were the historians of the period, and we know that all the learning of the time was in their keeping in common with the other ecclesiastics of the time. From the best information we are possessed of regarding the Order, we believe there can be little doubt that these learned clerks introduced the whole fabric of Craft Masonry into the body of the Templars, and that not only was the Speculative branch of the science by them incorporated with the laws and organization of the Knights, but to their Operative skill were the Templars indebted for their triumphs in architecture and fortification. And it is worthy of remark that in the records of the Order we find no mention of individual architects or builders; we may therefore not unfairly draw the inference that the whole body were made participators in the knowledge and mysteries of the Craft."

To this theory there is the same objection that has been already made to the other, that it is wholly unsupported by historical authority, and that it is a mere congeries of bold assumptions and fanciful conjectures. Very strange, indeed, is the reasoning which draws the inference that all the Templars were builders because there is no mention of such a class in the records of the Order. Such a silence would rather seem to indicate that there was no such class among the Knights. That they employed architects and builders, who may have belonged to the guilds of Traveling Freemasons before they went to Palestine, is by no means improbable; but there is no evidence, and it is by no means likely, that they would engage in anything more than the duties of their profession, or that there

---

[1] *Freemasons' Magazine and Masonic Mirror*, vol. iv., p. 962, London, 1858, Part I.

Strasbourg Cathedral

would be any disposition on the part of the Knights devoted to a warlike vocation to take any share in their peaceful association.

The second theory is that the Templars derived their secret doctrines and ceremonies from the sect of the Assassins, or from the Druses of Mount Lebanon, and that on their return to Europe they organized the Fraternity of Freemasons.   This theory is the direct opposite of the former, and, like it, has neither history to sustain its truth as a statement nor probability to support it as a conjecture.

It was the doctrine of a German writer, Adler, who advanced it in his treatise, *De Drusis Montis Libani*, published in 1786 at Rome.   But its most prominent advocate was Von Hammer, an avowed and prejudiced foe of both Templarism and Freemasonry, and who made it the basis of his charges against both institutions. Notwithstanding this, it has been accepted with his wonted credulity by Higgins in his ponderous work entitled *Anacalypsis*.

Brewster, in the work attributed to Lawrie on the *History of Freemasonry*, has adopted the same hypothesis.   " As the Order of the Templars," he says, " was originally formed in Syria, and existed there for a considerable time, it would be no improbable supposition that they received their Masonic knowledge from the Lodges in that quarter."

But as Brewster, or the author of the work called *Lawrie's History*, had previously, with equal powers of sophistry and with a similar boldness of conjecture, attributed the origin of Freemasonry to the ancient Mysteries, to the Dionysiac Fraternity of Artificers, to the Essenes, the Druids, and to Pythagoras, we may safely relegate his hypothesis of its Templar origin to the profound abyss of what ought to be, and probably are, exploded theories.   All these various arguments tend only to show how the prejudices of preconceived opinions may warp the judgment of the most learned scholars.

On the whole, I think that we will be safe in concluding that, whatever may have been the valiant deeds of the Crusaders, and especially of the Templars, in their unsuccessful attempt to rescue the Holy Sepulcher from the possession of the infidels, they could scarcely have diverted their attention to the prosecution of an enterprise so uncongenial with the martial spirit of their occupation as that of inventing or organizing a peaceful association of builders. With the Crusades and the Crusaders, Freemasonry had no con-

nection that can be sustained by historical proof or probable conjecture. As to the supposed subsequent connection of Templarism
with the Freemasonry of Scotland, that forms another and an entirely different legend, the consideration of which will engage our
attention in the following chapter.

CHAPTER XXIX

THE STORY OF THE SCOTTISH TEMPLARS

HE story which connects the Knights Templars with Freemasonry in Scotland, after their return from the Crusades and after the suppression of their Order, forms one of the most interesting and romantic legends connected with the history of Freemasonry. In its incidents the elements of history and tradition are so mingled that it is with difficulty that they can be satisfactorily separated. While there are some writers of reputation who accept everything that has been said concerning the connection in the 14th century of the Freemasons of Scotland with the Templars who were then in that kingdom, or who escaped to it as an asylum from the persecutions of the French monarch, as an authentic narrative of events which had actually occurred, there are others who reject the whole as a myth or fable which has no support in history.

Here, as in most other cases, the middle course appears to be the safest. While there are some portions of the story which are corroborated by historical records, there are others which certainly are without the benefit of such evidence. In the present chapter I shall endeavor, by a careful and impartial analysis, to separate the conflicting elements and to dissever the historical from the legendary or purely traditional portions of the relation.

But it will be necessary, in clearing the way for any faithful investigation of the subject, to glance briefly at the history of those events which were connected with the suppression of the ancient Order of Knights Templars in France in the beginning of the 14th century.

The Templars, on leaving the Holy Land, upon the disastrous termination of the last Crusade and the fall of Acre, had taken temporary refuge in the island of Cyprus. After some vain attempts to regain a footing in Palestine and to renew their contests with the infidels, who were now in complete possession of that country, the Knights had retired from Cyprus and repaired to their different Commanderies in Europe, among which those in France were the most wealthy and the most numerous.

At this period Philip IV., known in history by the soubriquet of Philip the Fair, reigned on the French throne, and Clement V. was the Pontiff of the Roman Church. Never before had the crown or the tiara been worn by a more avaricious King or a more treacherous Pope.

Clement, when Bishop of Bordeaux, had secured the influence of the French monarch toward his election to the papacy by engaging himself by an oath on the sacrament to perform six conditions imposed upon him by the king, the last of which was reserved as a secret until after his coronation.

This last condition bound him to the extermination of the Templars, an Order of whose power Philip was envious and for whose wealth he was avaricious.

Pope Clement, who had removed his residence from Rome to Poictiers, summoned the heads of the military Orders to appear before him for the purpose, as he deceitfully pretended, of concerting measures for the inauguration of a new Crusade.

James de Molay, the Grand Master of the Templars, accordingly repaired to the papal court. While there the King of France preferred a series of charges against the Order, upon which he demanded its suppression and the punishment of its leaders.

The events that subsequently occurred have been well called a black page in the history of the Order. On the 13th of October, 1307, the Grand Master and one hundred and thirty-nine Knights were arrested in the palace of the Temple, at Paris, and similar arrests were on the same day made in various parts of France. The arrested Templars were thrown into prison and loaded with chains. They were not provided with a sufficiency of food and were refused the consolations of religion. Twenty-six princes and nobles of the court of France appeared as their accusers; and before the judgment of their guilt had been determined by the tribunals, the infamous Pope Clement launched a bull of excommunication against all persons who should give the Templars aid or comfort.

The trials which ensued were worse than a farce, only because of their tragical termination. The rack and the torture were unsparingly applied. Those who continued firm in a denial of guilt were condemned either to perpetual imprisonment or to the stake. Addison says that one hundred and thirteen were burnt in Paris and others in Lorraine, in Normandy, at Carcassonne, and at Senlis.

The last scene of the tragedy was enacted on the 11th of March, 1314. James de Molay, the Grand Master of the Order, after a close and painful imprisonment of six years and a half, was publicly burnt in front of the Cathedral of Notre Dame, in Paris.

The Order was thus totally suppressed in France and its possessions confiscated. The other monarchs of Europe followed the example of the King of France in abolishing the Order in their dominions; but, in a more merciful spirit, they refrained from inflicting capital punishment upon the Knights. Outside of France, in all the other kingdoms of Europe, not a Templar was condemned to death.

The Order was, however, everywhere suppressed, and a spoil made of its vast possessions, notwithstanding that in every country beyond the influence of the Pope and the King of France its general innocence was sustained. In Portugal it changed its name to that of the Knights of Christ—everywhere else the Order ceased to exist.

But there are writers who, like Burnes,[1] maintain that the persecution of the Templars in the 14th century did not close the history of the Order, but that there has been a succession of Knights Templars from the 12th century down to these days. Dr. Burnes alluded to the Order of the Temple and the pretended transmission of the powers of de Molay to Larmenius.

With this question and with the authenticity of the so-called "Charter of Transmission," the topic which we are now about to discuss has no connection, and I shall therefore make no further allusion to it.

It is evident from the influence of natural causes, without the necessity of any historical proof, that after the death of the Grand Master and the sanguinary persecution and suppression of the Order in France, many of the Knights must have sought safety by flight to other countries. It is to their acts in Scotland that we are now to direct our attention.

---

[1] "Sketch of the History of the Knights Templars," by James Burnes, LL.D., F.R.S., etc., London, 1840, p. 39.

There are two Legends in existence which relate to the connection of Templarism with the Freemasonry of Scotland, each of which will require our separate attention. The first may be called the Legend of Bruce, and the other the Legend of d'Aumont.

In Scotland the possessions of the Order were very extensive. Their Preceptories were scattered in various parts of the country. A papal inquisition was held at Holyrood in 1309 to try and, of course, to condemn the Templars. At this inquisition only two knights, Walter de Clifton, Grand Preceptor of Scotland, and William de Middleton appeared. The others absconded, and as Robert Bruce was then marching to meet and repel the invasion of King Edward of England, the Templars are said to have joined the army of the Scottish monarch. Thus far the various versions of the Bruce Legend agree, but in the subsequent details there are irreconcilable differences.

According to one version, the Templars distinguished themselves at the battle of Bannockburn, which was fought on St. John the Baptist's Day, 1314, and after the battle a new Order was formed called the Royal Order of Scotland, into which the Templars were admitted. But Oliver thinks very justly that the two Orders were unconnected with each other.

Thory says that Robert Bruce, King of Scotland under the title of Robert I., created on the 24th of June, 1314, after the battle of Bannockburn, the Order of St. Andrew of the Thistle, to which was afterward added that of Heredom, for the sake of the Scottish Masons, who had made a part of the thirty thousand men who had fought with an hundred thousand English soldiers. He reserved for himself and his successors the title of Grand Master and founded at Kilwinning the Grand Lodge of the Royal Order of Heredom.[1]

The Manual of the Order of the Temple says that the Templars, at the instigation of Robert Bruce, ranged themselves under the banners of this new Order, whose initiations were based on those of the Templars. For this apostasy they were excommunicated by John Mark Larmenius, who is claimed to have been the legitimate successor of de Molay.[2]

None of these statements are susceptible of historical proof.

---

[1] " Acta Latomorum," tome i., p. 6.
[2] " Manuel des Chevaliers de l'Ordre du Temple," p. 8.

The Order of Knights of St. Andrew or of the Thistle was not created by Bruce in 1314, but by James II. in 1440.

There is no evidence that the Templars ever made a part of the Royal Order of Heredom. At this day the two are entirely distinct. Nor is it now considered as a fact that the Royal Order was established by Bruce after the Battle of Bannockburn, although such is the esoteric legend.

On the contrary, it is supposed to have been the fabrication of Michael Ramsay in the 18th century. On this subject the remarks of Bro. Lyon, who has made the Masonry of Scotland his especial study, are well worth citation.

"The ritual of the Royal Order of Scotland embraces," he says, "what may be termed a spiritualization of the supposed symbols and ceremonies of the Christian architects and builders of primitive times, and so closely associates the sword with the trowel as to lead to the second degree being denominated an order of Masonic knighthood, which its recipients are asked to believe was first conferred on the field of Bannockburn, as a reward for the valor that had been displayed by a body of Templars who aided Bruce in that memorable victory; and that afterward a Grand Lodge of the Order was established by the King at Kilwinning, with the reservation of the office of Grand Master to him and his successors on the Scottish throne. It is further asserted that the Royal Order and the Masonic Fraternity of Kilwinning were governed by the same head. As regards the claims to antiquity, and a royal origin that are advanced in favor of this rite, it is proper to say that modern inquiries have shown these to be purely fabulous. The credence that is given to that part of the legend which associates the Order with the ancient Lodge of Kilwinning is based on the assumed certainty that that Lodge possessed in former times a knowledge of other degrees of Masonry than those of St. John. But such is not the case. The fraternity of Kilwinning never at any period practiced or acknowledged other than the Craft degrees; neither does there exist any tradition worthy of the name, local or national, nor has any authentic document yet been discovered that can in the remotest degree be held to identify Robert Bruce with the holding of Masonic Courts, or the institution of a secret society at Kilwinning."[1]

---

[1] "History of the Lodge of Edinburgh," by David Murray Lyon, chap. xxxii., p. 307.

After such a statement made by a writer who from his position and opportunities as a Scottish Mason was better enabled to discover proofs, if there were any to be discovered, we may safely conclude that the Bruce and Bannockburn Legend of Scottish Templarism is to be deemed a pure myth, without the slightest historical element to sustain it.

There is another Legend connecting the Templars in Scotland with Freemasonry which demands our attention.

It is said in this Legend that in order to escape from the persecution that followed the suppression of the Order by the King of France, a certain Templar, named d'Aumont, accompanied by seven others, disguised as mechanics or Operative Masons, fled into Scotland and there secretly founded another Order ; and to preserve as much as possible the ancient name of Templars as well as to retain the remembrance of and to do honor to the Masons in whose clothing they had disguised themselves when they fled, they adopted the name of Masons in connection with the word Franc, and called themselves Franc Masons. This they did because the old Templars were for the most part Frenchmen, and as the word *Franc* means both *French* and *Free*, when they established themselves in England they called themselves Freemasons. As the ancient Order had been originally established for the purpose of rebuilding the Temple of Jerusalem, the new Order maintained their bond of union and preserved the memory and the design of their predecessors by building symbolically spiritual Temples consecrated to Virtue, Truth, and Light, and to the honor of the Grand Architect of the Universe.

Such is the Legend as given by a writer in the Dutch *Freemasons' Almanac*, from which it is cited in the London *Freemasons' Quarterly Review*.[1]

Clavel, in his *Picturesque History of Freemasonry*,[2] gives it more in detail, almost in the words of Von Hund.

After the execution of de Molay, Peter d'Aumont, the Provincial Grand Master of Auvergne, with two Commanders and five Knights, fled for safety and directed their course toward Scotland, concealing themselves during their journey under the disguise of Operative Masons. Having landed on the Scottish Island of Mull they

---

[1] See *Freemasons' Quarterly Review*, London, 1843, p. 501, where the Legend is given in full, as above.

[2] " Histoire Pitioresque de la Franc Maçonnerie," p. 184.

there met the Grand Commander George Harris and several other brethren, with whom they resolved to continue the Order. d'Aumont was elected Grand Master in a Chapter held on St. John's Day, 1313. To protect themselves from all chance of discovery and persecution they adopted symbols taken from architecture and assumed the title of Freemasons. In 1361 the Grand Master of the Temple transferred the seat of the Order to the old city of Aberdeen, and from that time it spread, under the guise of Freemasonry, through Italy, Germany, France, Portugal, Spain, and other places.

It was on this Legend that the Baron Von Hund founded his Rite of Strict Observance, and with spurious documents in his possession, he attempted, but without success, to obtain the sanction of the Congress of Wilhelmsbad to his dogma that every Freemason was a Templar.

This doctrine, though making but slow progress in Germany, was more readily accepted in France, where already it had been promulgated by the Chapter of Clermont, into whose Templar system Von Hund had been initiated.

The Chevalier Ramsay was the real author of the doctrine of the Templar origin of Freemasonry, and to him we are really indebted (if the debt have any value) for the d'Aumont Legend. The source whence it sprang is tolerably satisfactory evidence of its fictitious character. The inventive genius of Ramsay, as exhibited in the fabrications of high degrees and Masonic legends, is well known. Nor, unfortunately for his reputation, can it be doubted that in the composition of his legends he cared but little for the support of history. If his genius, his learning, and his zeal had been consecrated, not to the formation of new Masonic systems, but to a profound investigation of the true origin of the Institution, viewed only from an authentic historical point, it is impossible to say what incalculable benefit would have been derived from his researches. The unproductive desert which for three-fourths of a century spread over the continent, bearing no fruit except fanciful theories, absurd systems, and unnecessary degrees, would have been occupied in all probability by a race of Masonic scholars whose researches would have been directed to the creation of a genuine history, and much of the labors of our modern iconoclasts would have been spared.

The Masonic scholars of that long period, which began with Ramsay and has hardly yet wholly terminated, assumed for the most part rather the rôle of poets than of historians. They did not remember the wise saying of Cervantes, that the poet may say or sing, not as things have been, but as they ought to have been, while the historian must write of them as they really were, and not as he thinks they ought to have been. And hence we have a mass of traditional rubbish, in which there is a great deal of falsehood with very little truth.

Of this rubbish is the Legend of Peter d'Aumont and his resuscitation of the Order of Knights Templars in Scotland. Without a particle of historical evidence for its support, it has nevertheless exerted a powerful influence on the Masonic organization of even the present day. We find its effects looming out in the most important rites and giving a Templar form to many of the high degrees. And it cannot be doubted that the incorporation of Templarism into the modern Masonic system is mainly to be attributed to ideas suggested by this d'Aumont Legend.

As there appears to be some difficulty in reconciling the supposed heretical opinions of the Templars with the strictly Christian faith of the Scottish Masons, to meet this objection a third Legend was invented, in which it was stated that after the abolition of the Templars, the clerical part of the Order—that is, the chaplains and priests—united in Scotland to revive it and to transplant it into Freemasonry. But as this Legend has not met with many supporters and was never strongly urged, it is scarcely necessary to do more than thus briefly to allude to it.

Much as the Legend of d'Aumont has exerted an influence in mingling together the elements of Templarism and Freemasonry, as we see at the present day in Britain and in America, and in the high degrees formed on the continent of Europe, the dogma of Ramsay, that every Freemason is a Templar, has been utterly repudiated, and the authenticity of the Legend has been rejected by nearly all of the best Masonic scholars.

Dr. Burnes, who was a believer in the legitimacy of the French Order of the Temple, as being directly derived from de Molay through Larmenius, and who, therefore, subscribed unhesitatingly to the authenticity of the "Charter of Transmission," does not hesitate to call Von Hund "an adventurer" and his Legend of d'Aumont "a plausible tale."

Of that part of the Legend which relates to the transfer of the chief seat of the Templars to Aberdeen in Scotland, he says that "the imposture was soon detected, and it was even discovered that he had himself enticed and initiated the ill-fated Pretender into his fabulous order of chivalry. The delusions on this subject had taken such a hold in Germany, that they were not altogether dispelled until a deputation had actually visited Aberdeen and found amongst the worthy and astonished brethren there no trace either of very ancient Templars or of Freemasonry." [1]

In this last assertion, however, Burnes is in error, for it is alleged that the Lodge of Aberdeen was instituted in 1541, though, as its more ancient minutes have been, as it is said, destroyed by fire, its present records go no further back than 1670. Bro. Lyon concurs with Burnes in the statement that the Aberdeenians were much surprised when first told that their Lodge was an ancient center of the High Degrees. [2]

William Frederick Wilke, a German writer of great ability, has attacked the credibility of this Scottish Legend with a closeness of reasoning and a vigor of arguments that leave but little room for reply. [3] As he gives the Legend in a slightly different form, it may be interesting to quote it, as well as his course of argument.

"The Legend relates," he says, "that after the suppression of the Order the head of the Templar clergy, Peter of Boulogne, fled from prison and took refuge with the Commander Hugh, Wildgrave of Salm, and thence escaped to Scotland with Sylvester von Grumbach. Thither the Grand Commander Harris and Marshal d'Aumont had likewise betaken themselves, and these three preserved the secrets of the Order of Templars and transferred them to the Fraternity of Freemasons."

In commenting on this statement Wilke says it is true that Peter of Boulogne fled from prison, but whither he went never has been known. The Wildgrave of Salm never was in prison. But the legendist has entangled himself in saying that Peter left the Wildgrave Hugh and went to Scotland with Sylvester von Grumbach, for Hugh and Sylvester are one and the same person. His

---

[1] Burnes, "Sketch of the History of the Knights Templars," p. 71.

[2] "History of the Lodge of Edinburgh," p. 420.

[3] In his "Geschichte des Tempelherren's Orders." I have not been able to obtain the work, but I have availed myself of an excellent analysis of it in "Findel's History of Freemasonry," Lyon's Translation.

title was Count Sylvester Wildgrave, and Grumbach was the designation of his Templar Commandery. Hugh of Salm, also Wildgrave and Commander of Grumbach, never took refuge in Scotland, and after the abolition of the Order was made Prebendary of the Cathedral of Mayence.

Wilke thinks that the continuation of the Templar Order was attributed to Scotland because the higher degrees of Freemasonry, having reference in a political sense to the Pretender, Edward Stuart, were called Scotch. Scotland is, therefore, the cradle of the higher degrees of Masonry. But here I am inclined to differ from him and am disposed rather to refer the explanation to the circumstance that Ramsay, who was the inventor of the Legend and the first fabricator of the high degrees, was a native of Scotland and was born in the neighborhood of Kilwinning. To these degrees he gave the name of Scottish Masonry, in a spirit of nationality, and hence Scotland was supposed to be their birthplace. This is not, however, material to the present argument.

Wilke says that Harris and d'Aumont are not mentioned in the real history of the Templars and therefore, if they were Knights, they could not have had any prominence in the Order, and neither would have been likely to have been chosen by the fugitive Knights as their Grand Master.

He concludes by saying that of course some of the fugitive Templars found their way to Scotland, and it may be believed that some of the brethren were admitted into the building fraternities, but that is no reason why either the Lodges of builders or the Knights of St. John should be considered as a continuation of the Templar Order, because they both received Templar fugitives, and the less so as the building guilds were not, like the Templars, composed of chivalrous and free-thinking worldlings, but of pious workmen who cherished the pure doctrines of religion.

The anxiety of certain theorists to connect Templarism with Freemasonry, has led to the invention of other fables, in which the Hiramic Legend of the Master's degree is replaced by others referring to events said to have occurred in the history of the knightly Order. The most ingenious of these is the following :

Some time before the destruction of the Order of Templars, a certain Sub-prior of Montfauçon, named Carolus de Monte Carmel, was murdered by three traitors. From the events that accompanied and followed this murder, it is said that an important part of the ritual of Freemasonry has been derived.   The assassins of the Sub-prior of Montfauçon concealed his body in a grave, and in order to designate the spot, planted a young thorn-tree upon it.   The Templars, in searching for the body, had their attention drawn to the spot by the tree, and in that way they discovered his remains.   The Legend goes on to recite the disinterring of the body and its removal to another grave, in striking similarity with the same events narrated in the Legend of Hiram.

Another theory connects the martyrdom of James de Molay, the last Grand Master of the Templars, with the Legend of the third degree, and supposes that in that Legend, as now preserved in the Masonic ritual, Hiram has been made to replace de Molay, that the fact of the Templar fusion into Masonry might be concealed.

Thus the events which in the genuine Masonic Legend are referred to Hiram Abif are, in the Templar Legend, made applicable to de Molay ; the three assassins are said to be Pope Clement V., Philip the Fair, King of France, and a Templar named Naffodei, who betrayed the Order.   They have even attempted to explain the mystical search for the body by the invention of a fable that on the night after de Molay had been burnt at the stake, certain Knights diligently sought for his remains amongst the ashes, but could find only some bones to which the flesh, though scorched, still adhered, but which it left immediately upon their being handled ; and in this way they explain the origin of the substitute word, according to the mistranslation too generally accepted.

Nothing could more clearly show the absurdity of the Legend than this adoption of a popular interpretation of the meaning of this word, made by someone utterly ignorant of the Hebrew language. The word, as is now well known to all scholars, has a totally different signification.

But it is scarcely necessary to look to so unessential a part of the narrative for proof that the whole Legend of the connection of Templarism with Freemasonry is irreconcilable with the facts of history.

The Legend of Bruce and Bannockburn has already been disposed of.   The story has no historical foundation.

The other Legend, that makes d'Aumont and his companions founders of the Masonic Order in Scotland by amalgamating the

Knights with the fraternity of builders, is equally devoid of an historical basis. But, besides, there is a feature of improbability if not of impossibility about it. The Knights Templars were an aristocratic Order, composed of high-born gentlemen who had embraced the soldier's life as their vocation, and who were governed by the customs of chivalry. In those days there was a much wider line of demarkation drawn between the various casts of society than exists at the present day. The " belted knight " was at the top of the social scale, the mechanic at the bottom.

It is therefore almost impossible to believe that because their Order had been suppressed, these proud soldiers of the Cross, whose military life had unfitted them for any other pursuit except that of arms, would have thrown aside their swords and their spurs and assumed the trowel; with the use of this implement and all the mysteries of the builder's craft they were wholly unacquainted. To have become Operative Masons, they must have at once abandoned all the prejudices of social life in which they had been educated. That a Knight Templar would have gone into some religious house as a retreat from the world whose usage of his Order had disgusted him, or taken refuge in some other chivalric Order, might reasonably happen, as was actually the case. But that these Knights would have willingly transformed themselves into Stonemasons and daily workmen is a supposition too absurd to extort belief even from the most credulous.

We may then say that those legendists who have sought by their own invented traditions to trace the origin of Freemasonry to Templarism, or to establish any close connection between the two Institutions, have failed in their object.

They have attempted to write a history, but they have scarcely succeeded in composing a plausible romance.

CHAPTER XXX

HE theory that connects the royal house of the Stuarts with Freemasonry, as an Institution to be cultivated, not on account of its own intrinsic merit, but that it might serve as a political engine to be wielded for the restoration of an exiled family to a throne which the follies and even the crimes of its members had forfeited, is so repugnant to all that has been supposed to be congruous with the true spirit and character of Freemasonry, that one would hardly believe that such a theory was ever seriously entertained, were it not for many too conclusive proofs of the fact.

The history of the family of Stuart, from the accession of James I. to the throne of England to the death of the last of his descendants, the young Pretender, is a narrative of follies and sometimes of crimes. The reign of James was distinguished only by arts which could gain for him no higher title with posterity than that of a royal pedant. His son and successor Charles I. was beheaded by an indignant people whose constitutional rights and liberties he had sought to betray. His son Charles II., after a long exile was finally restored to the throne, only to pass a life of indolence and licentiousness. On his death he was succeeded by his brother James II., a prince distinguished only for his bigotry. Zealously attached to the Roman Catholic religion, he sought to restore its power and influence among his subjects, who were for the most part Protestants. To save the Established Church and the religion of the nation, his estranged subjects called to the throne the Protestant Prince of Orange, and James, abdicating the crown, fled to France, where he was hospitably received with his followers by Louis XIV., who could, however, say nothing better of him than that he had given three crowns for a mass. From 1688, the date of his abdication and flight, until the year 1745 the exiled family were engaged in repeated but unavailing attempts to recover the throne.

It is not unreasonable to suppose that in these attempts the partisans of the house of Stuart were not unwilling to accept the influence of the Masonic Institution, as one of the most powerful instruments whereby to effect their purpose.

It is true that in this, the Institution would have been diverted from its true design, but the object of the Jacobites, as they were called, or the adherents of King James was not to elevate the character of Freemasonry but only to advance the cause of the Pretender.

It must however be understood that this theory which connects the Stuarts with Masonry does not suppose that the third or Master's degree was invented by them or their adherents, but only that there were certain modifications in the application of its Legend. Thus, the Temple was interpreted as alluding to the monarchy, the death of its Builder to the execution of Charles I., or to the destruction of the succession by the compulsory abdication of James II., and the dogma of the resurrection to the restoration of the Stuart family to the throne of England.

Thus, one of the earliest instances of this political interpretation of the Master's Legend was that made after the expulsion of James II. from the throne and his retirement to France. The mother of James was Henrietta Maria, queen of Charles I. The Jacobites called her "the Widow," and the exiled James became "the Widow's son," receiving thus the title applied in the Masonic Legend to Hiram Abif, whose death they said symbolized the loss of the throne and the expulsion of the Stuarts from England.

They carried this idea to such an extent as to invent a new substitute word for the Master's degree, in the place of the old one, which was known to the English Masons at the time of the Revival in 1717.

This new word was not, as the significant words of Masonry usually are, of Hebrew origin, but was derived from the Gaelic. And this seems to have been done in compliment to the Highlanders, most of whom were loyal adherents of the Stuart cause.

The word *Macbenac* is derived from the Gaelic *mac*, a son, and *benach*, blessed, and literally means the "blessed son;" and this word was applied by the Jacobites to James, who was thus not only a "widow's son" but a "blessed" one, too. Masonry was here made subservient to loyalty.

They also, to mark their political antipathy to the enemies of the Stuart family, gave to the most prominent leaders of the republican cause, the names in which old Masonry had been appropriated to the assassins of the third degree. In the Stuart Masonry we find these assassins designated by names, generally unintelligible, but, when they can be explained, evidently referring to some well-known opponent of the Stuart dynasty. Thus, *Romvel* is manifestly an imperfect anagram of *Cromwell*, and *Jubelum Guibbs* doubtless was intended as an infamous embalmment of the name of the Rev. Adam Gib, an antiburgher clergyman, who, when the Pretender was in Edinburgh in 1745, hurled anathemas, for five successive Sundays against him.

But it was in the fabrication of the high degrees that the partisans of the Stuarts made the most use of Freemasonry as a political instrument.

The invention of these high degrees is to be attributed in the first place to the Chevalier Ramsay. He was connected in the most intimate relation with the exiled family, having been selected by the titular James III., or, as he was commonly known in England, the Old Pretender, as the tutor of his two sons, Charles Edward and Henry, the former of whom afterward became the Young Pretender, and the latter Cardinal York.

Ardently attached, by this relationship, by his nationality as a Scotchman, and by his religion as a Roman Catholic, to the Stuarts and their cause, he met with ready acquiescence the advances of those who had already begun to give a political aspect to the Masonic system, and who were seeking to enlist it in the Pretender's cause. Ramsay therefore aided in the modification of the old degrees or the fabrication of new ones, so that these views might be incorporated in a peculiar system; and hence in many of the high degrees invented either by Ramsay or by others of the same school, we will find these traces of a political application to the family of Stuart, which were better understood at that time than they are now.

Thus, one of the high degrees received the name of "Grand Scottish Mason of James VI." Of this degree Tessier says that it is the principal degree of the ancient Master's system, and was revived and esteemed by James VI., King of Scotland and of Great

Britain, and that it is still preserved in Scotland more than in any other kingdom.[1]

All of this is of course a mere fiction, but it shows that there has been a sort of official acknowledgment of the interference with Masonry by the Stuarts, who did not hesitate to give the name of the first founder of their house on the English throne to one of the degrees.

Another proof is found in the word *Jekson*, which is a significant word in one of the high Scottish or Ramsay degrees. It is thus spelled in the *Cahiers* or manuscript French rituals. There can be no doubt that it is a corruption of *Jacquesson*, a mongrel word compounded of the French *Jacques* and the English *son*, and denotes *The son of James*, that is, of James II. This son was the Old Pretender, or the Chevalier St. George, who after the death of his father assumed the empty title of James III., and whose son, the Young Pretender, was one of the pupils of the Chevalier Ramsay.

These, with many other similar instances, are very palpable proofs that the adherents of the Stuarts sought to infuse a political element into the spirit of Masonry, so as to make it a facile instrument for the elevation of the exiled family and the restoration of their head to the throne of England.

Of the truth of this fact, it is supposed that much support is to be found in the narrative of the various efforts for restoration made by the Stuarts.

When James II. made his flight from England he repaired to France, where he was hospitably received by Louis XIV. He took up his residence while in Paris at the Jesuitical College of Clermont. There, it is said, he first sought, with the assistance of the Jesuits, to establish a system of Masonry which should be employed by his partisans in their schemes for his restoration to the throne. After an unsuccessful invasion of Ireland he returned to France and repaired to St. Germain-en-Laye, a city about ten miles northwest of Paris, where he lived until the time of his death in 1701. It is one of the Stuart myths that at the Château of St. Germain some of the high degrees were fabricated by the adherents of James II., assisted by the Jesuits.

The story is told by Robison, a professed enemy of Freemasonry,

---

[1] "Manuel Générale de Maçonnerie," p. 148.

but who gives with correctness the general form of the Stuart Legend as it was taught in the last century.

Robison says: "The revolution had taken place, and King James, with many of his most zealous adherents, had taken refuge in France.

"But they took Freemasonry with them to the Continent, where it was immediately received by the French, and cultivated with great zeal in a manner suited to the taste and habits of that highly polished people. The Lodges in France naturally became the rendezvous of the adherents of the exiled king, and the means of carrying on a correspondence with their friends in England."[1]

Robison says that at this time the Jesuits took an active part in Freemasonry, and united with the English Lodges, with the view of creating an influence in favor of the re-establishment of the Roman Catholic religion in England. But the supposed connection of the Jesuits with Freemasonry pertains to an independent proposition, to be hereafter considered.

Robison further says that "it was in the Lodge held at St. Germain that the degree of *Chevalier Maçon Ecossais* was added to the three *symbolical* degrees of English Masonry. The Constitution, as imported, appeared too coarse for the refined taste of the French, and they must make Masonry more like the occupation of a gentleman. Therefore the English degrees of Apprentice, Fellowcraft, and Master were called *symbolical*, and the whole contrivance was considered either as typical of something more elegant or as a preparation for it. The degrees afterward superadded to this leave us in doubt which of these views the French entertained of our Masonry. But, at all events, this rank of Scotch Knight was called the *first* degree of the *Maçon Parfait*. There is a device belonging to this Lodge which deserves notice. A lion wounded by an arrow, and escaped from the stake to which he had been bound, with the broken rope still about his neck, is represented lying at the mouth of a cave, and occupied with mathematical instruments, which are lying near him. A broken crown lies at the foot of the stake. There can be little doubt but that this emblem alludes to the dethronement, the captivity, the escape, and the asylum of James II., and his hopes of re-establishment by the help of the

---

[1] "Proofs of a Conspiracy," p. 27.

loyal Brethren. This emblem is worn as the gorget of the Scotch Knight. It is not very certain, however, when this degree was added, whether immediately after King James's abdication or about the time of the attempt to set his son on the British throne."[1]

This extract from Robison presents a very fair specimen of the way in which Masonic history was universally written in the last century and is still written by a few in the present.

Although it cannot be denied that at a subsequent period the primitive degrees were modified and changed in their application of the death of Hiram Abif to that of Charles I., or the dethronement of James II., and that higher degrees were created with still more definite allusion to the destinies of the family of Stuart, yet it is very evident that no such measures could have been taken during the lifetime of James II.

The two periods referred to by Robison, the time of the abdication of James II., which was in 1688, and the attempt of James III., as he was called, to regain the throne, which was in 1715, as being, one or the other, the date of the fabrication of the degree of Scottish Knight or Master, are both irreconcilable with the facts of history. The symbolical degrees of Fellow Craft and Master had not been invented before 1717, or rather a few years later, and it is absurd to speak of higher degrees cumulated upon lower ones which did not at that time exist.

James II. died in 1701. At that day we have no record of any sort of Speculative Masonry except that of the one degree which was common to Masons of all ranks. The titular King James III., his son, succeeded to the claims and pretensions of his father, of course, in that year, but made no attempt to enforce them until 1715, at which time he invaded England with a fleet and army supplied by Louis XIV. But in 1715, Masonry was in the same condition that it had been in 1701. There was no Master's degree to supply a Legend capable of alteration for a political purpose, and the high degrees were altogether unknown. The Grand Lodge of England, the mother of all Continental as well as English Masonry, was not established, or as Anderson improperly calls it, "revived," until 1717. The Institution was not introduced into France until 1725, and there could, therefore, have been no political Masonry practiced in a

---

[1] Robison, "Proofs of a Conspiracy," p. 28.

country where the pure Masonry of which it must have been a corruption did not exist.   Scottish or Stuart Masonry was a superstructure built upon the foundation of the symbolic Masonry of the three
degrees.   If in 1715 there was, as we know, no such foundation, it
follows, of course, that there could have been no superstructure.

The theory, therefore, that Stuart Masonry, or the fabrication of
degrees and the change of the primitive rituals to establish a system
to be engaged in the support and the advancement of the falling
cause of the Stuarts, was commenced during the lifetime of James
II., and that the royal château of St. Germain-en-Laye was the
manufactory in which, between the years 1689 and 1701, these degrees and rituals were fabricated, is a mere fable not only improbable
but absolutely impossible in all its details.

Rebold, however, gives another form to the Legend and traces the
rise of Stuart Masonry to a much earlier period.   In his *History of
the Three Grand Lodges* he says that during the troubles which dis-
tracted Great Britain about the middle of the 17th century and after
the decapitation of Charles I. in 1649, the Masons of England, and
especially those of Scotland, labored secretly for the re-establishment
of the monarchy which had been overthrown by Cromwell.   For the
accomplishment of this purpose they invented two higher degrees
and gave to Freemasonry an entirely political character.   The dissensions to which the country was a prey had already produced a
separation of the Operative and the Accepted Masons—that is to say,
of the builders by profession and those honorary members who were
not Masons.   These latter were men of power and high position,
and it was through their influence that Charles II., having been received as a Mason during his exile, was enabled to recover the
throne in 1660.   This prince gratefully gave to Masonry the title of
the "Royal Art," because it was Freemasonry that had principally
contributed to the restoration of royalty.[1]

Ragon, in his *Masonic Orthodoxy*,[2] is still more explicit and
presents some new details.   He says that Ashmole and other
Brethren of the Rose Croix, seeing that the Speculative Masons
were surpassing in numbers the Operative, had renounced the simple
initiation of the latter and established new degrees founded on the

---

[1] " Histoire de Trois Grandes Loges," p. 32.
[2] Ragon, " Orthodoxie Maçonnique," p. 29.

Mysteries of Egypt and Greece. The Fellow Craft degree was fabricated in 1648, and that of Master a short time afterward. But the decapitation of King Charles I., and the part taken by Ashmole in favor of the Stuarts produced great modifications in this third and last degree, which had become of a Biblical character. The same epoch gave birth to the degrees of *Secret Master, Perfect Master*, and *Irish Master*, of which Charles I. was the hero, under the name of Hiram. These degrees, he says, were, however, not then openly practiced, although they afterward became the ornament of Ecossaism.

But the non-operative or "Accepted" members of the organization secretly gave to the Institution, especially in Scotland, a political tendency. The chiefs or protectors of the Craft in Scotland worked, in the dark, for the re-establishment of the throne. They made use of the seclusion of the Masonic Lodges as places where they might hold their meetings and concert their plans in safety. As the execution of Charles I. was to be avenged, his partisans fabricated a Templar degree, in which the violent death of James de Molay called for vengeance. Ashmole, who partook of that political sentiment, then modified the degree of Master and the Egyptian doctrine of which it was composed, and made it conform to the two preceding degrees framing a Biblical allegory, incomplete and inconsistent, so that the initials of the sacred words of these three degrees should compose those of the name and title of the Grand Master of the Templars.

Northouck,[1] who should have known better, gives countenance to these *supercheries* of history by asserting that Charles II. was made a Mason during his exile, although he carefully omits to tell us when, where, how, or by whom the initiation was effected; but seeks, with a flippancy that ought to provoke a smile, to prove that Charles II. took a great interest in Masonry and architecture, by citing the preamble to the charter of the Royal Society, an association whose object was solely the cultivation of the philosophical and mathematical sciences, especially astronomy and chemistry, and whose members took no interest in the art of building.

Dr. Oliver, whose unfortunate failing was to accept without careful examination all the statements of preceding writers, how-

---

[1] "Constitutions," p. 141.

ever absurd they might be, repeats substantially these apocryphal tales about early Stuart Masonry.

He says that, about the close of the 17th century, the followers of James II. who accompanied the unfortunate monarch in his exile carried Freemasonry to France and laid the foundation of that system of innovation which subsequently threw the Order into confusion, by the establishment of a new degree, which they called the *Chevalier Maçon Ecossais*, and worked the details in the Lodge at St. Germain. Hence, he adds, other degrees were invented in the Continental Lodges, which became the rendezvous of the partisans of James, and by these means they held communication with their friends in England.[1]

But as the high degrees were not fabricated until more than a third of the 18th century had passed, and as James died in 1701, we are struck with the confusion that prevails in this statement as to dates and persons.

It is very painful and embarrassing to the scholar who is really in search of truth to meet with such caricatures of history, in which the boldest and broadest assumptions are offered in the place of facts, the most absurd fables are presented as narratives of actual occurrences, chronology is put at defiance, anachronisms are coolly perpetrated, the events of the 18th century are transferred to the 17th, the third degree is said to have been modified in its ritual during the Commonwealth, when we know that no third degree was in existence until after 1717; and we are told that high degrees were invented at the same time, although history records the fact that the first of them was not fabricated until about the year 1728. Such writers, if they really believed what they had written, must have adopted the axiom of the credulous Tertullian, who said, *Credo quia impossible est*—"I believe because it is impossible." Better would it be to remember the saying of Polybius, that if we eliminate truth from history nothing will remain but an idle tale.

We must, then, reject as altogether untenable the theory that there was any connection between the Stuart family and Freemasonry during the life of James II., for the simple reason that at that period there was no system of Speculative Masonry existing

---

[1] "Historical Landmarks," II., p. 28.

which could have been perverted by the partisans of that family into a political instrument for its advancement. If there was any connection at all, it must be looked for as developed at a subsequent period.

The views of Findel on this subject, as given in his *History of Free-masonry*, are worthy of attention, because they are divested of that mystical element so conspicuous and so embarrassing in all the statements which have been heretofore cited. His language is as follows :

"Ever since the banishment of the Stuarts from England in 1688, secret alliances had been kept up between Rome and Scotland ; for to the former place the Pretender James Stuart had retired in 1719 and his son Charles Edward was born there in 1720; and these communications became the more intimate the higher the hopes of the Pretender rose. The Jesuits played a very important part in these conferences. Regarding the reinstatement of the Stuarts and the extension of the power of the Roman Church as identical, they sought at that time to make the Society of Freemasons subservient to their ends. But to make use of the Fraternity, to restore the exiled family to the throne, could not have been contemplated, as Freemasonry could hardly be said to exist in Scotland then. Perhaps in 1724, when Ramsay was a year in Rome, or in 1728, when the Pretender in Parma kept up an intercourse with the restless Duke of Wharton, a Past Grand Master, this idea was first entertained, and then when it was apparent how difficult it would be to corrupt the loyalty and fealty of Freemasonry in the Grand Lodge of Scotland, founded in 1736, this scheme was set on foot of assembling the faithful adherents of the banished royal family in the High Degrees! The soil that was best adapted for this innovation was France, where the low ebb to which Masonry had sunk had paved the way for all kinds of new-fangled notions, and where the Lodges were composed of Scotch conspirators and accomplices of the Jesuits. When the path had thus been smoothed by the agency of these secret propagandists, Ramsay, at that time Grand Orator (an office unknown in England), by his speech completed the preliminaries necessary for the introduction of the High Degrees; their further development was left to the instrumentality of others, whose influence produced a result somewhat different from that originally intended."[1]

---

[1] "Geschichte der Freimaurerei."—Translation of Lyon, p. 209.

After the death of James II. his son, commonly called the Chevalier St. George, does not appear to have actively prosecuted his claims to the throne beyond the attempted invasion of England in 1715. He afterward retired to Rome, where the remainder of his life was passed in the quiet observation of religious duties. Nor is there any satisfactory evidence that he was in any way connected with Freemasonry.

In the meantime, his sons, who had been born at Rome, were intrusted to the instructions of the Chevalier Michael Andrew Ramsay, who was appointed their tutor. Ramsay was a man of learning and genius—a Scotchman, a Jacobite, and a Roman Catholic—but he was also an ardent Freemason.

As a Jacobite he was prepared to bend all his powers to accomplish the restoration of the Stuarts to what he believed to be their lawful rights. As a Freemason he saw in that Institution a means, if properly directed, of effecting that purpose. Intimately acquainted with the old Legends of Masonry, he resolved so to modify them as to transfer their Biblical to political allusions. With this design he commenced the fabrication of a series of High Degrees, under whose symbolism he concealed a wholly political object.

These High Degrees had also a Scottish character, which is to be attributed partly to the nationality of Ramsay and partly to a desire to effect a political influence among the Masons of Scotland, in which country the first attempts for the restoration of the Stuarts were to be made. Hence we have to this day in Masonry such terms as " Ecossaim," " Scottish Knights of St. Andrew," " Scottish Master," " Scottish Architect," and the " Scottish Rite," the use of which words is calculated to produce upon readers not thoroughly versed in Masonic history the impression that the High Degrees of Freemasonry originated in Scotland—an impression which it was the object of Ramsay to make.

There is another word for which the language of Masonry has been indebted to Ramsay. This is *Heredom*, indifferently spelled in the old rituals, *Herodem*, *Heroden* and *Heredon*. Now the etymology of this word is very obscure and various attempts have been made to trace it to some sensible signification.

One writer[1] thinks that the word is derived from the Greek *hieros*—"holy," and *domos*—"house," and that it means "the *holy house*," that is, the Temple. This explanation is ingenious, and it has been adopted by some recent authorities.

Ragon,[1] however, offers a different etymology. He thinks that it is a corrupted form of the mediæval Latin *hæredum*, which signifies a "heritage," and that it refers to the Château of St. Germain, the residence for a long time of the exiled Stuarts and the only heritage which was left to them. If we accept this etymology, I should rather be inclined to think that the heritage referred to the throne of Great Britain, which they claimed as their lawful possession, and of which, in the opinion of their partisans, they had been unrighteously despoiled.

This derivation is equally as ingenious and just as plausible as the former one, and if adopted will add another link to the chain of evidence which tends to prove that the high degrees were originally fabricated by Ramsay to advance the cause of the Stuart dynasty.

Whatever may be the derivation of the word the rituals leave us in no doubt as to what was its pretended meaning. In one of these rituals, that of the Grand Architect, we meet with the following questions and answers :

" *Q*. Where was your first Lodge held ?

" *A*. Between three mountains, inaccessible to the profane, where cock never crew, lion roared, nor woman chattered ; in a profound valley.

" *Q*. What are these three mountains named ?

" *A*. Mount Moriah, in the bosom of the land of Gabaon, Mount Sinai, and the Mountain of Heredon.

" *Q*. What is this Mountain of Heredon ?

" *A*. A mountain situated between the West and the North of Scotland, at the end of the sun's course, where the first Lodge of Masonry was held : in that terrestrial part which has given name to Scottish Masonry.

" *Q*. What do you mean by a profound valley ?

" *A*. I mean the tranquillity of our Lodges."

From this catechism we learn that in inventing the word *Heredon* to designate a fabulous mountain, situated in some unknown part of Scotland, Ramsay meant to select that kingdom as the birth-

---

[1] " Orthodoxie Maçonnique," p. 91.

place of those Masonic degrees by whose instrumentality he expected to raise a powerful support in the accomplishment of the designs of the Jacobite party. The selection of this country was a tribute to his own national prejudices and to those of his countrymen.

Again : by the "profound valley," which denoted " the tranquillity of the Lodges," Ramsay meant to inculcate the doctrine that in the seclusion of these Masonic reunions, where none were to be permitted to enter except "the well-tried, true, and trusty," the plans of the conspirators to overthrow the Hanoverian usurpation and to effect the restoration of the Stuarts could be best conducted. Fortunately for the purity of the non-political character of the Masonic Institution, this doctrine was not generally accepted by the Masons of Scotland.

But there is something else concerning this word *Heredon,* in its connection with Stuart Freemasonry, that is worth attention.

There is an Order of Freemasonry, at this day existing, almost exclusively in Scotland. It is called the Royal Order of Scotland, and consists of two degrees, entitled " Heredon of Kilwinning," and " Rosy Cross." The first is said, in the traditions of the Order, to have originated in the reign of David I., in the 12th century, and the second to have been instituted by Robert Bruce, who revived the former and incorporated the two into one Order, of which the King of Scotland was forever to be the head. This tradition is, however, attacked by Bro. Lyon, in his *History of the Lodge of Edinburgh.* He denies that the Lodge at Kilwinning ever at any period practiced or acknowledged other than the Craft degrees, or that there exists any tradition, local or national, worthy of the name, or any authentic document yet discovered that can in the remotest degree be held to identify Robert Bruce with the holding of Masonic courts or the institution of a secret society at Kilwinning

" The paternity of the Royal Order," he says, " is now pretty generally attributed to a Jacobite Knight named Andrew Ramsay, a devoted follower of the Pretender, and famous as the fabricator of certain rites, inaugurated in France about 1735–40, and through the propagation of which it was hoped the fallen fortunes of the Stuarts would be retrieved."[1]

On September 24, 1745, soon after the commencement of his

---

[1] "History of the Lodge of Edinburgh," p. 307.

invasion of Britain, Charles Edward, the son of the Old Pretender, or Chevalier St. George, styled by his adherents James III., is said to have been admitted into the Order of Knights Templars, and to have been elected its Grand Master, a position which he held until his death.   Such is the tradition, but here again we are met by the authentic statements of Bro. Lyon that Templarism was not introduced into Scotland until the year 1798.[1]   It was then impossible that Charles Edward could have been made a Templar at Edinburgh in 1745.

It is, however, probable that he was invested with official supremacy over the high degrees which had been fabricated by Ramsay in the interest of his family, and it is not unlikely, as has been affirmed, that, resting his claim on the ritual provision that the Kings of Scotland were the hereditary Grand Masters of the Royal Order, he had assumed that title.   Of this we have something like an authentic proof, something which it is refreshing to get hold of as an oasis of history in this arid desert of doubts and conjectures and assumptions.

In the year 1747, more than twelve months after his return from his disastrous invasion of Scotland and England, Charles Edward issued a charter for the formation at the town of Arras in France of what is called in the instrument "a Sovereign Primordial Chapter of Rose Croix under the distinctive title of Scottish Jacobite."

In 1853, the Count de Hamel, Prefect of the Department in which Arras is situated, discovered an authentic copy of the charter in the Departmental archives.

In this document, the Young Pretender gives his Masonic titles in the following words :

"We, Charles Edward, King of England, France, Scotland, and Ireland, and as such Substitute Grand Master of the Chapter of H., known by the title of Knight of the Eagle and Pelican, and since our sorrows and misfortunes by that of Rose Croix," etc.

The initial letter " H." undoubtedly designates the Scottish Chapter of Heredon.   Of this body, by its ritual regulation, his father as King of Scotland, would have been the hereditary Grand Master, and he, therefore, only assumes the subordinate one of Substitute.

---

[1] " History of the Lodge of Edinburgh," p. 287.

This charter, of the authenticity of which, as well as the transaction which it records, there appears to be no doubt, settles the question that it was of the Royal Order of Scotland and not of the Knights Templars that Charles Edward was made Grand Master, or himself assumed the Grand Mastership, during his visit in 1745 to Edinburgh. As that Order and the other High Degrees were fabricated by the Chevalier Ramsay to promote the interests of his cause, his acceptance or assumption of the rank and functions of a presiding officer was a recognition of the plan to use Masonry as a political instrument, and is, in fact, the first and fundamental point in the history of the hypothesis of Stuart Masonry. We here for the first time get tangible evidence that there was an attempt to connect the Institution of Freemasonry with the fortunes and political enterprises of the Stuarts.

The title given to this primordial charter at Arras is further evidence that its design was really political; for the words *Ecosse Jacobite*, or Scottish Jacobite, were at that period universally accepted as a party name to designate a partisan of the Stuart pretensions to the throne of England.

The charter also shows that the organization of this chapter was intended only as the beginning of a plan to enlist other Masons in the same political design, for the members of the chapter were authorized "not only to make knights, but even to create a chapter in whatever town they might think proper," which they actually did in a few instances, among them one at Paris in 1780, which in 1801 was united to the Grand Orient of France.

A year after the establishment of the Chapter at Arras, the Rite of the *Veille Bru*, or the *Faithful Scottish Masons*, was created at Toulouse in grateful remembrance of the reception given by the Masons of that place to Sir Samuel Lockhart, the aide-de-camp of the Pretender. Ragon says that the favorites who accompanied this prince to France were accustomed to sell to certain speculators charters for mother Lodges, patents for Chapters, etc. These titles were their property and they did not fail to use them as a means of livelihood.

It has been long held as a recognized fact in Masonic history that the first Lodge established in France by a warrant from the Grand Lodge of England was held in the year 1725. There is no doubt that a Lodge of Freemasons met in that year at the house of

one Hure, and that it was presided over by the titular Earl of Derwentwater.   But the researches of Bro. Hughan have incontestably
proved that this was what we would now call a clandestine body,
and that the first French Lodge legally established by the Grand
Lodge of England was in 1732.   Besides the fact that there is no
record in that Grand Lodge of England of any Lodge in France at
the early date of 1725, it is most improbable that a warrant would
have been granted to so conspicuous a Jacobite as Derwentwater.
Political reasons of the utmost gravity at that time would have forbidden any such action.

Charles Radcliffe, with his brother the Earl of Derwentwater,
had been arrested in England for the part taken by them in the rebellion of 1715 to place James III. on the throne.   They were
both condemned to death and the earl was executed, but Radcliffe
made his escape to France, where he assumed the title which, as he
claimed, had devolved upon him by the death of his brother's son.
In the subsequent rebellion of 1745, having attempted to join the
Young Pretender, the vessel in which he sailed was captured by an
English cruiser, and being carried to London, he was decapitated in
December, 1746.

The titular Earl of Derwentwater was therefore a zealous Jacobite, an attainted rebel who had been sentenced to death for his
treason, a fugitive from the law, and a pensioner of the Old Pretender or Chevalier St. George, who, by the order of Louis XIV., had
been proclaimed King of England under the title of James III.

It is absurd, therefore, to suppose that the Grand Lodge of England would have granted to him and to his Jacobite associates a
warrant for the establishment of a Lodge.   Its statutes had declared
in very unmistakable words that a rebel against the State was not
to be countenanced in his rebellion.   But no greater countenance
could have been given than to make him the Master of a new
Lodge.

Such, however, has until very recently been universally accepted
as a part of the authentic history of Masonry in France.   In the
words of a modern feuilletonist, " the story was too ridiculous to be
believed, and so everybody believed it."

But it is an undeniable fact that in 1725 an English Lodge was
really opened and held in the house of an English confectioner
named Hure.   It was however without regular or legal authority—

was probably organized, although we have no recorded evidence to that effect, through the advice and instructions of Ramsay—and was a Jacobite Lodge consisting solely of the adherents and partisans of the Old Pretender.

This is the most explicit instance that we have of the connection of the Stuarts with Freemasonry. It was an effort made by the adherents of that house to enlist the Order as an instrument to restore its fallen fortunes. The principal members of the Lodge were Derwentwater, Maskelyne, and Heguertly or Heguety. Of Derwentwater I have already spoken ; the second was evidently a Scotchman, but the name of the third has been so corrupted in its French orthography that we are unable to trace it to its source. It has been supposed that the real name was Haggerty ; if so, he was probably an Irishman. But they were all Jacobites.

The Rite of Strict Observance, which at one time in the last century took so strong a hold upon the Masons of Germany, and whose fundamental doctrine was that of Ramsay—that Freemasonry was only a continuation of the Templar system—is said to have been originally erected in the interésts of the Stuarts, and the Brotherhood was expected to contribute liberally to the enterprises in favor of the Pretender.

Upon a review of all that has been written on this very intricate subject—the theories oftentimes altogether hypothetical, assumptions in place of facts, conjectures altogether problematical, and the grain of history in this vast amount of traditional and mythical trash so small—we may, I think, be considered safe in drawing a few conclusions.

In the first place it is not to be doubted that at one time the political efforts of the adherents of the dethroned and exiled family of the Stuarts did exercise a very considerable effect on the outward form and the internal spirit of Masonry, as it prevailed on the continent of Europe.

In the symbolic degrees of ancient Craft Masonry, the influence was but slightly felt. It extended only to a political interpretation of the Legend of the Master's degree, in which sometimes the decapitation of Charles I., and sometimes the forced abdication and exile of James II., was substituted for the fate of Hiram, and to a change in the substitute word so as to give an application of the phrase the " Widow's son " to the child of Henrietta Maria, the consort of Charles I. The effect of these changes, except that of the *word*, which still continues in some Rites, has long since disappeared, but their memory still remains as a relict of the incidents of Stuart Masonry.

But the principal influence of this policy was shown in the fabrication of what are called the "High Degrees," the "Hautes Grades" of the French. Until the year 1728 these accumulations to the body of Masonry were unknown. The Chevalier Ramsay, the tutor of the Pretender in his childhood, and subsequently his most earnest friend and ardent supporter, was the first to fabricate these degrees, although other inventors were not tardy in following in his footsteps.

These degrees, at first created solely to institute a form of Masonry which should be worked for the purpose of restoring the Pretender to the throne of his ancestors, have most of them become obsolete, and their names alone are preserved in the catalogues of collectors; but their effect is to this day seen in such of them as still remain and are practiced in existing Rites, which have been derived indirectly from the system invented in the Chapter of Clermont or the Château of St. Germain. The particular design has passed away but the general features still remain, by which we are enabled to recognize the relicts of Stuart Masonry.

As to the time when this system first began to be developed there can be but little doubt.

We must reject the notion that James II. had any connection with it. However unfitted he may have been by his peculiar temperament from entering into any such bold conspiracy, the question is set at rest by the simple fact that up to the time of his death there was no Masonic organization upon which he or his partisans could have acted.

His son the Chevalier St. George was almost in the same category. He is described in history as a prince—pious, pacific and without talents, incapable of being made the prominent actor in such a drama, and besides, Speculative Masonry had not assumed the proportions necessary to make it available as a part of a conspiracy until long after he had retired from active life to the practice of religious and recluse habits in Rome.

But his son Charles Edward, the Young Pretender as he was called, was of an ardent temperament; an active genius, a fair amount of talent, and a spirit of enterprise which well fitted him to accept the place assigned him by Ramsay. Freemasonry had then begun to excite public attention, and was already an institution that was rapidly gaining popularity.

Ramsay saw in it what he deemed a fitting lever to be used in the elevation of his patron to the throne, and Prince Charles Edward with eagerness met his propositions and united with him in the futile effort.

To the Chevalier Ramsay we must attribute the invention of Stuart Masonry, the foundations of which he began to lay early in the 18th century, perhaps with the tacit approval of the Old Pretender. About 1725, when the first Lodge was organized in Paris, under some illegitimate authority, he made the first public exposition of his system in the Scottish High Degrees which he at that time brought to light. And finally the workings of the system were fully developed when the Young Pretender began his unsuccessful career in search of a throne, which once lost was never to be recovered.

This conspiracy of Ramsay to connect Freemasonry with the fortunes of the Stuarts was the first attempt to introduce politics into the institution. To the credit of its character as a school of speculative philosophy, the attempt proved a signal failure.

CHAPTER XXXI

HE opinion has been entertained by several writers of eminence that the Company of Jesus, more briefly styled the Jesuits, sought, about the end of the 17th and the beginning of the 18th century, to mingle with the Freemasons and to bend the objects of that Institution to the ambitious designs of their own Order. This view has been denied by other writers of equal eminence, though it is admitted that Roman Catholic, if not Jesuitical, features are to be found in some of the high degrees.

It is contended by one German writer that the object of the Jesuits in seeking a control of the Masonic Institution was that they might be thus assisted in their design of establishing an aristocracy within themselves, and that they sought to accomplish this object by securing not only the direction of the Masonic Lodges, but also by obtaining a monopoly of the schools and churches, and all the pursuits of science, and even of business.

But the more generally accepted reason for this attempted interference with the Lodges is that they thus sought by their influence and secret working to aid the Stuarts to regain the throne, and then, as an expected result, to re-establish the Roman Catholic religion in England.

The first of these explanations is certainly more satisfactory than the second. While there is a great want of historical testimony to prove that the Jesuits ever mingled with Freemasonry—a question to be hereafter decided—there is no doubt of the egotistical and ambitious designs of the disciples of Loyola to secure a control of the public and private affairs of every government where they could obtain a foothold. It was a knowledge of these designs that led to the unpopularity of the Order among even Catholic sovereigns and caused its total suppression, in 1773, by Pope Clement XIV., from

which it was not relieved until 1814, when their privileges were renewed by Pope Pius VII.

But I think that we must concur with Gadeike in the conclusion
to which he had arrived, that it is proved by history to be a falsehood that Freemasonry was ever concealed under the mask of Jesuitism, or that it derived its existence from that source.[1] It is,
however, but fair that we should collate and compare the arguments
on both sides.

Robison, who, where Masonry was concerned, could find a spec-
ter in every bush, is, of course, of very little authority as to facts;
but he may supply us with a record of the opinions which were prevalent at the time of his writing. He says that when James II. fled
from England to France, which was in 1688, his adherents took
Freemasonry with them to the continent, where it was received and
cultivated by the French in a manner suited to the tastes and
habits of that people. But he adds that "at this time, also, the Jesuits took a more active hand in Freemasonry than ever. They
insinuated themselves into the English Lodges, where they were
caressed by the Catholics, who panted after the re-establishment of
their faith, and tolerated by the Protestant royalists, who thought no
concession too great a compensation for their services. At this
time changes were made in some of the Masonic symbols, particularly in the tracing of the Lodge, which bear evident marks of Jesuitical interference."[2]

Speaking of the High Degrees, the fabrication of which, however, he greatly antedates, he says that "in all this progressive
mummery we see much of the hand of the Jesuits, and it would
seem that it was encouraged by the church."[3] But he thinks that
the Masons, protected by their secrecy, ventured further than the
clergy approved in their philosophical interpretations of the symbols,
opposing at last some of "the ridiculous and oppressive superstitions of the church,"[4] and thus he accounts for the persecution of
Freemasonry at a later period by the priests, and their attempts to
suppress the Lodges.

The story, as thus narrated by Robison, is substantially that which
has been accepted by all writers who trace the origin of Freemasonry

---

[1] "Freimaurer Lexicon," art. "*Jesuiten.*"
[2] "Proofs of a Conspiracy," p. 27.
[3] Ibid., p. 30.
[4] Ibid.

to the Jesuits. They affirm, as we have seen, that it was instituted about the time of the expulsion of James II. from England, or that if it was not then fabricated as a secret society, it was at least modified in all its features from that form which it originally had in England, and was adapted as a political engine to aid in the restoration of the exiled monarch and in the establishment in his recovered kingdom of the Roman Catholic religion.

These theorists have evidently confounded primitive Speculative Masonry, consisting only of three degrees, with the supplementary grades invented subsequently by Ramsay and the ritualists who succeeded him. But even if we relieve the theory of this confusion and view it as affirming that the Jesuits at the College of Clermont modified the third degree and invented others, such as the Scottish Knight of St. Andrew, for the purpose of restoring James II. to the throne, we shall find no scintilla of evidence in history to support this view, but, on the contrary, obstacles in the way of anachronisms which it will be impossible to overcome.

James II. abdicated the throne in 1688, and, after an abortive attempt to recover it by an unsuccessful invasion of Ireland, took up his residence at the Château of St. Germain-en-Laye, in France, where he died in 1701.

Between the two periods of 1688, when James abdicated, and 1701, when he died, no one has been enabled to find either in England or elsewhere any trace of a third degree. Indeed, I am very sure that it can be proved that this degree was not invented until 1721 or 1722. It is, therefore, absolutely impossible that any modification could have been made in the latter part of the 17th century of that which did not exist until the beginning of the 18th. And if there was no Speculative Masonry, as distinguished from the Operative Art practiced by the mediæval guilds, during the lifetime of James, it is equally absurd to contend that supplementary grades were invented to illustrate and complete a superstructure whose foundations had not yet been laid.

The theory that the Jesuits in the 17th century had invented Freemasonry for the purpose of effecting one of their ambitious projects, or that they had taken it as it then existed, changed it, and added to it for the same purpose, is absolutely untenable.

Another theory has been advanced which accounts for the establishment of what has been called "Jesuitic Masonry," at about the middle of the 18th century. This theory is certainly free from the absurd anachronisms which we encounter in the former, although the proofs that there ever was such a Masonry are still very unsatisfactory.

It has been maintained that this notion of the intrusion, as it may well be called, of the Jesuits into the Masonic Order has been attributed to the Illuminati, that secret society which was established by Adam Weishaupt in Bavaria about the year 1776.

The original object of this society was, as its founder declared, to enable its members to attain the greatest possible amount of virtue, and by the association of good men to oppose the progress of moral evil. To give it influence it was connected with Freemasonry, whose symbolic degrees formed the substratum of its esoteric instructions. This has led it incorrectly to be deemed a Masonic Rite; it could really lay no claim to that character, except inasmuch as it required a previous initiation into the symbolic degrees to entitle its disciples to further advancement.

The charges made against it, that it was a political organization, and that one of its designs was to undermine the Christian religion, although strenuously maintained by Barruel, Robison, and a host of other adversaries, have no foundation in truth. The principles of the order were liberal and philosophical, but neither revolutionary nor anti-Christian.

As the defender of free thought, it came of course into conflict with the Roman Catholic Church and the Company of Jesus, whose tendencies were altogether the other way. The priests, therefore, became its most active enemies, and their opposition was so successful that it was suppressed in 1784.

There was also between Illuminism and the many Masonic Rites, which about the period of its popularity were constantly arising in Germany and in France, a species of rivalry. With the natural egotism of reformers, the Illuminati sought to prove the superiority of their own system to that of their rivals.

With this view they proclaimed that all the Lodges of Free masons were secretly controlled by the Jesuits; that their laws and their mysteries were the inventions of the same Order, of whom every Freemason was unconsciously the slave and the instrument. Hence they concluded that he who desired to possess the genuine mysteries of Masonry must seek them not among the degrees of Rose Croix or the Scottish Knights, or still less among the English Masons and the disciples of the Rite of Strict Observance in Germany, but only in the Eclectic Lodges that had been instituted by the Illuminati.

Such, says Barruel, was the doctrine of the Illuminati, advanced for the purpose of elevating the character and aims of their own institution. The French abbé is not generally trustworthy on any subject connected with Freemasonry, of which he was the avowed and implacable foe, but we must acknowledge that he was not far from wrong in calling this story of Jesuitic Masonry "a ridiculous and contemptible fable." For once we are disposed to agree with him, when he says in his fervent declamation, " If prejudice did not sometimes destroy the faculty of reasoning, we should be astonished that the Freemasons could permit themselves to be ensnared in so clumsy a trap. What is it, in fact, but to say to the Mother Lodge of Edinburgh, to the Grand Lodges of London and York, to their rulers, and to all their Grand Masters: ' You thought that you held the reins of the Masonic world, and you looked upon yourselves as the great depository of its secrets, the distributers of its diplomas; but you are not so, and, without even knowing it, are merely puppets of which the Jesuits hold the leading-strings, and which they move at their pleasure.'" [1]

I think that with a little trouble we may be able to solve this apparently difficult problem of the Jesuitical interference with Freemasonry.

The Jesuits appear to have taken the priests of Egypt for their model. Like them, they sought to be the conservators and the interpreters of religion. The vows which they took attached them to their Order with bonds as indissoluble as those that united the Egyptian priests in the sacred college of Memphis. Those who sought admission into their company were compelled to pass through trials of their fortitude and fidelity. Their ambition was as indomitable as their cunning was astute. They strove to be the confessors and the counsellors of kings, and to control the education of youth, that by these means they might become of importance in the state, and direct the policy of every government where they

---

[1] " Memoires pour servir à l'Histoire du Jacobanisme," T. N., p. 291.

were admitted. And this policy was on all occasions to be made subservient to the interests of the church.

At one time they had not less than an hundred schools or colleges in France, the most important being that of Clermont, which, though at one time suppressed, had received renewed letters patent from Louis XIV.

It was this College of Clermont, where James II. was a frequent guest, led there by his religious feelings, that is said to have been the seat of that conspiracy of the Stuart faction which was to terminate either in the invention or the adoption of Freemasonry as a means of restoring the monarch to his throne, and of resuscitating the Roman Catholic religion in heretical England.

Now we may readily admit that the Jesuits were exceedingly anxious to accomplish both these objects, and that for that purpose they would enter into any intrigue which would probably lead to success.

With this design there can be but little doubt that they united with the adherents of the Stuarts. But this conspiracy could not have had any reference to a Masonic organization, because Freemasonry was during the life of James II. wholly unknown in France, and known in England only as a guild of Operative Masons, into which a few non-Masons had been admitted through courtesy. It certainly had not yet assumed the form in which we are called upon to recognize it as the political engine used by the Jesuits. The Grand Lodge of England, the mother of all modern Speculative Masonry, had no existence until 1717, or sixteen years after the death of the king.

We are bound, therefore, if on the ground of an anachronism alone, to repudiate any theory that connects the Jesuits with Freemasonry during the life of James II., although we may be ready to admit their political conspiracy in the interests of that dethroned monarch.

During the life of his son and putative successor, the titular James III., Speculative Masonry was established in England and passed over into France.

The Lodge established in Paris in 1725 was, I have no doubt, an organization of the adherents of the Stuart family, as has already been shown. It is probable that most of the members were Catholics and under the influence of the Jesuits. But it is not likely that those priests took an active part in the internal organization of the Lodge. They could do their work better outside of it than within it.

In the Rose Croix and some other of the High Degrees we find the influences of a Roman Catholic spirit in the original rituals, but this might naturally arise from the religious tendencies of their founders, and did not require the special aid of Jesuitism.

After the year 1738 the bull of excommunication of Pope Clement XII. must have precluded the Jesuits from all connection with Freemasonry except as its denouncers and persecutors, parts which up to the present day they have uninterruptedly played.

In conclusion we must, I think, refuse to accept the theory which makes a friendly connection between Freemasonry and Jesuitism as one of those mythical stories which, born in the imagination of its inventors, has been fostered only by the credulity of its believers.

At this day I doubt if there is a Masonic scholar who would accept it as more than a fable not even " cunningly devised," though there was a time when it was received as a part of the authentic history of Freemasonry.

CHAPTER XXXII

THREE fables have been invented to establish a connection between Freemasonry and the dynasty of the Stuarts—one which made it the purpose of the adherents of James II. to use the Institution as a means of restoring that monarch to the throne ; a second in which the Jesuits were to employ it for the same purpose, as well as for the re-establishment of the Roman Catholic religion in England ; the third and most preposterous of these fables is that which attributes the invention of Freemasonry as a secret society to Oliver Cromwell, who is supposed to have employed it as a political engine to aid him in the dethronement of Charles I., in the abolition of the monarchy, and in the foundation of a republic on its ruins, with himself for its head.

The first and second of these fables have already been discussed. The consideration of the third will be the subject of the present chapter.

The theory that Freemasonry was instituted by Oliver Cromwell was not at first received like the other two by any large portion of the fraternity.   It was the invention of a single mind and was first made public in the year 1746, by the Abbé Larudan, who presented his views in a work entitled *Les Franc-Maçons écrassés*—a book which Klass, the bibliographer, says is the armory from which all the enemies of Masonry have since derived their weapons of abuse.

The propositions of Larudan are distinguished for their absolute independence of all historical authority and for the bold assumptions which are presented to the reader in the place of facts.

His strongest argument for the truth of his theory is that the purposes of the Masonic Institution and of the political course of Cromwell are identical, namely, to sustain the doctrines of liberty and equality among mankind.

Rejecting all the claims to antiquity that have been urged in be-half of the Institution, he thinks that it was in England where the Order of Freemasonry first saw the light of day, and that it is to Cromwell that it owes its origin.   And this theory he claims (with what truth we know not) to have received from a certain Grand Master with whose astuteness and sincerity he was well acquainted. But even this authority, he says, would not have been sufficient to secure his belief, had it not afterward been confirmed by his reading of the history of the English Protector and his mature reflections on the morals and the laws of the Order, where he detected at every step the presence of Cromwell.

The object of Cromwell, as it has been already said, was by the organization of a secret society, whose members would be bound by the most solemn ties of fraternity, to reconcile the various relig-ions and political sects which prevailed in England in the reign of Charles I. to the prosecution of his views, which were equally op-posed to the supremacy of the king and to the power of the Parlia-ment, and as a consequence of the destruction of both, to the eleva-tion of himself to the headship of affairs.

In the execution of this plan Cromwell proceeded with his usual caution and address.   He first submitted the outline to several of his most intimate friends, such as Algernon Sidney, Harrington, Monk, and Fairfax, and he held with them several private meetings. But it was not until the year 1648 that he began to take the neces-sary steps for bringing it to maturity.

In that year, at a dinner which he gave to a large number of his friends, he opened his designs to the company.   When his guests, among whom were many members of Parliament, both Presbyterians and Independents, the two rival religious sects of the day, had been well feasted, the host dexterously led the conversation to the subject of the unhappy condition of England.   He showed in a pathetic manner how the unfortunate nation had suffered distracting conflicts of politics and religion, and he declared that it was a disgrace that men so intelligent as those who then heard him did not make an exertion to put an end to these distracting contests of party.

Scarcely had Cromwell ceased to speak when Ireton, his son-in-law, who had been prepared for the occasion rose, and, seconding the sentiments of his leader, proceeded to show the absolute necessity for the public good of a conciliation and union of the many discordant parties which were then dividing the country.   He exclaimed with fervor that he would not, himself, hesitate to sacrifice his fortune and his life to remedy such calamities, and to show to the people the road they ought to take, to relieve themselves from the yoke which was oppressing them and to break the iron scepter under which they were groaning.   But to do this it was first necessary, he insisted, to destroy every power and influence which had betrayed the nation.   Then, turning to Cromwell, he conjured him to explain his views on this important matter, and to suggest the cure for these evils.

Cromwell did not hesitate to accept the task which had, apparently without his previous concurrence, been assigned to him.   Addressing his guests in that metaphorical style which he was accustomed to use, and the object of which was to confuse their intellects and make them more ready to receive his boldest propositions, he explained the obligation of a worship of God, the necessity to repel force by force, and to deliver mankind from oppression and tyranny.   He then concluded his speech, exciting the curiosity of his auditors by telling them that he knew a method by which they could succeed in this great enterprise, restore peace to England, and rescue it from the depth of misery into which it was plunged.   This method, he added, if communicated to the world, would win the gratitude of mankind and secure a glorious memory for its authors to the latest posterity.

The discourse was well managed and well received.   All of his guests earnestly besought him to make this admirable expedient known to them.   But Cromwell would not yield at once to their importunities, but modestly replying that so important an enterprise was beyond the strength of any one man to accomplish, and that he would rather continue to endure the evils of a bad government than, in seeking to remove them by the efforts of his friends, to subject them to dangers which they might be unwiling to encounter.

Cromwell well understood the character of every man who sat at the table with him, and he knew that by this artful address he should still further excite their curiosity and awaken their enthusiasm.

And so it was that, after a repetition of importunities, he finally consented to develop his scheme, on the condition that all the guests should take a solemn oath to reveal the plan to no one and to consider it after it had been proposed with absolutely unprejudiced mind.   This was unanimously assented to, and, the oath of secrecy having been taken, Cromwell threw himself on his knees and, extending his hands toward heaven, called on God and all the celestial powers to witness the innocence of his heart and the purity of his intentions.   All this the Abbé Larudan relates with a minuteness of detail which we could expect only from an eye-witness of the scene.

Having thus made a deep impression on his guests, Cromwell said that the precise moment for disclosing the plan had not arrived, and that an inspiration from heaven, which he had just received, instructed him not to divulge it until four days had elapsed.

The company though impatient to receive a knowledge of the important secret, were compelled to restrain their desires and to agree to meet again at the appointed time and at a place which was designated.

On the fourth day all the guests repaired to a house in King Street, where the meeting took place, and Cromwell proceeded to develop his plan.   (And here the Abbé Larudan becomes fervid and diffuse in the minuteness with which he describes what must have been a wholly imaginary scene.)

He commenced by conducting the guests into a dark room, where he prepared their minds for what was going to occur by a long prayer, in the course of which he gave them to understand that he was in communion with the spirits of the blessed.   After this he told them that his design was to found a society whose only objects would be to render due worship to God and to restore to England the peace for which it so ardently longed.   But this project, he added, required consummate prudence and infinite address to secure its success.   Then taking a censer in his hands, he filled the apartment with the most subtle fumes, so as to produce a favorable disposition in the company to hear what he had further to say.

He informed them that at the reception of a new adherent it was necessary that he should undergo a certain ceremony, to which all of them, without exception, would have to submit.   He asked them whether they were willing to pass through this ceremony, to which proposition unanimous consent was given.   He then chose from the company five assistants to occupy appropriate places and to perform prescribed functions.   These assistants were a Master, two Wardens, a Secretary, and an Orator.

Having made these preparations, the visitors were removed to another apartment, which had been prepared for the purpose, and in which was a picture representing the ruins of King Solomon's Temple. From this apartment they were transferred to another, and, being blindfolded, were finally invested with the secrets of initiation. Cromwell delivered a discourse on religion and politics, the purport of which was to show to the contending sects of Presbyterians and Independents, representatives of both being present, the necessity, for the public good, of abandoning all their frivolous disputes, of becoming reconciled, and of changing the bitter hatred which then inspired them for a tender love and charity toward each other.

The eloquence of their artful leader had the desired effect, and both sects united with the army in the establishment of a secret association founded on the professed principles of love of God and the maintenance of liberty and equality among men, but whose real design was to advance the projects of Cromwell, by the abolition of the monarchy and the establishment of a commonwealth of which he should be the head.

It is unfortunate for the completed symmetry of this rather interesting fable that the Abbé has refrained from indulging his imagination by giving us the full details of the form of initiation. He has, however, in various parts of his book alluded to so much of it as to enable us to learn that the instructions were of a symbolic character, and that the Temple of Solomon constituted the most prominent symbol.

This Temple had been built by divine command to be the sanctuary of religion and as a place peculiarly consecrated to the performance of its august ceremonies. After several years of glory and magnificence it had been destroyed by a formidable army, and the people who had been there accustomed to worship were loaded with chains and carried in captivity to Babylon. After years of servitude, an idolatrous prince, chosen as the instrument of Divine clemency, had permitted the captives to return to Jerusalem and to rebuild the Temple in its primitive splendor.

It was in this allegory, says the Abbé, that the Freemasons of Cromwell found the exact analogy of their society. The Temple in its first splendor is figurative of the primitive state of man. The religion and the ceremonies which were there practiced are nothing else than that universal law engraved on every heart whose principles are found in the ideas of equity and charity to which all men are obliged. The destruction of this Temple, and the captivity and slavery of its worshippers, symbolized the pride and ambition which have produced political subjection among men. The unpitying hosts of Assyrians who destroyed the Temple and led the people into captivity are the kings, princes, and magistrates whose power has overwhelmed oppressed nations with innumerable evils. And finally, the chosen people charged with the duty of rebuilding the Temple are the Freemasons, who are to restore men to their original dignity.

Cromwell had divided the Order which he founded into three classes or degrees. The third or Master's degree was of course not without its Hiramic legend, but the interpretation of its symbolism was very different from that which is given at the present day.

The Abbé thus explains it. The disorder of the workmen and the confusion at the Temple were intended to make a profound impression upon the mind of the candidate and to show him that the loss of liberty and equality, represented by the death of Hiram, is the cause of all the evils which affect mankind. While men lived in tranquillity in the asylum of the Temple of Liberty they enjoyed perpetual happiness. But they have been surprised and attacked by tyrants who have reduced them to a state of slavery. This is symbolized by the destruction of the Temple, which it is the duty of the Master Masons to rebuild; that is to say, to restore that liberty and equality which had been lost.

Cromwell appointed missionaries or emissaries, says Larudan, who propagated the Order, not only over all England, but even into Scotland and Ireland, where many Lodges were established.

The members of the Order or Society were first called Freemasons; afterward the name was repeatedly changed to suit the political circumstances of the times, and they were called Levelers, then Independents, afterward Fifth Monarchy Men, and finally resumed their original title, which they have retained to the present day.

Such is the fable of the Cromwellian origin of Freemasonry which we owe entirely to the inventive genius of the Abbé Larudan. And yet it is not wholly a story of the imagination, but is really founded on an extraordinary distortion of the facts of history.

Edmund Ludlow was an honest and honorable man who took at first a prominent part in the civil war which ended in the decapitation of Charles I., the dissolution of the monarchy, and the establishment of the Commonwealth.   He was throughout his whole life a consistent and unswerving republican, and was as much opposed to the political schemes of Cromwell for his own advancement to power as he was to the usurpation of unconstitutional power by the King.   In the language of the editor of his memoirs, "He was an enemy to all arbitrary government, though gilded over with the most specious pretences; and not only disapproved the usurpation of Cromwell, but would have opposed him with as much vigor as he had done the King, if all occasions of that nature had not been cut off by the extraordinary jealousy or vigilance of the usurpers."[1]

Having unsuccessfully labored to counteract the influence of Cromwell with the army, he abandoned public affairs and retired to his home in Essex, where he remained in seclusion until the restoration of Charles II., when he fled to Switzerland, where he resided until his death.

During his exile, Ludlow occupied his leisure hours in the composition of his *Memoirs*, a work of great value as a faithful record of the troublous period in which he lived and of which he was himself a great part.   In these memoirs he has given a copious narrative of the intrigues by which Cromwell secured the alliance of the army and destroyed the influence of the Parliament.

The work was published at Vevay, in Switzerland, under the title of *Memoirs of Edmund Ludlow, Esq.; Lieutenant-General of the Tories in Ireland, One of the Council of State, and a Member of the Parliament which began on November 3, 1640.*   It is in two volumes, with a supplementary one containing copies of important papers. The edition from which I cite bears the date of 1698.   There may have been an earlier one.   With these memoirs the Abbé Larudan appears to have been well acquainted.   He had undoubtedly read them carefully, for he has made many quotations and has repeatedly referred to Ludlow as his authority.

But unfortunately for the Abbé's intelligence, or far more probably for his honesty, he has always applied what Ludlow said of the intrigues of Cromwell for the organization of a new party as if it were meant to describe the formation of a new and secret society.

Neither Ludlow nor any other writer refers to the existence of Freemasonry as we now have it and as it is described by the Abbé

---

[1] Ludlow's "Memoirs," Preface, p. iv.

Larudan in the time of the civil wars. Even the Operative Masons were not at that period greatly encouraged, for, says Northouck, "no regard to science and elegance was to be expected from the sour minds of the puritanical masters of the nation between the fall of Charles I. and the restoration of his son." [1]

The Guild of Freemasons, the only form in which the Order was known until the 18th century, was during the Commonwealth discouraged and architecture was neglected. In the tumult of war the arts of peace are silent. Cromwell was, it is true, engaged in many political intrigues, but he had other and more effective means to accomplish his ends than those of Freemasonry, of whose existence at that time, except as a guild of workmen, we have no historical evidence, but a great many historical facts to contradict its probability.

The theory, therefore, that Freemasonry owes its origin to Oliver Cromwell, who invented it as a means of forwarding his designs toward obtaining the supreme power of the state, is simply a fable, the invention of a clerical adversary of the Institution, and devised by him plainly to give to it a political character, by which, like his successors Barruel and Robison, he sought to injure it.

---

[1] Northouck's "Constitutions," p. 141.

CHAPTER XXXIII

HE hypothesis that Freemasonry was instituted in the 17th century and in the reign of Charles II., by a set of philosophers and scientists who organized it under the title of the " Royal Society," is the last of those theories which attempts to connect the Masonic Order with the House of Stuart that we will have to investigate.

The theory was first advanced by an anonymous writer in the *German Mercury*, a Masonic journal published about the close of the last century at Weimar, and edited by the celebrated Christopher Martin Wieland.

In this article the writer says that Dr. John Wilkins, one of the most learned men of his time, and the brother-in-law of Oliver Cromwell, becoming discontented with the administration of Richard Cromwell, his son and successor, began to devise the means of re-establishing the royal authority. With this view he suggested the idea of organizing a society or club, in which, under the pretence of cultivating the sciences, the partisans of the king might meet together with entire freedom. General Monk and several other military men, who had scarcely more learning than would enable them to write their names, were members of this academy. Their meetings were always begun with a learned lecture, for the sake of form, but the conversation afterward turned upon politics and the interests of the king. And this politico-philosophical club, which subsequently assumed, after the Restoration, the title of the " Royal Society of Sciences," he asserts to have been the origin of the fraternity of Freemasons.

We have already had abundant reason to see, in the formation of Masonic theories, what little respect has been paid by their framers to the contradictory facts of history nor does the present hypothesis afford any exception to the general rule of dogmatic assumption and unfounded assertion.

Christopher Frederick Nicolai, a learned bookseller of Berlin, wrote and published, in 1783, an *Essay on the Accusations made against the Order of Knights Templars and their Mystery; with an Appendix on the Origin of the Fraternity of Freemasons.*[1]

In this work he vigorously attacks the theory of the anonymous writer in Wieland's *Mercury*, and the reasons on which he grounds his dissent are well chosen, but they do not cover the whole ground. Unfortunately, Nicolai had a theory of his own to foster, which also in a certain way connects Freemasonry with the real founders of the Royal Society, and the impugnment of the hypothesis of Wieland's contribution in its whole extent impugns also his own. Two negatives in most languages are equivalent to an affirmative, but nowhere are two fictions resolvable into a truth.

The arguments of Nicolai against the Wieland theory are, however, worth citation, before we examine his own.

He says that Wilkins could scarcely have been discontented with the government of Richard Cromwell, since it was equally as advantageous to him as that of his father. He was (and he quotes Wood in the *Athenæ Oxonienses* as his authority) much opposed to the court, and was a zealous Puritan before the rebellion.

In 1648 he was made the Master of Wadham College, in the place of a royalist who had been removed. In 1649, after the decapitation of Charles I., he joined the republican party and took the oath of allegiance to the Commonwealth. In 1656 he married the sister of Cromwell, and under Richard received the valuable appointment of Master of Trinity College, which, however, he lost upon the restoration of the monarchy in the following year.

"Is it credible," says Nicolai, "that this man could have instituted a society for the purpose of advancing the restoration of the king; a society all of whose members were of the opposite party? The celebrated Dr. Goddard, who was one of the most distinguished members, was the physician and favorite of Cromwell, whom, after the death of the King, he attended in his campaigns in Ireland and Scotland. It is an extraordinary assertion that a dis-

---

[1] "Versuch über die Besschuldigungen, welche dem Tempelherrn orden gemacht worden und über dessen Geheimniss ; nebst einem Anhange über das Enstehen der Freimaurergesellschaft," Berlin and Stettin, 1783.

content with the administration of Richard Cromwell should have given rise in 1658 to a society which was instituted in 1646. It is not less extraordinary that this society should have held its meetings in a tavern. It is very certain that in those days of somber Puritanism the few taverns to be found in London could not have been used as places of meeting for associations consisting of men of all conditions, as is now the custom. There would have been much imprudence in thus exposing secret deliberations on an affair equally dangerous and important to the inspection of all the spies who might be congregated in a tavern."

He asserts that the first meetings of the society were held at the house of Dr. Goddard and of another member, and afterward at Cheapside and at Gresham College. And these facts are proved by the records of the society, as published by its annalists.

As to the statement that Monk was one of the members of the society—a fact that would be important in strengthening the theory that it was organized by the friends of the monarchy and with a design of advancing its restoration—he shows the impossibility that it could be correct, because Monk was a prisoner in the Tower from 1643 until 1647, and after his release in that year spent only a month in London, not again visiting that city till 1659, when he returned at the head of an army and was engaged in the arrangement of such delicate affairs and was so narrowly watched that it is not possible to be believed that with his well-known caution he would have taken part in any sort of political society whatever, while the society would have acted very inconsiderately in admitting into its ranks military men who could scarcely write, and that too at a time when distrust had risen to its height.

But a better proof than any advanced by Nicolai, that Monk had nothing to do with the establishment of the Royal Society, whatever may have been its object, is that his name does not appear upon the list of original or early members, taken from the official records and published by Dr. Thompson in his history of the society.

Finally Nicolai asserts very truthfully that its subsequent history has shown that this society was really engaged in scientific pursuits, and that politics were altogether banished from its conferences. But he also contends, but with less accuracy, that the political principles of its members were opposed to the restoration of the monarchy, for which statement there is no positive authority.

Hence Nicolai concludes that "there is no truth in the statements of the anonymous writer in Wieland's *Mercury*, except that the restoration was opposed in secret by a certain society."

And now he advances his own theory, no less untenable than the one he is opposing, that this society "was the Freemasons, who had nothing in common with the other, except the date of foundation, and whose views in literature as well as in politics were of an entirely opposite character."

This was the theory of Nicolai—not that Freemasonry originated in the Royal Society, but that it was established by certain learned men who sought to advance the experimental philosophy which had just been introduced by Bacon. But the same idea was sought by the originators of the Royal Society, and as many of the founders of this school were also among the founders of the Royal Society, it seems difficult to separate the two theories so as to make of each a distinct and independent existence. But it will be better to let the Berlin bookseller explain his doctrine in his own language, before an attempt is made to apply to it the canons of criticism.

He commences by asserting that one of the effects of the labors of Andrea and the other Rosicrucians was the application of a wholesome criticism to the examination of philosophical and scientific subjects. He thinks even that the *Fama Fraternitatis*, the great work of Andrea, had first suggested to Bacon the notion of his immortal work on *The Advancement of Learning.* At the same time in which Bacon flourisheb and taught his inductive philosophy, the Rosicrucians had introduced a system of philosophy which was established on the phenomena of nature.

Lord Bacon had cultivated these views in his book *De Augmentis Scientiarum*, except that he rejected the Rosicrucian method of esoteric instruction. Everything that he taught was to be open and exoteric. Therefore, as he had written his great work in the Latin language, for the use of the learned, he now composed his *New Atlantis* in English, that all classes might be able to read it.

In this work is contained his celebrated romance of the House of Solomon, which Nicolai thinks may have had its influence in originating the society of Freemasons.

In this fictitious tale Bacon supposes that a vessel lands on an unknown island, called Bensalem, over which in days of yore a certain King Solomon reigned. This King had a large establishment, which was called the House of Solomon or the College of the Six Days' Work, in allusion to the six days of the Mosaic account of the creation. He afterward describes the immense apparatus which was there employed in physical researches. There were deep grottoes and tall bowers for the observation of the phenomena of nature ; artificial mineral-waters ; large buildings in which meteors, the wind, rain and thunder and lightning were imitated; extensive botanic gardens, and large fields in which all kinds of animals were collected for the study of their instinct and habits, and houses filled with all the wonders of nature and art. There were also a great number of learned men, to whom the direction of these things was intrusted. They made journeys into foreign countries, and observations on what they saw. They wrote, they collected, they determined results, and deliberated together as to what was proper to be published.

This romance, says Nicolai, which was in accord with the prevailing taste of the age, contributed far more to spread the views of Bacon on the observation of nature than his more learned and profound work had been able to do. The House of Solomon attracted the attention of everybody. King Charles I. was anxious to establish something like it, but was prevented by the civil wars. Nevertheless this great idea, associated with that of the Rosicrucians, continued to powerfully agitate the minds of the learned men of that period, who now began to be persuaded of the necessity of experimental knowledge.

Accordingly, in 1646, a society of learned men was established, all of whom were of Bacon's opinion, that philosophy and the physical sciences should be placed within the reach of all thinking minds. They held meetings at which—believing that instruction in physics was to be sought by a mutual communication of ideas—they made many scientific experiments in common. Among these men were John Wallis, John Wilkins, Jonathan Goddard, Samuel Foster, Francis Glisson, and many others, all of whom were, fourteen years afterward, the founders of the Royal Society.

But proceedings like these were not congenial with the intellectual condition of England at that period. A melancholy and somber spirit had overshadowed religion, and a mystical theology, almost Gnostic in its character, had infected the best minds. Devotion had passed into enthusiasm and that into fanaticism, and sanguinary wars and revolutions were the result.

It was then that such skillful hypocrites as Cromwell and Ireton took advantage of this weakness for the purpose of concealing and advancing their own designs.

The taint of this dark and sad character is met with in all the science, the philosophy, and even in the oratory and poetry of the period. Astrology and Theurgy were then in all their glory. Chemistry, which took the place of experimental science, was as obscure as every other species of learning, and its facts were enveloped in the allegories of the Alchemists and the Rosicrucians. A few learned men, disheartened by this obscuration of intellectual light, had organized a society in 1646; but as they were still imbued with a remnant of the popular prejudice, they were the partisans of the esoteric method of instruction, and did not believe that human knowledge should be exoterically taught so as to become accessible to all. Hence their society became a secret one. The first members of this society were, says Nicolai, Elias Ashmole, the celebrated antiquary; William Lilly, a famous astrologer; Thomas Wharton, a physician; George Wharton; William Oughtred, a mathematician; Dr. John Hewitt, and Dr. John Pearson, both clergymen, and several others. The annual festival of the Astrologers gave rise to this association. It had previously held one meeting at Warrington, in Lancashire, but it was first firmly established at London.

Its object was to build the House of Solomon in a literal sense; but the establishment was to remain as secret as the island of Bensalem in Bacon's *New Atlantis;* that is, they were to be engaged in the study of nature, but the instructions were to remain within the society in an esoteric form; in other words, it was to be a secret society. Allegories were used by these philosophers to express their ideas. First were the ancient columns of Hermes, by which Jamblichus pretended that he had enlightened all the doubts of Porphyry. You then mounted, by several steps, to a chequered floor divided into four regions, to denote the four superior sciences, after which came the types of the six days, which expressed the object of the society. All of which was intended to teach the doctrines that God created the world and preserves it by fixed principles, and that he who seeks to know these principles, by an investigation of the interior of nature, approximates to God and obtains from His grace the power of commanding nature. This, says Nicolai, was the essence of the mystical and alchemical doctrine of the age, so that we may conclude that the society which he has been describing was in reality an association of alchemists, or rather of astrologers.

In these allegories, for which Nicolai may have been indebted to the alchemical writings of that period, to which he refers, or for which he may have drawn on his own imagination—we are uncertain which, as he cites no authorities—we may plainly detect Masonic symbols, such as the pillars of the porch of the Temple, the mystical ladder of steps, and the mosaic pavement, and thus it is that he seems to find an analogy between Freemasonry and the secret society that he has been describing.

He still further pursues the hypothesis of their identity in the following remarks:

"It is known," he says, "that all who have the right of citizenship in London, whatever may be their rank or condition, must be recognized as members of some company or corporation. But it is always easy for a man of quality or of letters to gain admission into one of these companies. Now, several members of the society that has just been described were also members of the Company of Masons. This was the reason of their holding their meetings at Masons' Hall, in Masons' Alley, Basinghall Street. They all entered the company and assumed the name of *Free and Accepted Masons*, adopting, besides, all its external marks of distinction. *Free* is the title which every member of this body assumes in England; the right or franchise is called *Freedom;* the brethren call themselves *Freemen; Accepted* means, in this place, that this private society had been accepted or incorporated into that of the Masons, and thus it was that chance gave birth to that denomination of *Freemasons* which afterward became so famous, although it is possible that some allusion may also have been intended to the building of the House of Solomon, an allegory with which they were also familiar."

Hence, according to the theory of Nicolai, two famous associations, each of a character peculiar to itself, were at the same period indebted to the same cause for their existence. These were the Royal Society and the Freemasons. "Both," he says, "had the same object and the difference in their proceedings arose only from a difference in some of the opinions of their members. The one society had adopted as its maxim that the knowledge of nature and of natural science should be indiscriminately communicated to all classes of men, while the other contended that the secrets of nature should be restricted to a small number of chosen recipients. The former body, which was the Royal Society, therefore held open meetings; the latter, which was the Society of Freemasons, enveloped its transactions in mystery."

" In those days," says Nicolai, " the Freemasons were altogether devoted to the King and opposed to the Parliament, and they soon occupied themselves at their meetings in devising the means of sustaining the royal cause. After the death of Charles I., in 1649, the Royalists becoming still more closely united, and, fearing to be known as such, they joined the assemblies of the Freemasons for the purpose of concealing their own identity, and the good intentions of that society being well known many persons of rank were admitted into it. But as the objects which occupied their attention were no other than to diminish the number of the partisans of Parliament, and to prepare the way for the restoration of Charles II. to the throne, it would have been very imprudent to communicate to all Freemasons, without exception, the measures which they deemed it expedient to take, and which required an inviolable secrecy. Accordingly they adopted the method of selecting a certain number of their members, who met in secret, and this committee, which had nothing at all to do with the House of Solomon, selected allegories, which had no relation to the former ones, but which were very appropriate to their design. These new Masons took Death for their symbol. They lamented the death of their master, Charles I.; they nursed the hope of vengeance on his murderers; they sought to re-establish the *Word,* or his son, Charles II., for they applied to him the word *Logos,* which, in its theological sense, means both the *Word* and the *Son;* and the Queen, Henrietta Maria, the relict of Charles I., being thenceforth the head of the party, they designated themselves the *Widow's Sons.*

" They agreed also upon private signs and modes of recognition, by which the friends of the royal cause might be able to distinguish each other from their enemies. This precaution was of great utility to those who traveled, and especially to those of them who retired with the court to Holland, where, being surrounded by the spies of the Commonwealth, it was necessary to be exceedingly diligent in guarding their secret."

Nicolai then proceeds to show how, after the death of Oliver Cromwell and the abdication of his son Richard, the administration of affairs fell into the hands of the chiefs of various parties, whence resulted confusion and dissensions, which tended to render the cause of the monarchy still more popular.   The generals of the army were, however, still opposed to any notion of a restoration, and the hopes of the royalists centered upon General Monk, who commanded the army in Scotland, and who, it was known, had begun to look favorably on propositions which he had received in 1659 from the exiled King.

It then became necessary to bind their secret committee still more closely, that they might treat of Scottish affairs in reference to the interests of the King.   They selected new allegories, which symbolized the critical state to which they were reduced, and the virtues, such as prudence, pliancy, and courage, which were necessary to success.   They selected a new device and a new sign, "and in their meetings spoke allegorically of taking care, in that wavering and uncertain condition of falling, lest the arms should be broken."   It is probable that, in this last and otherwise incomprehensible sentence, Nicolai refers to some of the changes made in the High Degrees, fabricated about the middle of the 18th century, but whose invention he incorrectly, but like most Masonic historians of his day, attributes to an earlier date.

As some elucidation of what he says respecting the fact of *falling and the broken arm*, we find Nicolai afterward quoting a small dictionary which he says appeared about the beginning of the 18th century, and in which we meet with the following definition :

"*Mason's Wound*, An imaginary wound above the elbow, to represent a fracture of the arm occasioned by a fall from an elevated place."

"This," says Nicolai, "is the authentic history of the origin of the Society of Freemasons, and of the first changes that it underwent, changes which transformed it from an esoteric society of natural philosophers into an association of good patriots and loyal subjects ; and hence it was that it subsequently took the name of the Royal Art as applied to Masonry."

He concludes by affirming that the Society of Freemasons continued to assemble after the Restoration, in 1660, and even made, in 1663, several regulations for its preservation, but the zeal of its members was diminished by the changes which science and manners underwent during the reign of Charles II.   Its political character

ceased by the advent of the king, and its esoteric method of teaching the natural sciences must have been greatly interrupted.

The Royal Society, whose method had been exoteric and open,
and from whose conferences politics were excluded, although its
members were, in principle, opposed to the Restoration, had a more
successful progress, and was joined by many of the Freemasons, the
most prominent of whom was Elias Ashmole, who, Nicolai says,
changed his opinions and became a member of the Royal Society.

But, to prevent its dissolution, the Society of Freemasons made
several changes in its constitution, so as to give it a specific design.
This was undertaken and the symbols of the Society were altered
so as to substitute the Temple of Solomon in the place of Bacon's
House of Solomon, as a more appropriate allegory to express the
character of the new institution.   Nicolai thinks that the building
of St. Paul's Church and the persecutions endured by Sir Christopher Wren may have contributed to the selection of these new symbols.   But on this point he does not insist.

Such is the theory of Nicolai.   Rejecting the idea that the origin of the Order of Freemasonry is to be traced to the founders of
the Royal Society, he claims to have found it in a society of contemporaneous philosophers who met at Masons' Hall, in Basinghall
Street, and assumed the name of Free and Accepted Masons, and who,
claiming, in opposition to the views of the members of the Royal
Society, that all sciences should be communicated esoterically, therefore held their meetings in secret, their real object therefor being to
nourish a political conspiracy for the advancement of the cause of
the monarchy and the restoration of the exiled King.

Nicolai does not expressly mention the Astrologers, but it is very
evident that he alludes to them as the so-called philosophers who
originated this secret society, and to them, therefore, he attributes
the invention of the Masonic system, as it now exists, after the
necessary changes which policy and the vicissitudes of the times
had induced.

Nicholas de Bonneville, the author of the essay entitled *The
Jesuits chased out of Freemasonry*, entertained a similar opinion.
He says that in 1646 a society of Rosicrucians was formed at London, modeled on the ideas of the *New Atlantis* of Bacon.   It
assembled in Masons' Hall, where Ashmole and other Rosicrucians modified the formula of reception of the Operative Masons,

which had consisted only of a few ceremonies used by craftsmen, and substituted a mode of initiation founded in part on the mysteries of Ancient Egypt and Greece.   They then fabricated the first degree of Masonry as we now have it, and, to distinguish themselves from common Masons, called themselves Freemasons.   Thory cites this without comment in his *Acta Latomorum*, and gives it as a part of the authentic annals of the Order.

But ingenious and plausible as are these views, both of Nicolai and Bonneville, they unfortunately can not withstand the touchstone of all truth, the proofs of authentic history.

It will be seen that we have two hypotheses to investigate—first that advanced by the contributor to Wieland's *Mercury*, that the Society of Freemasons was originated by the founders of the Royal Society, and that maintained by Nicolai and Bonneville, that it owes its invention to the Astrologers who were contemporary with these founders.   Both hypotheses place the date of the invention in the same year, 1646, and give London as the place of the invention.

We must first direct our attention to the theory which maintains that the Royal Society was the origin of Freemasonry, and that the founders of that academy were the establishers of the Society of Freemasons.

This theory, first advanced, apparently, by the anonymous contributor to Wieland's *Mercury*, was exploded by Nicolai, in the arguments heretofore quoted, but something may be added to increase the strength of what he has said.

We have the explicit testimony of all the historians of that institution that it was not at all connected with the political contests of the day, and that it was founded only as a means of pursuing philosophical and scientific inquiries.

Dr. Thompson, who derives his information from the early records of the society, says that "it was established for the express purpose of advancing experimental philosophy, and that its foundation was laid during the time of the civil wars and was owing to the accidental association of several learned men who took no part in the disturbances which agitated Great Britain." [1]

He adds that "about the year 1645 several ingenious men who

---

[1] " History of the Royal Society," by Thomas Thompson, M.D., F.R.S., LL.D. London, 1812, p. 1.

resided in London and were interested in the progress of mathematics and natural philosophy agreed to meet once a week to discourse upon subjects connected with these sciences. These meetings were suspended after the resignation of Richard Cromwell, but revived in 1660, upon the Restoration." [1]

They met at first in private rooms, but afterward in Gresham College and then in Arundel House. Their earliest code of laws shows that their conferences were not in secret, but open to properly introduced visitors, as they still continue to be.

Weld, the librarian of the society, says that to it "attaches the renown of having from its foundation applied itself with untiring zeal and energy to the great objects of its institution." [2] He states that, although the society was not chartered until 1660, "there is no doubt that a society of learned men were in the habit of assembling together to discuss scientific subjects for many years previous to that time." [3]

Spratt, in his history of the society, says that in the gloomy season of the civil wars they had selected natural philosophy as their private diversion, and that at their meetings "they chiefly attended to some particular trials in Chymistry or Mechanics."

The testimony of Robert Boyle, Wallis, and Evelyn, contemporaries of the founders, is to the same effect, that the society was simply philosophical in its character and without any political design.

Dr. Wallis, who was one of the original founders, makes this statement concerning the origin and objects of the society in his *Account of some Passages in my own Life:* [4]

"About the year 1645, while I lived in London (at a time when, by our civil wars, academical studies were much interrupted in both our Universities), besides the conversation of divers eminent divines, as to matters theological, I had the opportunity of being acquainted with divers worthy persons inquisitive into natural philosophy and other parts of human learning, and particularly what has

---

[1] "History of the Royal Society," by Thomas Thompson, M.D., F.R.S., LL.D., London, 1812, p. 1.

[2] "A History of the Royal Society," with Memoirs of its Presidents, by Charles Richard Weld, Esq., 2 vols., London, 1848, I., 27.

[3] Ibid.

[4] In Hearne's edition of Langsteff's chronicle.

been called the *New Philosophy* or *Experimental Philosophy*. We did, by agreements, divers of us meet weekly in London on a certain day to treat and discourse of such affairs."

Wallis says that the subjects pursued by them related to physics, astronomy, and natural philosophy, such as the circulation of the blood, the Copernican system, the Torricellian experiment, etc.

In all these authentic accounts of the object of the society there is not the slightest allusion to it as a secret organization, nor any mention of a form of initiation, but only a reception by the unanimous vote of the members, which reception, as laid down in the bylaws consisted merely in the president taking the newly elected candidate by the hand and saluting him as a member or fellow of the society.

The fact is that at that period many similar societies had been instituted in different countries of Europe, such as the Academia del Corriento at Florence and the Academy of Sciences at Paris, whose members, like those of the Royal Society of London, devoted themselves to the development of science.

This encouragement of scientific pursuits may be principally attributed to many circumstances that followed the revival of learning; the advent of Greeks into Western Europe, imbued with Grecian literature; Bacon's new system of philosophy, which alone was enough to awaken the intellects of all thinking men; and the labors of Galileo and his disciples. All these had prepared many minds for the pursuit of philosophy by experimental and inductive methods, which took the place of the superstitious dogmas of preceding ages.

It was through such influences as these, wholly unconnected with any religious or political aspirations, that the founders of the Royal Society were induced to hold their meetings and to cultivate without the restraints of secrecy their philosophical labors, which culminated in 1660 in the incorporation of an institution of learned men which at this day holds the most honored and prominent place among the learned societies of the world.

But it is in vain to look in this society, either in the mode of its organization, in the character of its members, or in the nature of their pursuits, for any connection with Freemasonry, an institution entirely different in its construction and its objects. The theory, therefore, that Freemasonry is indebted for its origin to the Royal

Society of London must be rejected as wholly without authenticity or even plausibility.

But the theory of Nicolai, which attributes its origin to another contemporaneous society, whose members were evidently Astrologers, is somewhat more plausible, although equally incorrect. Its consideration must, however, be reserved as the subject of another chapter.

CHAPTER XXXIV

THE ASTROLOGERS AND THE FREEMASONS

E have seen, in the preceding chapter, that Nicolai had sought to trace the origin of Freemasonry to a society organized in 1646 by a sect of philosophers who were contemporary with, but entirely distinct from, those who founded the Royal Society. Though he does not explicitly state the fact, yet, from the names of the persons to whom he refers, there can be no doubt that he alluded to the Astrologers, who at that time were very popular in England.

Judicial astrology, or the divination of the future by the stars, was, of all the delusions to which the superstition of the Middle Ages gave birth, the most popular. It prevailed over all Europe, so that it was practiced by the most learned, and the predictions of its professors were sought with avidity and believed with confidence by the most wealthy and most powerful. Astrologers often formed a part of the household of princes, who followed their counsels in the most important matters relating to the future, while men and women of every rank sought these charlatans that they might have their nativities cast and secure the aid of their occult art in the recovery of stolen goods or the prognostications of happy marriages or of successful journeys.

Astrology was called the Daughter of Astronomy, and the scholars who devoted themselves to the study of the heavenly bodies for the purposes of pure science were often called upon to use their knowledge of the stars for the degrading purpose of astrological predictions. Kepler, the greatest astronomer of that age, was compelled against his will to pander to the popular superstition, that he might thus gain a livelihood and be enabled to pursue his nobler studies. In one of his works he complains that the scanty reward of an astronomer would not provide him with bread, if men did not entertain hopes of reading the future in the heavens.

And so he tampered with the science that he loved and adorned, and made predictions for inquisitive consulters, although, at the same time, he declared to his friends that "they were nothing but worthless conjecture."

Cornelius Agrippa, though he cultivated alchemy, a delusion but little more respectable than that of astrology, when commanded by his patroness, the Queen mother of France, to practice the latter, expressed his annoyance at the task. Of the Astrologers he said, in his great work on the *Vanity of the Arts and Sciences*, "these fortune tellers do find entertainment among princes and magistrates, from whom they receive large salaries; but, indeed, there is no class of men who are more pernicious to a commonwealth. For, as their skill lies in the adaptation of ambiguous predictions to events after they have happened, so it happens that a man who lives by falsehood shall by one accidental truth obtain more credit than he will lose by a hundred manifest errors."

The 16th and 17th centuries were the golden age of astrology in England. We know all that is needed of this charlatanism and of the character of its professors from the autobiography of William Lilly, himself an English astrologer of no mean note; perhaps, indeed, the best-educated and the most honest of those who practiced this delusion in England in the 17th century, and who is one of those to whom Nicolai ascribes the formation of that secret society, in 1646, which invented Freemasonry.

It will be remembered that Nicolai says that of the society of learned men who established Freemasonry, the first members were Elias Ashmole, the skillful antiquary, who was also a student of astrology, William Lilly, a famous astrologer, George Wharton, likewise an astrologer, William Oughtred, a mathematician, and some others. He also says that the annual festival of the Astrologers gave rise to this association. "It had previously held," says Nicolai, "one meeting at Warrington, in Lancashire, but it was first firmly established at London."

Their meetings, the same writer asserts, were held at Masons' Hall, in Masons' Alley, Basinghall Street. Many of them were members of the Masons' Company, and they all entered it and assumed the title of Free and Accepted Masons, adopting, besides, all its external marks of distinction.

Such is the theory which makes the Astrologers, incorporating themselves with the Operative Masons, who met at their Hall in Basinghall Street, the founders of the Speculative Order of Free and Accepted Masons as they exist at the present day.

It is surprising that in a question of history a man of letters of the reputation of Nicolai should have indulged in such bold assumptions and in statements so wholly bare of authority. But unfortunately it is thus that Masonic history has always been written.

I shall strive to eliminate the truth from the fiction in this narrative. The task will be a laborious one, for, as Goethe has well said in one of his maxims, " It is much easier to perceive error than to find truth. The former lies on the surface, so that it is easily reached ; the latter lies in the depth, which it is not every man's business to search for."

The Astrologers, to whose meeting in the Masons' Hall is ascribed the origin of the Freemasons, were not a class of persons who would have been likely to have united in such an attempt, which showed at least a desire for some intellectual progress. Lilly, perhaps the best-educated and the most honest of these charlatans, has in the narrative of his life, written by himself, given us some notion of the character of many of them who lived in London when he practiced the art in that city.[1]

Of Evans, who was his first teacher, he tells us that he was a clergyman of Staffordshire, whence he "had been in a manner enforced to fly for some offences very scandalous committed by him"; of another astrologer, Alexander Hart, he says " he was but a cheat." Jeffry Neve he calls a smatterer ; William Poole was a frequenter of taverns with "lewd people," and fled on one occasion from London under the suspicion of complicity in theft; John Booker, though honest, was ignorant of his profession ; William Hodges dealt with angels, but " his life answered not in holiness and sanctity to what it should," for he was addicted to profanity ; and John à Windsor was given to debauchery.

Men of such habits of life were not likely to interest themselves in the advancement of science or in the establishment of a society of speculative philosophers. It is true that these charlatans lived at an earlier period than that ascribed by Nicolai to the organization

---

[1] " The Life of William Lilly, Student in Astrology, wrote by himself in the 66th year of his Age, at Hersham, in the Parish of Walton upon Thames, in the County of Surrey. *Propria Manu*."

of the society in Masons' Hall, but in the few years that elapsed it is not probable that the disciples of astrology had much improved in their moral or intellectual condition.

Of certain of the men named by Nicolai as having organized the Society of Freemasons in 1646, we have some knowledge. Elias Ashmole, the celebrated antiquary, and founder of the Ashmolean Museum in the University of Oxford, is an historical character. He wrote his own life, in the form of a most minute diary, extending from July 2, 1633, to October 9, 1687. In this diary, in which he registers the most trivial as well as the most important events of his life—recording even the cutting of his wisdom teeth, or the taking of a sudorific—he does not make the slightest allusion to the transaction referred to by Nicolai. The silence of so babbling a chronicler as to such an important event is itself sufficient proof that it did not occur. What Ashmole has said about Freemasonry will be presently seen.

Lilly, another supposed actor in this scene, also wrote his life with great minuteness. His complete silence on the subject is equally suggestive. Nicolai says that the persons he cites were either already members of the Company of Masons or at once became so. Now, Lilly was a member of the Salter's Company, one of the twelve great livery companies, and would not have left it to join a minor company, which the Masons' was.

Oughtred could not have been united with Ashmole in organizing a society in 1646, for the latter, in a note to Lilly's life, traces his acquaintance with him to the residence of both as neighbors in Surrey. Now, Ashmole did not remove to Surrey until the year 1675, twenty-nine years after his supposed meeting with Oughtred at the Masons' Hall.

Between Wharton and Lilly, who were rival almanac-makers, there was, in 1646, a bitter feud, which was not reconciled until years afterward. In an almanac which Wharton published in 1645 he had called Lilly "an impudent, senseless fellow, and by name William Lilly." It is not likely that they would have been engaged in the fraternal task of organizing a great society at that very time.

Dr. Pearson, another one of the supposed founders, is celebrated in literary and theological history as the author of an *Exposition of the Creed*. Of a man so prominent as to have been the Master of

Jesus College, Cambridge, and afterward Bishop of Chester, Ashmole makes no mention in his diary. If he had ever met him or been engaged with him in so important an affair, this silence in so minute a journal of the transactions of his every-day life would be inexplicable.

But enough has been said to show the improbability of any such meeting as Nicolai records. Even Ashmole and Lilly, the two leaders, were unknown to each other until the close of the year 1646. Ashmole says in his diary of that year: "Mr. Jonas Moore brought and acquainted me with Mr. William Lilly: it was on a Friday night, and I think on the 20th Nov. (1646)."

That there was an association, or a club or society, of Astrologers about that time in London is very probable. Pepys, in his *Memoirs*, says that in October, 1660, he went to Mr. Lilly's, "there being a club that night among his friends." There he met Esquire Ashmole and went home accompanied by Mr. Booker, who, he says, "did tell me a great many fooleries, which may be done by nativities, and blaming Mr. Lilly for writing to please his friends, and not according to the rules of art, by which he could not well erre as he had done." The club, we may well suppose, was that of the Astrologers, held at the house of the chief member of the profession. That it was not a secret society we conclude from the fact that Pepys, who was no astrologer, was permitted to be present. We know also from Ashmole's diary that the Astrologers held an annual feast, generally in August, sometimes in March, July, or November, but never on a Masonic festival. Ashmole regularly attended it from 1649 to 1658, when it was suspended, but afterward revived, in 1682. In 1650 he was elected a steward for the following year. He mentions the place of meeting only three times, twice at Painters' Hall, which was probably the usual place, and once at the Three Cranes, in Chancery Lane. Had the Astrologers and the Masons been connected, Masons' Hall, in Basinghall Street, would certainly have been the place for holding their feast.

Again, it is said by Nicolai that the object of this secret society which organized the Freemasons was to advance the restoration of the King. But Lilly had made, in 1645, the year before the meeting, this declaration: "Before that time, I was more Cavalier than Roundhead, but after that I engaged body and soul in the cause of Parliament." He still expressed, it is true, his attachment to mon-

archy; but his life during the Commonwealth showed his devotion
to Cromwell, of whom he was a particular favorite.   After the Restoration he had to sue out a pardon, which was obtained by the influence of his friends, but which would hardly have been necessary
if he had been engaged in a secret society the object of which was
to restore Charles II. to the throne.

But Charles I. was not beheaded until 1649, so that a society
could not have been organized in 1646 for the restoration of his
son.   But it may be said that the Restoration alluded to was of the
monarchy, which at that time was virtually at an end.   So this objection may pass without further comment.

But the fact is that the whole of this fiction of the organization,
in 1646, of a secret society by a set of philosophers or astrologers,
or both, which resulted in the establishment of Freemasonry, arose
out of a misconception or a misrepresentation—whether willful or
not, I will not say—of two passages in the diary of Elias Ashmole.
Of these two passages, and they are the only ones in his minute diary
of fifty-four years in which there is any mention of Freemasonry,
the first is as follows :

" 1646, Octob. 16. 4 *Hor.* 30 minutes *post merid.*   I was made a
Free-Mason at Warrington in Lancashire, with Colonel Henry
Mainwarring of Karticham in Cheshire ; the names of those that
were then at the lodge, Mr. Richard Penket Warden, Mr. James
Collier, Mr. Richard Sankey, Henry Littler, John Ellam, and
Hugh Brewer."

And then, after an interval of thirty-five years, during which there
is no further allusion to Masonry, we find the following memo-
randum: " 1682, Mar. 10.   About 5 *Hor. post merid.*   I received
a summons to appear at a lodge to be held the next day at Masons
Hall, London.

"II. Accordingly I went, and about noon was admitted into
the fellowship of Free-Masons, by Sir William Wilson Knight,
Captain Richard Borthwick, Mr. William Wodman, Mr. William
Grey, Mr. Samuel Taylour, and Mr. William Wise.

" I was the senior fellow among them (it being thirty-five years
since I was admitted) there was present besides myself, the fellows
after mentioned.   Mr. Thomas Wise, Master of the Masons Company, this present year ; Mr. Thomas Shorthose, Mr. Thomas Shad-
bolt, —— Wardsfford, Esq ; Mr. Nicholas Young, Mr. John Short-

hose, Mr. William Hamon, Mr. John Thompson, and Mr. William Stanton.   We all dined at the Half-Moon-Tavern, in Cheapside, at a noble dinner prepared at the charge of the new accepted Masons."

Without the slightest show of reason or semblance of authority, Nicolai transmutes the Lodge at Warrington, in which Ashmole was made a Freemason, into an annual feast of the Astrologers.   The Society of Astrologers, he says, "had previously held one meeting at Warrington, in Lancashire, but it was first firmly established at London."   And he cites as his authority for this statement the very passage from Ashmole's diary in which that antiquary records his reception in a Masonic Lodge.

These events in the life of Ashmole, which connect him with the Masonic fraternity, have given considerable embarrassment to Masonic scholars who have been unable to comprehend the two apparently conflicting statements that he was made a Freemason at Warrington in 1646 and afterward received into the fellowship of the Freemasons, in 1682, at London.   The embarrassment and misapprehension arose from the fact that we have unfortunately no records of the meetings of the Operative Lodges of England in the 17th century, and nothing but traditional and generally mythical accounts of their usages during that period.

The sister kingdom of Scotland has been more fortunate in this respect, and the valuable work of Brother Lyon, on the *History of the Lodge of Edinburgh*, has supplied us with authentic records of the Scottish Lodges at a much earlier date.   These records will furnish us with some information in respect to the contemporaneous English Lodges, which we have every reason to suppose were governed by usages not very different from those of the Lodges in the adjacent kingdom.

Mr. Lyon has on this subject the following remarks, which may be opportunely quoted on the present occasion.

" The earliest date at which non-professionals are known to have been received into an English Lodge is 1646.   The evidence of this is derived from the diary of one of the persons so admitted ; but the preceding minutes[1] afford authentic instances of Speculative Masons having been admitted to the fellowship of the Lodge of

---

[1] Minutes of the Lodge of Cannongate, Kilwinning, for 1635, quoted by him in a preceding page.

Edinburgh twelve years prior to the reception of Colonel Main.
warring and Elias Ashmole in the Lodge of Warrington and
thirty-eight years before the date at which the presence of Gentleman Masons is first discernible in the Lodge of Kilwinning by
the election of Lord Cassillis to the deaconship.   It is worthy of remark that, with singularly few exceptions, the non-operatives who
were admitted to Masonic fellowship in the Lodges of Edinburgh
and Kilwinning, during the 17th century, were persons of quality,
the most distinguished of whom, as the natural result of its metro-
politan position, being made in the former Lodge.   Their admission
to fellowship in an institution composed of Operative Masons associated together for purposes of their Craft would in all probability origi-
nate in a desire to elevate its position and increase its influence, and
once adopted, the system would further recommend itself to the
Fraternity by the opportunities which it presented for cultivating
the friendship and enjoying the society of gentlemen to whom in
ordinary circumstances there was little chance of their ever being
personally known.   On the other hand, non-professionals connecting themselves with the Lodge by the ties of membership would, we
believe, be actuated partly by a disposition to reciprocate the feelings that had prompted the bestowal of the fellowship partly by
curiosity to penetrate the arcana of the Craft, and partly by the
novelty of the situation as members of a secret society and partici-
pants in its ceremonies and festivities.   But whatever may have
been the motives which animated the parties on either side, the tie
which united them was a purely honorary one." [1]

What is here said by Lyon of the Scottish Lodges may, I think,
be with equal propriety applied to those of England at the same
period.   There was in 1646 a Lodge of Operative Masons at Warrington, just as there was a similar one at Edinburgh.   Into this
Lodge Colonel Mainwarring and Elias Ashmole, both non-professional gentlemen, were admitted as honorary members, or, to use the
language of the latter, were "made Freemasons," a technical term
that has been preserved to the present day.

But thirty-five years afterward, being then a resident of London,
he was summoned to attend a meeting of the Company of Masons,
to be held at their hall in Masons' Alley, Basinghall Street, and

---

[1] Lyon, " History of the Lodge of Edinburgh," p. 81.

there, according to his own account, he was "admitted into the fellowship of Freemasons." How are we to explain this apparent double or renewed admission? But mark the difference of language. In 1646 he was "made a Freemason." In 1682 he was "admitted into the fellowship of Freemasons." The distinction is an important one.

The Masons' Company in 1682 constituted in London one of those many city companies which embraced the various trades and handicrafts of the metropolis. Stowe, in his *Survey of London*, says that "the Masons, otherwise termed Freemasons, were a society of ancient standing and good reckoning, by means of affable and kind meetings divers times, and as a loving brotherhood should use to do, did frequent their mutual assemblies in the time of King Henry IV., in the 12th year of whose most gracious reign they were incorporated."

In Cheswell's *New View of London*, printed in 1708, it is said that the Masons' Company "were incorporated about the year 1410, having been called the Free Masons, a Fraternity of great account, who have been honored by several Kings, and very many of the Nobility and Gentry being of their Society. They are governed by a Master, 2 Wardens, 25 Assistants, and there are 65 on the Livery."

Maitland, in his *London and its Environs*, says, speaking of the Masons: "This company had their arms granted by Clarencieux, King-at-Arms, in the year 1477, though the members were not incorporated by letters patent till they obtained them from King Charles II. in 1677. They have a small convenient hall in Masons' Alley, Basinghall Street."

There were then, in the time of Ashmole, two distinct bodies of men practicing the Craft of Operative Masonry, namely, the Lodges which were to be found in various parts of the country, and the Company of Masons, whose seat was at London.

Into one of the Lodges, which was situated at Warrington, in Lancashire, Ashmole had in 1646 received honorary membership, which, in compliance with the technical language of that and of the present day, he called being "made a Freemason." But this did not constitute him a member of the Masons' Company of London, for this was a distinct incorporated society, with its exclusive rules and regulations, and admission into which could only be obtained by the consent of the members. There were many Masons who were not members of the Company.

Ashmole, who had for thirty-five years been a Freemason, by virtue of his making at Warrington, was in 1682 elected a member of this Masons' Company, and this he styles being "admitted into the fellowship of Free-Masons"—that is, he was admitted to the fellowship or membership of the Company and made "free" of it.

From all of which we may draw the following conclusions: First, that in 1646, at the very date assigned by Nicolai for the organization of the Freemasons as a secret political society, under the leadership of Ashmole and Lilly, the former, being as yet unacquainted with the latter, was at Warrington, in Lancashire, where he found a Lodge of Masons already organized and with its proper officers and its members, by whom he was admitted as an honorary non-professional member of the Craft. And secondly, that while in London he was admitted, being already a Freemason, to the fellowship of the Masons' Company. And thirdly, that he was also a member of the fraternity of Astrologers, having been admitted probably in 1649, and regularly attended their annual feast from that year to 1658, when the festival, and perhaps the fraternity, was suspended until 1682, when it was again revived. But during all this time it is evident from the memoranda of Ashmole that the Freemasons and the Astrologers were two entirely distinct bodies. Lilly, who was the head of the Astrologers, was, we may say almost with certainty, not a Freemason, else the spirit of minuteness with which he has written his autobiography would not have permitted him to omit what to his peculiar frame of mind would have been so important a circumstance as connecting him still more closely with his admired friend, Elias Ashmole, nor would the latter have neglected to record it in his diary, written with even still greater minuteness than Lilly's memoirs.

Notwithstanding the clear historical testimony which shows that Lodges of Freemasons had been organized long before the time of Ashmole, and that he had actually been made a Freemason in one of them, many writers, both Masonic and profane, have maintained the erroneous doctrine that Ashmole was the founder of the Masonic Society.

Thus Chambers, in their *Encyclopædia*, say that "Masonry was founded by Ashmole and some of his literary friends," and De Quincey expressed the same opinion.

Mr. John Yarker, in his very readable *Notes on the Scientific and Religious Mysteries of Antiquity*, offers a modified view and a compromise of the subject. He refers to the meeting of the chemical adepts at Masons' Hall (a fact of which we have no evidence), and then to the "Feast of the Astrologers" which Ashmole attended. He follows Nicolai in asserting that their allegories were founded on Bacon's House of Solomon, and says that they used as emblems the sun, moon, square, triangle, etc. And he concludes, " it is possible that Ashmole may have consolidated the customs of the two associations, but there is *no evidence* that any Lodge of this, his speculative rite, came under the Masonic Constitution." [1]

We may also say that it is possible that Ashmole may have invented a speculative rite of some kind, but there is *no evidence* that he did so. Many things are possible that are not probable, and many probable that are not actual. History is made up of facts, and not of possibilities or probabilities.

Ashmole himself entertained a very different and much more correct notion of the origin of Masonry than any of those who have striven to claim him as its founder.

Dr. Knipe, of Christ Church, Oxford, in a letter to the publisher of Ashmole's Life, says : " What from Mr. E. Ashmole's collections I could gather was, that the report of our society's taking rise from a bull granted by the Pope in the reign of Henry III., to some Italian architects to travel over all Europe, to erect chapels, was illfounded. Such a bull there was, and these architects were Masons ; but this bull, in the opinion of the learned Mr. Ashmole, was confirmative only, and did not, by any means, create our Fraternity, or even establish them in this kingdom."

This settles the question. Ashmole could not have been the founder of Freemasonry in London in 1646, since he himself expressed the belief that the Institution had existed in England before the 13th century.

There is no doubt, as I have already said, that he was very intimately connected with the Astrologers. Dr. Krause, in his *Three Oldest Documents of the Masonic Brotherhood*,[2] quotes the following passage from Lilly's *History of my Life and Times*. (I can not

---

[1] " Notes on the Scientific and Religious Mysteries of Antiquity," p. 106.
[2] " Die drei ältesten Kunsturkunden der Freimaurerbrüderschaft," IV., 286.

find it in my own copy of that work, but the statements are corrob
orated by Ashmole's diary.)

"The King's affairs being now grown desperate, Mr. Ashmole
withdrew himself, after the surrender of the Garrison of Worcester,
into Cheshire, where he continued till the end of October, and then
came up to London, where he became acquainted with Master, afterwards Sir Jonas Moore, Mr. William Lilly, and Mr. John Booker,
esteemed the greatest astrologers in the world, by whom he was
caressed, instructed and received into their fraternity, which then
made a very considerable figure, as appeared by the great resort of
persons of distinction to their annual feast, of which Mr. Ashmole
was afterwards elected Steward."

Ashmole left Worcester for Cheshire July 24, 1646, and removed
from Cheshire to London October 25, of the same year. In that
interval of three months he was made a Freemason, at Warrington.
At that time he was not acquainted with Lilly, Moore, or Booker,
and knew nothing of astrology or of the great astrologers.

This destroys the accuracy of Nicolai's assertion that the meeting held at Masons' Hall, in 1682, by Ashmole, Lilly, and other
astrologers, when they founded the Society of Freemasons, was preceded by a similar and initiatory one, in 1646, at Warrington.

A few words must now be said upon the subject of Bacon's
House of Solomon, which Nicolai and others supposed to have first
given rise to the Masonic allegory which was afterward changed to
that of the Temple of Solomon.

Bacon, in his fragmentary and unfinished romance of the *New
Atlantis*, had devised the fable of an island of Bensalem, in which
was an institution or college called the House of Solomon, the fellows of which were to be students of philosophy and investigators
of science. He thus described their occupations :

"We have twelve that sail into foreign countries, who bring in
the books and patterns of experiments of all other parts ; these we
call merchants of light. We have three that collect the experiments
that are in all books ; these are called depredators. We have three
that collect experiments of all mechanical arts, and also of liberal
sciences, and also of practices which are not brought into the arts ;
these we call mystery men. We have three that try new experiments
such as themselves think good ; these we call pioneers or miners. We
have three that draw the experiments of the former four into titles and

tablets to give the better light for the drawing of observations and axioms out of them; these we call compilers. We have three that bind
themselves looking into the experiments of their fellows and cast
about how to draw out of them things of use and practice for man's life
and knowledge as well for works as for plain demonstrations and the
easy and clear discovering of the virtues and parts of bodies ; these
we call doing men and benefactors. Then after divers meetings
and consults of our whole number to consider of the former labors
and collections, we have three to take care out of them to direct new
experiments of higher light, more penetrating into nature than the
former ; these we call lamps. We have three others that do execute
the experiments so directed and report them ; these we call inocu-
lators. Lastly we have three that raise the former discoveries by
experiments into greater observations, axioms and aphorisms ; these
we call interpreters of nature." [1]

It is evident from this schedule of the occupations of the inmates
of the House of Solomon that it could not in the remotest degree
have been made the foundation of a Masonic allegory. In fact, the
suggestion of a Masonic connection could have been derived only
from a confused idea of the relation of the House to the Temple of
Solomon, a misapprehension which a reading of the *New Atlantis*
would readily remove.

As Plato had written his *Republic* and Sir Thomas More his
Utopia to give their ideas of a model commonwealth, so Lord Bacon
commenced his *New Atlantis* to furnish his idea of a model college
to be instituted for the study and interpretation of nature by experimental methods. These views were first introduced in his *Advancement of Human Learning*, and would have been perfected in his
New Atlantis had he ever completed it.

The new philosophy of Bacon had produced a great revolution
in the minds of thinking men, and that group of philosophers who
in the 17th century, as Dr. Whewell says, "began to knock at the
door where truth was to be found " would very wisely seek the key
in the inductive and experimental method taught by Bacon.

To the learned men, therefore, who first met at the house of Dr.
Goddard and the other members, and whose meetings finally ended
in the formation of the Royal Society, the allegory of the House of

---

[1] "New Atlantis," Works, vol. ii., p. 376.

Solomon very probably furnished valuable hints for the pursuit of their experimental studies.

To Freemasons in any age the allegory would have been useless and unprofitable, and could by no ingenious method have been twisted into a foundation for their symbolic science.   The hypothesis that it was adopted in 1646 by the founders of Freemasonry as a fitting allegory for their esoteric system of instruction is evidently too absurd to need further refutation.

In conclusion, we may unhesitatingly concur with Bro. W. J. Hughan in his opinion that the theory which assigns the foundation of Freemasonry to Elias Ashmole and his friends the Astrologers " is opposed to existing documents dating before and since his initiation."   It is equally opposed to the whole current of authentic history, and is unsupported by the character of the Institution and the nature of its symbolism.

CHAPTER XXXV

F all the theories which have been advanced in relation to the origin of Freemasonry from some one of the secret sects, either of antiquity or of the Middle Ages, there is none more interesting than that which seeks to connect it with the Hermetic philosophy, because there is none which presents more plausible claims to our consideration.

There can be no doubt that in some of what are called the High Degrees there is a very palpable infusion of a Hermetic element. This can not be denied, because the evidence will be most apparent to any one who examines their rituals, and some by their very titles, in which the Hermetic language and a reference to Hermetic principles are adopted, plainly admit the connection and the influence.

There is, therefore, no necessity to investigate the question whether or not some of those High or Philosophic Degrees which were fabricated about the middle of the last century are or are not of a Hermetic character, because the time of their invention, when Craft Masonry was already in a fixed condition, removes them entirely out of the problem which relates to the origin of the Masonic Institution. No matter when Freemasonry was established, the High Degrees were an afterthought, and might very well be tinctured with the principles of any philosophy which prevailed at the period of their invention.

But it is a question of some interest to the Masonic scholar whether at the time of the so-called Revival of Freemasonry, in the early part of the 18th century, certain Hermetic degrees did not exist which sought to connect themselves with the system of Masonry. And it is a question of still greater interest whether this attempt was successful so far, at least, as to impress upon the features of that early Freemasonry a portion of the characteristic tints of the Hermetic philosophy, some of the marks of which may still remain in our modern system.

But as the Hermetic philosophy was that which was invented and taught by the Rosicrucians, before we can attempt to resolve these important and interesting questions, it will be necessary to take a brief glance at the history and the character of Rosicrucianism. On the 17th of August, 1586, Johann Valentin Andreä was born at Herrenberg, a small market-town of what was afterward the kingdom of Würtemburg. After a studious youth, during which he became possessed of a more than moderate share of learning, he departed in 1610 on a pilgrimage through Germany, Austria, Italy, and France, supplied with but little money, but with an indomitable desire for the acquisition of knowledge. Returning home, in 1614, he embraced the clerical profession and was appointed a deacon in the town of Vaihingen, and by subsequent promotions reached, in 1634, the positions of Protestant prelate of the Abbey of Bebenhausen and spiritual counsellor of the Duchy of Brunswick. He died on the 27th of June, 1654, at the ripe age of sixty-eight years.

On the moral character of Andreä his biographers have lavished their encomiums. A philanthropist from his earliest life, he carried, or sought to carry, his plans of benevolence into active operation. Wherever, says Vaughan, the church, the school, the institute of charity have fallen into ruin or distress, there the indefatigable Andreä sought to restore them. He was, says another writer, the guardian genius and the comforter of the suffering ; he was a practical helper as well as a theoretical adviser; in the times of dearth and famine, many thousand poor were fed and clothed by his exertions, and the town of Kalw, of which, in 1720, he was appointed the superintendent, long enjoyed the benefit of many charitable institutions which owed their origin to his solicitations and zeal.[1]

It is not surprising that a man indued with such benevolent feelings and actuated by such a spirit of philanthropy should have viewed with deep regret the corruptions of the times in which he lived, and should have sought to devise some plan by which the condition of his fellow-men might be ameliorated and the dry, effete

---

[1] Biographical Sketch by Wm. Bell, in *Freemasons' Quarterly Magazine*, London, vol. ii., N. S., 1854, p. 27.

theology of the church be converted into some more living, active, humanizing system.

For the accomplishment of this purpose he could see no better method than the establishment of a practical philanthropical fraternity, one that did not at that time exist, but the formation of which he resolved to suggest to such noble minds as might be stimulated to the enterprise.

With this view he invoked the assistance of fiction, and hence there appeared, in 1615, a work which he entitled the *Report of the Rosicrucian Brotherhood*, or, in its original Latin, *Fama Fraternitatis Rosæ Crucis*.   An edition had been published the year before with the title of *Universal Reformation of the Whole World, with a Report of the Worshipful Order of the Rosicrucian Brotherhood, addressed to all the Learned Men and Nobility of Europe.*[1] There was another work, published in 1616, with the title of *Chemische Hochzeit*, or *Chemical Nuptials, by Christian Rosencreutz.*

All of these books were published anonymously, but they were universally attributed to the pen of Andreä, and were all intended for one purpose, that of discovering by the character of their reception who were the true lovers of wisdom and philanthropy, and of inducing them to come forward to the perfection of the enterprise, by transforming this fabulous society into a real and active organization.

The romantic story of Christian Rosencreutz, the supposed founder of the Order, is thus told by Andreä.   I have borrowed for the most part the language of Mr. Sloane,[2] who, although his views and deductions on the subject are for the most part erroneous, has yet given us the best English epitome of the myth of Andreä.

According to Andreä's tale, a certain Christian Rosencreutz, though of good birth, found himself compelled from poverty to enter the cloister at a very early period of life.   He was only sixteen years old when one of the monks purposed a pilgrimage to the Holy Sepulcher, and Rosencreutz, as a special favor, was permitted to accompany him.   At Cyprus the monk is taken ill, but Rosencreutz proceeds onward to Damascus with the intention of going on to

---

[1] " Allgemeine und General Reformation der ganzen, weiten Welt.   Beneben der Fama Fraternitatis des Löblichen Ordens des Rosencreutzes, an alle Gelehrte und Haüpter Europæ geschreiben," Cassel, 1614.
[2] " New Curiosities of Literature," vol. ii., p. 44.

Jerusalem. While detained in the former city by the fatigues of his journey, he hears of the wonders performed by the sages of Damascus, and, his curiosity being excited, he places himself under their direction.

Three years having been spent in the acquisition of their most hidden mysteries, he sets sail from the Gulf of Arabia for Egypt. There he studies the nature of plants and animals and then repairs, in obedience to the instructions of his Arabian masters, to Fez, in Africa. In this city it was the custom of the Arab and African sages to meet annually for the purpose of communicating to each other the results of their experience and inquiries, and here he passed two years in study. He then crossed over to Spain, but not meeting there with a favorable reception, he returned to his native country.

But as Germany was then filled with mystics of all kinds, his proposals for a reformation in morals and science meets with so little sympathy from the public that he resolves to establish a society of his own.

With this view he selects three of his favorite companions from his old convent. To them, under a solemn vow of secrecy, he communicates the knowledge which he had acquired during his travels. He imposes on them the duty of committing it to writing and of forming a magical vocabulary for the benefit of future students.

But in addition to this task they also undertook to prescribe gratuitously for all the sick who should ask their assistance, and as in a short time the concourse of patients became so great as materially to interfere with their other duties, and as a building which Rosencreutz had been erecting, called the Temple of the Holy Ghost, was now completed, he determines to increase the number of the brotherhood, and accordingly initiates four new members.

When all is completed, and the eight brethren are instructed in the mysteries of the Order, they separate, according to agreement, two only staying with Father Christian. The other six, after traveling for a year, are to return and communicate the results of their experience. The two who had stayed at home are then to be relieved by two of the travelers, so that the founder may never be alone, and the six again divide and travel for a year.

The laws of the Order as they had been prescribed by Rosencreutz were as follows:

1. That they should devote themselves to no other occupation than that of the gratuitous practice of physic.

2. That they were not to wear a particular habit, but were to conform in this respect to the customs of the country in which they might happen to be.

3. That each one was to present himself on a certain day in the year at the Temple of the Holy Ghost, or send an excuse for his absence.

4. That each one was to look out for a brother to succeed him in the event of his death.

5. That the letters R. C. were to be their seal, watchword, and title.

6. That the brotherhood was to be kept a secret for one hundred years.

When one hundred years old, Christian Rosencreutz died, but the place of his burial was unknown to any one but the two brothers who were with him at the time of his death, and they carried the secret with them to the grave.

The society, however, continued to exist unknown to the world, always consisting of eight members only, until another hundred and twenty years had elapsed, when, according to a tradition of the Order, the grave of Father Rosencreutz was to be discovered, and the brotherhood to be no longer a mystery to the world.

It was about this time that the brethren began to make some alterations in their building, and thought of removing to another and more fitting situation the memorial tablet, on which were inscribed the names of their associates. The plate, which was of brass, was affixed to the wall by means of a nail in its center, and so firmly was it fastened that in tearing it away a portion of the plaster of the wall became detached and exposed a concealed door. Upon this door being still further cleansed from the incrustation, there appeared above it in large letters the following words: POST CXX ANNOS PATEBO—*After one hundred and twenty years I will be opened.*

Although the brethren were greatly delighted at the discovery, they so far restrained their curiosity as not to open the door until the next morning, when they found themselves in a vault of seven sides, each side five feet wide and eight feet high. It was lighted by an artificial sun in the centre of the arched roof, while in the middle of the floor, instead of a tomb, stood a round altar covered with a small brass plate, on which was this inscription :

A. C. R. C. *Hoc, universi compendium, vivus mihi sepulchrum feci—i.e.,* while living, I made this epitome of the universe my sepulcher.

About the outer edge was :

Jesus mihi omnia—i.e., Jesus is all things to me.

In the center were four figures, each enclosed in a circle, with these words inscribed around them :

1. *Nequaquam vacuus.*
2. *Legis Jugum.*
3. *Libertas Evangelii.*
4. *Dei gloria intacta.*

That is—1. By no means void.   2. The yoke of the Law.   3. The liberty of the Gospel.   4. The unsullied Glory of God.

On seeing all this, the brethren knelt down and returned thanks to God for having made them so much wiser than the rest of the world.   Then they divided the vault into three parts, the roof, the wall, and the pavement.   The first and the last were divided into seven triangles, corresponding to the seven sides of the wall, each of which formed the base of a triangle, while the apices met in the center of the roof and of the pavement.   Each side was divided into ten squares, containing figures and sentences which were to be explained to the new initiates.   In each side there was also a door opening upon a closet, wherein were stored up many rare articles, such as the secret books of the Order, the vocabulary of Paracelsus, and other things of a similar nature.   In one of the closets they discovered the life of their founder ; in others they found curious mirrors, burning lamps, and a variety of objects intended to aid in rebuilding the Order, which, after the lapse of many centuries, was to fall into decay.

Pushing aside the altar, they came upon a strong brass plate, which being removed, they beheld the corpse of Rosencreutz as freshly preserved as on the day when it had been deposited, and under his arm a volume of vellum with letters of gold, containing, among other things, the names of the eight brethren who had founded the Order.

Such is an outline of the story of Christian Rosencreutz and his Rosicrucian Order as it is told in the *Fama Fraternitatis.* It is very evident that Andreä composed this romance—for it is nothing else—not to record the existence of any actual society, but only that it might serve as a suggestion to the learned and the philanthropic to engage in the establishment of some such benevolent association. "He hoped," says Vaughan, "that the few nobler minds whom he desired to organize would see through the veil of fiction in which he had invested his proposal; that he might communicate personally with some such, if they should appear, or that his book might lead them to form among themselves a practical philanthropic confederacy answering to the serious purpose he had embodied in his fiction." [1]

But his design was misunderstood then, as it has been since, and everywhere his fable was accepted as a fact. Diligent search was made by the credulous for the discovery of the Temple of the Holy Ghost. Printed letters appeared continually, addressed to the unknown brotherhood, seeking admission into the fraternity—a fraternity that existed only in the pages of the *Fama*. But the irresponsive silence to so many applications awoke the suspicions of some, while the continued mystery strengthened the credulity of others. The brotherhood, whose actual house "lay beneath the Doctor's hat of Valentin Andreä," was violently attacked and as vigorously defended in numerous books and pamphlets which during that period flooded the German press.

The learned men among the Germans did not give a favoring ear to the philanthropic suggestions of Andreä, but the mystical notions contained in his fabulous history were seized with avidity by the charlatans, who added to them the dreams of the alchemists and the reveries of the astrologers, so that the post-Andrean Rosicrucianism became a very different thing from that which had been devised by its original author. It does not, however, appear that the Rosicrucians, as an organized society, made any stand in Germany. Descartes says that after strict search he could not find a single lodge in that country. But it extended, as we will presently see, into England, and there became identified as a mystical association.

It is strange what misapprehension, either willful or mistaken, has existed in respect to the relations of Andreä to Rosicrucianism. We have no more right or reason to attribute the detection of such

---

[1] "Hours with the Mystics," vol. ii., p. 103.

a sect to the German theologian than we have to ascribe the discovery of the republic of Utopia to Sir Thomas More, or of the island of Bensalem to Lord Bacon. In each of these instances a fiction was invented on which the author might impose his philosophical or political thoughts, with no dream that readers would take that for fact which was merely intended for fiction.

And yet Rhigellini, in his *Masonry Considered as the Result of the Egyptian, Jewish, and Christian Religions*, while declining to express an opinion on the allegorical question, as if there might be a doubt on the subject, respects the legend as it had been given in the *Fama*, and asserting that on the return of Rosencreutz to Germany " he instituted secret societies with an initiation that resembled that of the early Christians." [1] He antedates the *Chemical Nuptials* of Andreä a century and a half, ascribes the authorship of that work to Christian Rosencreutz, as if he were a real personage, and thinks that he established, in 1459, the Rite of the Theosophists, the earliest branch of the Rose Croix, or the Rosicrucians; for the French make no distinction in the two words, though in history they are entirely different. History written in this way is worse than fable—it is an *ignis fatuus* which can only lead astray. And yet this is the method in which Masonic history has too often been treated.

Nicolai, although the deductions by which he connects Freemasonry with Rosicrucianism are wholly untenable, is yet, in his treatment of the latter, more honest or less ignorant. He adopts the correct view when he says that the *Fama Fraternitatis* only announced a general reformation and exhorted all wise men to unite in a proposed society for the purpose of removing corruption and restoring wisdom. He commends it as a charming vision, full of poesy and imagination, but of a singular extravagance very common in the writings of that age. And he notes the fact that while the Alchemists have sought in that work for the secrets of their mysteries, it really contains the gravest satire on their absurd pretensions.

The *Fama Fraternitatis* had undoubtedly excited the curiosity of the Mystics, who abounded in Germany at the time of its appearance, of whom not the least prominent were the Alchemists. These, having sought in vain for the invisible society of the Rosicrucians, as it had been described in the romance of Andreä, resolved to form

---

[1] " La Maçonnerie considerée comme le resultat des Religions Egyptienne, Juive et Chrétienne," L. iii., p. 108.

Symbols of Freemasonry

such a society for themselves.   But, to the disappointment and the displeasure of the author of the *Fama*, they neglected or postponed the moral reformation which he had sought, and substituted the visionary schemes of the Alchemists, a body of quasi-philosophers who assigned their origin as students of nature and seekers of the philosopher's stone and the elixir of immortality to a very remote period.

Thus it is that I trace the origin of the Rosicrucians, not to Valentin Andreä, nor to Christian Rosencreutz, who was only the coinage of his brain, but to the influence exerted by him upon certain Mystics and Alchemists who, whether they accepted the legend of Rosencreutz as a fiction or as a verity, at least made diligent use of it in the establishment of their new society.

I am not, therefore, disposed to doubt the statement of L. C. Orvius, as cited by Nicolai, that in 1622 there was a society of Alchemists at The Hague, who called themselves Rosicrucians and claimed Rosencreutz as their founder.

Michael Maier, the physician of the Emperor Rudolf II., devoted himself in the early part of the 17th century to the pursuits of alchemy, and, having adopted the mystical views of the Rosicrucians, is said to have introduced that society into England.   Maier was the author of many works in Latin in defense and in explanation of the Rosicrucian system.   Among them was an epistle addressed "To all lovers of true chemistry throughout Germany, and especially to that Order which has hitherto lain concealed, but is now probably made known by the Report of the Fraternity (*Fama Fraternitatis*) and their admirable Confession."[1]   In this work he uses the following language :

"What is contained in the ' Fama' and ' confessio' is true.   It is a very childish objection that the brotherhood have promised so much and performed so little.   The Masters of the Order hold out the Rose as a remote reward, but they impose the Cross on all who are entering.   Like the Pythagoreans and the Egyptians, the Rosicrucians extract vows of silence and secrecy.   Ignorant men have treated the whole as a fiction ; but this has arisen from the probation of five years to which they subject even well qualified novices,

---

[1] " Omnibus veræ chymiæ Amantibus per Germaniam, et preciperè illi Ordini adhue delitescenti, at Fama Fraternitatis et confessione suâ admiranda et probabile manifestato."

before they are admitted to the higher mysteries, and within that period they are taught how to govern their own tongues!"

Although Maier died in 1622, it appears that he had lived long enough to take part in the organization of the Rosicrucian sect, which had been formed out of the suggestions of Andreä. His views on this subject were, however, peculiar and different from those of most of the new disciples. He denied that the Order had derived either its origin or its name from the person called Rosencreutz. He says that the founder of the society, having given his disciples the letters R. C. as a sign of their fraternity, they improperly made out of them the words *Rose* and *Cross*. But these heterodox opinions were not accepted by the Rosicrucians in general, who still adhered to Andreä's legend as the source and the signification of their Order.

At one time Maier went to England, where he became intimately acquainted with Dr. Robert Fludd, the most famous as well as the earliest of the English Rosicrucians.

Robert Fludd was a physician of London, who was born in 1574 and died in 1637. He was a zealous student of alchemy, theosophy, and every other branch of mysticism, and wrote in defense of Rosicrucianism, of which sect he was an active member. Among his earliest works is one published in 1616 under the title of *A Compendious Apology clearing the Fraternity of the Rosy Cross from the stains of suspicion and infamy cast upon them.*[1]

There is much doubt whether Maier communicated the system of Rosicrucianism to Fludd or whether Fludd had already received it from Germany before the visit of Maier. The only authority for the former statement is De Quincey (a most unreliable one), and the date of Fludd's *Apology* militates against it.

Fludd's explanation of the name of the sect differs from that of both Andreä and Maier. It is, he says, to be taken in a figurative sense, and alludes to the cross dyed with the blood of Christ. In this explanation he approaches very nearly to the idea entertained by the members of the modern Rose Croix degree.

No matter who was the missionary that brought it over, it is very certain that Rosicrucianism was introduced from Germany, its birth-

---

[1] "Apologia Compendiaria, Fraternitatem de Rosea Cruce suspicionis et infamiæ maculis aspersum abluens."

place, into England at a very early period of the 17th century, and it is equally certain that after its introduction it flourished, though an exotic, with more vigor than it ever had in its native soil.

That there were in that century, and even in the beginning of the succeeding one, mystical initiations wholly unconnected with Freemasonry, but openly professing a Hermetic or Rosicrucian character and origin, may very readily be supposed from existing documents. It is a misfortune that such authors as Buhle, Nicolai, and Rhigellini, with many others, to say nothing of such non-masonic writers as Sloane and De Quincey, who were necessarily mere sciolists in all Masonic studies, should have confounded the two institutions, and, because both were mystical, and one appeared to follow (although it really did not) the other in point of time, should have proclaimed the theory (wholly untenable) that Freemasonry is indebted for its origin to Rosicrucianism.

The writings of Lilly and Ashmole, both learned men for the age in which they lived, prove the existence of a mystical philosophy in England in the 17th century, in which each of them was a participant. The Astrologers, who were deeply imbued with the Hermetic philosophy, held their social meetings for mutual instruction and their annual feasts, and Ashmole gives hints of his initiation into what I suppose to have been alchemical or Rosicrucian wisdom by one whom he reverently calls " Father Backhouse."

But we have the clearest documentary testimony of the existence of a Hermetic degree or system at the beginning of the 18th century, and about the time of what is called the Revival of Masonry in England, by the establishment of the Grand Lodge at London, and which, from other undoubted testimony, we know were not Masonic. This testimony is found in a rare work, some portions of whose contents, in reference to this subject, are well worthy of a careful review.

In the year 1722 there was published in London a work in small octavo bearing the following title :[1]

"Long Livers: A curious History of such Persons of both Sexes who have liv'd several Ages and grown Young again: With the rare Secret of Rejuvenescency of Arnoldus de Villa Nova. And

---

[1] A copy of this work, and, most probably, the only one in this country, is in the valuable library of Bro. Carson, of Cincinnati, and to it I am indebted for the extracts that I have made.

a great many approv'd and invaluable Rules to prolong Life : Also how to prepare the Universal Medicine. Most humbly dedicated to the Grand Master, Masters, Wardens, and Brethren of the Most Ancient and Honorable Fraternity of the FREE MASONS of Great Britain and Ireland. By Eugenius Philalethes, F.R.S., Author of the Treatise of the Plague. *Viri Fratres audite me.* Act. xv. 13. *Diligite Fraternitatem timete Deum honorate Regem.* I. Pet. ii. 17. LONDON. Printed for J. Holland, at the Bible and Ball, in St. Paul's Church Yard, and L. Stokoe, at Charing Cross, 1722." pp. 64–199.

Eugenius Philalethes was the pseudonym of Thomas Vaughn, a celebrated Rosicrucian of the 17th century, who published, in 1652, a translation of the *Fama Fraternitatis* into English. But, as he was born in 1612, it is not to be supposed that he wrote the present work. It is, however, not very important to identify this second Philalethes. It is sufficient for our purpose to know that it is a Hermetic treatise written by a Rosicrucian, of which the title alone—the references to the renewal of youth, one of the Rosicrucian secrets, to the recipe of the great Rosicrucian Villa Nova, or Arnold de Villaneuve, and to the Universal Medicine, the Rosicrucian Elixir Vitæ—would be sufficient evidence. But the only matter of interest in connection with the present subject is that this Hermetic work, written, or at least printed, in 1722, one year before the publication of the first edition of Anderson's *Constitutions*, refers explicitly to the existence of a higher initiation than that of the Craft degrees, which the author seeks to interweave in the Masonic system.

This is evidently shown in portions of the dedication, which is inscribed to "the Grand Master, Masters, Wardens, and Brethren of the Most Ancient and Most Honorable Fraternity of the Free Masons of Great Britain and Ireland"; and it is dedicated to them by their "Brother Eugenius Philalethes." This fraternal subscription shows that he was a Freemason as well as a Rosicrucian, and therefore must have been acquainted with both systems.

The important fact, in this dedication, is that the writer alludes, in language that can not be mistaken, to a certain higher degree, or to a more exalted initiation, to the attainment of which the primitive degrees of Ancient Craft Masonry were preparatory. Thus he says, addressing the Freemasons:

"I present you with the following sheets, as belonging more

properly to you than any else. But what I here say, those of you who are not far illuminated, who stand in the outward place and are not worthy to look behind the veil, may find no disagreeable or unprofitable entertainment; and those who are so happy as to have greater light, will discover under these shadows, somewhat truly great and noble and worthy the serious attention of a genius the most elevated and sublime—the spiritual, celestial cube, the only true, solid, and immovable basis and foundation of all knowledge, peace, and happiness." (Page iv.)

Another passage will show that the writer was not only thoroughly acquainted with the religious, philosophical, and symbolic character of the institution, but that he wrote evidently under the impression (rather I should say the knowledge) that at that day others besides himself had sought to connect Freemasonry with Rosicrucianism. He says:

"Remember that you are the salt of the earth, the light of the world, and the fire of the universe. Ye are living stones, built up a spiritual house, who believe and rely on the chief *Lapis Angularis*, which the refractory and disobedient builders disallowed; you are called from darkness to light; you are a chosen generation, a royal priesthood."

Here the symbolism is Masonic, but it is also Rosicrucian. The Masons had derived their symbol of the STONE from the metaphor of the Apostle, and like him had given it a spiritual signification. The Rosicrucians had also the *Stone* as their most important symbol. "Now," says one of them, "in this discourse will I manifest to thee the natural condition of the Stone of the Philosophers, apparelled with a triple garment, even this Stone of Riches and Charity, the Stone of Relief from Languishment—in which is contained every secret; being a Divine Mystery and Gift of God, than which there is nothing more sublime." [1]

It was natural that a Rosicrucian, in addressing Freemasons, should refer to a symbol common to both, though each derived its interpretation through a different channel.

In another passage he refers to the seven liberal arts, of which he calls Astronomy "the grandest and most sublime." This was the

---

[1] Dialogue of Arislaus in the Alchemist's Enchiridion, 1672. Quoted by Hitchcock in his "Alchemy and the Alchemists," p. 39.

Rosicrucian doctrine. In that of the Freemasons the precedency is given to Geometry. Here we find a difference between the two institutions which proves their separate and independent existence. Still more important differences will be found in the following passages, which, while they intimate a higher degree, show that it was a Hermetic one, which, however, the Rosicrucian writer was willing to ingraft on Freemasonry. He says:

"And now, my Brethren, *you of the higher class* (note that he does not call it a degree), permit me a few words, since you are but few; and these few words I shall speak to you in riddles, because to you it is given to know those mysteries which are hidden from the unworthy.

"Have you not seen then, my dearest Brethren, that stupendous bath, filled with the most limpid water, than which no pure can be purer, of such admirable mechanism, that makes even the greatest philosopher gaze with wonder and astonishment, and is the subject of the contemplation of the wisest men. Its form is a quadrate sublimely placed on six others, blazing all with celestial jewels, each angularly supported with four lions. Here repose our mighty King and Queen, (I speak foolishly, I am not worthy to be of you), the King shining in his glorious apparel of transparent, incorruptible gold, beset with living sapphires; he is fair and ruddy, and feeds among the lilies; his eyes, two carbuncles, the most brilliant, darting prolific never-dying fires; and his large, flowing hair, blacker than the deepest black or plumage of the long-lived crow; his royal consort vested in tissue of immortal silver, watered with emeralds, pearl and coral. O mystical union! O admirable commerce!

"Cast now your eyes to the basis of this celestial structure, and you will discover just before it a large basin of porphyrian marble, receiving from the mouth of a large lion's head, to which two bodies displayed on each side of it are conjoined, a greenish fountain of liquid jasper. Ponder this well and consider. Haunt no more the woods and forests; (I speak as a fool) haunt no more the fleet; let the flying eagle fly unobserved; busy yourselves no longer with the dancing idiot, swollen toads, and his own tail-devouring dragon; leave these as elements to your *Tyrones*.

"The object of your wishes and desires (some of you may, perhaps, have attained it, I speak as a fool), is that admirable thing which has a substance, neither too fiery nor altogether earthy, nor simply watery; neither a quality the most acute or most obtuse, but of a middle nature, and light to the touch, and in some manner soft, at least not hard, not having asperity, but even in some sort sweet to the taste, odorous to the smell, grateful to the sight, agreeable and delectable to the hearing, and pleasant to the thought; in short, that one only thing besides which there is no other, and yet everywhere possible to be found, the blessed and most sacred subject of the square of wise men, that is . . .   I had almost blabbed it out and been sacrilegiously perjured.   I shall therefore speak of it with a circumlocution yet more dark and obscure, that none but the Sons of Science and those who are illuminated with the sublimest mysteries and profoundest secrets of MASONRY may understand. . . .   It is then what brings you, my dearest Brethren, to that pellucid, diaphanous palace of the true disinterested lovers of wisdom, that triumphant pyramid of purple salt, more sparkling and radiant than the finest Orient ruby, in the center of which reposes inaccessible light epitomized, that incorruptible celestial fire, blazing like burning crystal, and brighter than the sun in his full meridian glories, which is that immortal, eternal, never-dying PYROPUS; the King of genius, whence proceeds everything that is great and wise and happy.

"These things are deeply hidden from common view, and covered with pavilions of thickest darkness, that what is sacred may not be given to dogs or your pearls cast before swine, lest they trample them under foot, and turn again and rend you."

All this is Rosicrucian thought and phraseology.   Its counterpart may be found in the writings of any of the Hermetic philosophers.   But it is not Freemasonry and could be understood by no Freemason relying for his comprehension only on the teaching he had received in his own Order.   It is the language of a Rosicrucian adept addressed to other adepts, who like himself had united with the Fraternity of Freemasons, that they might out of its select coterie choose the most mystical and therefore the most suitable candidates to elevate them to the higher mysteries of their own brotherhood.

That Philalethes and his brother Rosicrucians entertained an opinion of the true character of Speculative Masonry very different from that taught by its founders is evident from other passages of this Dedication.   Unlike Anderson, Desaguliers, and the writers purely

Masonic who succeeded them, the author of the Dedication establishes no connection between Architecture and Freemasonry. Indeed it is somewhat singular that although he names both David and Solomon in the course of his narrative, it is with little respect, especially for the latter, and he does not refer, even by a single word, to the Temple of Jerusalem. The Freemasonry of this writer is not architectural, but altogether theosophic. It is evident that as a Hermetic philosopher he sought to identify the Freemasons with the disciples of the Rosicrucian sect rather than with the Operative Masons of the Middle Ages. This is a point of much interest in the discussion of the question of a connection between the two associations, considering that this work was published only five years after the revival. It tends to show, not that Freemasonry was established by the Rosicrucians, but, on the contrary, that at that early period the latter were seeking to ingraft themselves upon the former, and that while they were willing to use the simple degrees of Craft Masonry as a nucleus for the growth of their own fraternity, they looked upon them only as the medium of securing a higher initiation, altogether unmasonic in its character and to which but few Masons ever attained.

Neither Anderson nor Desaguliers, our best because contemporary authority for the state of Masonry in the beginning of the 18th century, give the slightest indication that there was in their day a higher Masonry than that described in the *Book of Constitutions* of 1723. The Hermetic element was evidently not introduced into Speculative Masonry until the middle of the 18th century, when it was infused in a fragmentary form into some of the High Degrees which were at that time fabricated by certain of the Continental manufacturers of Rites.

But if, as Eugenius Philalethes plainly indicates, there were in the year 1721 higher degrees, or at least a higher degree, attached to the Masonic system and claimed to be a part of it, which possessed mystical knowledge that was concealed from the great body of the Craft, "who were not far illuminated, who stood in the outward place and were not worthy to look behind the veil"—by which it is clearly implied that there was another class of initiates *who were far illuminated, who stood within the inner place and looked behind the veil*—then the question forces itself upon us, why is it that neither Anderson nor Desaguliers nor any of the writers of that period, nor any of the rituals, make any allusion to this higher and more illuminated system ?

The answer is readily at hand. It is because no such system of initiation, so far as Freemasonry was concerned, existed. The Master's degree was at that day the consummation and perfection of Speculative Masonry. There was nothing above or beyond it. The Rosicrucians, who, especially in their astrological branch, were then in full force in England, had, as we see from this book, their own initiation into their Hermetic and theosophic system. Freemasonry then beginning to become popular and being also a mystical society, these mystical brethren of the Rosy Cross were ready to enter within its portals and to take advantage of its organization. But they soon sought to discriminate between their own perfect wisdom and the imperfect knowledge of their brother Masons, and, Rosicrucian-like, spoke of an arcana which they only possessed. There were some Rosicrucians who, like Philalethes, became Freemasons, and some Freemasons, like Elias Ashmole, who became Rosicrucians.

But there was no legitimate derivation of one from the other. There is no similarity between the two systems—their origin is different; their symbols, though sometimes identical, have always a different interpretation; and it would be an impossible task to deduce the one historically from the other.

Yet there are not wanting scholars whose judgment on other matters has not been deficient, who have not hesitated to trace Freemasonry to a Rosicrucian source. Some of these, as Buhle, De Quincey, and Sloane, were not Freemasons, and we can easily ascribe their historical errors to their want of knowledge, but such writers as Nicolai and Reghellini have no such excuse for the fallacy of which they have been guilty.

Johann Gottlieb Buhle was among the first to advance the hypothesis that Freemasonry was an offshoot of Rosicrucianism. This he did in a work entitled *On the Origin and the Principal Events of the Orders of Rosicrucianism and Freemasonry*,[1] published in 1804. His theory was that Freemasonry was invented in the year 1629, by John Valentin Andreä, and hence that it sprang out of the

---

[1] "Uber den Ursprung und die vornehmsten Schicksale des Ordens der Rosenkreutzen und Freimaurer."

Rosicrucian system or fiction which was the fabrication of that writer. His fallacious views and numerous inaccuracies met with many refutations at the time, besides those of Nicolai, produced in the work which has been heretofore cited. Even De Quincey himself, a bitter but flippant adversary of Freemasonry, and who translated, or rather paraphrased, the views of Buhle, does not hesitate to brand him as illogical in his reasoning and confused in his arrangement.

Yet both Nicolai and De Quincey have advanced almost the same hypothesis, though that of the former is considerably modified in its conclusions.

The flippancy and egotism of De Quincey, with his complete ignorance as a profane, of the true elements of the Masonic institution, hardly entitle his arguments to a serious criticism. His theory and his self-styled facts may be epitomized as follows:

He thinks that the Rosicrucians were attracted to the Operative Masons by the incidents, attributes, and legends of the latter, and that thus the two Orders were brought into some connection with each other. The same building that was used by the guild of Masons offered a desirable means for the secret assemblies of the early Freemasons, who, of course, were Rosicrucians. An apparatus of implements and utensils, such as was presented in the fabulous sepulcher of Father Rosencreutz, was introduced, and the first formal and solemn Lodge of Freemasons, on which occasion the name of Freemasons was publicly made known, was held in Masons' Hall, Masons' Alley, Basinghall Street, London, in the year 1646. Into this Lodge he tells us that Elias Ashmole was admitted. Private meetings, he says, may have been held, and one at Warrington in Lancashire, which is mentioned in Ashmole's Life, but the name of a Freemasons' Lodge, with the insignia, attributes, and circumstances of a Lodge, first, he assures us, came forward at the date above mentioned.

All of this, he tells us, is upon record, and thus refers to historical testimony, though he does not tell us where it is to be found. Now, all these statements we know, from authentic records, to be false. Ashmole is our authority, and he is the very best authority, because he was an eye-witness and a personal actor in the occurrences which he records.

It has already been seen, by the extracts heretofore given from Ashmole's diary, that there is no record of a Lodge held in 1646 at

Masons' Hall; that the Lodge was held, with all "the attributes and circumstances of a Lodge," at Warrington ; that Ashmole was then and there initiated as a Freemason, and not at London ; and finally, that the record of the Lodge held at Masons' Hall, London, which is made by the same Ashmole, was in 1683 and not in 1646, or thirty-five years afterward.

An historian who thus falsifies records to sustain a theory is not entitled to the respectful attention of a serious argument. And so De Quincey may be dismissed for what he is worth. I do not concede to him the excuse of ignorance, for he evidently must have had Ashmole's diary under his eyes, and his misquotations could only have been made in bad faith.

Nicolai is more honorable in his mode of treating the question. He does not attribute the use of Freemasonry directly and immediately from the Rosicrucian brotherhood. But he thinks that its mystical theosophy was the cause of the outspring of many other mystical associations, such as the Theosophists, and that, passing over into England, it met with the experimental philosophy of Bacon, as developed especially in his *New Atlantis*, and that the combined influence of the two, the esoteric principles of the one and the experimental doctrines of the other, together with the existence of certain political motives, led to a meeting of philosophers who established the system of Freemasonry at Masons' Hall in 1646. He does not explicitly say so, but it is evident from the names that he gives that these philosophers were Astrologers, who were only a sect of the Rosicrucians devoted to a specialty.

The theory and the arguments of Nicolai have already been considered in the preceding chapter of this work, and need no further discussion here.

The views of Rhigellini are based on the book of Nicolai, and differ from them only in being, from his Gallic ignorance of English history, a little more inaccurate. The views of Rhigellini have already been referred to on a preceding page.

And now we meet with another theorist, who is scarcely more respectful or less flippant than De Quincey, and who, not being a Freemason, labors under the disadvantage of an incorrect knowledge of the principles of the Order. Besides we can expect but little accuracy from one who quotes as authentic history the spurious Leland Manuscript.

Mr. George Sloane, in a very readable book published in London in 1849, under the title of *New Curiosities of Literature*, has a very long article in his second volume on *The Rosicrucians and Freemasons*. Adopting the theory that the latter are derived from the former, he contends, from what he calls proofs, but which are no proofs at all, that "the Freemasons are not anterior to the Rosicrucians; and their principles, so far as they were avowed about the middle of the 17th century, being identical, *it is fair to presume* that the Freemasons were, in reality, the first incorporated body of Rosicrucians or Sapientes."

As he admits that this is but a presumption, and as presumptions are not facts, it is hardly necessary to occupy any time in its discussion.

But he proceeds to confirm his presumption, in the following way.

"In the *Fama* of Andreä," he says, "we have the first sketch of a constitution which bound by oath the members to mutual secrecy, which proposed higher and lower grades, yet leveled all worldly distinctions in the common bonds of brotherhood, and which opened its privileges to all classes, making only purity of mind and purpose the condition of reception."

This is not correct. Long before the publication of the *Fama Fraternitatis* there were many secret associations in the Middle Ages, to say nothing of the Mysteries of antiquity, in which such constitutions prevailed, enjoining secrecy under the severest penalties, dividing their system of esoteric instruction into different grades, establishing a bond of brotherhood, and always making purity of life and rectitude of conduct the indispensable qualifications for admission. Freemasonry needed not to seek the model of such a constitution from the Rosicrucians.

Another argument advanced by Mr. Sloane is this:

"The emblems of the two brotherhoods are the same in every respect—the plummet, the level, the compasses, the cross, the rose, and all the symbolic trumpery which the Rosicrucians named in their writings as the insignia of their imaginary associations, and which they also would have persuaded a credulous world concealed truths ineffable by mere language; both, too, derived their wisdom from Adam, adopted the same myth of building, connected themselves in the same unintelligible way with Solomon's Temple, affected to be seeking *light from the East*—in other words, the Cabala—and accepted the heathen Pythagoras among their adepts."

In this long passage there are almost as many errors and misstatements as there are lines. The emblems of the two Orders were not the same in any respect. The square and compasses were not ordinary nor usual Rosicrucian emblems. In one instance, in a plate in the *Azoth Philosophorum* of Basil Valentine, published in the 17th century, we will, it is true, find these implements forming part of a Rosicrucian figure, but they are there evidently used as phallic symbols, a meaning never attached to them in Freemasonry, whose interpretation of them is derived from their operative use. Besides, we know, from a relic discovered near Limerick, in Ireland, that the square and the level were used by the Operative Masons as emblems in the 16th or, perhaps, the 15th century, with the same signification that is given to them by the Freemasons of the present day. The Speculative Masons derived nearly all of their symbols from the implements and the language of the Operative art; the Rosicrucians took theirs from astronomical and geometrical problems, and were connected in their interpretations with a system of theosophy and not with the art of building. The cross and the rose, referred to by Mr. Sloane, never were at any time, not even at the present day, emblems recognized in Craft Masonry, and were introduced into such of the High Degrees fabricated about the middle of the 18th century as had in them a Rosicrucian element. Again, the Rosicrucians had nothing to do with the Temple of Solomon. Their "invisible house," or their Temple, or "House of the Holy Ghost," was a religious and philosophic idea, much more intimately connected with Lord Bacon's House of Solomon in the Island of Bensalem than it was with the Temple of Jerusalem. And, finally, the early Freemasons, like their successors of the present day, in "seeking light from the East," intended no reference to the Cabala, which is never mentioned in any of their primitive rituals, but alluded to the East as the source of physical light—the place of sunrising, which they adopted as a symbol of intellectual and moral light. It would, indeed, be easier to prove from their symbols that the first Speculative Masons were sun-worshippers than that they were Rosicrucians, though neither hypothesis would be correct.

If any one will take the trouble of toiling through the three books of Cornelius Agrippa's *Occult Philosophy*, which may be considered as the text-book of the old Rosicrucian philosophy, he will see how little there is in common between Rosicrucianism and Freemasonry. The one is a mystical system founded on the Cabala ; the other the outgrowth of a very natural interpretation of symbols derived from the usages and the implements of an operative art. The Rosicrucians were theosophists, whose doctrines were of angels and demons, of the elements, of the heavenly bodies and their influence on the affairs of men, and of the magical powers of numbers, of suffumigations, and other sorceries.

The Alchemists, who have been called "physical Rosicrucians," adopted the metals and their transmutation, the elixir of life, and their universal solvent, as symbols, if we may believe Hitchcock,[1] by which they concealed the purest dogmas of a religious life.

But Freemasonry has not and never had anything of this kind in its system. Its founders were, as we will see when we come to the historical part of this work, builders, whose symbols, applied in their architecture, were of a religious and Christian character; and when their successors made this building fraternity a speculative association, they borrowed the symbols by which they sought to teach their philosophy, not from Rosicrucianism, not from magic, nor from the Cabala, but from the art to which they owed their origin. Every part of Speculative Masonry proves that it could not have been derived from Rosicrucianism. The two Orders had in common but one thing—they both had secrets which they scrupulously preserved from the unhallowed gaze of the profane.

Andreä sought, it is true, in his *Fama Fraternitatis*, to elevate Rosicrucianism to a more practical and useful character, and to make it a vehicle for moral and intellectual reform. But even his system, which was the only one that could have exerted any influence on the English philosophers, is so thoroughly at variance in its principles from that of the Freemasonry of the 17th century, that a union of the two, or the derivation of one from the other, must have been utterly impracticable.

It has been said that when Henry Cornelius Agrippa was in London, in the year 1510, he founded a secret society of Rosicrucians. This is possible, although, during his brief visit to London, Agrippa was the guest of the learned Dean Colet, and spent his time with his

---

[1] " Remarks upon Alchemy and the Alchemists," *passim.*

host in the study of the works of the Apostle to the Gentiles. " I labored hard," he says himself, "at the Epistles of St. Paul." Still he may have found time to organize a society of Rosicrucians. In the beginning of the 16th century secret societies "chiefly composed," says Mr. Morley, "of curious and learned youths had become numerous, especially among the Germans, and towards the close of that century these secret societies were developed into the form of brotherhoods of Rosicrucians, each member of which gloried in styling himself Physician, Theosophist, Chemist, and now, by the mercy of God, Rosicrucian."[1]

But to say of this society, established by Agrippa in England in 1510 (if one was actually established), as has been said by a writer of the last century, that "this practice of initiation, or secret incorporation, thus and then first introduced has been handed down to our own times, and hence, apparently, the mysterious Eleusinian confederacies now known as the Lodges of Freemasonry,"[2] is to make an assertion that is neither sustained by historical testimony nor supported by any chain of reasoning or probability.

I have said that while the hypothesis that Freemasonry was originally derived from Rosicrucianism, and that its founders were the English Rosicrucians in the 17th century, is wholly untenable, there is no doubt that at a later period, a century after this, its supposed origin, a Rosicrucian element, was very largely diffused in the *Hautes Grades* or High Degrees which were invented on the continent of Europe about the middle of the 18th century.

This subject belongs more appropriately to the domain of history than to that of legend, but its consideration will bring us so closely into connection with the Rosicrucian or Hermetic philosophy that I have thought that it would be more convenient not to dissever the two topics, but to make it the subject of the next chapter.

---

[1] "The Life of Henry Cornelius Agrippa von Netteshuri," by Henry Morley, vol. i., p. 58.

[2] *Monthly Review*, London, 1798, vol. xxv., p. 30.

CHAPTER XXXVI

THE ROSICRUCIANISM OF THE HIGH DEGREES

HE history of the High Degrees of Masonry begins with the inventions of the Chevalier Michael Ramsay, who about the year 1728 fabricated three which he called Ecossais, Novice, and Knight Templar. But the inventions of Ramsay had nothing in them of a Rosicrucian character. They were intended by him to support his hypothesis that Freemasonry originated in the Crusades, and that the first Freemasons were Templars. His degrees were therefore not philosophic but chivalric. The rite-manufacturers who succeeded him, followed for the most part in his footsteps, and the degrees that were subsequently invented partook of the chivalric and military character, so that the title of "Chevalier" or "Knight," unknown to the early Freemasons, became in time so common as to form the designation in connection with another noun of most of the new degrees. Thus we find in old and disused Rites, as well as in those still existing, such titles as "Knight of the Sword," "Knight of the Eagle," "Knight of the Brazen Serpent," and so many more that Ragon, in his *Nomenclature*, furnishes us with no less than two hundred and ninety-two degrees of Masonic Knighthood, without having exhausted the catalogue.

But it was not until long after the Masonic labors of Ramsay had ceased that the element of Hermetic philosophy began to intrude itself into still newer degrees.

Among the first to whom we are to ascribe the responsibility of this novel infusion is a Frenchman named Antoine Joseph Pernelty, who was born in 1716 and died in 1800, having passed, therefore, the most active and vigorous portion of his life in the midst of that flood of Masonic novelties which about the middle quarters of the 18th century inundated the continent of Europe and more especially the kingdom of France.

Pernelty was at first a Benedictine monk, but, having at the age of forty-nine obtained a dispensation from his vows, he removed from Paris to Berlin, where for a short time he served Frederick the Great as his librarian.   Returning to Paris, he studied and became infected with the mystical doctrines of Swedenborg, and published a translation of one of the most important of his works.   He then re-paired to Avignon, where he established a new Rite, which, on its transferrence to Montpellier, received the name of the "Academy of True Masons."   Into this Rite it may well be supposed that he introduced much of the theosophic mysticism of the Swedish sage, in parts of which there is a very strong analogy to Rosicrucianism, or at least to the Hermetic Doctrines of the Rosicrucians.   It will be remembered that the late General Hitchcock, who was learned on mystical topics, wrote a book to prove that Swedenborg was a Hermetic philosopher; and the arguments that he advances are not easily to be confuted.

But Pernelty was not a Swedenborgian only.   He was a man of multifarious reading and had devoted his studies, among other branches of learning, to theology, philosophy, and the mathematical sciences.   The appetite for a mystical theology, which had led him to the study and the adoption of the views of Swedenborg, would scarcely permit him to escape the still more appetizing study of the Hermetic philosophers.

Accordingly we find him inventing other degrees, and among them one, the "Knight of the Sun," which is in its original ritual a mere condensation of Rosicrucian doctrines, especially as developed in the alchemical branch of Rosicrucianism.

There is not in the wide compass of Masonic degrees, one more emphatically Rosicrucian than this.   The reference in its ritual to Sylphs, one of the four elementary spirits of the Rosicrucians; to the seven angels which formed a part of the Rosicrucian hierarchy; the dialogue between Father Adam and Truth in which the doctrines of Alchemy and the Cabala are discussed in the search of man for theosophic truth, and the adoption as its principal word of recogni-tion of that which in the Rosicrucian system was deemed the primal matter of all things, are all sufficient to prove the Hermetic spirit which governed the founder of the degree in its fabrication.

There have been many other degrees, most of which are now obsolete, whose very names openly indicate their Hermetic origin.

Such are the "Hermetic Knight," the "Adept of the Eagle" (the word *adept* being technically used to designate an expert Rosicrucian), the "Grand Hermetic Chancellor," and the "Philosophic Cabalist." The list might be increased by fifty more, at least, were time and space convenient. There have been whole rites fabricated on the basis of the Rosicrucian or Hermetic philosophy, such as the "Rite of Philalethes," the "Hermetic Rite," and the "Rite of Illuminated Theosophists," invented in 1767 by Benedict Chartanier, who united in it the notions of the Hermetic philosophy and the reveries of Swedenborg. Gadicke tells us also, in his *Freimaurer-Lexicon*, of a so-called Masonic system which was introduced by the Marquis of Lernais into Berlin in 1758, the objects of which were the Hermetic arcana and the philosopher's stone.

But the Hermetic degree which to the present day has exercised the greatest influence upon the higher grades of Masonry is that of the Rose Croix. This name was given to it by the French, and it must be noticed that in the French language no distinction has ever been made between the *Rosenkreutzer* and *Rose Croix;* or, rather, the French writers have always translated the *Rosenkreutzer* of the German and the *Rosicrucian* of the English by their own words *Rose Croix*, and to this philological inaccuracy is to be traced an historical error of some importance, to be soon adverted to.

The first that we hear in history of a Rosicrucian Masonry, under that distinctive name, is about the middle of the 18th century.

The society to which I allude was known as the "Gold-und-Rosenkreutzer," or the "Golden Rosicrucians." We first find this title in a book published at Berlin, in 1714, by one Samuel Richter, under the assumed name of Sincerus Renatus, and with the title of *A True and Complete Preparation of the Philosopher's Stone by the Order of the Golden Rosicrucians*. In it is contained the laws of the brotherhood, which Findel thinks bear unmistakable evidence of Jesuitical intervention.

The book of Richter describes a society which, if founded on the old Rosicrucians, differed essentially from them in its principles. Findel speaks of these "Golden Rosicrucians" as if originally formed on this work of Richter, and in the spirit of the Jesuits, to repress liberty of thought and the healthy development of the intellect. If formed at that early period, in the beginning of the 18th century, it could not possibly have had a connection with Free-masonry.

But the Order, as an appendant to Masonry, was not really per-fected until about the middle of the 18th century. Findel says after 1756. The Order consisted of nine degrees, all having Latin names, viz.: 1, Junior; 2, Theoreticus; 3, Practicus; 4, Philosophus; 5, Minor; 6, Major; 7, Adeptus; 8, Magister; 9, Magus. It based itself on the three primitive degrees of Freemasonry only as giving a right to entrance; it boasted of being descended from the ancient Rosicrucians, and of possessing all their secrets, and of being the only body that could give a true interpretation of the Masonic symbols, and it claimed, therefore, to be the head of the Order. There is no doubt that this brotherhood was a perfect in-stance of the influence sought to be cast, about the middle of the 18th century, upon Freemasonry by the doctrines of Rosicrucianism. The effort, however, to make it a Hermetic system failed. The Order of the Golden Rosicrucians, although for nearly half a cen-tury popular in Germany, and calling into its ranks many persons of high standing, at length began to decay, and finally died out, about the end of the last century.

Since that period we hear no more of Rosicrucian Masonry, except what is preserved in degrees like that of the Knight of the Sun and a few others, which are still retained in the catalogue of the Ancient and Accepted Scottish Rite.

I have said that the translation of the word *Rosicrucian* by *Rose Croix* has been the source of an important historical error. This is the confounding of the French degree of " Rose Croix," or " Knight of the Eagle and Pelican," with Rosicrucianism, to which it has not the slightest affinity. Thus Dr. Oliver, when speaking of this degree, says that the earliest notice that he finds of it is in the *Fama Fraternitatis*, evidently showing that he deemed it to be of Rosicrucian origin.

The modern Rose Croix, which constitutes the summit of the French Rite, and is the eighteenth of the Ancient and Accepted Scottish Rite, besides being incorporated into several other Masonic systems, has not in its construction the slightest tinge of Rosicru-cianism, nor is there in any part of its ritual, rightly interpreted, the faintest allusion to the Hermetic philosophy.

I speak of it, of course, as it appears in its original form. This has been somewhat changed in later days. The French Masons, objecting to its sectarian character, substituted for it a modification which they have called the " Philosophic Rose Croix."   In this they have given a Hermetic interpretation to the letters on the cross, an example that has elsewhere been more recently followed.

But the original Rose Croix, most probably first introduced to notice by Prince Charles Edward, the " Young Pretender," in the Primordial chapter which he established in 1747, at Arras, in France, was a purely Christian, if not a Catholic degree.   Its most prominent symbols, the rose, the cross, the eagle, and the pelican, its ceremonies, and even its words and signs of recognition, bore allusion to Jesus Christ, the expounder of the new law, which was to take the place of the old law that had ceased to operate when "the veil of the temple was rent."

The Rose Croix, as we find it in its pure and uncorrupted ritual, was an attempt to apply the rites, symbols, and legends of the primitive degrees of Ancient Craft Masonry to the last and greatest dispensation; to add to the first temple of Solomon, and the second of Zerubbabel, a third, which is the one to which Christ alluded when he said, " Destroy this temple, and in three days will I raise it up "— an expression wholly incomprehensible by the ignorant populace who stood around him at the time, but the meaning of which is perfectly intelligible to the Rose Croix Mason who consults the original ritual of his degree.

In all this there is nothing alchemical, Hermetic, or Rosicrucian and it is a great error to suppose that there is anything but Christian philosophy in the degree as originally invented.

The name of the degree has undoubtedly led to the confusion in its history.   But, in fact, the words " Rosa Crucis," common both to the ancient Rosicrucian philosophers and to the modern Rose Croix Masons, had in each a different meaning, and some have supposed a different derivation.   In the latter the title has by many writers been thought to allude to the *ros*, or dew, which was deemed by the alchemists to be a powerful solvent of gold, and to *crux*, the cross, which was the chemical hieroglyphic of light.   Mosheim says:

" The title of *Rosicrucians* evidently denotes the chemical philosophers and those who blended the doctrines of religion with the secrets of chemistry.   The denomination itself is drawn from the science of chemistry; and they only who are acquainted with the peculiar language of the chemists can understand its true signification and energy. It is not compounded, as many imagine, of the two words *rosa* and *crux*, which signify *rose* and *cross*, but of the latter of these words and the Latin word *ros*, which signifies *dew*. Of all natural bodies *dew* is the most powerful solvent of gold. The *cross*, in the chemical style, is equivalent to *light*, because the figure of the cross exhibits at the same time the three letters of which the word *lux*, i.e., *light*, is compounded. Now, *lux* is called by this sect the *seed* or *menstruum of the red dragon;* or, in other words, that gross and corporeal, when properly digested and modified, produces gold."[1]

Notwithstanding that this learned historian has declared that "all other explications of this term are false and chimerical," others more learned perhaps than he, in this especial subject, have differed from him in opinion, and trace the title to *rosa*, not to *ros*.

There is certainly a controversy about the derivation of *Rosicrucian* as applied to the Hermetic philosophers, but there is none whatever in reference to that of the Masonic *Rose Croix*. Everyone admits, because the admission is forced upon him by the ritual and the spirit of the degree, that the title comes from *rose* and *cross*, and that *rose* signifies Christ, and *cross* the instrument of his passion. In the Masonic degree, *Rose Croix* signifies *Christ on the cross*, a meaning that is carried out by the jewel, but one which is never attached to the rose and cross of the Rosicrucians, where *rose* most probably was the symbol of silence and secrecy, and the cross may have had either a Christian or a chemical application; most probably the latter.

Again, we see in the four most important symbols of the Rose Croix degree, as interpreted in the early rituals (at least in their spirit), the same Christian interpretation, entirely free from all taint of Rosicrucianism.

These symbols are the *eagle*, the *pelican*, the *rose*, and the *cross*, all of which are combined to form the beautiful and expressive jewel of the degree.

Thus the writer of the book of Exodus, in allusion to the be-

---

[1] Mosheim, "Ecclesiastical History," Maclane's Translation, cent. xvii., sec. i., vol. iii., p. 436, note.

lief that the eagle assists its feeble younglings in their first flights by bearing them on its pinions, represents Jehovah as saying, "Ye have seen what I did to the Egyptians, and how I bore you on eagle's wings and brought you unto myself." Hence, appropriating this idea, the Rose Croix Masons selected the eagle as a symbol of Christ in his divine character, bearing the children of his adoption in their upward course, and teaching them with unequalled love and tenderness to poise their unfledged wings, and soar from the dull corruptions of earth to a higher and holier sphere. And hence the eagle in the jewel is represented with expanded wings, as if ready for flight.

The pelican, "vulning herself and in her piety," as the heralds call it, is, says Mr. Sloane Evans, "a sacred emblem of great beauty and striking import, and the representation of it occurs not unfrequently among the ornaments of churches." [1] The allusion to Christ as a Saviour, shedding his blood for the sins of the world, is too evident to need explanation.

Of the rose and the cross I have already spoken. The rose is applied as a figurative appellation of Christ in only one passage of Scripture, where he is prophetically called the "rose of Sharon," but the flower was always accepted in the iconography of the church as one of his symbols. But the fact that in the jewel of the Rose Croix the blood-red rose appears attached to the center of the cross, as though crucified upon it, requires no profound knowledge of the science of symbolism to discover its meaning.

The cross was, it is true, a very ancient symbol of eternal life, especially among the Egyptians, but since the crucifixion it has been adopted by Christians as an emblem of him who suffered upon it. "The cross," says Didron, "is more than a mere figure of Christ; it is, in iconography, either Christ himself or his symbol." As such it is used in the Masonry of the Rose Croix.

It is evident, from these explanations, that the Rose Croix was, in its original conception, a purely Christian degree. There was no intention of its founders to borrow for its construction anything from occult philosophy, but simply to express in its symbolization a purely Christian sentiment.

I have, in what I have said, endeavored to show that while Rosi-

---

[1] "The Art of Blazon," p. 130.

crucianism had no concern, as has been alleged, with the origination of Freemasonry in the 17th century, yet that in the succeeding century, under various influences, especially, perhaps, the diffusion of the mystical doctrines of Swedenborg, a Hermetic or Rosicrucian element was infused into some of the High Degrees then newly fabricated.   But the diffusion of that element went no farther ; it never affected the pure Masonic system ; and, with the few exceptions which I have mentioned, even these degrees have ceased to exist.   Especially was it not connected with one of the most important and most popular of those degrees.

From the beginning of the 19th century Rosicrucianism has been dead to Masonry, as its exponent, the Hermetic philosophy, has been to literature.   It has no life now, and we preserve its relics only as memorials of a past obscuration which the sunbeams of modern learning have dispersed.

CHAPTER XXXVII

THE PYTHAGOREANS AND FREEMASONRY

HE theory which ascribes, if not the actual origin of Freemasonry to Pythagoras, at least its introduction into Europe by him, through the school which he established at Crotona, in Italy, which was a favorite one among our early writers, may very properly be placed among the legends of the Order, since it wants all the requisites of historical authority for its support.

The notion was most probably derived from what has been called the Leland Manuscript, because it is said to have been found in the Bodleian Library, in the handwriting of that celebrated antiquary. The author of the *Life of Leland* gives this account of the manuscript :

"The original is said to be the handwriting of King Henry VI. and copied by Leland by order of his highness, King Henry VIII. If the authenticity of this ancient monument of literature remains unquestioned, it demands particular notice in the present publication, on account of the singularity of the subject, and no less from a due regard to the royal writer and our author, his transcriber, indefatigable in every part of literature. It will also be admitted, acknowledgment is due to the learned Mr. Locke, who, amidst the closest studies and the most strict attention to human understanding, could unbend his mind in search of this ancient treatise, which he first brought from obscurity in the year 1796."[1]

This production was first brought to the attention of scholars by being published in the *Gentleman's Magazine* for September, 1753, where it is stated to have been previously printed at Frankfort, in Germany, in 1748, from a copy found in "the writing-desk of a deceased brother."

---

[1] " Life of John Leland," p. 67.

The title of it, as given in the magazine, is in the following words:

"Certeyne Questyons wyth Answeres to the same, concernynge the Mystery of Maconrye; wrytenne by the hande of Kynge Henrye the Sixthe of the Name, and faythefullye copyed by me Johan Ley-lande, Antiquarius, by the commaunde of His Highnesse."

The opinion of Masonic critics of the present day is that the document is a forgery. It was most probably written about the time and in the spirit in which Chatterton composed his imitations of the Monk Rowley, and of Ireland with his impositions of Shakespeare, and was fabricated as an unsuccessful attempt to imitate the archaic language of the 15th century, and as a pious fraud intended to elevate the character and sustain the pretensions of the Masonic Fraternity by furnishing the evidence of its very ancient origin.

Such were not, however, the views of the Masonic writers of the last and beginning of the present century.

They accepted the manuscript, or rather the printed copy of it —for the original codex has never been seen—with unhesitating faith as an authentic document. Hutchinson gave it as an appendix to his *Spirit of Masonry*, Preston published it in the second and enlarged edition of his *Illustrations*, Calcott in his *Candid Disquisition*, Dermott in his *Ahiman Rezon*, and Krause in his *Drei Altesten Kunslurkunden*. In none of these is there the faintest hint of its being anything but an authentic document. Oliver said: " I entertain no doubt of the genuineness and authenticity of this valuable Manuscript." The same view has been entertained by Reghellini among the French, and by Krause, Fessler, and Lenning among the Germans.

Mr. Halliwell was perhaps the first of English scholars to express a doubt of its genuineness. After a long and unsuccessful search in the Bodleian Library for the original, he came, very naturally, to the conclusion that it is a forgery. Hughan and Woodford, both excellent judges, have arrived at the same conclusion, and it is now a settled question that the Leland or Locke Manuscript (for it is known by both titles) is a document of no historic character.

It is not, however, without its value. To its appearance about the middle of the last century, and the unhesitating acceptance of its truth by the Craft at the time, we can, in all probability, assign the establishment of the doctrine that Freemasonry was of a Pythagorean origin, though it had been long before adverted to by Dr. Anderson.

Before proceeding to an examination of the rise and progress of this opinion, it will be proper to cite so much of the manuscript as connects Pythagoras with Masonry.   I do not quote the whole document, though it is short, because it has so repeatedly been printed, in even elementary Masonic works, as to be readily accessible to the reader.   In making my quotations I shall so far defer to the artifice of the fabricator as to preserve unchanged his poor attempt to imitate the orthography and style of the 15th century, and interpolate in brackets, when necessary, an explanation of the most unintelligible words.

The document purports to be answers by some Mason to questions proposed by King Henry VI., who, it would seem, must have taken some interest in the " Mystery of Masonry," and had sought to obtain from competent authority a knowledge of its true character.   The following are among the questions and answers :

" Q. Where dyd ytt [*Masonry*] begynne ?

" A. Ytt dyd begynne with the fyrst menne, yn the Este, which were before the fyrste Manne of the Weste, and comynge westlye, ytt hathe broughte herwyth alle comfortes to the wylde and comfortlesse.

" Q. Who dyd brynge ytt Westlye ?

" A. The Venetians [*Phœnicians*] who beynge grate Merchaundes, comed ffyrst ffrome the Este yn Venetia [*Phœnicia*] ffor the commodyte of Merchaundysinge beithe [*both*] Este and Weste bey the redde and Myddlelonde [*Mediterranean*] Sees.

" Q. Howe comede ytt yn Englonde ?

" A. Peter Gower [*Pythagoras*] a Grecian journeyedde ffor kunnynge yn Egypt and in Syria and in everyche Londe whereat the Venetians [*Phœnicians*] hadde plauntedde Maconrye and wynnynge Entraunce yn al Lodges of Maconnes, he lerned muche, and retournedde and woned [*dwelt*] yn Grecia Magna wachsynge [*growing*] and becommynge a myghtye wyseacre [*philosopher*] and gratelyche renouned and here he framed a grate Lodge at Groton [*Crotona*] and maked many Maconnes, some whereoffe dyd journeye yn Fraunce, and maked manye Maconnes wherefromme, yn processe of Tyme, the Arte passed yn Engelonde."

I am convinced that there was a French original of this document, from which language the fabricator translated it into archaic English.   The internal proofs of this are to be found in the numerous preservations of French idioms.   Thus we meet with *Peter Gower*, evidently derived from *Pythagore*, pronounced *Petagore*, the French for Pythagoras ; *Maconrye* and *Maconnes*, for *Masonry* and *Masons*, the French *c* in the word being used instead of the English *s ;* the phrase *wynnynge the Facultye of Abrac*, which is a pure Gallic idiom, instead of *acquiring the faculty*, the word *gayner* being indifferently used in French as signifying to *win* or to *acquire ;* the word *Freres* for *Brethren ;* and the statement, in the spirit of French nationality, that Masonry was brought into England out of France.

None of these idiomatic phrases or national peculiarities would have been likely to occur if the manuscript had been originally written by an Englishman and in the English language.

But be this as it may, the document had no sooner appeared than it seemed to inspire contemporary Masonic writers with the idea that Masonry and the school of Pythagoras, which he established at Crotona, in Italy, about five centuries before Christ, were closely connected—an idea which was very generally adopted by their successors, so that it came at last to be a point of the orthodox Masonic creed.

Thus Preston, in his *Illustrations of Masonry*, when commenting on the dialogue contained in this document, says that "the records of the fraternity inform us that Pythagoras was regularly initiated into Masonry ; and being properly instructed in the mysteries of the Art, he was much improved, and propagated the principles of the Order in other countries into which he afterwards travelled."

Calcott, in his *Candid Disquisition*, speaks of the Leland Manuscript as "an antique relation, from whence may be gathered many of the original principles of the ancient society, on which the institution of Freemasonry was ingrafted"—by the "ancient society" meaning the school of Pythagoras.

Hutchinson, in his *Spirit of Masonry*, quotes this "ancient Masonic record," as he calls it, and says that " it brings us positive evidence of the Pythagorean doctrine and Basilidian principles making the foundation of our religious and moral duties." Two of the lectures in his work are appropriated to a discussion of the doctrines of Pythagoras in connection with the Masonic system.

But this theory of the Pythagorean origin of Freemasonry does not owe its existence to the writers of the middle of the 18th century. It had been advanced at an early period, and soon after the Revival in 1717 by Dr. Anderson. In the first edition of the *Constitutions*, published in 1723, he alludes to Pythagoras as having borrowed great knowledge from the Chaldean Magi and the Babylonish Jews, but he is more explicit in his *Defense of Masonry*, published in 1730, wherein he says: "I am fully convinced that Freemasonry is very nearly allied to the old Pythagorean Discipline, from whence, I am persuaded, it may in some circumstances very justly claim a descent."

Now, how are we to explain the way in which this tradition of the connection of the Philosopher of Samos first acquired a place among the legends of the Craft? The solution of the problem does not appear to be very difficult.

In none of the old manuscript constitutions which contain what has been called the *Legend of the Guild*, or the *Legend of the Craft*, is there, with a single exception, any allusion to the name of Pythagoras. That exception is found in the Cooke MS., where the legendist, after relating the story of the two pillars inscribed with all the sciences, which had been erected by Jabal before the flood, adds, in lines 318–326, this statement:

" And after this flode many yeres as the cronycle telleth these ii were founde and as the polycronicon seyeth that a grete clerke that called putogaras [*Pythagoras*] fonde that one and hermes the philisophre fonde that other, and thei tought forthe the sciens that thei fonde therein ywritten."

Now, although the Cooke MS. is the earliest of the old records, after the Halliwell poem, none of the subsequent constitutions have followed it in this allusion to Pythagoras. This was because the writer of the Cooke MS., being in possession of the *Polychronicon* of the monk Ranulph Higden, an edition of which had been printed during his time by William Caxton, he had liberally borrowed from that historical work and incorporated parts of it into his Legend.

Of these interpolations, the story of the finding of one of the pillars by Pythagoras is one. The writer acknowledges his indebtedness for the statement to Higden's *Polychronicon*. But it formed no part of the *Legend of the Craft*, and hence no notice is taken of it in the subsequent manuscript copies of the Legend.   In none of them is Pythagoras even named.

It is evident, then, that in the 14th and following centuries, to the beginning of the 18th, the theory of the Pythagorean origin of Freemasonry, or of the connection of the Grecian philosopher with it, was not recognized by the Craft as any part of the traditional history of the Fraternity.   There is no safer rule than that of the old schoolmen, which teaches us that we must reason alike concerning that which does not appear and that which does not exist—" *de non apparentibus et de non existentibus, eadem est ratio.*"   The old craftsmen who fabricated the Legend were workmen and not scholars ; they were neither acquainted with the scholastic nor the ancient philosophy ; they said nothing about Pythagoras because they knew nothing about him.

But about the beginning of the 18th century a change took place, not only in the organization of the Masonic institution, but also in the character and qualifications of the men who were engaged in producing the modification, or we might more properly call it the revolution.

Although in the 17th, and perhaps in the 16th century, many persons were admitted into the Lodges of Operative Masons who were not professional builders, it is, I think, evident that the society did not assume a purely speculative form until the year 1717.   The Revival in that year, by the election of Anthony Sayer, " Gentleman," as Grand Master ; Jacob Lamball, a " Carpenter," and Joseph Elliott, a " Captain," as Grand Wardens, proves that the control of the society was to be taken out of the hands of the Operative Masons.

Among those who were at about that time engaged in the reconstruction of the Institution were James Anderson and Theophilus Desaguliers.   Anderson was a Master of Arts, and afterward a Doctor of Divinity, the minister of a church in London, and an author ; Desaguliers was a Doctor of Laws, a fellow of the Royal Society, and a teacher of Experimental Philosophy of no little reputation.

Both of these men, as scholars, were thoroughly conversant with the system of Pythagoras, and they were not unwilling to take advantage of his symbolic method of inculcating his doctrine, and to introduce some of his symbols into the symbolism of the Order which they were renovating.

Jamblichus, the biographer of Pythagoras, tells us that while the sage was on his travels he caused himself to be initiated into all the mysteries of Byblos and Tyre and those which were practiced in many parts of Syria. But as these mysteries were originally received by the Phœnicians from Egypt, he passed over into that country, where he remained twenty-two years, occupying himself in the study of geometry, astronomy, and all the initiations of the gods, until he was carried a captive into Babylon by the soldiers of Cambyses. There he freely associated with the Magi in their religion and their studies, and, having obtained a thorough knowledge of music, the science of numbers, and other arts, he finally returned to Greece.[1]

The school of philosophy which Pythagoras afterward established at the city of Crotona, in Italy, differed from those of all the other philosophers of Greece, in the austerities of initiation to which his disciples were subjected, in the degrees of probation into which they were divided, and in the method which he adopted of veiling his instructions under symbolic forms. In his various travels he had imbibed the mystical notions prevalent among the Egyptians and the Chaldeans, and had borrowed some of their modes of initiation into their religious mysteries, which he adopted in the method by which he communicated his own principles.

Grote, in his *History of Greece*, has very justly said that " Pythagoras represents in part the scientific tendencies of his age, in part also the spirit of mysticism and of special fraternities for religious and ascetic observance which became diffused throughout Greece in the 6th century before the Christian era."

Of the character of the philosophy of Pythagoras and of his method of instruction, which certainly bore a very close resemblance to that adopted by the founders of the speculative system, such cultivated scholars as Anderson and Desaguliers certainly were not ignorant. And if, among those who were engaged with them in the construction of this new and improved school of speculative Masonry, there were any whose limited scholastic attainments would not enable them to consult the Greek biographies of Pythagoras by Jamblichus and by Porphyry, they had at hand and readily accessible an English translation of M. Dacier's life of the philosopher, con-

---

[1] " Jamblichus de Pythagorica Vita," c. iii., iv.

taining also an elaborate explication of his symbols, together with a translation of the *Commentaries of Hierodes on the Golden Verses of Pythagoras*, all embraced in one volume and published in London in the year 1707, by the celebrated bibliopole Jacob Tonson.

There was abundant material and ready opportunity for the partially unlearned as well as for the more erudite to obtain a familiarity with the philosophy of Pythagoras, his method of initiation, and his system of symbols.

It is not, therefore, surprising that these "Revivalists," as they have been called, should have delighted, as Anderson has done in his *Defense of Masonry*, to compare the two schools of the Pythagoreans and the Freemasons; that they should have dwelt on their great similarity; and in the development of their speculative system should have adopted many symbols from the former which do not appear to have been known to or used by the old Operative Masons whom they succeeded.

Among the first Pythagorean symbols which were adopted by the Speculative Masons was the symbolism of the science of numbers, which appears in the earliest rituals extant, and of which Dr. Oliver has justly said, in his posthumous work entitled *The Pythagorean Triangle*, that "the Pythagoreans had so high an opinion of it that they considered it to be the origin of all things, and thought a knowledge of it to be equivalent to a knowledge of God."

This symbolism of numbers, which was adopted into Speculative Masonry at a very early period after the Revival, has been developed and enlarged in successive revisions of the lectures, until at the present day it constitutes one of the most important and curious parts of the system of Freemasonry. But we have no evidence that the same system of numerical symbolism, having the Pythagorean and modern Masonic interpretation, prevailed among the Craft anterior to the beginning of the 18th century. It was the work of the Revivalists, who, as scholars familiar with the mystical philosophy of Pythagoras, deemed it expedient to introduce it into the equally mystical philosophy of Speculative Masonry.

In fact, the Traveling Freemasons, Builders, or Operative Masons of the Middle Ages, who were the real predecessors of the Speculative Masons of the 18th century, did not, so far as we can learn from their remains, practice any of the symbolism of Pythagoras. Their symbols, such as the *vesica piscis*, the cross, the rose, or certain mathematical figures, were derived either from the legends of the church or from the principles of geometry applied to the art of building. These skillful architects who, in the dark ages, when few men could read or write, erected edifices surpassing the works of ancient Greece or Rome, and which have never been equalled by modern builders, were wonderful in their peculiar skill, but were wholly ignorant of metaphysics or philosophy, and borrowed nothing from Pythagoras.

Between the period of the Revival and the adoption of the Prestonian system, in 1772, the lectures of Freemasonry underwent at least seven revisions. In each of these, the fabricators of which were such cultivated scholars as Dr. Desaguliers, Martin Clare, a President of the Royal Society, Thomas Dunckerley, a man of considerable literary attainments, and others of like character, there was a gradual increment of Pythagorean symbols. Among these, one of the most noted is the forty-seventh proposition of Euclid, which is said to have been discovered by Pythagoras, and which the introducer of it into the Masonic system, in his explanation of the symbol, claims the sage to have been " an ancient brother."

For some time after the Revival, the symbols of Pythagoras, growing into gradual use among the Craft, were referred to simply as an evidence of the great similarity which existed between the two systems—a theory which, so far as it respects modern Speculative Masonry, may be accepted with but little hesitation.

The most liberal belief on this subject was that the two systems were nearly allied, but, except in the modified statement of Anderson, already quoted from his *Defense of Masonry*, there was no claim in the years immediately succeeding the Revival that the one was in direct descent from the other.

In none of the speeches, lectures, or essays of the early part of the last century, which have been preserved, is there any allusion to this as a received theory of the Craft.

Drake, in his speech before the Grand Lodge of York, delivered in 1726, does, indeed, speak of Pythagoras, not as the founder of Masonry, but only in connection with Euclid and Archimedes as great proficients in Geometry, whose works have been the basis " on which the learned have built at different times so many noble superstructures." And of Geometry, he calls it "that noble and useful science which must have begun and goes hand-in-hand with

Masonry," an assertion which, to use the old chorus of the Masons, "nobody will deny."

But to say that Geometry is closely connected with Operative Masonry, and that Pythagoras was a great geometrician, is very different from saying that he was a Mason and propagated Masonry in Europe.

Martin Clare, in his lecture on the *Advantages Enjoyed by the Fraternity*, whose date is 1735, does not even mention the name of Pythagoras, although, in one passage at least, when referring to "those great and worthy spirits with whom we are intimately related," he had a fair opportunity to refer to that illustrious sage.

In a *Discourse Upon Masonry*, delivered before a Lodge of England in 1742, now lying before me, in which the origin of the Order is fully discussed, there is not one word of reference to Pythagoras.

The same silence is preserved in a *Lecture on the Connection Between Freemasonry and Religion*, by the Rev. C. Brockwell, published in 1747.

But after the middle of the century the frequent references in the lectures to the Pythagorean symbols, and especially to that important one, in its Masonic as well as its geometrical value, the forty-seventh proposition, began to lead the members of the society to give to Pythagoras the credit of a relationship to the order to which historically he had no claim.

Thus, in *A Search After Truth*, delivered in the Lodge in 1752, the author says that "Solon, Plato, and Pythagoras, and from them the Grecian literati in general, in a great measure, were obliged for their learning to Masonry and the labors of some of our ancient brethren."

And then, when this notion of the Pythagorean origin of Freemasonry began to take root in the minds of the Craft, it was more firmly established by the appearance in 1753, in the *Gentleman's Magazine*, of that spurious document already quoted, in which, by a "pious fraud," the fabricator of it sought to give the form of an historical record to the statement that Pythagoras, learning his Masonry of the Eastern Magi, had brought it to Italy, and established a Lodge at Crotona, whence the institution was propagated throughout Europe, and from France into England.

As to this statement in the Leland MS., it may be sufficient to say that the sect of Pythagoras did not subsist longer than to the end of the reign of Alexander the Great. So far from disseminating its Lodges or schools after the Christian era, we may cite the authority of the learned Dacier, who says that "in after ages there were here and there some disciples of Pythagoras, but these were only private persons who never established any society, nor had the Pythagoreans any longer a public school."

And so the result of this investigation into the theory of the Pythagorean origin of Freemasonry may be briefly epitomized thus:

The mediæval Freemasons never entertained any such theory, nor in their architectural labors did they adopt any of his symbols.

The writer of the Cooke MS., in 1490, having at hand Higden's *Polychronicon*, in Trevisa's translation, a new edition of which had just been printed by Caxton, incorporated into the *Legend of the Craft* some of the historical statements (such as they were) of the Monk of Chester, but they were extraneous to and formed no part of the original Legend. Therefore, in all the subsequent *Old Records* these interpolations were rejected and the *Legend of the Craft*, as accepted by the writers of the manuscripts which succeeded that of the Cooke codex, from 1550 to 1701, contained no mention of Pythagoras.

Upon the Revival, in 1717, which was really the beginning of genuine Speculative Masonry, the scholars who fabricated the scheme, finding the symbolic teaching of Pythagoras very apposite, adopted some of its symbols, especially those relating to numbers in the new Speculative system which they were forming.

By the continued additions of subsequent ritualists these symbols were greatly increased, so that the name and the philosophy of Pythagoras became familiar to the Craft, and finally, in 1753, a forged document was published which claimed him as the founder and propagator of Masonry.

In later days this theory has continued to be maintained by a few writers, and the received rituals of the Order require it as a part of the orthodox Masonic creed, that Pythagoras was a Mason and an ancient brother and patron of the Order.

Neither early Masonic tradition nor any historical records exist which support such a belief.

CHAPTER XXXVIII

HE hypothesis which seeks to trace a connection between Gnosticism and Freemasonry, and perhaps even an origin of the latter from the former, has been repeatedly advanced, and is therefore worthy of consideration.

The latest instance is in a work of Mr. C. W. King, published in 1864, under the title of *The Gnostics and their Remains, Ancient and Mediæval.*

Mr. King is not a Freemason, and, like all the writers non-Masonic, such as Barnell, Robison, De Quincey, and a host of others, who have attempted to discuss the history and character of Freemasonry, he has shown a vast amount of ignorance. In fact, these self-constituted critics, when treating of subjects with which they are not and can not be familiar, remind one of the busybodies of Plautus, of whom he has said that, while pretending to know everything, they in fact know nothing—" *Qui omnia se simulant scise nec quicquam sciunt.*"

Very justly has Mr. Hughan called this work of King's, so far as its Masonic theories are concerned, one of an "unmasonic and unhistoric character."

But King, it must be admitted, was not the first writer who sought to trace Freemasonry to a Gnostic origin.

In a pamphlet published in 1725, a copy of which has been preserved in the Bodleian Library, among the manuscripts of Dr. Rawlinson, and which bears the title of *Two Letters to a Friend. The First concerning the Society of Free-Masons. The Second, giving an Account of the Most Ancient Order of Gormogons*, etc., we find, in the first letter, on the Freemasons, the following passage:

" But now, Sir, to draw towards a conclusion ; and to give my opinion seriously, concerning these prodigious Virtuosi ;—My belief is, that if they fall under any denomination at all, or belong to any sect of men, which has hitherto appeared in the world, they may be ranked among the GNOSTICS, who took their original from Simon Magus; these were a set of men, which ridiculed not only Christianity, but even rational morality; teaching that they should be saved by their capacious knowledge and understanding of no mortal man could tell what. They babbled of an amazing intelligence they had, from nobody knows whence. They amused and puzzled the hair-brained, unwary crowd with superstitious interpretations of extravagant talismanic characters and abstruse significations of uncommon Cabalistic words; which exactly agrees with the proceedings of our modern Freemasons."

Although the intrinsic value of this pamphlet was not such as to have preserved it from the literary tomb which would have consigned it to oblivion, had not the zeal of an antiquary preserved a single copy as a relic, yet the notion of some relation of Freemasonry to Gnosticism was not in later years altogether abandoned.

Hutchinson says that "under our present profession of Masonry, we allege our morality was originally deduced from the school of Pythagoras, and that the Basilidian system of religion furnished us with some tenets, principles, and hieroglyphics."[1] Basilides, the founder of the sect which bears his name, was the most eminent of the Egyptian Gnostics.

About the time of the fabrication of the High Degrees on the continent of Europe, a variety of opinions of the origin of Masonry —many of them absurd—sprang up among Masonic scholars. Among these theorists, there were not a few who traced the Order to the early Christians, because they found it, as they supposed, among the Gnostics, and especially its most important sect, the Basilidians.

Some German and French writers have also maintained the hypothesis of a connection, more or less intimate, between the Gnostics and the Masons.

I do not know that any German writer has positively asserted the existence of this connection. But the doctrine has, at times, been alluded to without any absolute disclaimer of a belief in its truth.

Thus Carl Michaeler, the author of a *Treatise on the Phœnician*

---

[1] " Spirit of Masonry," lect. x., p. 106.

Mysteries, has written some observations on the subject in an article published by him in 1784, in the Vienna *Journale für Freimaurer*, on the analogy between the Christianity of the early times and Freemasonry. In this essay he adverts to the theory of the Gnostic origin of Freemasonry. He is, however, very guarded in his deductions, and says conditionally that, if there is any connection between the two, it must be traced to the Gnosticism of Clement of Alexandria, and on which simply as a school of philosophy and history it may have been founded, while the differences between the two now existing must be attributed to changes of human conception in the intervening centuries.

But, in fact, the Gnosticism of Clement was something entirely different from that of Basilides, to whom Hutchinson and King attribute the origin of our symbols, and whom Clement vigorously opposed in his works. It was what he himself calls it, "a true gnosis or Christian philosophy on the basis of faith." It was that higher knowledge, or more perfect state of Christian faith, to which St. Paul is supposed to allude when he says, in his First Epistle to the Corinthians, that he made known to those who were perfect a higher wisdom.

Reghellini speaks more positively, and says that the symbols and doctrines of the Ophites, who were a Gnostic sect, passed over into Europe, having been adapted by the Crusaders, the Rosicrucians, and the Templars, and finally reached the Masons.[1]

Finally, I may refer to the Leland MS., the author of which distinctly brought this doctrine to the public view, by asserting that the Masons were acquainted with the "facultye of Abrac," by which expression he alludes to the most prominent and distinctive of the Gnostic symbols. That the fabricator of this spurious document should thus have intimated the existence of a connection between Gnosticism and Freemasonry would lead us to infer that the idea of such a connection was not wholly unfamiliar to the Masonic mind at that period—an inference which will be strengthened by the passage already quoted from the pamphlet in the Rawlinson collection, which was published about a quarter of a century before.

But before we can enter into a proper discussion of this im-

---

[1] "Maçonnerie consideries comme re Resultat des Relig. Egypt. Juive et Chretienne," tom. i., p. 291.

portant question, it will be expedient for the sake of the general reader that something should be said of the Gnostics and of the philosophical and religious system which they professed.

I propose, therefore, very briefly to reply to the questions, What is Gnosticism, and Who were the Gnostics?

Scarcely had the light of Christianity dawned upon the world before a multitude of heresies sprang up to disturb the new religion. Among these Gnosticism holds the most important position. The title of the sect is derived from the Greek word γνῶσις (gnosis), "wisdom or knowledge," and was adopted in a spirit of ostentation, to intimate that the disciples of the sect were in possession of a higher degree of spiritual wisdom than was attainable by those who had not been initiated into their mysteries.

At so early a period did the heresy of Gnosticism arise in the Christian Church, that we find the Apostle Paul warning the converts to the new faith of the innovations on the pure doctrine of Christ, and telling his disciple Timothy to avoid "profane and vain babblings, and oppositions of science, falsely so called." The translators of the authorized version have so rendered the passage. But, in view of the greater light that has since their day been thrown upon the religious history and spirit of the apostolical age, and the real nature of the Gnostic element which disturbed it, we may better preserve the true sense of the original Greek by rendering it "oppositions of the false gnosis."

There were then two kinds of *Gnosis*, or Gnosticism—the true and the false, a distinction which St. Paul himself makes in a passage in his Epistle to the Corinthians, in which he speaks of the wisdom which he communicated to the perfect, in contradistinction to the wisdom of the world.

Of this true Gnosticism, Clement declared himself to be a follower. With it and Freemasonry there can be no connection, except that modified one admitted by Michaeler, which relates only to the investigation of philosophical and historical truth.

The false *Gnosis* to which the Apostle refers is the Gnosticism which is the subject of our present inquiry.

When John the Baptist was preaching in the Wilderness, and for some time before, there were many old philosophical and religious systems which, emanating from the East, all partook of the mystical character peculiar to the Oriental mind. These various systems were then, in consequence of the increased communication of different nations which followed the conquests of Alexander of Macedon, beginning to approximate each other. The disciples of Plato were acquiring some of the doctrines of the Eastern Magi, and these in turn were becoming more or less imbued with the philosophy of Greece. The traditions of India, Persia, Egypt, Chaldea, Judea, Greece, and Rome were commingling in one mass, and forming out of the conglomeration a mystical philosophy and religion which partook of the elements of all the ingredients out of which it was composed, and yet contained within its bosom a mysticism which was peculiar to itself.

This new system was Gnosticism, which derived its leading doctrines from Plato, from the Zend-Avesta, the Cabala, the Vedas, and the hieroglyphs of Egypt. It taught as articles of faith the existence of a Supreme Being, invisible, inaccessible, and incomprehensible, who was the creator of a spiritual world consisting of divine intelligences called *æons*, emanating from him, and of matter which was eternal, the source of evil and the antagonist of the Supreme Being.

One of these *æons*, the lowest of all, called the Demiurge, created the world out of matter, which, though eternal, was inert and formless.

The Supreme Father, or First Principle of all things, had dwelt from all eternity in a *pleroma*, or fullness of inaccessible light, and hence he was called *Bythos*, or the Abyss, to denote the unfathomable nature of his perfections. "This Being," says Dr. Burton, in his able exposition of the Gnostic system, in the *Bampton Lectures*, "by an operation purely mental, or by acting upon himself, produced two other beings of different sexes, from whom by a series of descents, more or less numerous according to different schemes, several pairs of beings were formed, who were called *æons*, from the periods of their existence before time was, or *emanations* from the mode of their production. These successive *æons* or *emanations* appear to have been inferior each to the preceding ; and their existence was indispensable to the Gnostic scheme, that they might account for the creation of the world, without making God the author of evil. These *æons* lived through countless ages with their first Father. But the system of *emanations* seems to have resembled that of concentric circles, and they gradually deteriorated as they

approached nearer and nearer to the extremity of the *pleroma*. Beyond this *pleroma* was matter, inert and powerless, though co-eternal
with the Supreme God, and like him without beginning. At length
one of the *æons* (the Demiurge) passed the limits of the *pleroma*,
and, meeting with matter, created the world after the form and
model of an ideal world, which existed in the *pleroma* or the mind
of the Supreme God."

It is not necessary to enter into a minute recapitulation of the
other points of doctrine which were evolved out of these three. It
is sufficient to say that the old Gnosticism was not an original system, but was really a cosmogony, a religion and a philosophy which
was made up of portions of the older Grecian and Oriental systems,
including the Platonism of the Greeks, the Parsism of the Persians,
and the Cabala of the Jews.

The advent of Christianity found this old Gnosticism prevailing
in Asia and in Egypt. Some of its disciples became converts to the
new religion, but brought with them into its fold many of the mystical views of their Gnostic philosophy and sought to apply them to
the pure and simple doctrines of the Gospel.

Thus it happened that the name of Gnosticism was applied to a
great variety of schools, differing from each other in their interpretations of the Christian faith, and yet having one common principle
of unity—that they placed themselves in opposition to the conceptions of Christianity as it was generally received by its disciples.
And this was because they deemed it insufficient to afford any germs
of absolute truth, and therefore they claimed for themselves the
possession of an amount of knowledge higher than that of ordinary
believers.

"They seldom pretended," says the Rev. Dr. Wing, "to demon-
strate the principles on which their systems were founded by historical evidence or logical reasonings, since they rather boasted that
these were discovered by the intuitional powers of more highly endowed minds, and that the materials thus obtained, whether through
faith or divine revelation, were then worked up into a scientific form,
according to each one's natural power and culture. Their aim
was to construct, not merely a theory of redemption, but of the
universe—a cosmogony. No subject was beyond their investigations. Whatever God could reveal to the finite intellect they looked
upon as within their range. What to others seemed only specula-

tive ideas, were by them hypostatized or personified into real beings or historical facts. It was in this way that they constructed systems of speculation on subjects entirely beyond the range of human knowledge, which startle us by their boldness and their apparent consciousness of reality." [1]

Such was the Gnosticism whose various sects intruded with their mystical notions and their allegorical interpretations into the Church, before Christianity had been well established. Although denounced by St. Paul as "vain babblers," they increased in strength and gave rise to many heresies which lasted until the 4th century.

The most important of these sects, and the one from which the moderns have derived most of their views of what Christian Gnosticism is, was established in the 2d century by Basilides, the chief of the Egyptian Gnostics.

The doctrine of Basilides and the Basilidians was a further development of the original Gnostic system. It was more particularly distinguished by its adoption from Pythagoras of the doctrine of numbers and its use and interpretation of the word *Abraxas*—that word the meaning of which, according to the Leland MS., so greatly puzzled the learned Mr. Locke.

In the system of Basilides the Supreme God was incomprehensible, non-existent, and ineffable. Unfolded from his perfection were seven attributes or personified powers, namely, *Mind, Reason, Thought, Wisdom, Power, Holiness*, and *Peace*. Seven was a sacred number, and these seven powers referred to the seven days of the week. Basilides also supposed that there were seven similar beings in every stage or region of the spiritual world, and that these regions were three hundred and sixty-five in number, thus corresponding to the days in the solar year. These three hundred and sixty-five regions were so many heavenly mansions between the earth and the empyrean, and he supposed the existence of an equal number of angels. The number three hundred and sixty-five was in the Basilidian system one of sacred import. Hence he fabricated the word A B R A X A S, because the Greek letters of which it is composed have the numerical value, when added together, of exactly three hundred and sixty-five. The learned German theologian, Bellerman,

---

[1] Strong and McClintock's "Cyclopædia of Biblical, Theological, and Ecclesiastical Literature."

thinks that he has found the derivation in the Captu, or old Egyptian language, where the words *abrah*, signifying "word," and *sadsch*, signifying "blessed," "holy," or "adorable," and therefore *abrahsadsch*, Hellenized into *Abraxas*, would denote "the holy, blessed, or adorable Word," thus approximating to the spirit of the Jewish Cabalists in their similar use of a Holy Name.

Whether the word was thus derived or was invented by Basilides on account of the numerical value of its letters, is uncertain. He, however, applied it in his system as the name of the Supreme God.

This word *Abraxas*, like the *Tetragrammaton* of the Jews, became one of great importance to the sect of Basilidians. Their reverence for it gave origin to what are called "abraxas gems."

These are gems, plates, or tablets of metal, which have been discovered principally in Egypt, but have also been found in France and Spain. They are inscribed with the word *Abraxas* and an image supposed to designate the Basilidian god. Some of them have on them Jewish words, such as *Jehovah* or *Adonai*, and others contain Persian, Egyptian, or Grecian symbols.

Montfaucon, who has treated the subject of "abraxas gems" elaborately, divides them into seven classes. 1. Those inscribed with the head of a cock as a symbol of the sun. 2. Those having the head of a lion, to denote the heat of the sun, and the word *Mithras*. 3. Those having the image of the Egyptian god *Serapis*. 4. Those having the images of sphinxes, apes, and other animals. 5. Those having human figures with the words *Iao, Sabaoth, Adonai, etc.* 6. Those having inscriptions without figures. 7. Those having monstrous forms.

From these gems we have derived our knowledge of the Gnostic or Basilidian symbols, which are said to have furnished ideas to the builders of the Middle Ages in their decorative art, and which Mr. King and some other writers have supposed to have been transmitted to the Freemasons.

The principal of these Gnostic symbols is that of the Supreme God, *Abraxas*. This is represented as a human figure with the head of a cock, the legs being two serpents. He brandishes a sword in one hand (sometimes a whip) and a shield in the other.

The serpent is also a very common symbol, having sometimes the head of a cock and sometimes that of a lion or of a hawk.

Other symbols, known to be of a purely Gnostic or rather Basilidian origin, from the accompanying inscription, *Abraxas*, or *Iao*, or both, are *Horus*, or the Sun, seated on a lotus flower, which is supported by a double lamp, composed of two phallic images conjoined at their bases ; the dog ; the raven ; the tancross surmounted by a human head ; the Egyptian god, *Anubis;* and Father *Nilus*, in a bending posture and holding in his hand the double, phallic lamp of *Horus*. This last symbol is curious because the word *Heilos*, like *Mithras*, which is also a Gnostic symbol, and *Abraxas*, expresses, in the value of the Greek letters of which it is composed, the number three hundred and sixty-five.

All these symbols, it will be seen, make some reference to the sun, either as the representative of the Supreme God or as the source of light, and it might lead to the supposition that in the later Gnosticism, as in the Mithraic Mysteries, there was an allusion to sun-worship, which was one of the earliest and most extensively diffused of the primitive religions. Evidently in both the Gnostic and the Mithraic symbolism the sun plays a very important part.

While the architects or builders of the Middle Ages may have borrowed, and probably did borrow, some suggestions from the Gnostics in carrying out the symbolism of their art, it is not probable, from their ecclesiastical organization and their religious character, that they would be more than mere suggestions. Certainly they would not have been accepted by these orthodox Christians with anything of their real Gnostic interpretation.

We may apply to the use of Gnostic symbols by the mediæval architects the remarks made by Mr. Paley on the subject of the adoption of certain Pagan symbols by the same builders. Their Gnostic origin was a mere accident. They were employed not as the symbolism of any Gnostic doctrine, but in the spirit of Christianity, and " the Church, in perfecting their development, stamped them with a purer and sublimer character." [1]

On a comparison of these Gnostic symbols with those of Ancient Craft or Speculative Masonry, I fail to find any reason to subscribe to the opinion of Hutchinson, that " the Basilidian system of religion furnished Freemasonry with some tenets, principles, and hieroglyphics." As Freemasons we will have to repudiate the " tenets and principles" of the sect which was condemned by

---

[1] " Manual of Gothic Architecture," p. 4.

Clement and by Irenæus; and as to its "hieroglyphics," by which is meant its symbols, we will look in vain for their counterpart or any approximation to them in the system of Speculative Masonry.

That the Masons at a very early period exhibited a tendency to the doctrine of sacred numbers, which has since been largely developed in the Masonry of the modern High Degrees, is true, but this symbolism was derived directly from the teachings of Pythagoras, with which the founders of the primitive rituals were familiar.

That the sun and the moon are briefly referred to in our rituals and may be deemed in some sort Masonic symbols, is also true, but the use made of this symbolism, and the interpretation of it, very clearly prove that it has not been derived from a Gnostic source.

The doctrine of the metempsychosis, which was taught by the Basilidians, is another marked point which would widely separate Freemasonry from Gnosticism, the dogma of the resurrection being almost the foundation-stone on which the whole religious philosophy of the former is erected.

Mr. King, in his work on the Gnostics, to which allusion has already been made, seeks to trace the connection between Freemasonry and Gnosticism through a line of argument which only goes to prove his absolute and perhaps his pardonable ignorance of Masonic history. It requires a careful research, which must be stimulated by a connection with the Order, to enable a scholar to avoid the errors into which he has fallen.

"The foregoing considerations," he says, "seem to afford a rational explanation of the manner in which the genuine Gnostic symbols (whether still retaining any mystic meaning or kept as mere lifeless forms, let the Order declare) have come down to these times, still paraded as things holy and of deep significance. Treasured up amongst the dark sectaries of the Lebanon and the Sofis of Persia, communicated to the Templars, and transmitted to their heirs, the Brethren of the Rosy Cross, they have kept up an unbroken existence."[1]

In the line of history which Mr. King has here pursued, he has presented a mere jumble of non-consecutive events which it would be impossible to disentangle. He has evidently confounded the old Rosicrucians with the more modern Rose Croix, while the only

---

[1] "The Gnostics and their Remains," p. 191.

connection between the two is to be found in the apparent similarity of name.   If he meant the former, he has failed to show a relation between them and the Freemasons; if the latter, he was wholly ignorant that there is not a Gnostic symbol in their system, which is wholly constructed out of an ecclesiastical symbolism.   Such inconsequential assertions need no refutation.

Finally he says that "Thus those symbols, in their origin, embodying the highest mysteries of Indian theosophy, afterward eagerly embraced by the subtle genius of the Alexandrian Greeks, and combined by them with the hidden wisdom of Egypt, in whose captivating and profound doctrines the few bright spirits of the Middle Ages sought a refuge from the childish fables then constituting orthodoxy, engendered by monkery upon the primal Buddhistic stock; these sacred symbols exist even now, but serve merely for the insignia of what at best is but a charitable, probably nothing more in its present form than a convivial institution."

These last lines indicate the precise amount of knowledge that he possesses of the character and the design of Freemasonry.   It is to be regretted that he had not sought to explain the singular anomaly that "what at best is but a charitable, and probably nothing more than a convivial institution" has been made the depository of the symbols of an abstruse theosophy.   Benevolent societies and convivial clubs do not, as a rule, meddle with matters of such high import.

But to this uncritical essay there need be no reply.   When anyone shall distinctly point out and enumerate the Gnostic symbols that made a part of the pure and simple symbolism of the primitive Speculative Masons, it will be time enough to seek the way in which they came there.

For the present we need not undergo the needless labor of searching for that which we are sure can not be found.

CHAPTER XXXIX

THE SOCINIANS AND FREEMASONRY

HILE some of the adversaries of Freemasonry have pretended that its origin is to be found in the efforts of the Jesuits, who sought to effect certain religious and political objects through the influence of such a society, one, at least, has endeavored to trace its first rise to the Socinians, who sprang up as a religious sect in Italy about the middle of the 16th century.

This hypothesis is of so unhistorical a character that it merits a passing notice in the legendary history of the Institution.

It was first promulgated (and I do not know that it has ever since been repeated) by the Abbé Le Franc, the Superior of the House of the Eudists, at Caën, in a book published by him in the year 1791, under the title of *Le Voile levé pour les curieux, ou le secret des Révolutions, révelé à l'aide de la Franc-Maçonnerie;* i.e., "The Veil lifted for the Inquisitive, or the Secret of Revolutions revealed by the assistance of Freemasonry." This work was deemed of so much importance that it was translated in the following year into Italian.

In this essay Le Franc, as a loyal Catholic ecclesiastic, hating both the Freemasons and the Socinians, readily seized the idea, or at all events advanced it, that the former was derived from the latter, whose origin he assigns to the year 1546.

He recapitulates, only to deny, all the other theories that have been advanced on the subject, such as that the origin of the Institution is to be sought in the fraternities of Operative Masons of the Middle Ages, or in the assembly held at York under the auspices of King Athelstane, or in the builders of King Solomon's Temple, or in the Ancient Mysteries of Egypt. Each of these hypotheses he refuses to admit as true.

On the contrary, he says the Order can not be traced beyond the famous meeting of Socinians, which was held at the City of Vicenza, in Italy, in the year 1546, by Lælius Socinus, Ochirius, Gentilis, and others, who there and then established the sect which repudiated the doctrine of the Trinity, and whose successors, with some modification of tenets, still exist under the name of Unitarians, or Liberal Christians.

But it is to Faustus Socinus, the nephew of Lælius, he asserts, that the real foundation of Freemasonry as a secret and symbolical society is to be ascribed. This "artful and indefatigable sectary," as he calls him, having beheld the burning of Servetus at Geneva by Calvin, for maintaining only a part of the system that he advocated, and finding that both Catholics and Protestants were equally hostile to his views, is said to have concealed it under symbols and mysterious ceremonies, accompanied by oaths of secrecy, in order that, while it was publicly taught to the people in countries where it was tolerated, it might be gradually and safely insinuated into other states, where an open confession of it would probably lead its preachers to the stake.

The propagation of this system, he further says, was veiled under the enigmatical allegory of building a temple whose extent, in the very words of Freemasonry, was to be "in length from the east to the west, and in breadth from north to south." The professors of it were therefore furnished, so as to carry out the allegory, with the various implements used in building, such as the square, the compasses, the level, and the plumb. And here it is that the Abbé Le Franc has found the first form and beginning of the Masonic Institution as it existed at the time of his writing.

I have said that, so far as I have been able to learn, Le Franc is the sole author or inventor of this hypothesis. Reghellini attributes it to three distinct writers, the author of the *Voile levé*, Le Franc, and the Abbé Barruel. But in fact the first and second of these are identical, and Barruel has not made any allusion to it in his *History of Jacobinism*. He attributes the origin of Freemasonry to the Manicheans, and makes a very elaborate and learned collation of the usages and ceremonies of the two, to show how much the one has taken from the other.

Reghellini, in commenting on this theory of the Abbé Le Franc, says that all that is true in it is that there was at the same period, about the middle of the 16th century, a learned society of philosophers and literary men at Vicenza, who held conferences on the theological questions which at that time divided Europe, and particularly Germany.

The members of this celebrated academy, he says, looked upon all these questions and difficulties concerning the mysteries of the Christian religion as points of doctrine which pertained simply to the philosophy of the ancient Egyptians, Greeks, and Christians, and had no relation whatever to the dogmas of faith.[1]

Considering that out of these meetings of the philosophers at Vicenza issued a religious sect, whose views present a very important modification of the orthodox creeds, we may well suppose that Reghellini is as much in error in his commentary as Le Franc has been in his text.

The society which met at Vicenza and at Venice, though it sought to conceal its new and heterodox doctrines under a veil of secrecy, soon became exposed to the observation of the Papal court, through whose influence the members were expelled from the Venetian republic, some of them seeking safety in Germany, but most of them in Poland, where their doctrines were not only tolerated, but in time became popular. In consequence, flourishing congregations were established at Cracow, Lublin, and various other places in Poland and in Lithuania.

Lælius Socinus had, soon after the immigration of his followers into Poland, retired to Zurich, in Switzerland, where he died. He was succeeded by his nephew, Faustus Socinus, who greatly modified the doctrines of his uncle, and may be considered as the real founder of the Socinian sect of Christians.

Now, authentic history furnishes us with these few simple facts.

In the 16th century secret societies were by no means uncommon in various countries of Europe. In Italy especially many were to be found. Some of these coteries were established for the cultivation of philosophical studies, some for the pursuit of alchemy, some for theological discussions, and many were of a mere social character. In all of them, however, there was an exclusiveness which shut out the vulgar, the illiterate, or the profane.

Thus there was founded at Florence a club which called itself the " Società della Cucchiara," or the *Society of the Trowel.* The

---

[1] Reghellini, " La Maçonnerie," tom. iii., p. 60.

name and the symbols it used, which were the trowel, the hammer, the square, and the level, have led both Lenning and Reghellini to suppose that it was a Masonic association.   But the account given of it by Vasari, in his *Lives of the Painters and Sculptors*, shows that it was merely a social club of Florentine artists, and that it derived its existence and its name from the accidental circumstance that certain painters and sculptors dining together once upon a time, in a certain garden, discovered, not far from their table, a heap of mortar in which a trowel was sticking.   In an exuberance of spirits they began to throw the mortar on each other, and to call for the trowel to scrape it off.   In the same sportive humor they then and there resolved to form an association which should annually thereafter dine together, and to commemorate the ludicrous event which had given rise to their association, they called it the Society of the Trowel, and adopted as emblems certain tools connected with the mystery of bricklaying.

Every city in Italy in which science was cultivated had its academy, many of which, like the Platonic Academy, established at Florence in 1540, held their sessions in secret, and admitted none but members to participate in their mystical studies.   In Germany the secret societies of the Alchemists were abundant.   These spread also into France and England.   To borrow the language of a modern writer, mystical interpretation ran riot, everything was symbolized, and metaphors were elaborated into allegories.[1]

It is a matter of historical record that in 1546 there was a society of this kind, consisting of about forty persons, eminent for their learning, who, in the words of Mosheim,[2] "held secret assemblies, at different times, in the territory of Venice, and particularly at Vicenza, in which they deliberated concerning a general reformation of the received systems of religion, and, in a more especial manner, undertook to refute the peculiar doctrines that were afterwards publicly rejected by the Socinians."

Mosheim, who was rigorous in the application of the canons of criticism to all historical questions that came under his review, says, in a note appended to this passage : " Many circumstances and relations sufficiently prove that immediately after the reformation had

---

[1] Vaughan, "Hours with the Mystics," I., p. 119.
[2] "Ecclesiast. Hist. XVI. Cent.," Part III., chap. iv.

taken place in Germany, secret assemblies were held and measures proposed in several provinces that were still under the jurisdiction of Rome, with a view to combat the errors and superstitions of the times."

Such was the character of the secret society at Vicenza to which Le Franc attributes the origin of Freemasonry. It was an assembly of men of advanced thought, who were compelled to hold their meetings in secret, because the intolerance of the church and the jealous caution of the state forbade the free and open discussion of opinions which militated against the common sentiments of the period.

The further attempt to connect the doctrines of Socinus with those of Freemasonry, because, when speaking of the new religion which he was laboring to establish, he compared it to the building of a new temple, in which his disciples were to be diligent workers, is futile. The use of such expressions is to be attributed merely to a metaphorical and allegorical spirit by no means uncommon in writers of every age. The same metaphor is repeatedly employed by St. Paul in his various Epistles, and it is not improbable that from him Socinus borrowed the idea.

There is, therefore, as I conceive, no historical evidence whatever to support the theory that Faustus Socinus and the Socinians were the founders of Freemasonry. At the very time when he was establishing the sect whose distinctive feature was its denial of the dogma of the Trinity, the manuscript constitutions of the Masons were beginning their *Legend of the Craft*, with an invocation to "the Might of the Father, the Wisdom of the Glorious Son, and the Goodness of the Holy Ghost, three Persons and one God."

The idea of any such connection between two institutions whose doctrines were so antagonistic was the dream—or rather the malicious invention—of Le Franc, and has in subsequent times received the amount of credit to which it is entitled.

CHAPTER XL

FREEMASONRY AND THE ESSENES

AWRIE—or I should rather say Brewster—was the first to discover a connection between the Freemasons and the Jewish sect of the Essenes, a doctrine which is announced in his *History of Freemasonry*. He does not indeed trace the origin of the Masonic Institution to the Essenes, but only makes them the successors of the Masons of the Temple, whose forms and tenets they transmitted to Pythagoras and his school at Crotona, by whom the art was disseminated throughout Europe.

Believing as he did in the theory that Freemasonry was first organized at the Temple of Solomon by a union of the Jewish workmen with the association of Dionysian Artificers—a theory which has already been discussed in a preceding chapter—the editor of Lawrie's *History* meets with a hiatus in the regular and uninterrupted progress of the Order which requires to be filled up. The ingenious mode in which he accomplishes this task may be best explained in his own words:

"To these opinions it may be objected, that if the Fraternity of Freemasons flourished during the reign of Solomon, it would have existed in Judea in after ages, and attracted the notice of sacred or profane historians. Whether or not this objection is well founded, we shall not pretend to determine; but if it can be shown that there did exist, after the building of the temple, an association of men resembling Freemasons, in the nature, ceremonies, and object of their institution, the force of the objection will not only be taken away, but additional strength will be communicated to the opinion which we have been supporting. The association here alluded to is that of the Essenes, whose origin and sentiments have occasioned much discussion among ecclesiastical historians. They are all, however, of

one mind concerning the constitution and observances of this religious order."[1]

The peace-making quality of "if" is here very apparent.   "If it
can be shown" that there is a chronological sequence from the builders of the Temple to the Essenes, and that there is a resemblance
of both to the Freemasons in "the nature, ceremonies, and object of
their institution," the conclusion to which Brewster has arrived will
be better sustained than it would be if these premises are denied or
not proved.

The course of argument must therefore be directed to these
points.

In the first place we must inquire, who were the Essenes and
what was their history?   This subject has already been treated to
some extent in a previous portion of this work.   But the integrity of
the present argument will require, and I trust excuse, the necessity
of a repetition.

The three sects into which the Jews were divided in the time of
Christ were the Pharisees, the Sadducees, and the Essenes.   Of
these, while the Saviour makes repeated mention of the first two, he
never alludes in the remotest manner to the third.   This singular
silence of Jesus has beèn explained by some imaginative Masonic
writers, such, for instance, as Clavel, by asserting that he was probably
an initiate of the sect.   But scholars have been divided on this subject, some supposing that it is to be attributed to the fact (which,
however, has not been established) that the Essenes originated in
Egypt at a later period; others that they were not an independent
sect, but only an order or subdivision of Pharisaism.   However, in
connection with the present argument, the settlement of this question is of no material importance.

The Essenes were an association of ascetic celibates whose numbers were therefore recruited from the children of the Jewish community in which they lived.   These were carefully trained by proper
instructions for admission into the society.   The admission into the
interior body of the society and to the possession of its mystical doctrine was only attained after a long probation through three stages
or degrees, the last of which made the aspirant a participant in the
full fellowship of the community.

---

[1] Lawrie's " History of Freemasonry," p. 33.

The history of the Essenes has been so often written by ancient and modern authors, from Philo and Josephus to Ginsburg, that an inquirer can be at no loss for a knowledge of the sect.   The Masonic student will find the subject discussed in the author's *Encyclopædia of Freemasonry*, and the ordinary reader may be referred to the able article in McClintock and Strong's *Cyclopædia of Biblical, Theological, and Ecclesiastical Literature*.   I shall content myself, in fairness to the theory, with quoting the brief but compendious description given by the editor of Lawrie's *History*.   It is in the main correct and sustained by other authorities, except a few deductions which must be attributed to the natural inclination of every theorist to adapt facts to his hypothesis.   A few interpolations will be necessary to correct manifest errors.

"When a candidate was proposed for admission, the strictest scrutiny was made into his character.   If his life had been hitherto exemplary, and if he appeared capable of curbing his passions and regulating his conduct according to the virtuous though austere maxims of their order, he was presented, at the expiration of his novitiate, with a white garment, as an emblem of the regularity of his conduct and the purity of his heart."

It was not at the termination, but at the beginning of the novitiate, that the white garment or robe was presented, and it was accompanied by the presentation of an apron and a spade.

"A solemn oath was then administered to him that he would never divulge the mysteries of the Order ; that he would make no innovations on the doctrines of the society ; and that he would continue in that honorable course of piety and virtue which he had begun to pursue."

This is a mere abstract of the oath, which is given at length by Josephus.   It was not, however, administered until the candidate had passed through all the degrees or stages, and was ready to be admitted into full fellowship.

"Like Freemasons, they instructed the young member in the knowledge which they derived from their ancestors."

He might have said, like all other sects, in which the instruction of the young member is an imperative duty.

"They admitted no women into their Order."

Though this is intended by the editor to show a point of identity with Freemasonry, it does no such thing.   It is the common rule of all masculine associations. It distinguishes the Essenes from other religious sects, but it by no means essentially likens them to the Freemasons.

" They had particular signs for recognizing each other, which have a strong resemblance to those of Freemasons."

This is a mere assumption. That they had signs for mutual recognition is probable, because such has been in all ages the custom of secret societies. We have classical authority that they were employed in the ancient Pagan Mysteries. But there is no authority for saying that these signs of the Essenes bore any resemblance to those of the Freemasons. The only allusion to this subject is in the treatise of Philo Judæus, *De Vita Contemplativa*, where that author says that " the Essenes meet together in an assembly and the right hand is laid upon the part between the chin and the breast, while the left hand hangs straight by the side." But Philo does not say that it was used as a sign of recognition, but rather speaks of it as an attitude or posture assumed in their assemblies. Of the resemblance every Mason can judge for himself.

"They had colleges, or places of retirement, where they resorted to practice their rites, and settle the affairs of the society ; and after the performance of these duties, they assembled in a large hall, where an entertainment was provided for them by the president, or master, of the college, who allotted a certain quantity of provisions to every individual."

This was the common meal, not partaken on set occasions and in a particular place, as the writer intimates, but every day, in their usual habitation and at the close of daily labor.

" They abolished all distinctions of rank ; and if preference was ever given, it was given to piety, liberality, and virtue. Treasurers were appointed in every town to supply the wants of indigent strangers. The Essenes pretended to higher degrees of piety and knowledge than the uneducated vulgar, and though their pretensions were high, they were never questioned by their enemies. Austerity of manners was one of the chief characteristics of the Essenian Fraternity. They frequently assembled, however, in convivial parties, and relieved for awhile the severity of those duties which they were accustomed to perform."

In concluding this description of an ascetic religious sect, the writer of Lawrie's *History* says that " this remarkable coinci-

dence between the chief features of the Masonic and Essenian Fraternities can be accounted for only by referring them to the same
origin." Another, and, perhaps, a better reason to account for these
coincidences will be hereafter presented.

While admitting that there is a resemblance in some points of
the two institutions to each other, such as their secrecy, their classification into different degrees, although there is no evidence that the
Essenian initiation had any form except that of a mere passage from
a lower to a higher grade, and their cultivation of fraternal love,
which resemblances may be found in many other secret associations,
I fail to see the identity "in the nature, the object, and the external
forms of the two institutions" which Brewster claims.

On the contrary, there is a total dissimilarity in each of these
points.

The nature of the Essenian institution was that of an ascetic
and a bigoted religious sect, and in so far has certainly no resemblance to Freemasonry.

The object of the Essenes was to preserve in its most rigid re-
quirements the observance of the Mosaic law; that of Freemasonry
is to diffuse the tolerant principles of a universal religion, which
men of every sect and creed may approve.

As to the external form of the two institutions, what little we
know of those of the Essenes certainly does not exhibit any other
resemblance than that which is common to all secret associations,
whatever may be their nature and objects.

But the most fatal objection to the theory of a connection between them, which is maintained by the author of Lawrie's *History*,
has been admitted with some candor by himself.

"There is one point, however," he says, "which may, at first
sight, seem to militate against this supposition. The Essenes appear in no respects connected with architecture; nor addicted to
those sciences and pursuits which are subsidiary to the art of
building."

This objection, I say, is fatal to the theory which makes the Essenes the successors of the builders of Solomon's Temple and the
forerunners of the Operative Masons of the Middle Ages, out of
whom sprang the Speculative Masons of the 18th century. Admitting for a moment the reality of the organization of Masonry at the
building of the Temple in Jerusalem, any chain which unites that

body of builders with the Freemasonry of the present day must show, in every link, the presence and the continuance of pursuits and ideas connected with the operative art of building. Even the Speculative Masons of the present day have not disturbed that chain, because, though the fraternity is not now composed, necessarily, of architects and builders, yet the ideas and pursuits of those professions are retained in the Speculative science, all of whose symbolism is founded on the operative art.

The Essenes were not even Speculative Masons. Their symbolism, if they had any, was not founded on nor had any reference to the art of building. The apron which they presented to their novice was intended to be used, according to their practice, in baptism and in bathing ; and the spade had no symbolic meaning, but was simply intended for practical purposes.

The defense made by the author of the *History*, that in modern times there are " many associations of Freemasons where no architects are members, and which have no connection with the art of building," hardly needs a reply. There never has been an association of Freemasons, either Operative or Speculative, which did not have a connection with the art of building, in the former case practically, in the latter symbolically.

It is absurd to suppose the interpolation between these two classes of an institution which neither practically nor symbolically cultivated the art on which the very existence of Freemasonry in either condition is based.

But another objection, equally as fatal to the theory which makes the Essenes the uninterrupted successors of the Temple builders, is to be found in the chronological sequence of the facts of history. If this succession is interrupted by any interval, the chain which connects the two institutions is broken, and the theory falls to the ground.

The Temple of Solomon was finished about a thousand years before the Christian era, and, according to the Masonic legendary account, the builders who were engaged in its construction immediately dispersed and traveled into foreign countries to propagate the art which they had there acquired. This, though merely a legend, is not at all improbable. It is very likely that the Tyrian workmen, at least (and they constituted the larger number of those employed in the building), returned to their homes after the tasks for which

they had been sent to Solomon, by the King of Tyre, had been accomplished.   If there were any Jewish Masons at all, who were not
mere laborers, it is not unreasonable to suppose that they would
seek employment elsewhere, in the art of building which they had
acquired from their Tyrian masters.   This is a proper deduction
from the tradition, considered as such.

Who, then, were left to continue the due succession of the fraternity?   Brewster, in Lawrie's *History*, and Oliver, in his *Antiquities*, affirm that it was the Essenes.

But we do not hear of this sect as an organized body until eight
centuries afterward.   The apocryphal statement of Pliny, that they
had been in being for thousands of years—"*per seculorum millia*"—
has met with no reception from scholars.   It is something which, as
he himself admits, is incredible; and Pliny is no authority in Jewish
affairs.

Josephus speaks of them, as existing in the days of Jonathan the Maccabæan; but this was only 143 years before Christ.
They are never mentioned in any of the books of the Old Testament, written subsequently to the building of the Temple, and
the silence of the Saviour and the Apostles concerning them has
been attributed to the fact that they were not even at that time an
organized body, but merely an order of the Pharisees.   The Rabbi
Nathan distinctly says that "those Pharisees who live in a state of
celibacy are Essenes;" and McClintock collates from various authorities fourteen points of resemblance, which are enumerated to
show the identity in the most important usages of the two institutions.   At all events, we have no historic evidence of the existence
of the Essenes as a distinct organization before the war of the Maccabees, and this would separate them by eight centuries from the
builders of Solomon's Temple, of whom the theory under review
erroneously supposes them to be the direct descendants.

But Brewster[1] seeks to connect the Essenes and the builders of
Solomon through the Assideans, whom he also calls "an order of
the KNIGHTS OF THE TEMPLE OF JERUSALEM, who bound themselves to adorn the porches of that magnificent structure and to pre-

---

[1] The unfairness of the author of Lawrie's "History" is apparent when he quotes the
"Histoire des Juifs," by Basnage, as authority for the existence of the Essenes three hundred years before the Christian era.   Basnage actually says that they existed in the reign
of Antigonus, but this was only 105 B.C.

serve it from injury and decay." He adds that "this association was composed of the greatest men of Israel, who were distinguished for their charitable and peaceful dispositions; and always signalized themselves by their ardent zeal for the purity and preservation of the temple." Hence he argues that "the Essenes were not only an ancient fraternity, but that they originated from an association of architects who were connected with the building of Solomon's temple."

All this is very ingenious, but it is very untrue. It is, however, the style, now nearly obsolete, it is to be hoped, in which Masonic history has been written.

The fact is that the Assideans were not of older date than the Essenes. They are not mentioned by the canonical writers of the Scriptures, nor by Josephus, but the word first occurs in the book of Maccabees, where it is applied, not, as Brewster calls them, to men of "peaceful dispositions," but to a body of devoted and war-like heroes and patriots who, as Kitto says, rose at the signal for armed resistance given by Mattathias, the father of the Maccabees, and who, under him and his successors, upheld with the sword the great doctrine of the unity of God, and stemmed the advancing tide of Grecian manners and idolatries.

Hence the era of the Assideans, like that of the Essenes, is re-moved eight centuries from the time of the building of the Solo-monic Temple.

Scaliger, who is cited in Lawrie's *History* as authority, only says that the Assideans were a confraternity of Jews whose principal de-votion consisted in keeping up the edifices belonging to the Temple; and who, not content with paying the common tribute of half a shekel a head, appointed for Temple repairs, voluntarily imposed upon themselves an additional tax.

But as they are not known to have come into existence until the wars of the Maccabees, it is evident that the Temple to which they devoted their care must have been the second one, which had been built after the return of the Jews from their Babylonian captivity. With the Temple of Solomon and with its builders the Assideans could not have had any connection.

Prideaux says that the Jews were divided, after the captivity, into two classes—the Zadikim or righteous, who observed only the written law of Moses, and the Chasidim or pious, who superadded the traditions of the elders. These latter, he says, were the Assideans, the change of name resulting from a common alteration of the sounds of the original Hebrew letters.

But if this division took place after the captivity, a period of nearly five centuries had then elapsed since the building of Solomon's Temple, and an uninterrupted chain of sequences between that monarch's builders and the Essenes is not preserved.

After the establishment of the Christian religion we lose sight of the Essenes. Some of them are said to have gone to Egypt, and there to have founded the ascetic sect of Therapeutists. Others are believed to have been among the first converts to Christianity, but in a short time they faded out of all notice. I think, from what has been said, that there can be no hesitation in pronouncing the theory of the descent of Freemasonry to modern times through the Assideans and the Essenes to be wholly untenable and unsupported by historical testimony.

In relation to what has been called the "remarkable coincidences" to be met with in the doctrines and usages of this Jewish sect and the Freemasons, giving to them all the weight demanded, the rational explanation appears to be such as I have elsewhere given, and which I may repeat here.

The truth is that the Essenes and the Freemasons derive whatever similarity or resemblance they may have from that spirit of brotherhood which has prevailed in all ages of the civilized world, the inherent principles of which, as the natural results of any fraternization, where all the members are engaged in the same pursuit and governed by one common bond of unity, are brotherly love, charity, and generally that secrecy and exclusiveness which secures to them an isolation, in the practice of their rites, from the rest of the world. And hence, between all fraternities, ancient and modern, these "remarkable coincidences" will be apt to be found.

CHAPTER XLI

THE LEGEND OF ENOCH

EFORE concluding this series of essays, as they might be called, on the legendary history of Freemasonry, it will be necessary, so that a completion may be given to the subject, to refer to a few Legends of a peculiar character, which have not yet been noticed. These Legends form no part of the original *Legend of the Craft*. There are, however, brief allusions in that document to them; so brief as almost to attract no especial observation, but which might possibly indicate that some form, perhaps a very mutilated one, of these Legends was familiar to the Mediæval Masons, or, perhaps, which is more probable, that they have suggested a foundation for the fabrication of these legendary narratives at a later period by the Speculative Freemasons of the 18th century.

Or it may be supposed that both those views are correct, and that while the imperfect and fragmentary Legend was known to the Freemasons of the Middle Ages, its completed form was thereby suggested to the Fraternity at a later period, and after the era of the Revival.

Whichever of these views we may accept, it is at least certain that at the present day, and in the present condition of the Order, these Legends form an important part of the ritualism of the Order. They can not be rejected in their symbolic interpretation, unless we are willing with them to reject the whole fabric of Freemasonry, into which they have been closely interwoven.

Of these Legends and of some minor ones of the same class, Dr. Oliver has spoken with great fairness in his *Historical Landmarks*, in the following words:

"It is admitted that we are in possession of numerous legends which are not found in holy writ, but being of very ancient date, are entitled to consideration, although their authenticity may be questioned and their aid rejected. I shall not, however, in any case, use their evidence as a *prima facie* means of proving any doubtful proposition, but merely in corroboration of an argument which might probably be complete without their aid. Our system of typical or legendary tradition adds to the dignity of the institution by its general reference to sublime truths, which were considered necessary to its existence or its consistency, although some of the facts, how pure soever at their first promulgation, may have been distorted and perverted by passing through a multitude of hands in their transmission down the stream of time, amidst the fluctuation of the earth and the downfall of mighty states and empires."

Without discussing the question of their great antiquity, or of their original purity and subsequent distortion and perversion, I propose to present these Legends to the Masonic reader, because they are really not so much traditional narratives of events that are supposed to have at some time occurred, but because they are to be considered really as allegorical attempts to symbolize certain ethical or religious ideas, the expression of which lies at the very foundation of the Masonic system.

So considered, they must be deemed of great value. Their interest will also be much enhanced by a comparison of the facts of history that are interwoven with them, and to certain traditions of the ancient Oriental nations which show the existence of the same Legends among them. These may, indeed, have been the foundation on which the Masonic ones have been built, the "distortion or perversion" being simply those variations which were necessary to connect the legendary statements more intimately and consistently with the Masonic symbolic ideas.

The first of these to which our attention will be directed is the *Legend of Enoch*, the seventh of the Patriarchs, of whom Milton has said:

> .   .   .   "him the Most High,
> (Rapt in a balmy cloud with winged steeds)
> Did, as thou seest, receive to walk with God
> High in salvation and the claims of bliss,
> Exempt from death."

I shall first present the reader with the Masonic Legend, and then endeavor to trace out the idea which it was intended to convey, by a comparison of it with historical occurrences, with Oriental traditions of a similar nature, and with the Masonic symbolism which it seems to embody. The Legend as accepted by the Craft, from a time hereafter to be referred to, runs to the following effect.

Enoch, being inspired by the Most High, and in obedience to a vision, constructed underground, in the bosom of Mount Moriah, an edifice consisting of nine brick vaults situated perpendicularly beneath each other and communicating by apertures left in the arch of each vault.

He then caused a triangular plate of gold to be made, each side of which was a cubit long; he enriched it with the most precious stones, and engraved upon it the ineffable name of God. He then encrusted the plate upon a stone of agate of the same form, which he placed upon a cubical stone of marble, and deposited the whole within the ninth or innermost vault.

When this subterranean building was completed, Enoch made a slab or door of stone, and, attaching to it a ring of iron, by which it might, if necessary, be raised, he placed it over the aperture of the uppermost arch, and so covered it over with soil that the opening could not easily be discovered. Enoch himself was not permitted to enter it more than once a year, and on his death or translation all knowledge of this building and of the sacred treasure which it contained was lost until in succeeding ages it was accidentally discovered while Solomon was engaged in building a temple above the spot, on the same mountain.

The Legend proceeds to inform us that after Enoch had finished the construction of the nine vaults, fearing that the principles of the arts and sciences which he had assiduously cultivated would be lost in that universal deluge of which he had received a prophetic vision, he erected above-ground two pillars, one of marble, to withstand the destructive influences of fire, and one of brass, to resist the action of water. On the pillar of brass he engraved the history of the creation, the principles of the arts and sciences, and the doctrines of Speculative Masonry as they were then practiced; and on the pillar of marble he inscribed in hieroglyphic characters the information that near the spot where they stood a precious treasure was deposited in a subterranean vault.

Such is the *Legend of Enoch*, which forms a very important part of the legendary history of the High Degrees. As a traditional narrative it has not the slightest support of authentic history, and the events that it relates do not recommend themselves by an air of probability. But, accepted as the expression of a symbolic idea, it undoubtedly possesses some value.

That part of the Legend which refers to the two pillars is undoubtedly a perversion of the old Craft Legend of Lamech's sons, which has already been treated in this work. It will need no further consideration.

The germ of the Legend is the preservation through the efforts of the Patriarch of the Ineffable Name. This is in fact the true symbolism of the Legend, and it is thus connected with the whole system of Freemasonry in its Speculative form.

There is no allusion to this story in the *Legend of the Craft*. None of the old manuscript Constitutions contain the name of Enoch, nor does he appear to have been deemed by the Mediæval Masons to be one of the worthies of the Craft. The Enoch spoken of in the Cooke MS. is the son of Cain, and not the seventh Patriarch. We must conclude, therefore, that the Legend was a fabrication of a later day, and in no way suggested by anything contained in the original Craft Legend.

But that there were traditions outside of Masonry, which prevailed in the Middle Ages, in reference to subterranean caves in Mount Moriah is evident from the writings of the old historians. Thus there was a tradition of the Talmudists that when King Solomon was building the Temple, foreseeing that at some future time the edifice would be destroyed, he caused a dark and intricate vault to be constructed underground, in which the ark might be concealed whenever such a time of danger should arrive ; and that Josiah, being warned by Huldah, the prophetess, of the approaching peril, caused the ark to be hidden in the crypt which had been built by Solomon. There was also in this vault, as in that of Enoch, a cubical stone, on which the ark was placed.[1]

There is a tradition also, among the Arabians, of a sacred stone found by Abraham beneath the earth, and made by him the stone of foundation of the temple which Jehovah ordered him to erect—a temple the tradition of which is confined to the Mohammedans.

But the most curious story is one told by Nicephorus Callistus, a Greek historian of the 14th century, in his *Ecclesiastical Histories*.

---

[1] Lightfoot, " Prospect of the Temple," ch. xv.

When detailing the events that occurred while Julian the Apostate was making his attempt to rebuild the Temple of Jerusalem, he narrates the following fable, but of whose fabulous character the too credulous monk has not the slightest notion. .

"When the foundations were being laid, as has been said, one of the stones attached to the lowest part of the foundation was removed from its place and showed the mouth of a cavern which had been cut out of the rock. But as the cave could not be distinctly seen, those who had charge of the work, wishing to explore it, that they might be better acquainted with the place, sent one of the workmen down tied to a long rope. When he got to the bottom he found water up to his legs. Searching the cavern on every side, he found by touching with his hands that it was of a quadrangular form. When he was returning to the mouth, he discovered a certain pillar standing up scarcely above the water. Feeling with his hand, he found a little book placed upon it, and wrapped up in very fine and clean linen. Taking possession of it, he gave the signal with the rope that those who had sent him down, should draw him up. Being received above, as soon as the book was shown all were struck with astonishment, especially as it appeared untouched and fresh notwithstanding that it had been found in so dismal and dark a place. But when the book was unfolded, not only the Jews but the Greeks were astounded. For even at the beginning it declared in large letters: IN THE BEGINNING WAS THE WORD WITH GOD, AND THE WORD WAS GOD. To speak plainly, the writing embraced the whole Gospel which was announced in the Divine tongue of the Virgin disciple." [1]

It is true that Enoch has been supposed to have been identical with Hermes, and Keriher says, in the *Œdipus Egyptiacus*, "Idris, among the Hebrews, has been called Enoch, among the Egyptians Osiris and Hermes, and he was the first who before the Flood had any knowledge of astronomy and geometry." But the authors of the *Legend of the Craft* were hardly likely to be acquainted with this piece of archæology, and the Hermes to whom, with a very corrupt spelling, they refer as the son of Cush, was the Hermes Trismegistus, popularly known as the "Father of Wisdom."

Enoch is first introduced to the Craft as one of the founders of

---

[1] Nicephori Callisti "Ecclesiasticæ Historiæ," tom. ii., lib. x., cap. xxxiii.

Geometry and Masonry, by Anderson, in the year 1723, who, in the *Constitutions* printed in that year, has the following passage :

" By some vestiges of antiquity we find one of them (the offspring of Seth) prophesying of the final conflagration at the day of Judgment, as St. Jude tells, and likewise of the general deluge for the punishment of the world. Upon which he erected his two large pillars (though some ascribe them to Seth), the one of stone and the other of brick, whereon were engraven the liberal sciences, etc. And that the stone pillar remained in Syria until the days of Vespasian, the Emperor." [1]

Fifteen years afterward, when he published the second edition of the *Constitutions*, he repeated the Legend, with the additional statement that Enoch was "expert and bright both in the science and the art" of Geometry and Masonry, an abridgment of which he placed on the pillars which he had erected. He adds that "the old Masons firmly believed this tradition," but as there is no appearance of any such tradition in the old records, of which since his date a large number have been recovered (for in them the building of the pillars is ascribed to the sons of Lamech), we shall have to accept this assertion with many grains of allowance, and attribute it to the general inaccuracy of Anderson when citing legendary authority.

But as the first mention of Enoch as a Freemason is made by Anderson, and as we not long afterward find him incorporated into the legendary history of the Order, we may, I think, attribute to him the suggestion of the Legend, which was, however, afterward greatly developed.

It was not, however, adopted into the English system, since neither Entick nor Northouck, who subsequently edited the *Book of Constitutions*, say anything more of Enoch than had already been said by Anderson. They, indeed, correct to some extent his statement, by ascribing the pillars either to Seth or to Enoch, leaning, therefore, to the authority of Josephus, but, equally with Anderson, abandoning the real tradition of the old Legend, which gave them to the children of Lamech.

It is, I think, very evident that the *Legend of Enoch* was of Continental origin, and I am inclined conjecturally to assign its invention to the fertile genius of the Chevalier Ramsay, the first fab-

---

[1] " Constitutions," 1723, p. 3, notes.

ricator of High Degrees, or to some of his immediate successors in the manufactory of Masonic Rites.

Ramsay was too learned a man to be ignorant of the numerous Oriental traditions, Arabic, Egyptian, and Rabinical, concerning Enoch, that had been long in existence. Of this we have evidence in a very learned work on *The Philosophical Principles of Natural and Revealed Religion*, published by him in 1749.

In this work [1] he refers to the tradition extant in all nations, of a great man or legislator who was the first author of sacred symbols and hieroglyphics, and who taught the people their sacred mysteries and religious rites. This man, he says, was, among the Phœnicians, Thaut; the Greeks, Hermes; the Arabians, Edris. But he must have known that Thaut, Hermes, and Edris were all synonymous of Enoch, for he admits that "all these lived some time before the universal deluge, and they were all the same man, and consequently some antediluvian patriarch."

And, finally, he adds that "some think that this antediluvian patriarch was Enoch himself." And then he presents, in the following language, those views which most probably supplied the suggestions that were afterward developed by himself, or some of his followers, in the full form of the Masonic Legend of Enoch.

"Whatever be in these conjectures," says Ramsay, "it is certain, from the principles laid down, that the antediluvian or Noevian patriarchs ought to have taken some surer measures for transmitting the knowledge of divine truths to their posterity, than by oral tradition, and, consequently, that they either invented or made use of hieroglyphics or symbols to preserve the memory of these sacred truths." And these he calls the Enochian symbols.

He does not, indeed, make any allusion to a secret depository of these symbols of Enoch, and supposes that they must have been communicated to the sons of Noah and their descendants, though in time they lost their true meaning. But the change made in the Masonic Legend was necessary to adapt it to a peculiar system of ritualism.

It is singular how Enoch ever became among the ancients a type of the mysteries of religion. The book of Genesis devotes only

---

[1] Vol. ii., p. 12 *et seq.*

three short verses to an account of him, and nothing is there said of him, his deeds, or his character, except an allusion to his piety.

The Oriental writers, however, abound in traditionary tales of the learning of the Patriarch. One tradition states that God bestowed upon him the gift of knowledge, and that he received thirty volumes from Heaven, filled with all the secrets of the most mysterious sciences. The Babylonians supposed him to have been intimately acquainted with the nature of the stars, and they attribute to him the invention of astrology.

The Jewish Rabbins maintained that he was taught by Adam how to sacrifice and to worship the Deity aright. The Cabalistic book of Raziel says that he received the divine mysteries through the direct line of the preceding Patriarchs.

Bar Hebræus, a Jewish writer, asserts that Enoch was the first who invented books and writing; that he taught men the art of building cities—thus evidently confounding him with another Enoch, the son of Cain; that he discovered the knowledge of the Zodiac and the course of the stars; and that he inculcated the worship of God by religious rites.

There is a coincidence in the sacred character thus bestowed upon Enoch with his name and the age at which he died, and this may have had something to do with the mystical attributes bestowed upon him by the Orientalists.

The word *Enoch* signifies, in the Hebrew, *initiated* or *consecrated*, and would seem, as all Hebrew names are significant, to have authorized, or, perhaps, rather suggested the idea of his connection with a system of initiation into sacred rites.

He lived, the Scriptures say, three hundred and sixty-five years. This, too, would readily be received as having a mystical meaning, for 365 is the number of the days in a solar year and was, therefore, deemed a sacred number. Thus we have seen that the letters of the mystical word *Abraxas*, which was the Gnostic name of the Supreme Deity, amounted, according to their numerical value in the Greek alphabet, to 365, which was also the case with *Mithras*, the god to whom the Mithraic mysteries were dedicated. And this may account for the statement of Bar Hebræus that Enoch appointed festivals and sacrifices to the sun at the periods when that luminary entered each of the zodiacal signs.

Goldziher, one of the latest of the German ethnologists, has advanced a similar idea in his work on *Mythology Among the Hebrews*. He says:

" The solar character of Enoch admits of no doubt. He is brought into connection with the building of towns—a solar feature. He lives exactly three hundred and sixty-five years, the number of days of the solar year; which can not be accidental. And even then he did not die, but ' Enoch walked with Elohim, and was no more (to be seen), for Elohim *took him away.*' In the old times when the figure of Enoch was imagined, this was doubtless called Enoch's Ascension to heaven, as in the late traditional legends Ascensions to heaven are generally acknowledged to be solar features."[1]

These statements and speculations have been objected to, because they would tend to make Enoch an idolater and a sun-worshipper. This is a consequence by no means absolutely necessary, but, as the whole is merely traditionary, we need waste no time in defending the orthodox character of the Patriarch's religious views.

After all, it would appear that the *Legend of Enoch*, being wholly unknown to the Fraternity in the Middle Ages, unrecognized in the *Legend of the Craft*, and the name even, not mentioned in any of the old records, was first introduced into the rituals of some of the higher degrees which began to be fabricated toward the middle of the 18th century; that it was invented by the Chevalier Ramsay, or by some of those ritual-mongers who immediately succeeded him, and that in its fabrication very copious suggestions were borrowed from the Rabbinical and Oriental traditions on the same subject.

It is impossible then to assign to this Legend the slightest historical character. It is made up altogether out of traditions which were the inventions of Eastern imagination.

We must view it, therefore, as an allegory; but as one which has a profound symbolic character. It was intended to teach the doctrine of Divine Truth by the symbol of the Holy Name—the Tetragrammaton—the Name most reverently consecrated in the Jewish system as well as in others, and which has always constituted one of the most important and prominent symbols of Speculative Masonry.

In the Continental system of the High Degrees, this symbol is

---

[1] Chap. v., sect. viii., p. 127, Martineau's Translation.

presented in the form of the *Legend of Enoch*. From the English system of Ancient Craft Masonry, that Legend is rejected, or rather it never has been admitted into it. In its place, there is another esoteric Legend, which, differing altogether in details, is identical in result and effects the same symbolism. But this will be more appropriately discussed when the symbolism of Freemasonry is treated, in a future part of this work.

CHAPTER XLII

NOAH AND THE NOACHITES

IN reality, there is no Legend of Noah to be found in any of the Masonic Rituals. There is no myth, like that of Enoch or Euclid, which intimately connects him with the legendary history of the institution. And yet the story of his life has exercised a very important influence in the origin and the development of the principles of Speculative Masonry.

Dr. Oliver has related a few traditions of Noah which, he says, are Masonic, but they never had any general acceptance among the Craft, as they are referred to by no other writer, and, if they ever existed, are now happily obsolete.

The influence of Noah upon Masonic doctrine is to be traced to the almost universal belief of men in the events of the deluge, and the consequent establishment in many nations of a system of religion known to ethnologists as the "Arkite worship." Of this a brief notice must be taken before we can proceed to investigate the connection of the name of Noah with Speculative Masonry.

The character and the actions of Noah are to be looked upon from a twofold stand-point, the historic and the legendary.

The historic account of Noah is contained in portions of the sixth and seventh chapters of the Book of Genesis, and are readily accessible to every reader, with which, however, they must already be very familiar.

The legendary account is to be found in the almost inexhaustible store of traditions which are scattered among almost all the nations of the world where some more or less dim memory of a cataclysm has been preserved.

If we examine the ancient writers, we shall find ample evidence that among all the pagan peoples there was a tradition of a deluge which, at some remote period, had overwhelmed the earth. This tradition was greatly distorted from the biblical source, and the very name of the Patriarch who was saved was forgotten and replaced by some other, which varied in different countries. Thus, in different places, he had received the names of Xisuthrus, Prometheus, Deucalion, Ogyges, and many others, where the name has been rendered very unlike itself by terminations and other idiomatic changes. But everywhere the name was accompanied by a tradition, which also varied in its details, of a deluge by which mankind had been destroyed, and the race had, through the instrumentality of this personage, been renewed.

It is to be supposed that so important an event as the deluge would have been transmitted by the Patriarch to his posterity, and that in after times, when, by reason of the oral transmission of the history, the particular details of the event would be greatly distorted from the truth, a veneration for this new founder of the race of men would be retained. At length, when various systems of idolatry began to be established, Noah, under whatever name he may have been known, would have been among the first to whom divine honors would be paid. Hence arose that system known to modern scholars as the "Arkite worship," in whose rites and mysteries, which were eventually communicated to the other ancient religions, there were always some allusions to the events of the Noachic flood—to the ark, as the womb of Nature, to the eight persons saved in it, as the ogdoad or sacred number—and to the renovation of the world, as symbolizing the passage from death to immortal life.

It is not, therefore, surprising that Noah should have become a mystical personage, and that the modern Speculative Masons should have sought to incorporate some reference to him in their symbolic system, though no such idea appears to have been entertained by the Operative Masons who preceded them.

On examining the old records of the Operative Masons it will be found that no place is assigned to Noah, either as a Mason or as one of the founders of the "science." He receives only the briefest mention.

In the Halliwell Poem his name and the flood are merely referred to as denoting an era of time in the world's history. It is only a statement that the tower of Babel was begun many years after "Noees flod."

In the Cooke MS. the record is a little more extended, but still is but an historical narrative of the flood, in accordance with the biblical details.

In the Dowland MS. and in all the other manuscripts of the *Legend of the Craft* that succeeded it, the reference to Noah is exceedingly meager, his name only being mentioned, and that of his sons, from whom descended Hermes, who found one of the pillars and taught the science thereon described to other men. So far, Noah has had no part in Masonry.

Anderson, who, in the *Book of Constitutions* modified and enlarged the old Craft Legends at his pleasure, calls Noah and his three sons "all Masons true," and says that they brought over from the flood the traditions and arts of the antediluvians and communicated them to their growing offspring. And this was perhaps the first time that the Patriarch was presented to the attention of the Fraternity in a Masonic character.

Anderson seems to have cherished this idea, for in the second edition of the *Constitutions* he still further develops it by saying that the offspring of Noah, "as they journeyed from the East (the plains of Mount Ararat, where the ark rested) towards the West, they found a plain in the land of Shinar, and dwelt there together as NOACHIDÆ, or sons of Noah." And, he adds, without the slightest historical authority, that this word "Noachidæ" was "the first name of Masons, according to some old traditions." It would have puzzled him to specify any such tradition.

Having thus invented and adopted the name as the distinctive designation of a Mason, he repeats it in his second edition or revision of the "Old Charges" appended to the *Book of Constitutions*. The first of these charges, in the *Constitutions* of 1723, contained this passage: "A Mason is obliged by his tenure to obey the moral law." In the edition of 1738, Dr. Anderson has, without authority, completed the sentence by adding the words "as a true Noachida." This interpolation was rejected by Entick, who edited the third and fourth editions in 1756 and 1767, and by Northouck, who published the fifth in 1784, both of whom restored the old reading, which has ever since been preserved in all the Constitutions of the Grand Lodge of England.

Dermott, however, who closely followed the second edition of Anderson, in the composition of his *Ahiman Rezon*, of course adopted the new term.

About that time, or a little later, a degree was fabricated on the continent of Europe, bearing the name of "Patriarch Noachite," one peculiar feature of which was that it represented the existence of two classes or lines of Masons, the one descending from the Temple of Solomon, and who were called Hiramites, and the other tracing their origin to Noah, who were styled Noachites.

Neither Preston nor Hutchinson, nor any other writer of the 18th century, appear to have accepted the term. But it was a favorite with Dr. Oliver, and under his example it has become of so common use that *Noachida* and *Freemason* have come to be considered as synonymous terms.

What does this word really signify, and how came Anderson to adopt it as a Masonic term? The answers to these questions are by no means difficult.

Noachida, or Noachides, from which we get the English Noachite, is a gentilitial name, or a name designating the member of a family or race, and is legitimately formed according to Greek usage, where Atrides means a descendant of Atreus, or Heraclides a descendant of Heracles. And so Noachides, or its synonyms Noachida or Noachites, means a descendant of Noah.

But why, it may be asked, are the Freemasons called the descendants of Noah? Why has he been selected alone to represent the headship of the Fraternity? I have no doubt that Dr. Anderson was led to the adoption of the word by the following reason.

After Noah's emergence from the ark, he is said to have promulgated seven precepts for the government of the new race of men of whom he was to be the progenitor.

These seven precepts are: 1, to do justice; 2, worship God; 3, abstain from idolatry; 4, preserve chastity; 5, do not commit murder; 6, do not steal; 7, do not eat the blood.

These seven obligations, says the Rev. Dr. Raphall,[1] are held binding on all men, inasmuch as all are descendants of Noah, and the Rabbins maintain that he who observes them, though he be not an Israelite, has a share in the future life, and it is the duty of every Jew to enforce their due observance whenever he has the power to do so.

In consequence of this, the Jewish religion was not confined

---

[1] " Genesis, with Translation and Notes," by Rev. Morris J. Raphall, p. 52.

during its existence in Palestine to the Jewish nation only, but proselytes of three kinds were freely admitted. One of these classes was the "proselytes of the gate." These were persons who, without undergoing the rite of circumcision or observing the ritual prescribed by the law of Moses, engaged to worship the true God and to observe the seven precepts of Noah, and these things they were to do whether they resided in Judea or in foreign lands. They were not, however, admitted to all the privileges of the Jewish religion; marriage with Israelites was forbidden, and they were not permitted to enter within the sacred inclosure of the temple. So that, although they were Noachidæ, they were not considered equal to the true children of Abraham.

Anderson, who was a theologian, was, of course, acquainted with these facts, but, with a more tolerant spirit than the Jewish law, which gave the converted Gentiles only a qualified reception, he was disposed to admit into the full fellowship of Freemasonry all the descendants of Noah who would observe the precepts of the Patriarch, these being the only moral laws inculcated by Masonry.

In giving the history of the introduction of the word into Masonry, I have not cited among the authorities the document known as the Stonehouse MS., because it was verified by a person of that name, but more usually the Krause MS., because it was first published in a German translation by Dr. Krause in his *Three Oldest Documents*. It is alleged to be a copy of the *York Constitutions*, enacted in 926, but is generally admitted by scholars to be spurious. Yet, as it is probable that it was originally written by a contemporary of Anderson, and about the time of the publishing of the *Constitutions* of 1738, it may be accepted, so far as it supplies us with a suggestion of the motive that induced Anderson to interpolate the word "Noachida" into the "Old Charges."

In the Krause MS., under the head of "The Laws or Obligations laid before his Brother Masons by Prince Edwin," we find the following article. (I translate from the German of Krause, because the original English document is nowhere to be found.)

"The first obligation is that you shall sincerely honor God and obey the laws of the Noachites, because they are divine laws, which should be obeyed by all the world. Therefore, you must avoid all heresies and not thereby sin against God."

The language of this document is more precise than that of Anderson, though both have the same purpose. The meaning is that the only religious laws which a Freemason is required to obey are those which are contained in the code that has been attributed to Noah. This sentiment is still further expressed toward the close of the "Old Charges," where it is said that the Mason is obliged only " to that religion in which all men agree," excluding, therefore, atheism, and requiring the observance of such simple laws of morality as are enjoined in the precepts of Noah.

Anderson had, however, a particular object in the use of the word " Noachida." The Krause MS. says that the Mason "must obey the laws of the Noachites ; " that is, that he is to observe the seven precepts of Noah, without being required to observe any other religious dogmas outside of these—a matter which is left to himself.

But Anderson says he "must obey the moral law as a true Noachida," by which he intimates that that title is the proper designation of a Mason. And he has shown that this was his meaning by telling us, in a preceding part of his book, that " Noachidæ was the first name of Masons, according to some old traditions."

Now the object of Anderson in introducing this word into the second edition of the *Constitutions* was to sustain his theory that Noah was the founder of the science of Freemasonry after the flood. This was the theory taught by Dr. Oliver a century afterward, who followed Anderson in the use of the word, with the same meaning and the same object, and his example has been imitated by many recent writers. But when Anderson speaks of a Noachida or a Noachite as a word synonymous with Freemason, he is in error; for although all Freemasons are necessarily the descendants of Noah, all the descendants of Noah are not Freemasons.

And if by the use of the word he means to indicate that Noah was the founder of post-diluvian Freemasonry, he is equally in error ; for that theory, it has heretofore been shown, can not be sustained, and his statement that Noah and his three sons were " all Masons true " is one for which there is no historical support, and which greatly lacks an element of probability.

It is better, therefore, when we speak or write historically of Freemasonry, that this word Noachida, or Noachite, should be avoided, since its use leads to a confusion of ideas, and possibly to the promulgation of error.

CHAPTER XLIII

THE LEGEND OF HIRAM ABIF

HIS is the most important of all the legends of Freemasonry. It will therefore be considered in respect to its origin, its history, and its meaning.

Before, however, proceeding to the discussion of these important subjects, and the investigation of the truly mythical character of Hiram Abif, it will be proper to inquire into the meaning of his name, or rather the meaning of the epithet that accompanies it.

In the places in Scripture in which he is mentioned he is called at one time (in 2 Chronicles ii., 13), by the King of Tyre, in the letter written by him to King Solomon, CHURAM ABI; in another place (in 2 Chronicles iv., 16), where the writer of the narrative is recording the work done by him for Solomon, CHURAM ABIV, or, as it might be pronounced according to the sound of the Hebrew letters, ABIU. But Luther, in his German translation of the Bible, adopted the pronunciation ABIF, exchanging the flat *v* for the sharp *f*. In this he was followed by Anderson, who was the first to present the full name of *Hiram Abif* to the Craft. This he did in the first edition of the English book of *Constitutions*.

And since his time at least the appellation of Hiram Abif has been adopted by and become familiar to the Craft as the name of the cunning or skillful artist who was sent by Hiram, King of Tyre, to assist King Solomon in the construction of the Temple. In *Chronicles* and *Kings* we find Churam or Huram, as we may use the initial letter as a guttural or an aspirate, and Chiram or Hiram, the vowel *u* or *i* being indifferently used. But the Masonic usage has universally adopted the word *Hiram*.

Now, the *Abi* and *Abiv*, used by the King of Tyre, in the book of Chronicles form no part of the name, but are simply inflections of the possessive pronouns my and his suffixed to the appellative *Ab*.

Ab in Hebrew means *father*, *i* is *my*, and *in*, *iv*, or *if* is *his*. *Abi* is therefore *my father*, and so he is called by the King of Tyre when he is describing him to Solomon, "Hiram my father;" *Abif* is *his father*, and he is so spoken of by the historian when he recounts the various kinds of work which were done for King Solomon by "Hiram his father."

But the word *Ab* in Hebrew, though primarily signifying a male parent, has other derivative significations. It is evident that in none of the passages in which he is mentioned is it intended to intimate that he held such relationship to either the King of Tyre or the King of Israel.

The word "father" was applied by the Hebrews as a term of honor, or to signify a station of pre-eminence. Buxtorf[1] says it sometimes signified *Master*, and he cites the fourth chapter of Genesis, where Jabal is called the father of cattle and Jubal the father of musicians.

Hiram Abif was most probably selected by the King of Tyre to be sent to Solomon as a skillful artificer of pre-eminent skill that he might execute the principal works in the interior of the Temple and fabricate the various utensils intended for the sacred services. He was a master in his art or calling, and properly dignified with a title which announced his distinguished character. The title of Father, which was given to him, denotes, says Smith,[2] the respect and esteem in which he was held, according to the similar custom of the people of the East at the present day.

I am well pleased with the suggestion of Dr. McClintock that "*Hiram my father* seems to mean *Hiram my counsellor ;* that is to say, *foreman* or *master-workman*."[3]

Applying this meaning to the passages in Chronicles which refer to this artist, we shall see how easily every difficulty is removed and the Craftsman Hiram placed in his true light.

When King Hiram, wishing to aid the King of Israel in his contemplated building, writes him a letter in which he promises to comply with the request of Solomon to send him timber from Lebanon and wood-cutters to hew it, as an additional mark of his friendship and his desire to contribute his aid in building "a house for Je-

---

[1] "Lexicon Talmudicum." [2] " Cyclopædia of Biblical Literature."
[3] "Cyclopædia of Biblical, Theological, and Classical Literature."

hovah," he gives him the services of one of his most skillful artisans and announces the gift in these words: "And now I have sent a skillful man, endued with understanding, my master-workman Hiram."

And when the historian who wrote the *Chronicles* of the kingdom had recapitulated all the work that Hiram had accomplished, such as the pillars of the porch, the lavers and the candlesticks, and the sacred vessels, he concludes by saying that all these things were made for King Solomon by *his master-workman* Hiram, in the Hebrew *gnasah Huram Abif Lammelech Schelomoh.*

Hiram or Huram was his proper name. *Ab, father of his trade* or *master-workman*, his title, and *i* or *if, my* or *his*, the possessive pronominal suffix, used according to circumstances. The King of Tyre calls him *Hiram Abi*, "*my* master-workman." When the chronicler speaks of him in his relation to King Solomon, he calls him *Hiram Abif* "*his* master-workman." And as all his Masonic relations are with Solomon, this latter designation has been adopted, from Anderson, by the Craft.

Having thus disposed of the name and title of the personage who constitutes the main point in this Masonic Legend, I proceed to an examination of the origin and progressive growth of the myth.

"The Legend of the Temple-Builder," as he is commonly but improperly called, is so intimately connected in the ritual with the symbolic history of the Temple, that we would very naturally be led to suppose that the one has always been contemporary and coexistent with the other. The evidence on this point is, however, by no means conclusive or satisfactory, though a critical examination of the old manuscripts would seem to show that the writers of those documents, while compiling from traditional sources the *Legend of the Craft*, were not altogether ignorant of the rank and services that have been subsequently attributed by the Speculative Masons of the present day to Hiram Abif. They certainly had some notion that in the building of the Temple at Jerusalem King Solomon had the assistance of a skillful artist who had been supplied to him by the King of Tyre.

The origin of the Legend must be looked for in the Scriptural account of the building of the Temple of Jerusalem. The story, as told in the books of Kings and Chronicles, is to this effect.

On the death of King David, his son and successor, Solomon, resolved to carry into execution his father's long-contemplated design of erecting a Temple on Mount Moriah for the worship of Jehovah. But the Jews were not a nation of artisans, but rather of agriculturists, and had, even in the time of David, depended on the aid of the Phœnicians in the construction of the house built for that monarch at the beginning of his reign. Solomon, therefore, applied to his ally, Hiram, King of Tyre, to furnish him with trees from Lebanon and with hewers to prepare them, for, as he said in his letter to the Tyrian King, " thou knowest that there is not any among us that can skill to hew timber like unto the Sidonians."

Hiram complied with his request, and exchanged the skilled workmen of sterile Phœnicia for the oil and corn and wine of more fertile Judea.

Among the artists who were sent by the King of Tyre to the King of Israel, was one whose appearance at Jerusalem seems to have been in response to the following application of Solomon, recorded in the second book of Chronicles, the second chapter, seventh verse :

" Send me now therefore a man cunning to work in gold, and in silver, and in brass, and in iron, and in purple and in crimson, and blue, and that can skill to grave with the cunning men that are with me in Judah, and in Jerusalem, whom David my father did provide."

In the epistle of King Hiram, responsive to this request, contained in the same book and chapter, in the thirteenth and fourteenth verses, are the following words :

" And now I have sent a cunning man, endued with understanding, of Huram my father's. The son of a woman of the daughters of Dan, and his father was a man of Tyre, skillful to work in gold and in silver, in brass, in iron, in stone, and in timber, in purple, in blue, and in fine linen, and in crimson ; also to grave any manner of graving, and to find out every device which shall be put to him, with thy cunning men, and with the cunning men of my lord David, thy father."

A further description of him is given in the seventh chapter of the first book of Kings, in the thirteenth and fourteenth verses, and in these words :

" And King Solomon sent and fetched Hiram out of Tyre. He was a widow's son of the tribe of Naphtali—and his father was a man of Tyre, a worker in brass; and he was filled with wisdom and understanding, and cunning to work all works in brass, and he came to King Solomon and wrought all his work."

It is very evident that this was the origin of the Legend which was incorporated into the Masonic system, and which, on the institution of Speculative Freemasonry, was adopted as the most prominent portion of the Third Degree.

The mediæval Masons were acquainted with the fact that King Solomon had an assistant in the works of the Temple, and that that assistant had been sent to him by King Hiram.   But there was considerable confusion in their minds upon the subject, and an ignorance of the scriptural name and attributes of the person.

In the Halliwell MS., the earliest known to us, the Legend is not related.   Either the writers of the two poems of which that manuscript is composed were ignorant of it, or in the combination of the two poems there has been a mutilation and the Hiramic Legend has been omitted.

In the Cooke MS., which is a hundred years later, we meet with the first allusion to it and the first error, which is repeated in various forms in all the subsequent manuscript constitutions.

That manuscript says: "And at the makyng of the temple in Salamonis tyme as hit is seyd in the bibull in the iii boke of Regum in tertio Regum capitulo quinto, that Salomon had iiii score thousand masons at his werke.   And the kyngis sone of Tyry was his master mason."

The reference here made to the third book of Kings is according to the old distribution of the Hebrew canon, where the two books of Samuel are called the first and second books of Kings.   According to our present canon, the reference would be to the fifth chapter of the first book of Kings.   In that chapter nothing is said of Hiram Abif, but it is recorded there that "Adoniram was over the levy." Now the literal meaning of Adoniram is *the lord Hiram*.   As the King of Tyre had promised to send his workmen to Lebanon, and as it is stated that Adoniram superintended the men who were there hewing the trees, the old legendist, not taking into account that the levy of thirty thousand, over whom Adoniram presided, were Israelites and not Phœnicians, but supposing that they had been sent to Lebanon by Hiram, King of Tyre, and that he had sent Adoniram with them, and viewing the word as meaning *the lord Hiram*, hastily came to the conclusion that this Lord or Prince Hiram was the son of the King.   And hence he made the mistake of saying that the son of the King of Tyre was the person sent to Solomon to be his master-mason or master-builder.

This error was repeated in nearly all the succeeding manuscripts, for they are really only copies of each other, and the word *Adon*, as meaning *lord* or prince, seems to have been always assumed in some one or other corrupted form as the name of the workman sent by King Hiram to King Solomon, and whom the Freemasons of the present day know as Hiram Abif.

Thus in the Dowland MS., conjecturally dated at A.D. 1550, it is said :

" And furthermore there was a Kinge of another region that men called IRAM, and he loved well Kinge Solomon and he gave him tymber to his worke.   And he had a sonn that height (was called) AYNON, and he was a Master of Geometrie and was chief Master of all his Masons, and was Master of all his gravings and carvinge and of all manner of Masonrye that longed to the Temple."

There can be no doubt that *Aynon* is here a corruption of *Adon*.

In the Landsdowne MS., whose date is A.D. 1560, the language is precisely the same, except that it says King Iram " had a sonne that was called *a man*."

It seems almost certain that the initial letter *a* in this name has been, by careless writing, dislocated from the remaining letters, man, and that the true reading is *Aman*, which is itself an error, instead of *Amon*, and this a manifest corruption of *Adon*.   This is confirmed by the York MS., Number 1, which is about forty years later (A.D. 1600), where the name is spelled *Amon*.   This is also the name in the Lodge of Hope MS., dated A.D. 1680.

In the Grand Lodge MS., date of A.D. 1632, he is again called the son of the King of Tyre, but his name is given as *Aynone*, another corrupted form of *Adon*.   In the Sloane MS., Number 3,848, A.D. 1646, it is *Aynon*, the final *e* being omitted.   In the Harleian MS., Number 1,942, dated A.D. 1670, both the final *e* and the medial *y* are omitted, and the name becoming *Anon*, approximates still nearer to the true *Adon*.

In the Alnwick MS., of A.D. 1701, the name is still further corrupted into *Ajuon*.   In all of these manuscripts the Legend continues to call this artist the son of the King of Tyre, whose name is said to be *Hiram*, or more usually *Iram;* and hence the corrupted orthography of *Amon, Aynon,* or *Anon,* being restored to the true form of *Adon,* with which word the old Masons were acquainted, as signifying *Lord* or *Prince,* we get, by prefixing it to his father's name, *Adon-Iram* or *Adoniram,* the Lord or Prince Hiram. And hence arose the mistake of confounding Hiram Abif with Adoniram, the chief of the workmen on Mount Lebanon, who was a very different person.

The Papworth MS., whose date is A.D. 1714, is too near the time of the Revival and the real establishment of Speculative Masonry to be of much value in this inquiry. It, however, retains the statement from the Old Legend, that the artist was the son of King Hiram. But it changes his name to that of *Benaim.* This is probably an incorrect inflection of the Hebrew word *Boneh,* a builder, and shows that the writer, in an attempt to correct the error of the preceding legendists who had corrupted *Adon* into *Anon* or *Amon,* or *Ajuon,* had in his smattering of Hebrew committed a greater one.

The Krause MS. is utterly worthless as authority. It is a forgery, written most probably, I think I may say certainly, after the publication of the first edition of Anderson's *Constitutions,* and, of course, takes the name from that work.

The name of Hiram Abif is first introduced to public notice by Anderson in 1723, in the book of *Constitutions* printed in that year.

In this work he changes the statement made in the *Legend of the Craft,* and says that the King of Tyre sent to King Solomon " his namesake Hiram Abif, the prince of architects."

Then quoting in the original Hebrew a passage from the second book of Chronicles, where the name of Hiram Abif is to be found, he explains it " by allowing the word *Abif* to be the surname of Hiram the Mason;" furthermore he adds that in the passage where the King of Tyre calls him " Huram of my father's," the meaning is that Huram was "the chief Master Mason of my father, King Abibalus," a most uncritical attempt, because he intermixes, as its foundation, the Hebrew original and the English version. He had not discovered the true explication, namely, that *Hiram* is the name, and *Ab* the title, denoting, as I have before said, *Master Workman,* and that *in,* or *iv,* or *if,* is a pronominal suffix, meaning *his*, so that when speaking of him in his relation to King Solomon, he is called *Hiram Abif*, that is *Hiram, his* or *Solomon's Master Workman.*

But Anderson introduced an entirely new element in the Legend when he said, in the same book, that " the wise King Solomon was Grand Master of the Lodge at Jerusalem, King Hiram was Grand Master of the Lodge at Tyre, and the inspired Hiram Abif was Master of Work."

In the second or 1738 edition of the *Constitutions*, Anderson considerably enlarged the Legend, for reasons that will be adverted to when I come, in the next part of this work, to treat of the origin of the Third Degree, but on which it is here unnecessary to dwell.

In that second edition, he asserts that the tradition is that King Hiram had been Grand Master of all Masons, but that when the Temple was finished he surrendered the pre-eminence to King Solomon. No such tradition, nor any allusion to it, is to be found in any of the Old Records now extant, and it is, moreover, entirely opposed by the current of opinion of all subsequent Masonic writers.

From these suggestions of Anderson, and from some others of a more esoteric character, made, it is supposed, by him and by Dr. Desaguliers about the time of the Revival, we derive that form of the *Legend of Hiram Abif* which has been preserved to the present day with singular uniformity by the Freemasons of all countries.

The substance of this Legend, so far as it is concerned in the present investigation, is that at the building of the Temple there were three Grand Masters—Solomon, King of Israel ; Hiram, King of Tyre, and Hiram Abif, and that the last was the architect or chief builder of the edifice.

As what relates to the fate of Hiram Abif is to be explained in an altogether allegorical or symbolical sense, it will more appropriately come under consideration when we are treating, in a subsequent part of this work, of the Symbolism of Freemasonry.

Our present study will be the legendary character of Hiram Abif as the chief Master Mason of the Temple, and our investigations will be directed to the origin and meaning of the myth which has now, by universal consent of the Craft, been adopted, whether correctly or not we shall see hereafter.

The question before us, let it be understood, is not as to the historic truth of the Hiramic legend, as set forth in the Third Degree of the Masonic ritual—not as to whether this be the narrative of an actual occurrence or merely an allegory accompanied by a moral signification—not as to the truth or fallacy of the theory which finds the origin of Freemasonry in the Temple of Jerusalem—but how it has been that the Masons of the Middle Ages should have incorporated into their *Legend of the Craft* the idea that a worker in metal—in plain words, a smith—was the chief builder at the Temple. This thought, and this thought alone, must govern us in the whole course of our inquiry.

Of all the myths that have prevailed among the peoples of the earth, hardly any has had a greater antiquity or a more extensive existence than that of the *Smith* who worked in metals, and fabricated shields and swords for warriors, or jewelry for queens and noble ladies. Such a myth is to be found among the traditions of the earliest religions,[1] and being handed down through ages of popular transmission, it is preserved, with various natural modifications, in the legends of the Middle Ages, from Scandinavia to the most southern limit of the Latin race. Long before this period it was to be found in the mythology and the folk-lore of Assyria, of India, of Greece, and of Rome.

Freemasonry, in its most recent form as well as in its older Legend, while adopting the story of Hiram Abif, once called Adon Hiram, has strangely distorted its true features, as exhibited in the books of Kings and Chronicles; and it has, without any historical authority, transformed the Scriptural idea of a skillful smith into that of an architect and builder. Hence, in the Old Legend he is styled a "Master of Geometry and of all Masonry," and in the modern ritual of Speculative Masonry he is called "the Builder," and to him, in both, is supposed to have been intrusted the superintendence of the Temple of Solomon, during its construction, and the government and control of those workmen—the stone squarers and masons—who were engaged in the labor of its erection.

To divest this Legend of its corrupt form, and to give to Hiram

---

[1] "Vala, one of the names of Indra, in the Aryan mythology, is traced," says Mr. Cox, " through the Teutonic lands until we reach the cave of Wayland Smith, in Warwickshire." " Mythology of the Aryan Nations," vol. ii., p. 326.

Abif, who was actually an historic personage, his true position among the workmen at the Temple, can not affect, in the slightest degree, the symbolism of which he forms so integral a part, while it will rationally account for the importance that has been attributed to him in the old as well as in the new Masonic system.

Whether we make Hiram Abif the chief Builder and the Operative Grand Master of Solomon's Temple, or whether we assign that position to Anon, Amon, or Ajuon, as it is in the Old Legend, or to Adoniram, as it is done in some Masonic Rites, the symbolism will remain unaffected, because the symbolic idea rests on the fact of a Chief Builder having existed, and it is immaterial to the development of the symbolism what was his true name. The instruction intended to be conveyed in the legend of the Third Degree must remain unchanged, no matter whom we may identify as its hero; for he truly represents neither Hiram nor Anon nor Adoniram nor any other individual person, but rather the idea of man in an abstract sense.

It is, however, important to the truth of history that the real facts should be eliminated out of the mythical statements which envelop them. We must throw off the husk, that we may get at the germ. And besides, it will add a new attraction to the system of Masonic ritualism if we shall be able to trace in it any remnant of that oldest and most interesting of the myths, the *Legend of the Smith*, which, as I have said, has universally prevailed in the most ancient forms of religious faith.

Before investigating this *Legend of the Smith* in its reference to Freemasonry and to this particular *Legend of Hiram Abif* which we are now considering, it will be proper to inquire into the character of the Legend as it existed in the old religions and in the mediæval myths. We may then inquire how this Legend, adopted in Freemasonry in its stricter ancient form of the Legend of Tubal Cain, became afterward confounded with another legend of a Temple-Builder.

If we go back to the oldest of all mythologies, that which is taught in the Vedic hymns, we shall find the fire-god Agni, whose flames are described as being "luminous, powerful, fearful, and not to be trusted."

The element of fire thus worshipped by the primeval Aryans, as an instrument of good or of evil, was subsequently personified by

the Greeks; the Vedic hymns, referring to the continual renovation of the flame, as it was fed by fuel, called it the fire-god Agni ;
also Gavishtha, that is, the ever young. From this the Greeks got
their Hephæstus, the mighty workman, the immortal smith who
forged the weapons of the gods, and, at the prayer of Thetis, fabricated the irresistible armor of Achilles. The Romans were indebted to their Aryan ancestors for the same idea of the potency
of fire, and personified it in their Vulcan, a name which is evidently
derived from the Sanscrit *Ulka*, a firebrand, although a similarity
of sound has led many etymologists to deduce the Roman Vulcan
from the Semitic Tubal Cain. Indeed, until the modern discoveries in comparative philology, this was the universal opinion of the
learned.

Among the Babylonians an important god was Bil-can. He was
the fire-god, and the name seems to be derived from Baal, or Bel,
and Cain, the god of smiths, or the master smith. George Smith,
in his *Chaldæan Account of Genesis*, thinks that there is possibly
some connection here with the Biblical Tubal Cain and the classical
Vulcan.

From the fragments of Sanchoniathon we learn that the Phœnicians had a hero whom he calls Chrysor. He was worshipped after
his death, in consequence of the many inventions that he bestowed
on man, under the name of Diamichius; that is, the great inventor.
To him was ascribed the invention of all those arts which the
Greeks attributed to Hephæstus, and the Romans to Vulcan.
Bishop Cumberland derives the name of Chrysor from the Hebrew
Charatz, or the *Sharpener*, an appropriate designation of one who
taught the use of iron tools. The authorized version of Genesis,
which calls Tubal Cain " an instructor of every artificer in brass
and iron," is better rendered in the Septuagint and the Vulgate as
"a sharpener of every instrument in brass and iron."

Tubal Cain has been derived, in the English lectures of Dr. Hemming, and, of course, by Dr. Oliver, from a generally received etymology that *Cain* meant *worldly possessions*, and the true symbolism of the name has been thus perverted. The true derivation is
from *kin*, which, says Gesenius, has the especial meaning to *forge
iron*, whence comes *Kain*, a spear or lance, an instrument of iron
that has been forged. In the cognate Arabic it is *Kayin*. " This
word," says Dr. Goldziher in his work on *Mythology Among the He-*

brews, "which with other synonymous names of trades occurs several times on the so-called Nabatean Sinaitic inscriptions, signifies *Smith*, maker of agricultural implements,[1] and has preserved this meaning in the Arabic *Kayin* and the Aramaic *kinaya*, whilst in the later Hebrew it was lost altogether, being probably suppressed through the Biblical attempt to derive the proper name Cain etymologically from *kana*, "*to gain*." Here it is that Hemming and Oliver got their false symbolism of "worldly possessions."

Goldziher attempts to identify mythologically Cain the fratricide with the son of Lamech. Whether he be correct or not in his theory, it is at least a curious coincidence that Cain, which I have shown to mean a smith, should have been the first builder of a city, and that the same name should have been assigned to the first forger of metals, while the old Masonic Legend makes the master smith, Hiram of Tyre, also the chief builder of Solomon.

It will, I think, be interesting to trace the progress of the myth which has given in every age and every country this prominent position among artisans to the smith.

Hephæstus, or Vulcan, kindling his forges in the isle of Lemnos, and with his Cyclops journeymen beating out and shaping and welding the red-hot iron into the forms of spears and javelins and helmets and coats of mail, was the southern development of the Aryan fire-god Agni. "Hephæstus, or Vulcan," says Diodorus Siculus, "was the first founder in iron, brass, gold, silver, and all fusible metals, and he taught the uses to which fire might be applied by artificers." Hence he was called by the ancients the god of blacksmiths.

The Scandinavians, or northern descendants of the Aryan race, brought with them, in their emigration from Caucasus, the same reverence for fire and for the working of metals by its potent use. They did not, however, bring with them such recollections of Agni as would invent a god of fire like the Hephæstus and Vulcan of the Greeks and Romans. They had, indeed, Loki, who derived his name, it is said by some, from the Icelandic *logi*, or flame. But he was an

---

[1] He confines the expression to "agricultural" to enforce a particular theory then under consideration. He might correctly have been more general and included all other kinds of implements, warlike and mechanical as well as agricultural.

evil principle, and represented rather the destructive than the crea-
tive powers of fire.

But the Scandinavians, interpolating, like all the northern nations, their folk-lore into their mythology, invented their legends
of a skillful smith, beneath whose mighty blows upon the yielding
iron swords of marvelous keenness and strength were forged, or
by whose wonderful artistic skill diadems and bracelets and jewels
of surpassing beauty were constructed.   Hence the myth of a won-
derfully cunning artist was found everywhere, and the *Legend of the
Smith* became the common property of all the Scandinavian and
Teutonic nations, and was of so impressive a character that it continued to exist down to mediæval times, and traces of it have extended to the superstitions of the present day.   May we not justly
look to its influence for the prominence given by the old Masonic
legendists to the Master Smith of King Hiram among the workmen of Solomon?

Among the Scandinavians we have the Legend of Völund, whose
story is recited in the Völunddarkvitha, or Lay of Völund, contained
in the *Edda* of Sæmund.   Völund (pronounced as if spelled *Wayland*) was one of three brothers, sons of an Elf-king; that is
to say, of a supernatural race.   The three brothers emigrated to
Ulfdal, where they married three Valkyries, or choosers of the slain,
maidens of celestial origin, the attendants of Odin, and whose attributes were similar to those of the Greek Parcæ, or Fates.   After
seven years the three wives fled away to pursue their allotted duty
of visiting battle-fields.   Two of the brothers went in search of their
errant wives; but Völund remained in Ulfdal.   He was a skillful
workman at the forge, and occupied his time in fabricating works
in gold and steel, while patiently awaiting the promised return of
his beloved spouse.

Niduth, the king of the country, having heard of the wonderful
skill of Völund as a forger of metals, visited his home during his
absence and surreptitiously got possession of some of the jewels
which he had made, and of the beautiful sword which the smith had
fabricated for himself.

Völund, on his return, was seized by the warriors of Niduth and
conducted to the castle.   There the queen, terrified at his fierce
looks, ordered him to be hamstrung.   Thus, maimed and deprived
of the power of escape or resistance, he was confined to a small

island in the vicinity of the royal residence and compelled to fabricate jewels for the queen and her daughter, and weapons of war for
the king.[1]

It were tedious to recount all the adventures of the smith while
confined in his island prison. It is sufficient to say that, having
constructed a pair of wings by which he was enabled to fly (by
which we are reminded of the Greek fable of Dædalus), he made
his escape, having by stratagem first dishonored the princess and
slain her two brothers.

This legend of "a curious and cunning workman" at the forge
was so popular in Scandinavia that it extended into other countries,
where the *Legend of the Smith* presents itself under various modifications.

In the Icelandic legend Völund is described as a great artist in
the fabrication of iron, gold, and silver. It does not, however, connect him with supernatural beings, but attributes to him great skill
in his art, in which he is assisted by the power of magic.

The Germans had the same legend at a very early period. In
the German Legend the artificer is called Wieland, and he is represented as the son of a giant named Wade. He acquires the art of
a smith from Minner, a skillful workman, and is perfected by the
Dwarfs in all his operations at the forge as an armorer and goldsmith. He goes of his own accord to the king, who is here called
Nidung, where he finds another skillful smith, named Amilias, with
whom he contends in battle, and kills him with his sword, Mimung.
For this offense he is maimed by the king, and then the rest of the
story proceeds very much like that of the Scandinavian legend.

Among the Anglo-Saxons the legend is found not varying
much from the original type. The story where the hero receives the
name of Weland is contained in an ancient poem, of which fragments, unfortunately, only remain. The legend had become so familiar to the people that in the metrical romance of Beowulf the
coat of mail of the hero is described as the work of Weland; and
King Alfred, in his translation of the *Consolation of Philosophy*, by
Boethius, where the author alludes to the bones of the Consul Fabricius, in the passage "*ubi sunt ossa Fabricie?*" (where now are the
bones of Fabricius?), thus paraphrases the question: "Where now

---

[1] All these smiths of mythology and folk-lore are represented as being lame, like
Hephæstus, who broke his leg in falling from heaven.

are the bones of the wise Weland, the goldsmith that was formerly so famed?" Geoffrey of Monmouth afterward, in a Latin poem, speaks of the gold, and jewels, and cups that had been sculptured by Weland, which name he Latinizes as Gueilandus.

In the old French chronicles we repeatedly encounter the legend of the skillful smith, though, as might be expected, the name undergoes many changes. Thus, in a poem of the 6th century, entitled *Gautier à la main forte, or Walter of the strong hand*, it is said that in a combat of Walter de Varkastein he was protected from the lance of Randolf by a cuirass made by Wieland.

Another chronicle, of the 12th century, tells us that a Count of Angoulême, in a battle with the Normans, cut the cuirass and the body of the Norman King in twain at a single stroke, with his sword Durissima, which had been made by the smith Walander. A chronicle of the same period, written by the monk John of Marmontier, describes the magnificent habiliments of Geoffrey Plantagenet, Duke of Normandy, among which, says the author, was " a sword taken from the royal treasury and long since renowned. Galannus, the most skillful of armorers, had employed much labor and care in making it." Galans, for Walans (the *G* being substituted for the *W*, as a letter unknown in the French alphabet), is the name bestowed in general on this skillful smith, and the romances of the Trouvères and Troubadours of northern and southern France, in the 12th and 13th centuries, abound in references to swords of wondrous keenness and strength that were forged by him for the knights and paladins.

Whether the name was given as *Völund*, or *Wieland*, or *Weland*, or *Galans*, it found its common origin in the Icelandic *Völundr*, which signifies a *smith*. It is a generic term, from which the mythical name has been derived. So the Greeks called the skillful workman, the smith of their folk-lore, *Dædalus*, because there is a verb in their language *daidallo*, which means *to do skillful or ornamental work*.

Here it may not be irrelevant to notice the curious fact that concurrently with these legends of a skillful smith there ran in the Middle Ages others, of which King Solomon was the subject. In many of these old romances and metrical tales, a skill is attributed to him which makes him the rival of the subordinate artisan. Indeed, the artistic reputation of Solomon was so proverbial at the very time when these legends of the smith were prevalent, that in the poems of those days we meet with repeated uses of the expression "l'uevre Salemon," or "the work of Solomon," to indicate any production of great artistic beauty.

So fully had the Scandinavian sagas, the German chronicles, and the French romances spoken of this mythical smith that the idea became familiar to the common people, and was handed down in the popular superstitions and the folk-lore, to a comparatively modern period. Two of these, one from Germany and one from England, will suffice as examples, and show the general identity of the legends and the probability of their common origin.[1]

Herman Harrys, in his *Tales and Legends of Lower Saxony*, tells the story of a smith who dwelt in the village of Hagen, on the side of a mountain, about two miles from Osnabrück. He was celebrated for his skill in forging metals; but, being discontented with his lot, and murmuring against God, he was supernaturally carried into a cavernous cleft of the mountain, where he was condemned to be a metal-king, and, resting by day, to labor at night at the forge for the benefit of men, until the mine in the mountain should cease to be productive.

In the coolness of the mine, says the legend, his good disposition returned, and he labored with great assiduity, extracting ore from its veins, and at first forging household and agricultural implements. Afterward he confined himself to the shoeing of horses for the neighboring farmers. In front of the cavern was a stake fixed in the ground, to which the countryman fastened the horse which he wished to have shod, and on a stone near by he laid the necessary fee. He then retired. On returning in due time he would find the task completed; but the smith, or, as he was called, the *Hiller*, i.e., Hider, would never permit himself to be seen.

Similar to this is the English legend, which tells us that in a vale of Berkshire, at the foot of White Horse Hill, evidently, from the stones which lay scattered around, the site of a Druidic monument, formerly dwelt a person named Wayland Smith. It is easily

---

[1] For many of the details of these two legends, as well as for much that has already been said of the mythological smith of the Middle Ages, I have been indebted to the learned Dissertation of MM. Depping and Michel. It has been ably translated from the French, with additions by Mr. S. W. Singer, London, 1847.

understood that here the handicraft title has been incorporated with the anglicized name, and that it is the same as the mediæval Weland the Smith. No one ever saw him, for the huge stones afforded him a hiding-place. He, too, was a *Hiller;* for the word in the preceding legend does not mean "the man of the hill," but is from the German *hüllen,* to cover or conceal, and denotes the man who conceals himself. In this studious concealment of their persons by both of these smiths we detect the common origin of the two legends. When his services were required to shoe a horse, the animal was left among the stones and a piece of money placed on one of them. The owner then retired, and after some time had elapsed he returned, when he found that the horse was shod and the money had disappeared. The English reader ought to be familiar with this story from the use made of it by Sir Walter Scott in his novel of *Kenilworth.*

It is very evident, from all that has been here said, that the smith, as the fabricator of weapons for the battle-field and jewels for the *boudoir,* as well as implements of agriculture and household use, was a most important personage in the earliest times, deified by the ancients, and invested by the moderns with supernatural gifts. It is equally evident that this respect for the smith as an artificer was prevalent in the Middle Ages. But in the very latest legends, by a customary process of degeneration in all traditions, when the stream becomes muddled as it proceeds onward, he descended in character from a forger of swords, his earliest occupation, to be a shoer of horses, which was his last.

It must be borne in mind, also, that in the Middle Ages the respect for the smith as a "curious and cunning" workman began by the introduction of a new element, brought by the Crusaders and pilgrims from the East to be shared with King Solomon, who was supposed to be invested with equal skill.

It is not, therefore, strange that the idea should have been incorporated into the rituals of the various secret societies of the Middle Ages, and adopted by the Freemasons, at first by the Operative branch and afterward, in a more enlarged form, by the Speculative Masons.

In all of the old manuscript constitutions of the Operative Masons we find the *Legend of the Craft,* and with it, except in one instance, and that the earliest, a reference to Tubal Cain as the one who "found [that is, invented] the Smith Craft of gold and silver, iron and copper and steel."

Nothing but the universal prevalence of the mediæval legend of the smith, Völund or Weland, can, I think, account for this reference to the Father of Smith Craft in a legend which should have been exclusively appropriated to Stone Craft. There is no connection between the forge and the trowel which authorized on any other ground the honor paid by stone-masons to a forger of metals—an honor so marked that in time the very name of Tubal Cain came to be adopted as a significant and important word in the Masonic ritual, and the highest place in the traditional labors of the Temple was assigned to a worker in gold and brass and iron.

Afterward, when the Operative Art was superseded by the Speculative Science, the latter supplemented to the simple *Legend of the Craft* the more recondite *Legend of the Temple*. In this latter Legend, the name of that Hiram whom the King of Tyre had sent with all honor to the King of Israel, to give him aid in the construction of the Temple, is first introduced under his biblical appellation. But this is not the first time that this personage is made known to the fraternity. In the older Legends he is mentioned, always with a different name but always, also, as "King Solomon's Master Mason."

In the beginning of the 18th century, when what has been called the Revival took place, there was a continuation of the general idea that he was the chief Mason at the Temple; but the true name of Hiram Abif is, as we have already said, then first found in a written or printed record. Anderson speaks of his architectural abilities in exaggerated terms. He calls him in one place "the most accomplished Mason on earth," and in another "the prince of architects." This character has adhered to him in all subsequent times, and the unwritten Legend of the present day represents him as the "Chief Builder of the Temple," the "Operative Grand Master," and the "Skillful Architect" by whose elaborate designs on his trestle-board the Craft were guided in their labors and the edifice was constructed.

Now, it will be profitable in the investigation of historic truth to compare these attributes assigned to Hiram Abif by the older and more recent legendists with the biblical accounts of the same person which have already been cited.

In the original Hebrew text of the passage in the book of

Chronicles, the words which designate the profession of Hiram Abif are *khoresh nekhoshet;* literally, a worker in brass. The Vulgate, which was the popular version in those days and from which the old legendists must have derived their knowledge of biblical history, thus translates the letter of King Hiram to King Solomon: "Therefore I have sent to thee a wise and most skillful man, Hiram the workman or smith, my father"—*Hiram fabrem patrem meum.*

Indeed, in the close of the verse in the Authorized Version he is described as being "cunning to work all works in brass." And hence Dr. Adam Clarke, in his *Commentaries*, calls him "a very intelligent coppersmith."

The error into which the old legendists and the modern Masonic writers have fallen, in supposing him to have been a stone-mason or an architect, has arisen from the mistranslation in the Authorized Version of the passage in Chronicles where he is said to have been "skillful to work in gold and in silver, in brass, in iron, in stone, and in timber." The words in the original are *Baabanim vebagnetsim,* in *stones* and in *woods;* that is, in *precious stones* and in *woods of various kinds.* That is to say, besides being a coppersmith he was a lapidary and a carver and gilder. The words in the original Hebrew are in the plural, and therefore the translation "in wood and in timber" is not correct. Gesenius says—and there is no better authority for a Hebraism—that the word *eben* is used by way of excellence, to denote a precious stone, and its plural, *abanim,* means, therefore, precious stones. In the same way *gnetz,* which in the singular signifies a tree, in the plural denotes *materials of wood,* for any purpose.

The work that was done by Hiram Abif in the Temple is fully recounted in the first book of Kings, the seventh chapter, from the fifteenth to the fortieth verse, and is briefly recapitulated in verses forty-one to fifty. It is also enumerated in the third and fourth chapters of second Chronicles, and in both books care is taken to say that when this work was done the task of Hiram Abif was completed. In the first book of Kings (vii. 40) it is said: "So Hiram made an end of doing all the work that he made King Solomon for the house of the Lord." In the second book of Chronicles (iv. 2) the statement is repeated thus: "And Hiram finished the work that he was to make for King Solomon for the house of God."

The same authority leaves us in no doubt as to what that work was to which the skill of Hiram Abif had been devoted. "It was," says the book of Chronicles, " the two pillars, and the pommels and the chapiters which were on the top of the pillars ; and four hundred pomegranates on the two wreaths; two rows of pomegranates on each wreath, to cover the two pommels of the chapiters which were upon the pillars. He made also bases, and lavers made he upon the bases ; one sea and twelve oxen under it. The pots also, and the shovels and the flesh hooks and all their instruments, did Huram his father (Hiram Abif) make to King Solomon, for the house of the Lord, of bright brass."

Enough has been said to show that the labors of Hiram Abif in the Temple were those of a worker in brass and in precious stones, in carving and in gilding, and not those of a stonemason. He was the decorator and not the builder of the Temple. He owes the position which he holds in the legends and in the ritual of Freemasonry, not to any connection which he had with the art of architecture, of which there is not the slightest mention by the biblical authorities, but, like Tubal Cain, to his skill in bringing the potency of fire under his control and applying it to the forging of metals.

The high honor paid to him is the result of the influence of that *Legend of the Smith*, so universally spread in the Middle Ages, which recounted the wondrous deeds of Völund, or Wieland, or Wayland. The smith was, in the mediæval traditions, in the sagas of the north and in the romances of the south of Europe, the maker of swords and coats of mail ; in the Legends of Freemasonry he was transmuted into the fabricator of holy vessels and sacred implements.

But the idea that of all handicrafts smith-craft was the greatest was unwittingly retained by the Masons when they elevated the skillful smith of Tyre, the "cunning" worker in brass, to the highest place as a builder in their Temple legend.

The spirit of critical iconoclasm, which strips the exterior husk from the historic germ of all myths and legends, has been doing much to divest the history of Freemasonry of all fabulous assumptions. This attempt to give to Hiram Abif his true position, and to define his real profession, is in the spirit of that iconoclasm.

But the doctrine here advanced is not intended to affect in the slightest degree the part assigned to Hiram Abif in the symbolism of the Third Degree. Whatever may have been his profession, he must have stood high in the confidence of the two kings, of him who sent him and him who received him, as "a master workman ;"

and he might well be supposed to be entitled in an allegory to the exalted rank bestowed upon him in the *Legend of the Craft* and in the modern ritual.

Allegories are permitted to diverge at will from the facts of history and the teachings of science. Trees may be made to speak, as they do in the most ancient fable extant, and it is no infringement of their character that a worker in brass may be transmuted into a builder in stone to suit a symbolic purpose.

Hence this "celebrated artist," as he is fairly called, whether smith or mason, is still the representative, in the symbolism of Freemasonry, of the abstract idea of man laboring in the temple of life, and the symbolic lesson of his tried integrity and his unhappy fate is still the same.

As Freemasons, when we view the whole Legend as a myth intended to give expression to a symbolic idea, we may be content to call him an architect, the first of Masons, and the chief builder of the Temple ; but as students of history we can know nothing of him and admit nothing concerning him that is not supported by authentic and undisputed authority.

We must, therefore, look upon him as the ingenious artist, who worked in metals and in precious stones, who carved in cedar and in olive-wood, and thus made the ornaments of the Temple.

He is only the Völund or Wieland of the olden legend, changed, by a mistaken but a natural process of transmuting traditions, from a worker in brass to a worker in stone.

CHAPTER XLIV

HE Leland Manuscript, so called because it is said to have been discovered by the celebrated antiquary John Leland, and sometimes called the Locke Manuscript in consequence of the supposititious annotations appended to it by that metaphysician, has for more than a century attracted the attention and more recently excited the controversies of Masonic scholars. After having been cited with approbation by such writers as Preston, Hutchinson, Oliver, and Krause, it has suffered a reverse under the crucial examination of later critics. It has by nearly all of these been decided to be a forgery—a decision from which very few at this day would dissent.

It is in fact one of those "pious frauds" intended to strengthen the claim of the Order to a great antiquity and to connect it with the mystical schools of the ancients. But as it proposes a theory concerning the origin of the Institution, which was long accepted as a legend of the Order, it is entitled to a place in the legendary history of Freemasonry.

The story of this manuscript and the way in which it was introduced to the notice of the Craft is a singular one.

In the *Gentleman's Magazine* for September, 1753, the so-called manuscript was printed for the first time under the title of "Certayne Questyons with Awnserers to the same, Concernynge the Mystery of Maconrye, wrytenne by the Hande of Kynge Henrye the Sixthe of the Name, and faythfullye copyed by me Johan Leylande Antiquaries, by the Commaunde of His Highnesse." That is, King Henry the Eighth, by whom Leland was employed to search for antiquities in the libraries of cathedrals, abbeys, priories, colleges, and all places where any ancient records were to be found.

The article in the *Gentleman's Magazine* is prefaced with these words :

"The following Treatise is said to be printed at Franckfort, Germany, 1748, under the following Title. Ein Brief Vondem Beruchmten Herr Johann Locke, betreffend die Frey-Maureren. So auf einem Schrieb-Tisch enines verstorbnen Bruders ist gefunden worden. *That is*, A Letter of the famous Mr. John Locke relating to Freemasonry ; found in the Desk or Scritoir of a deceased Brother."

The claim, therefore, is that this document was first published at Frankfort in 1748, five years before it appeared in England. But this German original has never been produced, nor is there any evidence before us that there ever was such a production. The laborious learning of Krause would certainly have enabled him to discover it had it ever been in existence. But, although he accepts the so-called manuscript as authentic, he does not refer to the Frankfort copy, but admits that, so far as he knows, it first made its appearance in Germany in 1780, in J. G. L. Meyer's translation of Preston's *Illustrations*.[1]

Kloss, it is true, in his *Bibliography*, gives the title in German, with the imprint of "Frankfort, 12 pages." But he himself says that the actuality of such a document is to be wholly doubted.[2]

Besides, it is not unusual with Kloss to give the titles of books that he has never seen, and for whose existence he had no other authority than the casual remark of some other writer. Thus he gives the titles of the *Short Analysis of the Unchanged Rites and Ceremonies of Freemasons*, said to have been printed in 1676, and the *Short Charge*, ascribed to 1698, two books which have never been found. But he applies to them the epithet of "doubtful" as he does to the Frankfort edition of the *Leland Manuscript*.

But before proceeding to an examination of the external and internal evidence of the true character of this document, it will be expedient to give a sketch of its contents. It has been published in so many popular works of easy access that it is unnecessary to present it here in full.

It is introduced by a letter from Mr. Locke (the celebrated

---

[1] "Kunsturkunden der Freimaurerei," I., 14.
[2] "Bibliographie der Freimaurerei," No. 329.

author of the *Essay on the Human Understanding*), said to be addressed to the Earl of Pembroke, under date of May 6, 1696, in which he states that by the help of Mr. C——ns he had obtained a copy of the MS. in the Bodleian Library, which he therewith had sent to the Earl. It is accompanied by numerous notes which were made the day before by Mr. Locke for the reading of Lady Masham, who had become very fond of Masonry.

Mr. Locke says: "The *manuscript* of which this is a copy, appears to be about 160 years old. Yet (as your Lordship will observe by the title) it is itself a copy of one yet more ancient by about 100 years. For the original is said to have been the handwriting of K. H. VI. Where the Prince had it is at present an uncertainty, but it seems to me to be an examination (taken perhaps before the king) of some one of the Brotherhood of Masons; among whom he entered himself, as 'tis said, when he came out of his minority, and thenceforth put a stop to the persecution that had been raised against them."

The "examination," for such it purports to be, as Mr. Locke supposes, consists of twelve questions and answers. The style and orthography is an attempted imitation of the language of the 15th century. How far successful the attempt has been will be discussed hereafter.

Masonry is described to be the skill of Nature, the understanding of the might that is therein and its various operations, besides the skill of numbers, weights and measures, and the true manner of fashioning all things for the use of man, principally dwellings and buildings of all kinds, and all other things that may be useful to man.

Its origin is said to have been with the first men of the East, who were before the Man of the West, by which Mr. Locke,[1] in his note, says is meant Pre-Adamites, the "Man of the West" being Adam. The Phœnicians, who first came from the East into Phœnicia, are said to have brought it westwardly by the way of the Red and Mediterranean seas.

It was brought into England by Pythagoras, who is called in the document "Peter Gower," evidently from the French spelling of the name, "Pétagore," he having traveled in search of knowl-

---

[1] It will be seen that in this and other places I cite the name of Mr. Locke as if he were really the author of the note, a theory to which I by no means desire to commit myself. The reference in this way is merely for convenience.

edge into Egypt, Syria, and every other land where the Phœnicians had planted Masonry. Having obtained a knowledge of the art in the Lodges of Masons into which he gained admission, on his return to Europe he settled in Magna Grecia (the name given by the ancients to Southern Italy), and established a Grand Lodge at Crotona, one of its principal cities, where he made many Masons. Some of these traveled into France and made many Masons, whence in process of time the art passed over into England.

Such is the history of the origin and progress of Masonry which is given in the *Leland Manuscript.* The remainder of the document is engaged in giving the character and the objects of the Institution.

Thus it is said, in relation to secrecy, that Masons have at all times communicated to mankind such of their secrets as might generally be useful, and have kept back only those that might be harmful in evil hands—those that could be of no use unless accompanied by the teachings of the Lodge, and those which are employed to bind the brethren more strongly together.

The arts taught by Masons to mankind are enumerated as being Agriculture, Architecture, Astronomy, Geometry, Arithmetic, Music, Poetry, Chemistry, Government, and Religion.

Masons are said to be better teachers than other men, because the first of them received from God the art of finding new arts, and of teaching them, whereas the discoveries of other men have been but few, and acquired only by chance. This art of discovery the Masons conceal for their own profit. They also conceal the art of working miracles, the art of foretelling future events, the art of changes (which Mr. Locke is made in a note to interpret as signifying the transmutation of metals), the method of acquiring the faculty of Abrac, the power of becoming good and perfect without the aid of fear and hope, and the universal language.

And lastly it is admitted that Masons do not know more than other men, but only have a better opportunity of knowing, in which many fail for want of capacity and industry. And as to their virtue, while it is acknowledged that some are not so good as other men, yet it is believed that for the most part they are better than they would be if they were not Masons. And it is claimed that Masons greatly love each other, because good and true men, knowing each other to be such, always love the more the better they are.

"And here endethe the Questyonnes and Awnsweres."

There does not appear to be any great novelty or value in this document. The theory of the origin of Masonry had been advanced by others before its appearance in public, and the characteristics of Masonry had been previously defined in better language.

But no sooner is it printed in the *Gentleman's Magazine* for the month of September, and year 1753, than it is seized as a *bonne bouche* by printers and writers, so that being first received with surprise, it was soon accepted as a genuine relic of the early age of English Masonry and incorporated into its history, a position that it has not yet lost, in the opinion of some. The forgeries of Chatterton and of Ireland met a speedier literary death.

Of the genuine publications of this document, so much as this is known.

It was first printed, as we have seen, in the *Gentleman's Magazine*, in September, 1753. Kloss records a book as published in 1754, with no place of publication, but probably it was London, with the title of *A Masonic Creed, with a curious letter by Mr. Locke*. This, we can hardly doubt, was the *Leland Manuscript* with a new title. The republications in England pursued the following succession. In 1756 it was printed in Entick's edition of the *Constitutions* and in Dermott's *Ahiman Rezon;* in 1763, in the *Free-Masons' Pocket Companion;* in 1769, in Wilkinson's *Constitutions* of the Grand Lodge of Ireland, and in Calcott's *Candid Disquisition;* in 1772, in Huddesford's *Life of Leland*, and in Preston's *Illustrations of Masonry;* in 1775, in Hutchinson's *Spirit of Masonry;* and in 1784, in Northouck's edition of the *Constitutions*.

In Germany it first appeared in 1776, says Krause, in J. G. L. Meyer's translation of Preston; in 1780, in a translation of Hutchinson, published at Berlin; in 1805, in the *Magazin für Freimaurer* of Professor Seehass; in 1807, in the collected Masonic works of Fessler; in 1810, by Dr. Krause in his *Three Oldest Documents;* and in 1824, by Mossdorf in his edition of Lenning's *Encyclopädie*.

In France, Thory published a translation of it, with some comments of his own, in 1815, in the *Acta Latomorum*.

In America it was, so far as I know, first published in 1783, in Smith's *Ahiman Rezon* of the Grand Lodge of Pennsylvania; it was also published in 1817, by Cole, in his *Ahiman Rezon* of Maryland, and it has been copied into several other works.

In none of these republications, with one or two exceptions, is there an expression of the slightest doubt of the genuineness of the document. It has on the contrary been, until recently, almost everywhere accepted as authentic, and as the detail of an actual examination of a Mason or a company of Masons, made by King Henry VI., of England, or some of his ministers, in the 15th century.

Of all who have cited this pretended manuscript, Dr. Carl Christian Friederich Krause is perhaps the most learned, and the one who from the possession of great learning, we should naturally expect would have been most capable of detecting a literary forgery, speaks of it, in his great work on *The Three Oldest Documents of the Fraternity of Freemasons*, as being a remarkable and instructive document and as among the oldest that are known to us. In England, he says, it is, so far as it is known to him, accepted as authentic by the learned as well as by the whole body of the Craft, without a dissenting voice. And he refers as evidence of this to the fact that the Grand Lodge of England has formally admitted it into its *Book of Constitutions*, while the Grand Lodge of Scotland has approved the work of Lawrie, in which its authenticity is supported by new proofs.

And Mossdorf, whose warm and intimate relations with Krause influenced perhaps to some extent his views on this as well as they did on other Masonic subjects, has expressed a like favorable opinion of the *Leland Manuscript*. In his additions to the *Encyclopädie* of Lenning, he calls it a remarkable document, which, notwithstanding a singularity about it, and its impression of the ancient time in which it originated, is instructive, and the oldest catechism which we have on the origin, the nature, and the design of Masonry.

The editor of Lawrie's *History* is equally satisfied of the genuine character of this document, to which he confidently refers as conclusive evidence that Dr. Plot was wrong in saying that Henry VI. did not patronize Masonry.

Dr. Oliver is one of the most recent and, as might be expected from his peculiar notions in respect to the early events of Masonry, one of the most ardent defenders of the authenticity of the manuscript, although he candidly admits "that there is some degree of mystery about it, and doubts have been entertained whether it be not a forgery."

But, considering its publicity at a time when Freemasonry was beginning to excite a considerable share of public attention, and that the deception, if there was one, would have been publicly exposed by the opponents of the Order, he thinks that their silence is presumptive proof that the document is genuine.

" Being thus universally diffused," he says, " had it been a suspected document, its exposure would have been certainly attempted— if a forgery, it would have been unable to have endured the test of a critical examination. But no such attempt was made, and the presumption is that the document is authentic."

But, on the other hand, there are some writers who have as carefully investigated the subject as those whom I have referred to, but the result of whose investigations have led them irresistibly to the conclusion that the document never had any existence until the middle of the 18th century, and that the effort to place it in the time of Henry VI. is, as Mounier calls it, " a Masonic fraud."

As early as 1787, while the English Masons were receiving it as a document of approved truth, the French critics had begun to doubt its genuineness. At a meeting of the Philalethes, a Rite of Hermetic Masonry which had been instituted at Paris in 1775, the Marquis de Chefdebien read a paper entitled *Masonic Researches for the use of the Primitive Rite of Narbonne*.[1] In this paper he presented an unfavorable criticism of the *Leland Manuscript*. In 1801 M. Mounier published an essay *On the Influence attributed to the Philosophers, the Freemasons and the Illuminati in the French Revolution*,[2] in which he pronounces the document to be a forgery and a Masonic fraud.

Lessing was the first of the German critics who attacked the genuineness of the document. This he did in his *Ernst und Falk*, the first edition of which was published in 1778. Others followed, and the German unfavorable criticisms were closed by Findel, the editor of the *Bauhütte*, and author of a *History of Freemasonry*, first published in 1865, and which was translated in 1869 by Bro. Lyon. He says: "There is no reliance, whatever, to be placed on any assertions based on this spurious document; they all crumble to dust. Not even in England does any well-informed Mason of the present day, believe in the genuineness of this bungling composition."

In England it is only recently that any doubts of its authentic-

---

[1] " Recherches Maçonniques à l'usage des Frères du Régime Premitif de Narbonne."
[2] " De l'Influence attribuée aux Philosophes, aux Franc-Maçons et aux Illuminés sur la Revolution de France," per F. F. Mounier.

ity have been expressed by Masonic critics. The first attack upon it was made in 1849, by Mr. George Sloane, in his *New Curiosities of Literature.* Sloane was not a Freemason, and his criticism, vigorous as it is, seems to have been inspired rather by a feeling of enmity to the Institution than by an honest desire to seek the truth. His conclusions, however, as to the character of the document are based on the most correct canons of criticism. Bro. A. F. A. Woodford is more cautious in the expression of his judgment, but admits that "we must give up the actual claim of the document to be a *manuscript* of the time of King Henry VI., or to have been written by him or copied by Leland." Yet he thinks "it not unlikely that we have in it the remains of a Lodge catechism conjoined with a Hermetic one." But this is a mere supposition, and hardly a plausible one.

But a recent writer, unfortunately anonymous, in the *Masonic Magazine,*[1] of London, has given an able though brief review of the arguments for and against the external evidence of authenticity, and has come to the conclusion that the former has utterly failed and that the question must fall to the ground.

Now, amid such conflicting views, an investigation must be conducted with the greatest impartiality. The influence of great names, especially among the German writers, has been enlisted on both sides, and the most careful judgment must be exercised in determining which of these sides is right and which is wrong.

In the investigation of the genuineness of any document we must have resort to two kinds of evidence, the external and the internal. The former is usually more clear and precise, as well as more easily handled, because it is superficial and readily comprehended by the most unpracticed judgment. But when there is no doubt about the interpretation, and there is a proper exercise of skill, internal evidence is freer from doubt, and therefore the most conclusive. It is, says a recent writer on the history of our language, the pure reason of the case, speaking to us directly, by which we can not be deceived, if we only rightly apprehend it. But, although we must sometimes dispense with external evidence, because it may be unattainable, while the internal evidence is always existent, yet the combination of the two will make the conclusion to

---

[1] Vol. vi., No. 64, October, 1878, p. 148.

which we may arrive more infallible than it could be by the application of either kind alone.

If it should be claimed that a particular document was written in a certain century, the mention of it, or citations from it, by contemporary authors would be the best external evidence of its genuineness. It is thus that the received canon of the New Testament has been strengthened in its authority, by the quotation of numerous passages of the Gospels and the Epistles which are to be found in the authentic writings of the early Fathers of the Church. This is the external evidence.

If the language of the document under consideration, the peculiar style, and the archaic words used in it should be those found in other documents known to have been written in the same century, and if the sentiments are those that we should look for in the author, are in accord with the age in which he lived, this would be internal evidence and would be entitled to great weight.

But this internal evidence is subject to one fatal defect. The style and language of the period and the sentiments of the pretended author and of the age in which he lived may be successfully imitated by a skillful forger, and then the results of internal evidence will be evaded. So the youthful Chatterton palmed upon the world the supposititious productions of the monk Rowley, and Ireland forged pretended plays of Shakespeare. Each of these made admirable imitations of the style of the authors whose lost productions they pretended to have discovered.

But when the imitation has not been successful, or when there has been no imitation attempted, the use of words which were unknown at the date claimed for the document in dispute, or the reference to events of which the writer must be ignorant, because they occurred at a subsequent period, or when the sentiments are incongruous to the age in which they are supposed to have been written, then the internal evidence that it is a forgery, or at least a production of a later date, will be almost invincible.

It is by these two classes of evidence that I shall seek to inquire into the true character of the *Leland Manuscript.*

If it can be shown that there is no evidence of the existence of the document before the year 1753, and if it can also be shown that neither the language of the document, the sentiments expressed in it, nor the character attributed to the chief actor, King Henry VI., are in conformity with a document of the 15th century, we shall be authorized in rejecting the theory that it belongs to such a period as wholly untenable, and the question will admit of no more discussion.

But in arriving at a fair conclusion, whatever it may be, the rule of Ulpian must be obeyed, and the testimonies must be well considered and not merely counted. It is not the number of the whole but the weight of each that must control our judgment.

Those who defend the genuineness of the *Leland Manuscript* are required to establish these points:

1. That the document was first printed at Frankfort, in Germany, whence it was copied into the *Gentleman's Magazine* for September, 1753.

2. That the original manuscript was, by command of King Henry VIII., copied by John Leland from an older document of the age of Henry VI.

3. That this original manuscript, of which Leland made a copy, was written by King Henry VI.

4. That the manuscript of Leland was deposited in the Bodleian Library.

5. That a copy of this manuscript of Leland was made by a Mr. C——ns, which is said to mean Collins, and given by him to John Locke, the celebrated metaphysician.

6. That Locke wrote notes or annotations on it in the year 1696, which were published in Frankfort in 1748, and afterward in England, in 1753.

The failure to establish by competent proof any one of these six points will seriously affect the credibility of the whole story, for each of them is a link of one continuous chain.

1. Now as to the first point, *that the document was first printed at Frankfort in the year 1748.* The Frankfort copy has never yet been seen, notwithstanding diligent search has been made for it by German writers, who were the most capable of discovering it, if it had ever existed. The negative evidence is strong that the Frankfort copy may be justly considered as a mere myth. It follows that the article in the *Gentleman's Magazine* is an original document, and we have a right to suppose that it was written at the time for some purpose, to be hereafter considered, for, as the author of it has given a false reference, we may conclude that if he had copied it

at all he would have furnished us with the true one. Kloss, it is true, has admitted the title into his catalogue, but he has borrowed his description of it from the article in the *Gentleman's Magazine*, and speaks of this Frankfort copy as being doubtful. He evidently had never seen it, though he was an indefatigable searcher after Masonic books. Krause's account of it is, that it first was found worthy of Locke's notice in England ; that thence it passed over into Germany—"how, he does not know"—appeared in Frankfort, and then returned back to England, where it was printed in 1753. But all this is mere hearsay, and taken by Krause from the statement in the *Gentleman's Magazine*. He makes no reference to the Frankfort copy in his copious notes in his *Kunsturkunden*, and, like Kloss, had no personal knowledge of any such publication. In short, there is no positive evidence at all that any such document was printed at Frankfort-on-the-Main, but abundant negative evidence that it was not. The first point must therefore be abandoned.

2. The second point that requires to be proved is *that the man. uscript was, by command of King Henry VIII., copied by John Leland from an older document of the age of Henry VI.* Now, there is not the slightest evidence that a manuscript copy of the original document was taken by Leland, except what is afforded by the printed article in the *Gentleman's Magazine*, the authenticity of which is the very question in dispute, and it is a good maxim of the law that no one ought to be a witness in his own cause. But even this evidence is very insufficient. For, admitting that Locke was really the author of the annotations (an assertion which also needs proof), he does not say that he had seen the Leland copy, but only a copy of it, which had been made for him by a friend. So that even at that time the *Leland Manuscript* had not been brought to sight, and up to this has never been seen. Amid all the laborious and indefatigable researches of Bro. Hughan in the British Museum, in other libraries, and in the archives of lodges, while he has discovered many valuable old records and Masonic Constitutions which until then had lain hidden in these various receptacles, he has failed to unearth the famous *Leland Manuscript*. The hope of ever finding it is very faint, and must be entirely extinguished if other proofs can be adduced of its never having existed.

Huddesford, in his *Life of Leland*, had, it is true, made the following statement in reference to this manuscript : " It also appears

that an ancient *manuscript* of Leland's has long remained in the Bodleian Library, unnoticed in any account of our author yet published.
This Tract is entitled *Certayne Questyons with Awnsweres to the
same concernynge the mystery of Maconrye.*   The original is said
to be the handwriting of K. Henry VI., by order of his highness
K. Henry VIII."[1]   And he then proceeds to dilate upon the importance of this "ancient monument of literature, *if its authenticity remains unquestioned.*"

But it must be remembered that Huddesford wrote in 1772, nine-
teen years after the appearance of the document in the *Gentleman's
Magazine*, which he quotes in his Appendix, and from which it is
evident that he derived all the knowledge that he had of the pseudo-
manuscript.   But the remarks on this subject of the anonymous
writer in the *London Masonic Magazine*, already referred to, are so
apposite and conclusive that they justify a quotation.

"Though Huddesford was keeper of the Ashmolean Library, in
the Bodleian, he does not seek to verify even the existence of the
manuscript, but contents himself with 'it also appears' that it is from
the *Gentleman's Magazine* of 1753.   He surely ought not to have put
in here such a statement, that an ancient *manuscript* of Leland has
long remained in the Bodleian, without inquiry or collation.   Either
he knew the fact to be so, as he stated it, or he did not ; but in either
case his carelessness as an editor is, to my mind, utterly inexcusable.
Nothing would have been easier for him than to verify an alleged
manuscript of Leland, being an officer in the very collection in which
it was said to exist.   Still, if he did not do so, either the *manuscript*
did exist, and he knew it, but did not think well, for some reason,
to be more explicit about it, or he knew nothing at all about it, and
by an inexcusable neglect of his editorial duty, took no pains to
ascertain the truth, and simply copied others, by his quasi recognition of a professed *manuscript* of Leland."

But it is utterly incredible that Huddesford could have known
and yet concealed his knowledge of the existence of the *manuscript*.
There is no conceivable motive that could be assigned for such concealment and for the citation at the same time of other authority for
the fact.   It is therefore a fair inference that his only knowledge of
the document was derived from the *Gentleman's Magazine*.   There

---

[1] Huddesford's "Life of John Leland," p. 67.

is, therefore, no proof whatever that Leland ever copied any older manuscript.

Referring to certain obvious mistakes in the printed copy, such as *Peter Gower* for *Pythagoras*, it has been said that it is evident that the document was not printed from Leland's original transcript, but rather from a secondary copy of an unlearned. Huddesford adopts this view, but if he had ever seen the *manuscript* of Leland he could have better formed a judgment by a collation of it with the printed copy than by a mere inference that a man of Leland's learning could not have made such mistakes. As he did not do so, it follows that he had never seen *Leland's Manuscript*. The second point, therefore, falls to the ground.

3. The third point requiring proof is *that the original manuscript, of which Leland made a copy, was written by King Henry VI*. There is a legal rule that when a deed or writing is not produced in court, and the loss of it is not reasonably accounted for, it shall be treated as if it were not existent. This is just the case of the pretended manuscript in the handwriting of Henry VI. No one has ever seen that manuscript, no one has ever had any knowledge of it; the fact of its ever having existed depends solely on the statement made in the *Gentleman's Magazine* that it had been copied by Leland. Of a document "in the clouds" as this is, whose very existence is a mere presumption built on the very slightest foundation, it is absurd to predicate an opinion of the handwriting. Time enough when the manuscript is produced to inquire who wrote it. The third point, therefore, fails to be sustained.

4. The fourth point is *that the manuscript of Leland was deposited in the Bodleian Library*. This has already been discussed in the argument on the first and third point. It is sufficient now to say that no such manuscript has been found in that library. The writer in the *London Masonic Magazine*, whom I have before quoted, says that he had had a communication with the authorities of the Bodleian Library, and had been informed that nothing is known of it in that collection. Among the additional manuscripts of the British Museum are some that were once owned by one Essex, an architect, who lived late in the last century. Among these is a copy of the *Leland Manuscript*—evidently a copy made by Essex from the *Gentleman's Magazine*, or some one of the other works in which it had been printed. I say evidently, because in the

same collection is a copy of the *Grand Mystery*, transcribed by him as he had transcribed the *Leland Manuscript*, as a, to him perhaps, curious relic. The original *Leland Manuscript* is nowhere to be found, and there the attempt to prove the fourth point is unsuccessful.

5. The fifth point is *that a copy of Leland's MS. was made by a Mr. C——ns, and given by him to Locke.* The *Pocket Companion* printed the name as " Collins," upon what authority I know not. There were only two distinguished men of that name who were contemporaries of Locke—John Collins, the mathematician, and Anthony Collins, the celebrated skeptical writer. It could not have been the former who took the copy from the Ashmolean Library in 1696, for he died in 1683. There is, however, a strong probability that the latter was meant by the writer of the prefatory, since he was on such relations with Locke as to have been appointed one of his executors,[1] and it is an ingenious part of the forgery that he should be selected to perform such an act of courtesy for his friend as the transcription of an old manuscript. Yet there is an uncertainty about it, and it is a puzzle to be resolved why Mr. Locke should have unnecessarily used such a superabundance of caution, and given only the initial and final letters of the name of a friend who had been occupied in the harmless employment of copying for him a manuscript in a public library. This is mysterious, and mystery is always open to suspicion. For uncertainty and indefiniteness the fifth point is incapable of proof.

6. The sixth and last point is *that the notes or annotations were written by Mr. Locke in 1696, and fifty-two years afterward printed in Frankfort-on-the-Main.* We must add to this, because it is a part of the story, that the English text, with the annotations of Locke, said to have been translated into German, the question—was it translated by the unknown brother in whose desk the document was found after his death ?—and then retranslated into English for the use of the *Gentleman's Magazine*.

It is admitted that if we refuse to accept the document printed in the magazine in 1753 as genuine, it must follow that the notes

---

[1] It is strange that the idea that the Collins mentioned in the letter was Collins, the friend and executor of Locke, should not have suggested itself to any of the defenders or oppugners of the document. The writer in the " London Masonic Magazine " intimates that he was " a book-collector, or dealer in MSS."

supposed to have been written by Locke are also spurious. The two questions are not necessarily connected. Locke may have been deceived, and, believing that the manuscript presented to him by C——ns, or Collins, if that was really his name, did take the trouble, for the sake of Lady Masham, to annotate it and to explain its difficulties.

But if we have shown that there is no sufficient proof, and, in fact, no proof at all, that there ever was such a manuscript, and therefore that Collins did not transcribe it, then it will necessarily follow that the pretended notes of Locke are as complete a forgery as the text to which they are appended. Now, if the annotations of Locke were genuine, why is it that after diligent search this particular one has not been found? It is known that Locke left several manuscripts behind him, some of which were published after his death by his executors, King and Collins, and several unpublished manuscripts went into the possession of Lord King, who in 1829 published the *Life and Correspondence of Locke.* But nowhere has the notorious *Leland Manuscript* appeared. "If John Locke's letter were authentic," says the writer already repeatedly referred to, "a copy of this *manuscript* would remain among Mr. Locke's papers, or at Wilton House, and the original *manuscript* probably in the hands of this Mr. Collins, whoever he was, or in the Bodleian."

But there are other circumstances of great suspicion connected with the letter and annotations of Locke, which amount to a condemnation of their authenticity. In concluding his remarks on what he calls "this old paper," Locke is made to say: "It has so raised my curiosity as to induce me to enter myself into the fraternity; which I am determined to do (if I may be admitted) the next time I go to London, and that will be shortly."

Now, because it is known that at the date of the pseudo-letter, Mr. Locke was actually residing at Oates, the seat of Sir Francis Masham, for whose lady he says that the annotations were made, and because it is also known that in the next year he made a visit to London, Oliver says that there "he was initiated into Masonry." Now, there is not the slightest proof of this initiation, nor is it important to the question of authenticity whether he was initiated or not, because if he was not it would only prove that he had abandoned the intention he had expressed in the letter. But I cite the unsupported remark of Dr. Oliver to show how Masonic history has hitherto been written—always assumptions, and facts left to take care of themselves.

But it is really most probable that Mr. Locke was not made a Freemason in 1697 or at any other time, for if he had been, Dr. Anderson, writing the history of Masonry only a few years afterward, would not have failed to have entered this illustrious name in the list of "learned scholars" who had patronized the Fraternity.

It appears, from what is admitted in reference to this subject, that the *Leland Manuscript*, having been obtained by Mr. Collins from the Bodleian Library, was annotated by Mr. Locke, and a letter, stating the fact, was sent with the *manuscript* and annotations to a nobleman whose rank and title are designated by stars (a needless mystery), but who has been subsequently supposed to be the Earl of Pembroke.   All this was in the year 1696.   It then appears to have been completely lost to sight until the year 1748, when it is suddenly found hidden away in the desk of a deceased brother in Germany. During these fifty-two years that it lay in abeyance, we hear nothing of it.   Anderson, the Masonic historian, could not have heard of it, for he does not mention it in either the edition of the *Constitutions* published in 1723, or in that more copious one of 1738.   If anyone could have known of it, if it was in existence, it would have been Anderson, and if he had ever seen or heard of it he would most certainly have referred to it in his history of Masonry during the reign of Henry VI.

He does say, indeed, that according to a record in the reign of Edward IV. "the *charges* and *laws* of the Freemasons have been seen and perused by our late Sovereign, King Henry VI., and by the Lords of his most honourable Council, who have allowed them and declared that they be right good and reasonable to be holden as they have been drawn out and collected from the records of ancient times," etc.[1]

But it is evident that this is no description of the *Leland Manuscript*, which does not consist of "charges and laws," but is simply a history of the origin of Masonry, and a declaration of its character and objects.   And yet the fact that there is said to have been something submitted by the Masons to Henry VI. and his Council was

---

[1] Anderson's " Constitutions," edition of 1738, p. 75.

enough to suggest to the ingenious forger the idea of giving to his pseudo-manuscript a date corresponding to the reign of that monarch. But he overleaped the bounds of caution in giving the peculiar form to his forgery. Had he fabricated a document similar to those ancient constitutions, many genuine manuscripts of which are extant, the discovery of the fraud would have been more difficult.

But to continue the narrative: The *manuscript*, having been found in the desk of this unknown deceased brother, is forthwith published at Frankfort, Germany, in a pamphlet of twelve pages and in the German language.

Here again there are sundry questions to be asked, which can not be answered. Had the tale been a true one, and the circumstances such as always accompany the discovery of a lost document, and which are always put upon record, the replies and explanations would have been ready.

Was the letter of Locke, including of course the catechism of the *Leland Manuscript*, which was found in the desk of the unknown brother, the original document, or was it only a copy? If the latter, had it been copied in English by the brother, or translated by him into German? If not translated by him, by whom was it translated? Was the pamphlet printed in Frankfort merely a German translation, or did it also contain, in parallel columns, the English original, as Krause has printed the English documents in his *Kunsturkunden*, and as, in fact, he has printed this very document? These are questions of very great importance in determining the value and authenticity of the Frankfort pamphlet. And yet not one of them can be answered, simply because that pamphlet has never been found, nor is it known that anyone has ever seen it.

The pamphlet next makes its appearance five years afterward in England, and in an English translation in the *Gentleman's Magazine* for September, 1753. Nobody can tell, or at least nobody has told, how it got there, who brought it over, who translated it from the German, how it happened that the archaic language of the text and the style of Locke have been preserved. These are facts absolutely necessary to be known in any investigation of the question of authenticity, and yet over them all a suspicious silence broods.

Until this silence is dissipated and these questions answered by the acquisition of new knowledge in the premises, which it can hardly now be expected will be obtained, the stain of an imposture

must remain upon the character of the document. The discov-
erer of a genuine manuscript would have been more explicit in his
details.

As to internal evidence, there is the most insuperable difficulty
in applying here the canons of criticism which would identify the
age of the manuscript by its style.

Throwing aside any consideration of the Frankfort pamphlet on
account of the impossibility of explaining the question of translation, and admitting, for the time, that Mr. Locke did really annotate a copy of a manuscript then in the Bodleian Library, which
copy was made for him by his friend Collins, how, with this admission, will the case stand?

In Mr. Locke's letter (accepting it as such) he says : " The *manuscript*, of which this is a copy, appears to be about 160 years old."
As the date of Locke's letter is 1696, this estimate would bring us to
1536, or the thirty-first year of the reign of Henry VIII. Locke could
have derived his knowledge of this fact only in two ways : from the
date given in the manuscript, or from its style and language as belonging, in his opinion, to that period.

But if he derived his knowledge from the date inserted at the
head of the manuscript, that knowledge would be of no value, because it is the very question which is at issue. The writer of a
forged document would affix to it the date necessary to carry out
his imposture, which of course would be no proof of genuineness.

But if Locke judged from the style, then it must be said that,
though a great metaphysician and statesman, and no mean theologian, he was not an archæologist or antiquary, and never had any
reputation as an expert in the judgment of old records. Of this we
have a proof here, for the language of the *Leland Manuscript* is
not that of the period in which Leland lived. The investigator
may easily satisfy himself of this by a collation of Leland's genuine works, or of the Cranmer Bible, which is of the same date.

But it may be said that Locke judged of the date, not by the style,
but by the date of the manuscript itself. And this is probably true,
because he adds : " Yet (as your Lordship will observe by the title)
it is itself a copy of one yet more ancient by about 100 years : For
the original is said to have been in the handwriting of K. H. VI."

Locke then judged only by the title—a very insufficient proof,
as I have already said, of authenticity. So Locke seems to have

thought, for he limits the positiveness of the assertion by the quali-
fying phrase " it is said." If we accept this for what it is worth, the
claim will be that the original manuscript was written in the reign of
Henry VI., or about the middle of the 15th century. But here
again the language is not of that period. The new English, as it is
called, was then beginning to take that purer form which a century
and a half afterward culminated in the classical and vigorous style of
Cowley. We find no such archaisms as those perpetrated in this
document in the *Repressor of over-much Blaming of the Clergy*,
written in the same reign, about 1450, by Bishop Pecock, nor in
the Earl of Warwick's petition to Duke Humphrey, written in 1432,
nor in any other of the writings of that period. It is not surprising,
therefore, that the glossary or list of archaic words used in the document, by which from internal evidence we could be enabled to fix its
date, has, according to Mr. Woodford, " always been looked upon
with much suspicion by experts."

If I may advance an hypothesis upon the subject, I should say
that the style is a rather clumsy imitation of that of Sir John Mandeville, whose *Voiage and Travaile* was written in 1356, about a
century before the pretended date of the *Leland Manuscript*.

An edition of this book was published at London in 1725. It
was, therefore, accessible to the writer of the Leland document.
He being aware of the necessity of giving an air of antiquity to his
forgery, and yet not a sufficiently skillful philologist to know the
rapid strides that had taken place in the progress of the language
between the time of Mandeville and the middle of the reign of
Henry VI., adopted, to the best of his poor ability, the phraseology
of that most credulous of all travelers, supposing that it would well
fit into the period that he had selected for the date of his fraudu-
lent manuscript. His ignorance of philology has thus led to his
detection. I am constrained, from all these considerations, to in-
dorse the opinion of Mr. Halliwell Phillips, that " it is but a clumsy
attempt at deception, and quite a parallel to the recently discovered
one of the first *Englishe Mercurie*."

But the strangest thing in this whole affair is that so many men
of learning should have permitted themselves to become the dupes
of so bungling an impostor.

George Washington